STUDIES IN
Shakespeare, Bibliography,
and Theater

Sponsoring Committee

Matthew W. Black, *University of Pennsylvania*

Fredson Bowers, *University of Virginia*

Giles E. Dawson, *Folger Shakespeare Library*

Sir Frank C. Francis, *British Museum*

Charlton Hinman, *University of Kansas*

Richard Hosley, *University of Arizona*

Mrs. Donald F. Hyde, *Shakespeare Association of America*

Arthur C. Kirsch, *University of Virginia*

Kemp Malone, *The Johns Hopkins University*

Dorothy E. Mason, *Folger Shakespeare Library*

Charles D. Murphy, *University of Maryland*

Allardyce Nicoll, *University of Birmingham*

George Winchester Stone, *New York University*

John W. Velz, *University of Texas*

Virgil K. Whitaker, *Stanford University*

Editors

RICHARD HOSLEY

ARTHUR C. KIRSCH

JOHN W. VELZ

STUDIES IN

Shakespeare, Bibliography, and Theater

JAMES G. McMANAWAY

NEW YORK
THE SHAKESPEARE ASSOCIATION OF AMERICA
1969

Published by The Shakespeare Association of America, Inc.
P.O. Box 2653, Grand Central Station, New York City 10017

Printed in the United States of America
by the WILLIAM BYRD PRESS, Richmond, Virginia

The essays in this volume are reprinted by permission of the editors or publishers of the journals, annuals, and books in which they first appeared. Grateful acknowledgement is accordingly made to the editors of *English Literary History, Essays Honoring Lawrence C. Wroth, The Library, Modern Language Quarterly, Papers of the Bibliographical Society of America, PMLA, Shakespeare Quarterly, Shakespeare Studies* (Tokyo), *Shakespeare Survey* (Cambridge University Press), *Studies in Bibliography,* and *Theatre Miscellany* (Luttrell Society); and to the following publishers: Le Centre National de la Recherche Scientifique (*Le Lieu théâtral à la Renaissance*), the Clarendon Press (*Elizabethan and Jacobean Studies Presented to Frank Percy Wilson*), the Folger Shakespeare Library (*The Authorship of Shakespeare*), the Shakespeare Association of America (*Shakespeare 400*), the State University of Iowa (*Studies in English Drama Presented to Baldwin Maxwell*), the University of Missouri Press (*Studies in Honor of A.H.R. Fairchild*), and the University of Texas (*Studies in Honor of DeWitt T. Starnes*).

For

Mary Ruthven McManaway

Foreword

HIS volume is designed to pay homage to the scholarship of James G. McManaway and at the same time to make the best of it available to a wider audience. The essays reprinted here testify to the quality of that scholarship—what they may not reveal so clearly, and what deserves special comment, is the diversity and richness of their author's professional life.

James McManaway was graduated from the University of Virginia in 1919 and took his M.A. there one year later. He served as an instructor and Dean of the Faculty at Virginia Junior College from 1923 to 1927, and as an associate professor of English at Mississippi Agricultural and Mechanical College in 1927-28. In 1928 he entered the graduate school of The Johns Hopkins University, where he earned a Ph.D. in English in 1931. At Johns Hopkins he served as Secretary to the Graduate Department of English (1928-36), as an instructor (1930-33), and as a research associate in the School of Higher Studies (1933-36). He was a member of the group which produced the Variorum Spenser, and he contributed both collations and critical commentaries to that edition. In the years at Johns Hopkins he also cultivated his interest in rare books and was an active member of the Tudor and Stuart Club as well as an adviser to John C. French, Librarian of the Club and of the University.

In 1936 James McManaway was asked by Joseph Quincy Adams to become his assistant at the Folger Shakespeare Library. He was appointed Assistant Director at the Folger in 1943, Acting Director in 1946, and Consultant in Literature and Bibliography in 1948, a position which he held until his retirement in 1968. During all these years he was instrumental in building the Folger's holdings and providing bibliographical descriptions of them. With Adams and other senior members of the Folger staff he was involved in the acquisition in 1938 of the Renaissance collection of Sir Leicester Harmsworth—the acquisition which more than any other brought the Folger into the front rank of the world's

research libraries. But he will probably be remembered best at the Folger
for his enthusiam and efficiency in helping scholars with their research.
His knowledge of the Folger Library is as great as his knowledge of the
period, and he has always been willing to share both with those who
have come to him for help. There are now generations of Folger readers
who are personally indebted to his generosity and kindness.

His energies have not been confined to the Folger Library, however,
particularly during the last two decades. Always active in the Modern
Language Association of America, he was appointed Chairman of the
MLA Shakespeare Variorum Standing Committee in 1948. At about the
same time he began his annual reviews of Shakespearian textual scholarship in *Shakespeare Survey*. As General Editor of the Variorum Shakespeare (since 1958), he has seen two new volumes and a supplement
through the press: *Troilus and Cressida* (ed. H. N. Hillebrand and T. W.
Baldwin, 1953), *Richard II* (ed. Matthew W. Black, 1955), and a supplement to *1 Henry IV* (G. Blakemore Evans, 1956); and he is at present
administering the work on seventeen volumes which are in progress.
Both his work as Variorum General Editor and his reviews for *Shakespeare Survey* have been informed by his authority as an analytical bibliographer as well as by his wide-ranging knowledge of Shakespeare. Extensive selections from those reviews are reprinted in the present volume.
Taken together they provide both a discriminating history of Shakespearian textual scholarship during the last twenty years and a continuing exposition of the principles which have guided the Variorum Shakespeare.

In 1951 James McManaway was asked by the Shakespeare Association
of America to assume the editorship of *Shakespeare Quarterly,* a position
which he has held ever since and in which he has become most widely
known. To this post he has devoted much of his energy and powers, and
the resulting virtues of the *Quarterly* are in large measure his own: erudition, receptivity to new ideas (and new scholars), an emphasis upon
theatrical history, freedom from cant, and honest reviewing. It is for
these qualities that the *Quarterly* is respected not only by scholars but also
by the directors and actors who are producing Shakespeare in the contemporary theater.

In all these years, and with these many roles, James McManaway has
also been a teacher, and students and colleagues testify that his teaching
is marked by the same distinction as his scholarship. While at the Folger
he taught regularly in the graduate school of the University of Maryland,
and from time to time he accepted visiting professorships at universities

throughout the country, including the Catholic University of America, the University of Colorado, the University of Kansas, the University of Missouri, New York University, Rice University, and the University of Southern California. He has continued to teach since his retirement from the Folger. In 1968-69 he taught at the University of Texas in Austin, and in 1969-70 he will teach at the University of Arizona.

James McManaway has had a full and distinguished career, and those who know him are aware of how his devotion to learning has illuminated his life. The editors and sponsors of this selection from his writings join in paying him tribute.

R. H.

A. C. K.

J. W. V.

Editorial Note.—The plan to publish this book was conceived by the editors and developed through consultation with other members of the Sponsoring Committee. The choice of essays was made by the editors. The essays are reprinted as they first appeared, except that differing editorial styles of the original printings have been normalized. In addition, the author, who cheerfully accepted the editors' invitations to correct both printer's copy and proof, has added a number of afterthoughts within square brackets, and upon occasion he has silently altered the original text in order to correct a minor error, improve the style, or achieve greater clarity. The list of the author's publications was compiled by Cathryn A. Nelson.

CONTENTS

LIST OF PLATES

23. Richard Southern's reconstruction of a playhouse designed by Sir
    Christopher Wren 230
24. A page of text in John Roberts's "transcript" of the Covent Garden
    Promptbook of *Richard II* 257
25. Plan for the Combat Scene of *Richard II* at Covent Garden in 1738 .. 260
26. Plan for the Parliament Scene of *Richard II* at Covent Garden in 1738 261
27. An engraving from Robert Glover's *Nobilitas politica vel civilis* (1608) 262

LIST OF ABBREVIATIONS

B.M.: British Museum

C.S.P.: Calendar of State Papers

DNB: Dictionary of National Biography

ELH: English Literary History

G.M.: Gentleman's Magazine

HLQ: Huntington Library Quarterly

JEGP: Journal of English and Germanic Philology

L.C.: Lord Chamberlain's Warrants (P.R.O.)

MLN: Modern Language Notes

MLQ: Modern Language Quarterly

MLR: Modern Language Review

MP: Modern Philology

N&Q: Notes and Queries

PBSA: Papers of the Bibliographical Society of America

PMLA: Publications of the Modern Language Association of America

P.R.O.: Public Record Office, London

PQ: Philological Quarterly

RES: Review of English Studies

RN: Renaissance News

RQ: Renaissance Quarterly (= RN)

SAB: Shakespeare Association Bulletin

SEL: Studies in English Literature

SJ: Shakespeare Jahrbuch

SP: Studies in Philology

SQ: Shakespeare Quarterly

S.R.: Stationers' Register

STC: Short-Title Catalogue (Pollard and Redgrave)

TLS: Times Literary Supplement

TN: Theatre Notebook

STUDIES IN

Shakespeare, Bibliography,

and Theater

Philip Massinger and the Restoration Drama

[1934]

THE CONTINUITY of English drama in the 17th century, formerly a disputed point, is no longer seriously questioned. Opinion still differs, however, about the relative importance of English tradition and of French and Spanish romance and drama in the development of such genres as the comedy of manners and heroic tragedy. One approach to the problem is by way of studies of individual Caroline dramatists and their contribution to dramatic tradition. Shakespeare and Beaumont and Fletcher have thus been studied.[1] I propose to examine briefly some of the plays of Philip Massinger in an attempt to discover his treatment of certain situations and characters familiar in Restoration drama and then to estimate his influence by tracing the stage history of his plays and their adaptations from 1660 to 1700.

First let us mention some of the qualities of Massinger's plays. Every commentator has agreed that Massinger possessed marked ability in the construction of plots. His closely knit plots, in which catastrophe usually grows out of character, are in marked contrast to the episodic plays of Fletcher. To him was given by his collaborators the task of writing the opening, expository scenes, and many of the closing scenes, in which the various actions are brought to an end. In characterization Massinger was less successful; most of his characters are types, and many of them become merely the mouthpieces of the author in his social

---

[1] G. C. D. Odell, *Shakespeare from Betterton to Irving* (New York, 1920); Montague Summers, *Shakespeare Adaptations* (London, 1922); Hazelton Spencer, *Shakespeare Improved* (Harvard University Press, 1927); A. C. Sprague, *Beaumont and Fletcher on the Restoration Stage* (Harvard University Press, 1926); J. H. Wilson, *The Influence of Beaumont and Fletcher on Restoration Drama* (Ohio State University Press, 1928).

English Literary History, I (1934), 276-304.

criticism. But they vary in their natures less wildly with the exigencies of the plot than do the characters in the plays of Massinger's contemporaries. Massinger was influenced by both Shakespeare and Jonson in his handling of characters. He never quite succeeded, like Shakespeare, in depicting the growth or decay of a complex character buffeted by fate,[2] but the attempt gave warmth and humanity to more than one play. None of his characters are quite like those in Jonson's comedies of humors, but such names as Signior Sylli, Stargaze, and Adorio, and even such dominating personalities as Sir Giles Overreach and Luke Frugal, owe much to Jonsonian influence.

All of Massinger's critics have recognized the seriousness of his moral purpose and his insistence upon the didactic functions of the stage.[3] It is not surprising, then, to find that his plays contain fewer episodic situations involving questionable morality than those of Beaumont and Fletcher, fewer licentious characters, less of "that witty obscenity . . . which like poison infused in pleasant liquor is always the more dangerous the more delightful."[4] Massinger's first impulse was to instruct the individual and criticize society by the dramatic opposition of virtuous and vicious characters. But like many another moralist, he found his means defeating his end. It is a fact that virtuous characters on the stage tend to become self-conscious and priggish and their conduct dull and stodgy, whereas their opposites often speak and act gaily and appear to live glamorously. Witty inconstants, gay deceivers, scenes of purple passion are more apt to linger in the memory than sober characters or temperate lives.

Another danger beset Massinger. No reader of his plays can believe for an instant that he could feel at home in an amoral society. Human conduct was something about which he was deadly serious. He was at his best when ridiculing folly or castigating vice. But social criticism was not relished by the Court and theatergoers in the time of James I and Charles I. They wanted sprightly amusement. So in spite of himself Massinger had frequently to write in Fletcherian vein. The language of passion and obscenity, however unnatural to him, was not unknown, but

[2] R. S. Telfer, ed., *The Unnatural Combat* (Princeton University Press, 1932), pp. 47 ff., thinks Malefort an illustration of Shakespeare's influence.

[3] See, for instance, "Philip Massinger" by B. T. Spencer, in *Seventeenth Century Studies,* ed. Robert Shafer (Princeton University Press, 1933), pp. 3-119.

[4] Richard Flecknoe says that Fletcher's plays first had this quality. See his *Short Discourse on the English Stage* (1664), reprinted in *Critical Essays of the Seventeenth Century,* ed. J. E. Spingarn (Oxford University Press, 1908), II, 91-96.

it did not come trippingly from the tongue. Often the results are less witty than disgusting. Situations that Fletcher would handle deftly by insinuation are stated by Massinger with an explicitness that is positively erotic.

Licentiousness seems really to have had a fascination for him. Though he punishes Corisca (*The Bondman*) and Iolante (*The Guardian*) for their sins, nothing could be much more stimulating than the scenes (*The Bondman*, II. ii; *The Guardian*, II. ii, III. iv) in which their vices are displayed. In the same way the voluptuousness of Donusa (*The Renegado*) is depicted *con amore*; pure love does not win her to repentance until passion has held full sway. For a somewhat different, but still heavy-handed effect, read the "stallion" scenes in *The Custom of the Country,* which are generally attributed to Massinger.

Despite the presence of occasional scenes and characters of this sort, Massinger's plays declined in popularity as Shirley's and Brome's won public favor. The reason, I think, was what I have indicated: Massinger was too much the moralist; he was not naturally, or wittily, salacious.

The play in which Massinger comes nearest to urbanity and suavity is *The Guardian,* licensed 31 October 1633. Its most entertaining features—in the Restoration sense—are Adorio, "a young libertine"; Durazzo, the Guardian, with "the colt's tooth still in [his] mouth"; and Mirtilla, a pert maid. Adorio's philosophy of life is familiar to readers of Fletcher's *Wild Goose Chase* and of the Restoration comedies of manners. To Calista, who pursues him almost as shamelessly as Oriana does Mirabel, the Wild Goose, he says (I. i):

> You are a virgin . . . ,
> A noble virgin, for whose grace and favours
> Th' Italian princes might contend as rivals;
> Yet unto me, a thing far, far beneath you,
> (A noted libertine I profess myelf)
> In your mind there does appear one fault so gross,
> Nay, I might say unpardonable at your years,
> If justly you consider it, that I cannot
> As you desire, affect you. . . .
> You are too honest,
> And, like your mother, too strict and religious,
> And talk too soon of marriage; I shall break,
> If at that rate I purchase you. Can I part with

> My uncurb'd liberty, and on my neck
> Wear such a heavy yoke? hazard my fortunes,
> With all th' expected joys my life can yield me,
> For one commodity, before I prove it?
> Venus forbid on both sides! . . .
> 　　　　　　　　If you love me
> I' the way young people should, I'll fly to meet it,
> And we'll meet merrily. . . .
> 　　　　　　　　Think upon't a close friend,
> Or private mistress, is court rhetoric;
> A wife, mere rustic solecism.

Durazzo, who overhears this speech, so much approves the sentiments that he exclaims:

> A well-bred gentleman!
> I am thinking now if ever in the dark,
> Or drunk, I met his mother: he must have
> Some drops of my blood in him, for at his years
> I was much of his religion.

Durazzo has a positive theory of education. In answer to the reproaches of his friends, he tells them that his nephew and ward, Caldoro, is not being reared extravagantly.

> They [the critics] would have me
> Train up my ward a hopeful youth, to keep
> A merchant's book; or at the plough, and clothe him
> In canvas or coarse cotton; while I fell
> His woods, grant leases, which he must make good
> When he comes to age, or be compelled to marry
> With a cast whore and three bastards; let him know
> No more than how to cipher well, or do
> His tricks by the square root; grant him no pleasure
> But quoits and nine-pins. . . .
> He wears rich clothes, I do so; keeps horses, games, and wenches;
> 'Tis not amiss, so it be done with decorum:
> In an heir 'tis ten times more excusable
> Than to be over-thrifty.

This sounds much like the opinion of Sir Edward Belfond in Shadwell's *Squire of Alsatia* (Drury Lane, May 1688). Both dramatists may have had in mind the *Adelphi* of Terence.

As for the pert maid, Mirtilla, let the following conversation with

her mistress, Calista, introduce her. Calista, who has just been repri-
manded by her mother, is not unlike her Restoration nieces.

> *Calista.* Not stir abroad!
> The use and pleasure of our eyes denied us!
> *Mirtilla.* Insufferable.
> *Calista.* Nor write, nor yet receive
> An amorous letter!
> *Mirtilla.* Not to be endured.
> *Calista.* Nor look upon a man out of a window!
> *Mirtilla.* Flat tyranny, insupportable tyranny,
> To a lady of your blood. . . .
> Run away from't;
> Take any course.
> *Calista.* But without means, Mirtilla,
> How shall we live?
> *Mirtilla.* What a question's that! as if
> A buxom lady could want maintenance
> In any place in the world, where there are men,
> Wine, meat, or money stirring. . . .
> I grant your honour is a specious dressing,
> But without conversation of men,
> A kind of nothing. . . .
>   If she would allow you
> A dancer in the morning to well breathe you,
> A songster in the afternoon, a servant
> To air you in the evening; give you leave
> To see the theatre twice a week, to mark
> How the old actors decay, the young sprout up,
> (A fitting observation) you might bear it;
> But not to see, or talk, or touch a man,
> Abominable!
> *Calista.* Do not my blushes speak
> How willingly I would assent?
> *Mirtilla.* Sweet lady,
> Do something to deserve them, and blush after.

The roles of Paris in *The Roman Actor* (licensed 11 October 1626)
and Pisander in *The Bondman* (licensed 3 December 1623) afford excellent opportunities to a good actor. Of the two characters, Pisander has
more of the qualities of the lover of heroic drama. His love for Cleora
is as extravagant and his submission to her will as complete as in the

later plays. The fate of the city-state hangs in the balance as Pisander's fortunes vary. Finally he wins Cleora, but not by virtue of his own exertions; she has to take matters into her own hands.

It is safe, I think, to say that Massinger is the best link between the early drama and the later. His career as a playwright began, probably, before the death of Shakespeare and possibly before his retirement; it ended with his death, in March 1639, just three years before the closing of the theaters. At times he attains to something almost Shakespearian in characterization and Jonsonian in seriousness; at other times he indulges in romance, borders on the heroic, and plays with intrigue much as John Fletcher did before him and as Restoration wits would do later on. How well he was known to playwrights and audiences after the Restoration, we shall presently see.

Of the nineteen or more plays usually included in the Beaumont and Fletcher canon in which Massinger had a hand (the number varies according to whether we follow Boyle, Fleay, Chelli, or Oliphant), I have taken no account, for they are included in the studies of Sprague and Wilson.[5] Nineteen plays by Massinger have survived, of which two, *Believe as You List* and *The Parliament of Love*, were in manuscript and probably not available during the years 1660-1700. A third, *The Old Law* (1656), written in collaboration with Middleton and Rowley, is never credited to Massinger in Restoration play lists (Chelli, p. 95, thinks he had no part in it). Eleven of the seventeen printed plays were adapted wholly or in part (*The Bondman, The City Madam, The Guardian, The Bashful Lover, A New Way to Pay Old Debts, The Renegado, The Great Duke of Florence, The Roman Actor, A Very Woman, The Virgin Martyr, The Fatal Dowry*) before the death of Thomas Betterton, and several of the plays were acted in a form about which we have no specific record (*The Bondman, The Renegado, The Roman Actor, A New Way to Pay Old Debts, The Virgin Martyr*). Almost as high a proportion of Massinger's plays was on the stage, then, as of Shakespeare's (twenty-nine out of thirty-seven) or of Beaumont and Fletcher's (thirty-nine out of fifty-three). Figures mean comparatively little, how-

---

[5] Of the nineteen plays listed by Chelli, *Étude sur la collaboration de Massinger avec Fletcher et son groupe* (Paris, 1926), pp. 53-97, as the product of the collaboration of Massinger with Beaumont and Fletcher, twelve were revived between 1660 and 1720; see Wilson, pp. 135-43. If we include these plays with those in the strict Massinger canon, twenty-three out of thirty-six plays were revived in one form or another, an impressive total.

ever, for we have only a fragmentary record of performances, and do not even know the names of all the plays that were revived.[6]

The Restoration history of Philip Massinger's plays begins, as far as we know, with the organization of Rhodes's company at the Cockpit in Drury Lane about March 1660. One of the first plays acted was Massinger's *The Bondman,* in which Thomas Betterton won high applause as Pisander (*Roscius Anglicanus,* p. 18). The presumption is that *The Bondman* was performed a number of times during the summer and fall of 1660, but specific information is lacking.

The first dated performance was of another play and by a different company. *The Virgin Martyr* was acted on 16 February 1660/61, by the King's Company at the Theatre Royal in Vere Street. Pepys is our authority.

I dined with my Lord and then to the Theatre, where I saw "The Virgin Martyr," a good but too sober a play for the company.

Sometime during the year appeared Q 1661 of *The Virgin Martyr,* the only play by Massinger to be printed without alteration during the Restoration period.[7] No more unaltered plays were published until Dodsley brought out the eighth volume of *A Select Collection of Old Plays* in 1744.

Another performance of *The Virgin Martyr* seems to have been given on 10 January 1661/62, by the King's Men. This is one of the performances for which Sir Henry Herbert tried to collect fees and for which Killigrew, on 4 June 1662, promised to make payment.[8] The list includes a revival of *The Renegado* on 6 June 1662. No more is heard of *The Virgin Martyr* for another six years, except in the Browne Manuscript, to which I shall refer presently; it may well have remained in repertory. Its influence, if any, would have been (1) in the direction of obscene comedy, because of the Hircius-Spungius scenes; (2) toward the development of scenic and operatic effects, because of the appearing and disappearing of Angelo and Harpax and

[6] John Downes's list of plays acted soon after the opening of the theaters ends with the significant phrase, "With divers others" (*Roscius Anglicanus,* ed. Joseph Knight, London, 1886, pp. 17-19).

[7] Contrary to what seems to have been the usual practice, it was reprinted from a Commonwealth quarto, that of 1651, instead of from the last pre-Wars quarto, 1631, as will be shown by collation of the texts.

[8] J. Q. Adams, ed., *The Dramatic Records of Sir Henry Herbert* (Yale University Press, 1917), pp. 116-18.

of the spirits of Dorothea and others; and (3) in additional suggestions for the character of the Platonic heroine of the heroic plays. Dorothea permits her lover to address her in only the chastest language.[9] And though for love of her he refuses to marry the daughter of the Roman emperor, and thus become heir to the throne, the former gives no evidence of affection for him, merely acquiescing before her martyrdom in his suggestion that when he has died of a broken heart his soul may wait on hers in paradise.

Approximately a year after its first revival, *The Bondman* was still being acted.[10] Pepys's entry for 1 March 1660/61 is to the effect that he saw the play at the Whitefriars, where Davenant's company had been acting since its organization about 5 November 1660.[11] "An excellent play, and well done," he writes, "but above all that ever I saw, Betterton do the Bondman the best." This may mean that Pepys had seen *The Bondman* acted previously by Betterton here or at the Cockpit in Drury Lane, or that he had seen other actors give inferior performances, or merely that Betterton was better as Marullo than in any other of his roles. In any event, Pepys idolized Betterton, and his interest in this play continued for seven years, when, after having seen it acted at least seven times, he read it again (2 November 1666), "which the oftener I read the more I like."

The second dated performance, but certainly not the second seen by Pepys, was 10 March 1661. One week later, Pepys went again, this time with his wife. They sat in the pit at Salisbury Court and saw the play "done to admiration." He bought a copy of the play in Paul's Church-yard on 25 May,[12] perhaps about the time that it was being revived by the Red Bull actors.

This group contained Charles Hart, Michael Mohun, John Lacy, Walter Clun, William Cartwright, and others, who had acted before the Wars, and many of whom had fought for Charles I. They had begun acting at the Red Bull but now were organized as the King's Company

[9] My attention was directed to this by Martin Krebs, who mentions it in "The Character and Origin of the English Heroic Play" (unpublished M.A. thesis, Johns Hopkins University, 1930), p. 27.

[10] The stage history of Massinger's plays was worked out before the publication of Spencer's edition of *The Bondman* and Kirk's edition of *The City Madam*. I shall have occasion later to make two specific statements of indebtedness to these editors.

[11] Leslie Hotson, *The Commonwealth and Restoration Stage* (Harvard University Press, 1928), p. 239.

[12] Sprague, p. 17 n., records a performance on this date, by a misreading, probably, of this entry in the *Diary*.

under Thomas Killigrew at Gibbons's Tennis Court, after a stay at
the Cockpit in Drury Lane and a short return to the Red Bull. Betterton's
success in *The Bondman* may have inspired the revival by the other
company. We learn of it from the list in Sir Henry Herbert's records
referred to above. Discussion of the significance of the inclusion of
The Bondman must be postponed until some consideration can be
given to the date of the performance. The plays first mentioned in the
list (*Argalus and Parthenia* and those preceding) have specific dates for
their performance, and so do those that follow *The Dancing Master*.
No such specific date is given for *The Bondman* or the six other
plays grouped with it. Perhaps the play was acted in May 1661, for
the title appears opposite that month in Halliwell-Phillips's arrangement,[13]
but it is possible that Mohun and the others who compiled the document may not have remembered the exact date but wished merely to
indicate that the play had been presented by them.

The revival of a Jacobean play by two different companies raises the
question of the rights of the various Restoration troupes in old plays.
At least two other plays, *The Tamer Tamed* and *The Unfortunate
Lovers,* were performed by two different companies (Sprague, p. 11),
but this took place before the formal organization of the actors. In the
case of *The Bondman,* there may have been a definite encroachment
by one company on the other's rights. It has been argued that the old
plays were divided between Killigrew and Davenant on the basis of
possession of pre-Wars promptbooks, but it seems to me extremely unlikely that the theatrical libraries of the pre-Wars companies could have
been kept intact to descend to the Restoration companies.[14] We know, for
instance, that manuscripts had to be collected from all sources for the
publication of the Beaumont and Fletcher folio of 1647 (*The Wild
Goose Chase* was not included because the manuscript became available
too late). Many other dramatic manuscripts first reached the printer
during the Commonwealth period, including those of Shirley's *Six New
Plays* (1652-53), Massinger's *Three New Plays* (1655), and Brome's
Five New Plays (1659). Furthermore, Andrew Pennycuicke, an actor

---

[13] In *A Collection of Ancient Documents Respecting the Office of Master of the Revels*
(London, 1870), p. 34. Sprague, p. 16, and Adams, pp. 116-18, have slightly different
arrangements of the titles and dates; a fourth is given by Edmond Malone, *Variorum
Shakespeare* (1821), III, 272-76.

[14] Hazelton Spencer, "The Restoration Play-Lists," *RES,* I (1925), 443-46; for the
opposing view see Allardyce Nicoll, "The Rights of Beeston and D'Avenant in Elizabethan
Plays," *ibid.,* pp. 84-91, and his rejoinder to Spencer, *ibid.,* p. 446.

at the old Cockpit, published not only *The Sun's Darling* (1656), that
had belonged to his own company, but also Massinger's *The City Madam*
(1658), from a prompt copy that had belonged to the rival Blackfriars
actors.[15] If, as seems likely, the manuscripts were usually lost or destroyed by the printer after he finished with them, very few prompt
copies could have survived in the possession of the actors, who would
thus be forced to use pre-Wars quartos. It was to prevent unlimited
competition in the use of these (and the surviving manuscript promptbooks) that on 12 December 1660 Davenant was granted exclusive
rights to certain plays and rights for a period of two months in certain
others.[16] *The Bondman* is not named among the plays granted to
Davenant, nor does it appear in the list of plays allotted to Davenant
on 20 August 1668 (L. C. 5/139, p. 375; quoted by Nicoll, p. 315),
or those confirmed to Killigrew about 12 January 1668/69 (L. C. 5/12,
p. 212; see Nicoll, pp. 315-16). In view of the fact that seven of
Massinger's plays (*The Duke of Milan, The Guardian, The
Bashful Lover, The Emperour of the East, The Fatal Dowry, The
Roman Actor,* and *The Unnatural Combat*) are in Killigrew's list, it is
surprising that no mention is made of plays as popular as *The Bondman*
and *The Virgin Martyr.* Perhaps unnamed plays were regarded as
common property.

In June 1661 Davenant opened his new theater, the Opera, in Lincoln's
Inn Fields, with *The Siege of Rhodes,* and here on the 4th of November
1661, Pepys saw *The Bondman* with his wife but thought the acting
inferior to that at Salisbury Court. On the 25th of the month he left a
performance of *The Country Captain* at the Theatre to see the last act of
The Bondman at the Opera.

About this time Dr. Edward Browne saw three plays at "Salisbury
or Dorset Court," two by Beaumont and Fletcher and the third, Massinger's *The Bondman.*[17] The exact dates of the performances witnessed
by Browne and the identity of the company acting at Dorset Court are
more difficult to ascertain. Lawrence dates Browne's arrival in London

---

[15] A. K. McIlwraith, "Pen-and-Ink Corrections in Books of the Seventeenth Century,"
RES, VII (1931), 204-7.

[16] L. C. 5/137, p. 343, quoted in part by Nicoll, pp. 314-15. References are to the
first edition of Nicoll, except where otherwise stated.

[17] I am indebted to Professor E. A. Strathmann of Pomona College for a transcript of
the relevant portions of Browne's Memorandum Book, British Museum Sloane MS. 1900.
It is printed with certain differences in readings in W. W. Greg's article, "Theatrical
Repertories of 1662," *Gentleman's Magazine,* CCCI (1906), 69-72.

late in 1662 and observes that Browne refers in one place to the "Kings playhouse in Convent Garden," which was not in use until May 1663.[18] We may safely conclude that Browne saw *The Bondman* during the season 1662-63 (see also Sprague, pp. 21-24). Sprague believes it "likely that Betterton and his fellows, who had already put on all three pieces [referred to above], were the actors. If the performances in question took place in 1662-63, they had probably quitted their resplendent 'Opera' temporarily—perhaps while it underwent repairs—to play at their former house, still standing at the time" (p. 23). Nicoll, on the other hand, assumes that at this time Jolly's Men were acting at Salisbury Court; and if, as has been suggested, these three plays were not the exclusive property of one of the major companies, he is probably correct. The performances must have taken place, then, before 23 July 1663, when Jolly's license of 24 December 1660 was revoked; probably they were given before 27 January 1662/63, the date of his license to act in the provinces (see Nicoll, 2nd ed., pp. 276-77).

In these formative months, we have found specific records of eight performances of *The Bondman* and evidence that there were others. It was presented by Rhodes's, Davenant's, and Killigrew's, and possibly by Jolly's Men. So popular a play could hardly have failed to exert a strong influence on the taste of the audiences and on the writers of new plays.

[18] W. J. Lawrence, "A Forgotten Restoration Playhouse," *ES*, XXXV (1905), 279-89. The Browne Manuscript is generally dated 1662 because of the date of the mileage table on fol. 60^r and because the record of plays seems to accord with the known facts of the years 1662-63. The *terminus ad quem* is fixed by the fact that Browne departed from England in 1664. But there is no reason to suppose that Browne saw no plays in London until after he left Cambridge in 1662. In fact, Greg remarks of the entries that they were not all written at one time. One notation in the manuscript lends weight to the belief that Browne may have seen some of the plays before 1662 or early in that year. On fol. 62^v, opposite the entry for *Doctor Fostus*, are words which Strathmann records as "K Licens: Players" (Hotson, p. 179 and n., agrees), but which Greg prints "Quens (?) Players." Now we have a record of the organization of a group of actors under that name in warrant L. C. 5/137, p. 333, dated 17 December 1661 (Nicoll, 2nd ed., p. 274 and n.), and references to a group, originally at the Red Bull, as "Queen's actors" in L. C. 5/137, p. 43, on 5 February 1661 (Nicoll thinks this is "probably 1661/62"), and again on 29 December 1663, in L. C. 5/138, p. 10. Another such reference occurs in L. C. 5/137, p. 173, on 4 November 1662, and still others come in 1665/66 and 1669 (see Nicoll, 2nd ed., pp. 325-26). The earliest of these manuscripts includes Betterton with some of the Red Bull actors in a troupe to be known as "the Queenes Comoedians." Are we to suppose that Browne witnessed a performance by a "Royal Company" (the phrase is Nicoll's, 2nd ed., p. 274) at the Cockpit? If so, did the success of *Fostus* encourage a minor troupe to revive the play in the following spring at the Red Bull, where Pepys saw it on 26 May 1662 and found it "so wretchedly and poorly done, that we were sick of it"?

Possibly the pornographic scene (II. ii) between the lascivious Corisca and her foolish stepson was deleted, but few changes would have been necessary in the character of Marullo, a perfectly chaste, perfectly self-controlled, almost Platonic lover.

We now turn again to the King's Company. Their third known venture with a play of Massinger's was another performance of *The Virgin Martyr* on 10 January 1662. This is one of the performances for which Herbert had tried to collect (p. 9 above). The play was still in repertory in 1662/63, for Dr. Browne saw it at the "New Theatre in Lincoln's Inn fields." Opposite the name of the play Browne usually records the amount paid for admission; admission to *The Virgin Martyr* cost him nothing, perhaps because of the presence of "Mr. Wild," whose name appears on the line with the title.

In the same season Browne saw a performance of *The Renegado* at Lincoln's Inn Fields for which he paid 2s. 6d. The exact date is, of course, unknown, but it must have been earlier than 6 May 1663, when the King's Men left this house. This calls to mind the fact that the King's Men had acted the play on 6 June 1662 (see p. 9). As in the case of *The Virgin Martyr* above, the performance listed by Herbert may have been the one seen by Browne, but it may just as well have been another. Unlike *The Virgin Martyr* and *The Bondman,* which we have no reason for thinking were altered, *The Renegado* was probably changed for representation. MS. Rawlinson Poet. 20 in the Bodleian Library is a version of *The Renegado* "written in a late seventeenth-century hand, and evidently made for a revival of the play. . . . No cast is given and the manuscript bears no indication of having been used as a prompt copy."[19] After examining a photostat of the text, I agree that the manuscript is not a prompt copy.

The manuscript version changes the name of Vitelli's servant from Gazet to Iseppo, usually alters the spelling of Carazie to Corazie, and adds Muftie, Janizaries, and a Spye-Eunuch. The major changes are the excision of a bawdy scene (III. iv); the expansion of II. iv, the courtship of Vitelli by Donusa; and the alteration of the concluding scene to make it more spectacular. For a colloquy between Asambeg and Mustapha and a Messenger's account of the lovers' escape, the adapter substitutes an attack on the castle by Grimaldi and his sailors. Far from being anticlimactic, as in Massinger, the scene closes with stirring

[19] The opinion of W. J. Lawrence, who first called attention to the manuscript, "The Renegado," *TLS,* 24 October 1929, p. 846.

action. An important stylistic change is the breaking up of long de-
clamatory speeches by the introduction in their midst of brief questions
of fact that require explicit answers. The altered dialogue is much more
like ordinary conversation. Minor changes are in the direction of (1)
the modernization of manners and of diction, (2) the deletion or
modification of obscene, indelicate, and low words and phrases, (3)
the omission of Latin and other learned phrases, and (4) the avoidance
of anything that might be regarded as irreverent (in V. iii the audience
hears an account of the baptism of Donusa instead of seeing it on the
stage).

About this time a fourth play by Massinger was revived. It has been
customary to say that *A New Way to Pay Old Debts,* which held the
stage in the 18th and 19th centuries better than any other non-Shakespearian play, was not revived until 1748.[20] We are indebted again to Edward
Browne's manuscript for the record of the performance, which was
at "the King's Armes, Norwich."[21] It was acted by Jolly's provincial
company, presumably some time after he received his license on 27
January 1662/63 and before Browne left England in 1664. Nothing is
known about the text of the play used for the performance.

Massinger's other realistic comedy, *The City Madam* (II. ii) may have
suggested to John Dryden a brief passage (III. i) in his *Wild Gallant,*
produced at the Theatre Royal in February 1662/63, but the resemblance is not great.[22]

In July of the following year (*i.e.,* 1664), Pepys saw what must have
been the first performance of *The Bondman* in that season. His entry
for 28 July records that the actors "for want of practice . . . had many
of them forgot their parts a little; but Betterton and my poor Ianthe
outdo all the world. There is nothing more taking in the world with
me than that play." This, as far as we know, is the last time Pepys

---

[20] A. H. Cruickshank, ed., *A New Way to Pay Old Debts* (Oxford University Press,
1926), p. x. Wilson, p. 126, lists a performance in 1708, but this seems to have been of
The Debauchee, or A New Way to Pay Old Debts (see Genest, II, 405), the same play
that Wilson lists in 1677 with the alternate title, *The Credulous Cuckold.* It is an adaptation of Brome's *Mad Couple Well Matched,* generally attributed to Mrs. Behn. See Langbaine's comment: "Crafty Book sellers, whose custom it is as frequently to vent old
Plays with new Titles, as it has been the use of the Theatres to dupe the Town, by acting
old Plays under new Names, as if newly writ and never acted before; as, . . . *The
Debauchee,* another [old Play] of Brome's" (*Momus Triumphans,* London, 1688, sig. A4).
[21] B. M. Wagner, "George Jolly at Norwich," *RES,* VI (1930), 449-52.
[22] Suggested by Kathleen M. Lynch, "D'Urfé's *L'Astrée* and the 'Proviso' Scenes in
Dryden's Comedy," *PQ,* IV (1925), 302-8; called to my attention by Mr. G. W. Knipp.

saw the play. His delight in it continued, however, for he was reading it with increased enjoyment on 2 November 1666.

I find no further trace of revivals of Massinger's plays until 1668,[23] when Killigrew offered *The Virgin Martyr* in what may well have been a revised form. In 1661 Pepys thought it "a good but too sober a play for the company." This time (27 February 1667/68) he liked it better.

The first time it hath been acted a great while: and it is mighty pleasant; not that the play is worth much, but it is finely acted by Becke Marshall.

Fortunately, for we have no text of this date, Pepys gives us several clues to the features of the performance.

But that which did please me beyond any thing in the whole world was the wind-musique when the angel comes down, which is so sweet that it ravished me, and indeed, in a word, did wrap up my soul so that it made me really sick, just as I have formerly been when in love with my wife; that neither then, nor all the evening going home, and at home, I was able to think of any thing, but remained all night transported, so as I could not believe that ever any musick hath that real command over the soul of a man as this did upon mee.

Small wonder that on 2 March he went to hear the music again, "which at this hearing the second time, do still commend me as nothing ever did, and the other musique is nothing to it." He did not attend the performance witnessed by King Charles on 20 March.[24] Instead he spent

---

[23] The anonymous author of "An Elegy Upon the Death of S[r]. WILLIAM DAVENANT" must have been a lover of the old drama. He imagines the late poet laureate surrounded by the "Great Souls who once admired him here":

> First, *Johnson* doth demand a share in him,
> For both their Muses whip'd the Vice of time:
> Then *Shakespear* next a Brothers part doth claim,
> Because their quick Inventions were the same.
> *Beaumont* and *Fletcher* their Petitions joyn,
> This, for clear Style, that for his deep Design:
> *Tom Randolph* asks a Portion 'mongst the rest,
> Because they both were apt to break a Jest.
> *Shirley* and *Massinger* comes in for shares,
> For that his Language was refin'd as theirs. . . .

Reprinted from the original folio-broadside by G. Thorn-Drury in *A Little Ark* . . . (London, 1921), pp. 35-37. Davenant died 7 April 1668, and this elegy was composed shortly thereafter. This is the only contemporary criticism I know that praises Massinger for his refinement of language.

[24] Warrant dated 29 August 1668 (L. C. 5/139, p. 129), abstracted by Nicoll, pp. 304-5; also warrant (L. C. 5/12, p. 17). Nicoll notes that the second warrant gives the date as 2 March instead of 20 March. Since Pepys makes no mention of the King's

the time practising the violin "in order to be inventing a better theory of musique than hath yet been abroad; and I think verily I shall do it."

Speculation about changes in the text is idle; doubtless they were much like those in *The Renegado*. The stage directions of the quartos of *The Virgin Martyr* offer abundant material for a manager in search of spectacular effects. At IV. iii Angelo enters *"in the Angels habit"*; in V. i he materializes—to the accompaniment of music—to Theophilus, Roman persecutor of the Christians, *"with a basket filled with fruit and flowers"* and after a few words vanishes. Later in the scene Harpax disappears beneath the stage and mocks Theophilus from first one trap-door and then another, in imitation of the Ghost in *Hamlet*.[25] He reenters *"in a fearfull shape, fire flashing out of the studie."* There are other such exits and entries. The one Pepys enjoyed so much is probably that in V. i. Angelo's other materialization from the spirit world (V. ii) is in the company of four others. The stage direction makes no mention of music or of descending figures. Perhaps such a heavenly host would have overtaxed the capacity of Killigrew's machinery.[26]

The question of the rights of the King's and Duke's Companies in the old plays seems to have been acute in 1668. Reference has already been made to two warrants (L. C. 5/139, p. 375, dated 20 August 1668; L. C. 5/12, p. 212, of date *c*. 12 January 1668/69) which confirmed 23 plays to Davenant and 108 to Killigrew. No Massinger titles appear in the first list, but in the second (Killigrew's) are *The Duke of Milan, The Unnatural Combat, The Bashful Lover, The Emperour of the East, The Fatal Dowry, The Roman Actor*, and "The Gardian." The temptation is to assert that all the plays mentioned in the two lists were revived on the Restoration stage. The ownership of the exclusive rights to an old play was not an academic question. And I am the more persuaded that every play named was actually revived, because such plays as *The Bondman* and *The Virgin Martyr*, known to have

presence on 2 March, the correct date for the warrant is probably 20 March; but it is possible that the King attended both performances.

Nicoll records a performance on 19 March of which I have found no trace; see his note on p. 103 of the 2nd ed.

[25] But see the discussion of this point in W. J. Lawrence's lecture, *"Hamlet as Shakespeare Staged It,"* delivered under the auspices of the Tudor and Stuart Club, as printed in *The Johns Hopkins Alumni Magazine*, XIV (1925), 451-68.

[26] But see the stage directions for *"several Spirits in horrid shapes flying down amongst the Sailers, then rising and crossing in the Air,"* and *"a number of Aerial Spirits in the Air, Ariel flying from the Sun . . . ,"* quoted from the Shadwell version of *The Tempest* presented at Dorset Garden, 1674, by Spencer, pp. 204-9.

been acted by both companies, were excluded from the lists. In the
case of the seven plays just named (perhaps this is true of other plays
in the lists also), however, direct evidence is wanting. It is safe to say
only that Killigrew had sufficient interest in these titles at this time (and,
if the warrant be a reissue of one originally granted in 1660, as some
have supposed—see Wilson, p. 120—at that time too) to wish to reserve
them to himself.

One of the plays in Killigrew's list requires special notice. Was "The
Gardian" Massinger's play or Abraham Cowley's *Cutter of Coleman
Street?* The method of grouping the titles suggests the former.[27] The
plan of the list, to group the plays more or less by authors, is admittedly followed least toward the close, where "The Gardian" occurs
between a play by Massinger and one by Suckling. I am inclined,
nevertheless, to agree with A. H. Nethercot that the play allotted to
Killigrew was Massinger's,[28] for the play called *The Guardian* which
was presented before royalty by the Duke's Company at Lincoln's Inn
Fields on 9 August 1668 and at Dorset Garden on 17 November 1672 and
8 January 1674/75[29] was certainly Cowley's, despite the fact that when
it was revived in 1661 in altered form the title used was *Cutter of
Coleman Street.*[30] Why was the play acted under the title *Guardian* but
printed as *Cutter?* Perhaps *Cutter* brought to mind memories of the
early failure in 1661.[31] Inasmuch, then, as the Duke's Company owned

[27] The first 14 plays are by Jonson; then follow 15 (or 16) plays by Beaumont and
Fletcher, 3 by Shakespeare, 23 by Beaumont and Fletcher, 11 by Shakespeare, 1 by Cartwright (*The Royal Slave,* 1639, based in part on Massinger's *Bondman,* as pointed out
by W. G. Rice, "Sources of William Cartwright's *The Royall Slave,*" *MLN,* XLV (1930),
515-18), 7 by Shakespeare, 4 (or 5) by Shirley, 1 by Howard, 1 by Massinger, 1 that cannot be identified, 1 by Massinger, then "The Gardian," 1 by Suckling, 3 by Carlell, 1 by
Massinger, 1 by Chapman, 1 by Suckling, 2 by the Duke of Newcastle, 1 by Massinger,
1 by Carlell, 1 by Suckling, 1 by Massinger, 1 by Berkeley, an anonymous play, 2 by
Middleton, 2 by Brome, 1 by Carlell, 1 by Massinger, 1 by Jonson and others, and finally
1 by Chapman.

[28] "Abraham Cowley as Dramatist," *RES,* IV (1928), 1-24.

[29] See warrants L. C. 5/139, p. 125, and L. C. 5/141, pp. 2, 216, excerpted by Nicoll,
pp. 309-19.

[30] Pepys saw a performance on 5 August 1668 and was much disgusted to find it only
Cutter of Coleman Street under a different name. A failure at its first revival after the
Restoration, it was a distinct success in later years (see Cowley's preface to the 1663 edition
and Downes, ed. Knight, p. 25).

[31] For another play that was revived under a new title but afterwards known by its
first, see Nicoll, 2nd ed., p. 379, where he discusses Boyle's *General,* which was known
also as *Altamira.*

and acted Cowley's *The Guardian* in 1668 and later, the play secured
to the King's Men must have been written by Massinger.

In the next play to be discussed, we meet the first printed adaptation
of Massinger in the Restoration. *The Life of Mother Shipton. A New
Comedy,* although "acted Nineteen dayes together with great Applause"
(or so the title-page avers), was printed without date and with only
the initials of the author, "T. T." Fortunately, T. T. wrote another play
(printed in 1668) with signed dedication to one Mrs. Alice Barret.
Langbaine first spotted the indebtedness to Massinger's *The City Madam*
and added that the plot was "from a Book so called in Prose, 4°" (*Momus
Triumphans,* p. 25). In 1691 he expanded this account and commented
on the use of only the author's initials.

This Play has not the Author's Name to it, but the two first Letters: it may be
he was asham'd to set his Name to other Mens Labours.[32]

He also gave Kirkman the credit for expanding T. T. into Thomas
Thompson.[33] He made the mistake, however, of saying that the play
was "acted Nine Days together" instead of nineteen, and there has
been confusion about the matter ever since. Nineteen days was a long
but not impossible run in those days. Biographical information about
Thompson is entirely lacking. The British Museum has a poem of
his, *Midsummer-Morn; or, The Livery Man's Complaint* (1682), and
he wrote the other play referred to above, *The English Rogue* (1668). It is
entirely probable that there was some connection between Thompson and
Richard Head, who wrote the first part of *The English Rogue* (1665) in
association with Francis Kirkman and a pamphlet, *The Life and Death
of Mother Shipton* (1677). In addition to the similarities of titles, there
is identity of subject matter, not in the two *English Rogues,* but in
the two accounts of Mother Shipton. The earliest account of Shipton
in the British Museum Catalogue is dated 1641. Others with varying
titles appeared in 1642, 1643, 1648, 1662, 1663, 1677, 1684, 1685, 1687, 1697,
1740, 1775, 1797, 1810, 1811, 1815, 1825, 1870 1871, 1873, and 1882. The
early pamphlets contain the jingling prophecies attributed to Mother
Shipton, but the first I have seen that has narrative resembling the play
is that of 1687, written by Head, which as we have seen was published

---

[32] *An Account of the English Dramatick Poets* (Oxford, 1691), pp. 503-4.

[33] Francis Kirkman, "An Exact Catalogue of all English Stage-Plays printed, till this
present Year 1671," added to *Nicomede* by John Dancer (1671).

also in 1677.[34] If it were not for the date of the earliest known quarto (1677), I should say without hesitation that the pamphlet was Thompson's source. But we know from Kirkman's list that the play was in existence at least by 1671. The parallels are obvious and are of such a nature that Head could not easily have borrowed from Thompson. For example, in the prose narrative, the first part of a double charm which Mother Shipton repeats at the instance of the devil is as follows: "*Raziel* ellimihammirammish*ziragia Psonthonphanchia* Raphaelelhaverunatapinotambecazmitzphecat jarid cuman hapheah Gabriel Heydon turris dungeonis philonomostarkes sophecord hankim." Such stuff is not easy to memorize; in the play Thompson uses only the italicized portions, giving them thus: "Raziel, Ziragia, Phonthonfancia." It may be that Head's narrative was written much earlier than 1677, the date of the earliest known quarto. In fact, this seems probable, for the account closes with the Great Fire of 1666, and the title-page states that the prophecies are collected "until this present year 1667." In the Stationers' Register, furthermore, there is an entry to Mrs. Ann Maxwell dated 30 August 1667: "The life and death of Mother Shipton, or true Relačon of what ... shee did and spakt."[35] If this was an earlier edition of Head's narrative, Thompson may well have used it.[36]

[34] *The Life and Death of Mother Shipton. Being not only a true Account of her strange Birth; the most important Passages of her Life; but also all her Prophesies, now newly Collected ... until this present Year 1667* (London, ... W. Harris ... , 1687). Reprinted by Edwin Pearson (Westminster, 1871). The prefatory remarks are signed by Head, who says he secured the manuscript from a family which may have come into possession of it at the destruction of the monasteries in the time of Henry VIII. Pearson suggests in his Critical Preface that William Lilly (1602-81) was the original of "Mother Shipton."

[35] It is worth noting that Mrs. Ann Maxwell was the widow of David Maxwell, who died about 1665. David Maxwell published *Mercurius Publicus* until the time of his death, when Peter Lilliecrap took it up. Peter Lilliecrap was the printer of Thompson's *Mother Shipton*. See H. R. Plomer, *A Dictionary of the Booksellers and Printers ... from 1641 to 1667* (London, 1907).

[36] Another possibility presents itself, but it is merest conjecture, and it is apparently negatived at the outset by the existence of Thompson's poem, *Midsummer-Morn*, referred to above. Head returned to London from Ireland in 1663 and printed his play, *Hic et Ubique*. Other works appeared rapidly until 1666 or 1667. There is then a gap in his publications until 1672. After that Head continued prolific. Throughout this whole period, according to the *DNB*, Head was in straitened circumstances and made a living doing hack work. Now "T.T.'s" plays were printed in 1668 and, as we shall see, between that date and 1671. This is the interval during which Head published nothing under his own name. Did Head write the "T.T." plays, borrowing the title of one from his own *English Rogue*, and basing the other on his *Life of Mother Shipton?*

There is another possible point of contact between *Mother Shipton* and Head: in the

The date of *Mother Shipton* has been variously given as "1660?" by Nicoll (p. 375); "about 1668" (Halliwell-Phillips's *Dictionary of Old English Plays*, p. 175); and "1671" (Baker's *Companion to the Play-house*, 1764, vol. I, sig. Gg5ᵛ; vol. II, sig. O6ᵛ; *Playhouse Pocket-Companion*, 1779, p. 114). The later limit is 1671, the date of Kirkman's list. The history of Thomas Passinger, the bookseller who handled the play, helps fix the earlier limit of publication. He succeeded to his master's business in 1664 (Plomer, p. 145). The interval of 1664 to 1671 is narrowed by three years if Head's narrative *Life of Mother Shipton* was actually printed in 1667; it is narrowed still further by the Prologue to Thompson's other play, printed in 1668. These are the significant lines:

> Ye'r welcome to the labour of a Muse;
> Who do's implore (and 'tis your pitty worth)
> Your helping hands to bring her firstling forth,
> And let me tell ye, 'tis most necessary
> Since 'tis her first you act more kind and wary.[37]

If the Prologue may be relied on, Thompson wrote *Mother Shipton* after *The English Rogue*. And if the plays were printed in the order

play there is a group of beggars who praise their calling as enthusiastically as those in Brome's *Jovial Crew;* Head wrote a *Canting Dictionary* in 1673.

Why should Head have wished to conceal his identity? Perhaps for the same reason that he refused to continue *The English Rogue* with Kirkman, because people insisted that all the scandalous and criminal episodes were autobiographical. In the prefatory note to his *Life of Mother Shipton,* Head was careful to point out that he was acting merely as the editor of an old manuscript. His reputation was such that he could ill afford to be suspected of any connection with witchcraft.

Why the initials "T.T."? They were very popular with anonymous writers of the time. A great many pamphlets signed "T.T." have survived, the best known of which is, I suppose, *Quaker's Quibbles* (1675).

This conjecture has its origin in the fact that we know nothing about the Thomas Thompson named by Kirkman in his list dated 1671. There are records of men of this name, however; see the following: (1) a London bookseller (?), who received his freedom 6 July 1635 and whose name appears in the imprint of several pamphlets dated 1642; (2) a gentleman, widower, of Isle of Ely, who married Katherine Burroughs of St. Margaret's, Westminster, widow, in London on 8 April 1661; (3) a gentleman, bachelor, of Canterbury, who married Mrs. Phoebe Hammond of Canterbury at St. Bride's, London, on 29 June 1663; (4) a clerk, rector of Skegnes, co. Lincs., who on 29 October 1672 married Mary Parish of Fishtoft, Lincolnshire. The first is named in Plomer's *Dictionary of Booksellers and Printers;* the others, in Joseph Foster's *London Marriage Licenses 1521-1869* (London, 1887).

[37] For an accurate transcript of this prologue, I am indebted to Mr. C. K. Edmonds of the Henry E. Huntington Library, the quarto I have consulted in the Library of Congress being imperfect. [The original printer failed to set the closing parenthesis in the second line quoted.]

in which they were written, *Mother Shipton* can be dated with some certainty as having been printed between 1668 and 1671. Since plays were usually printed soon after their appearance on the stage, *Mother Shipton* was probably written in these same years.[38]

The quarto of *Mother Shipton* is badly printed. Turned letters and misspelled words are frequent. Punctuation is scanty in some places but excellent in others. Whoever prepared the manuscript for printing was careful to indicate act- and scene-divisions (except at V. vi) and to insert brief stage directions.[39] But blank verse is always printed as prose. Only the songs and the couplets are printed in verse form. The quarto may have been printed from a reported version, for the scenes are very short—many are only one page in length, and not more than three or four exceed two pages—and a number of scenes open with a soliloquy which is intended to introduce some character and narrate what has happened since he last appeared.

The Life of Mother Shipton has two plots, one involving Mother Shipton and Radamon and derived from the accounts of the life of the witch, and another, a complicated intrigue based chiefly on Middleton's *Chaste Maid in Cheapside*. The scenes which owe most to Massinger's *City Madam* are *Mother Shipton* I. v and V. v, but Thompson took other hints. The characters in the two plots are never brought together; they are connected by a third group which comes into contact with each of the other groups just once. The characters are carefully balanced, with five couples: the Whorehounds, the Shiftwells, Maria and Moneylack, Shipton and Radamon, Pluto and Proserpina. In addition, Hairbrain, Swagger, and the Captain pair off with Priscilla and the two whores. At the end of the play, all the characters in the intrigue plot are connections by blood or marriage. The dialogue is very poor except for the passages taken over from Massinger and Middleton. And only in the borrowed scenes is there much action on the stage. The method of the plagiarist was to find suitable passages

---

[38] If this dating is correct, the play cannot be identified with *Mother Rumming,* as suggested by W. W. Greg (*A List of Masques, Pageants, &c.,* London, 1902, Appendix II, p. xc). Nothing more is known of *Mother Rumming* than that the title appears in Archer's list printed at the end of Massinger's *Old Law* (1656).

[39] A stage direction on p. 49 seems to imply that a Restoration stage might sometimes have a partition like the inside wall of a house to produce the effect of two adjoining rooms: *"The Scene a Tavern. Sir Oliver. Shiftwel, Moneylack David and a Scrivener, Shiftwells wife Maria and Sir Olivers wife apart as in another room."* But perhaps the two groups stayed at opposite ends of the stage and left the audience to imagine a partitioning wall between them.

in one of his sources and to rearrange them with the minimum of verbal changes. The play's success must have resulted from the outspokenness of the men and women in the intrigue plot and from the spectacular effects made possible by the introduction of witches, devils, beggars, and an angel.

A brief notice of *The Virgin Martyr* in 1672 indicates its continued popularity. Softhead in Lacy's *Dumb Lady* exclaims (I. ii.): "You lie! and for the honour of squirehood I'll die a virgin martyr."[40] The reference may be to the revival of *The Virgin Martyr* in 1668, for Lacy's play was first acted at the Theatre Royal in 1669.

During the next few years there are no records of revivals of Massinger's plays. In 1677-78, however, Shadwell's *The True Widow* (Dorset Garden, *c.* March) appeared with a scene built around an incident borrowed from *A New Way to Pay Old Debts,* V. i. Lady Cheatly abuses and defrauds her creditors by means of disappearing ink and wax, as Marrall deludes Sir Giles Overreach.[41] About two years later, Lee's *Theodosius; or, The Force of Love* (*c.* September 1680) was brought out at the same theater. Baker seems to have been the first to comment on the fact that the play deals with the same central characters as Massinger's *Emperour of the East* and to suggest that Lee may have

borrowed some Hints from this Play; particularly that of *Theodosius's* Negligence as to public Affairs extending to such a Length, as the giving his Sister *Pulcheria* an absolute Power even over the Life of his beloved *Athenais,* by means of a Blank signed and delivered to her.[42]

The chief characters are indeed the same, but they are conceived in an entirely different spirit. Lee based his play on a translation (1666) of La Calprenède's *Pharamond,* as Langbaine (*Dramatick Poets,* p. 327) pointed out in detail; he took (*Theodosius,* IV. i) from Massinger (*Emperour of the East,* III. ii, iv) only the incident noted by Baker.

The plundering of Massinger began in earnest in 1680, with *The Guardian* as the chief victim. As in so many other cases, Langbaine was the first to record the plagiarism in *Love Lost in the Dark; or, The Drunken Couple. Acted at New-Market.* (*Momus Triumphans,* p. 31

---

[40] Genest I, 97; J. Maidment and W. H. Logan, eds., *The Dramatic Works of John Lacy, Comedian* (Edinburgh, 1875), p. 3.

[41] Called to my attention by Mr. W. B. Terwilliger, this indebtedness was first noted by Saintsbury, Mermaid ed. of Shadwell, p. 121.

[42] *Companion to the Play-House,* vol. II, sig. G2.

n.; *Dramatick Poets,* p. 542. He did not particularize because he did not have the play at hand.) Genest (X, 146) classified *Love Lost in the Dark* as "unacted" and explained that "nearly the whole of this F[arce] is stolen from Massinger—the bulk of it is from the Guardian—some parts of it are from a Very Woman, and the Bashful Lover." Cruickshank noted the fact that one character, Calandrino, derives his name from *The Great Duke of Florence.*[43] *Love Lost in the Dark* was printed in 1680 with two other farces, *The Merry Milkmaid of Islington; or, The Rambling Gallants Defeated* and *The Politick Whore; or, The Conceited Cuckold,* under the general title, *The Muse of Newmarket.* The three were entered separately to James Vade in the *Term Catalogue* (I, 440) at Easter 1681; so the printing must have been done about the turn of the year (January to March), 1680/81, and the plays were probably written and acted not long before, possibly at the time of the races in the previous fall, when we know that Pepys attended on Charles II at Newmarket (*Diary,* ed. Wheatley, I, xxxv). The identity of the first adapter of *The Guardian* is unknown, and we know no more about the company that acted the play. Since, as we have seen, *The Guardian* was probably awarded to Killigrew in 1668/69, some member of his company may have hashed up the adaptation. The droll is so wretchedly put together that I think it was intended for use by the minor actors or some provincial company. And from the fact that the few "original" portions are given to Calandrino and Moggulla, the low comedians, and that these insertions are almost unprintable gags, I believe the actors playing these two parts may well have prepared the adaptation.[44]

[43] A. H. Cruickshank, *Philip Massinger* (Oxford University Press, 1920), pp. 24-25.

[44] It is possible that the three farces are from the pen of one adapter. If so, he was probably not a Londoner and possibly not an actor. The Prologue to *The Merry Milkmaid* pleads with the audience:

> For once be courteous to a Country Muse
> Vntaught, such Tricks the Wits of London use;
> And in short time, he may find out the way
> To write fine Poppet Plays as well as they.

The Epilogue to this farce suggests that the three adaptations were acted as one evening's entertainment, comparing the pleasure of three short plays to that of one long one.

That the farces were acted by a provincial company is strongly suggested by some lines from the Prologue to *Love Lost in the Dark:*

> Our Habits and our Acting such appears,
> Like weather-beaten weary Travellers:
> Who have endur'd more then may here be told,

What the adapter (or adapters) did was to take a copy of *Three New Playes* (1655), which contains *The Guardian, The Bashful Lover,* and *A Very Woman,* and from these patch up a play. He did not take the trouble even to arrange as verse the passages lifted bodily from the originals. The droll was hastily prepared, or else the manuscript supplied the printer was very inferior, for mistakes abound. The play is straight farce, free from classical allusions, descriptive and moralizing passages, and romantic characters and incidents. Every effort is made towards simplicity and directness, and all the emphasis is on intrigue and obscenity.

Two years later Mrs. Aphra Behn tried her hand at adapting *The Guardian.* "'Tis true indeed," writes Langbaine (*Momus Triumphans,* sig. a3),

what is borrow'd from Shakspeare or Fletcher, is usually own'd by our Poets, because every one would be able to convict them of Theft, should they endeavour to conceal it. But in what has been stolen from Authors not so generally known, as Murston [*sic*], Middleton, Massenger, &c. we find our Poets playing the parts of Bathyllus to Virgil, and robbing them of that Fame, which is . . . justly their due.

Langbaine describes the indebtedness in detail (*Momus Triumphans,* p. 2, and again in *Dramatick Poets,* pp. 17-19); Baker adds to the account the statement that "Mrs. Behn has also introduced into this Play a great Part of the Inner Temple Masque, by Middleton" (*Companion to the Play-House,* vol. II, sig. D5ᵛ). As Summers points out in his edition of Mrs. Behn's *Works* (II, 198), "this charge is absolutely unfounded." Chelli has suggested, only to deny it, a possible indebtedness to *A New Way to Pay Old Debts* (p. 258 n.). He must have in mind the relationship of uncle to nephew which is found in each play, but this is much more satisfactorily traced to Middleton's *A Mad*

From Eastern blasts and sharper Northern cold.
Which keeps our sadded Hearts in deep suspence.
Wanting a place to fix our Residence.
Yet if these Radiant Beauties will but please
To smile on our Endeavours, 'twill much ease
Our cares, abate our Feares: well knowing then,
Their Influence creates Favours in those Men:
Whom noble Bounty and Compassion may,
Transform our sable Night to chearful Day.
So by your Goodness with your mercy mixt,
We wandring Planets may in time be fixt.

World, My Masters, the other play which Mrs. Behn draws on in writing *The City Heiress.*

One of the most amusing political plays of the Restoration is *The City Heiress; or, Sir Timothy Treaty-all.* It opened at Dorset Garden on 15 May 1682,[45] with a brilliant cast, but its run was short, possibly because of the political satire. It was, however, revived in 1707 (Genest, II, 374) and adapted by Charles Johnson in 1715; this adaptation was altered in turn by later playwrights. Mrs. Behn took from Massinger and Middleton whatever would complicate her intrigue plot and add sprightliness to her lines. She added enough, however, to integrate the material and make a sparkling though very naughty play. The difference between pre-Wars and Restoration comedy may be easily indicated by reference to the changes Mrs. Behn has made in her characters and incidents. Her Sir Anthony is Massinger's Durazzo without his sturdiness; Wilding, who is both Adorio and Follywit, is wilder, more eloquent, more fascinating than either. He agrees to marriage at the end of Act V, not in the middle of Act II, as Adorio does. Equally significant is the fact that Mrs. Behn gives him success with his whore, an assignation with his mistress, success in the theft of his uncle's papers, and, finally, the hand of the beautiful heiress who eloped with him. To the uncle is given the cast-off whore. Not so in Middleton. There the uncle retains most of his property, and the young libertine is gulled into marrying his uncle's cast-off mistress. Notice, too, that Massinger depicts the abandoned passion of an elderly matron in such a manner that we are thoroughly disgusted with her. Middleton depicts a scene of seduction, but makes his lovers repent and reform. The pre-Wars plays may in their characters and situations have been quite as immoral as *The City Heiress,* but Mrs. Behn's attitude and treatment are different. She stimulates the senses in a way that would have shocked the moralist in Massinger and the realist in Middleton.

After the union of the King's and Duke's Companies in 1682, a play in the possession of the former became available for Betterton's use. Davies is the authority for the statement that Betterton acted the role of Paris in *The Roman Actor. The Bondman,* he says, "was the only Play of Massinger revived after the Restoration; till Mr. Betterton took a fancy to the Part of Paris, in the *Roman Actor.*"[46] The revival may have occurred about this time, 1682, or as late as 1692, when Genest

---

[45] Summers gives this date in his edition of *Roscius Anglicanus,* p. 227. See also p. 226.

[46] Note signed "D." in *Roscius Anglicanus,* ed. Waldron (London, 1789), p. 26.

(III, 82) lists a performance, apparently quoting indirectly from a play-bill. If the play was indeed a favorite with Betterton, the version which was printed in 1722 may owe something to him.

At the death of John Lacy (17 September 1681), a play was found which derives in part from *The City Madam* and perhaps *A New Way to Pay Old Debts*. This is *Sir Hercules Buffoon; or, The Poetical Squire,* which was first acted at Dorset Garden in 1684, three years after Lacy's death. The initial situation of the serious plot is probably suggested by *The City Madam*. Sir Marmaduke Seldin is just as thorough-going a scoundrel as Luke Frugal and almost as much of a hypocrite. His plan is to ship his wards out of the country, not to America to be victims of savages, but to the north of Norway, where they are to be devoured by bears (perhaps suggested by *The Winter's Tale*). The heiresses are saved by a sentimental turn of the plot. At the end of the play (V. ii), Lord Armiger attempts to convert Sir Marmaduke with a device used in *The City Madam,* V. ii. At this point, Lacy turns from *The City Madam* to *A New Way,* makes Seldin rave at his daughters as Overreach does at Margaret, and sends him to a madman's death, like Overreach's.[47]

There is no reason for thinking that Dryden was at all influenced by Massinger's *Believe as You List* (then still in manuscript form only) in writing *Don Sebastian*. The only similarity is that Massinger's play in its original form and Dryden's play deal with the same historical character.

The last major plagiarism to be treated in this paper is that of Edward Ravenscroft, who in his *Canterbury Guests; or A Bargain Broken,* took material from *A New Way*. This play, which appeared first at Drury Lane in 1697, is not an adaptation of *A New Way,* but rather an alteration of Ravenscroft's own *Careless Lovers* (Dorset

---

[47] Mariana's reasons for renouncing her suitor, Lord Armiger, are of unusual interest:

> You made love to an impostor, a false woman; and now you know the cheat, are you so weak to think your honour is engaged to make that courtship good to that impostor? . . . My Lord, this heart and every drop of blood within it has more love for you than Dido quitted life for; yet all this can I conquer to be just, therefore must not in point of honour marry.

These are sentiments that about the turn of the century will be found in sentimental comedy. They are noteworthy here because Lacy had no high moral purpose; he designed only to cater to his public. And we may be reasonably sure that he worked into his plays only the elements that he knew from observation would please. 1681 is an early date for a sentimental heroine like Mariana.

Garden, March 1672/73), with additions from his *King Edgar and Alfreda* (Drury Lane, about December 1677), Molière's *Monsieur de Pourceaugnac,* and *A New Way to Pay Old Debts.* The first performance, according to Nicoll (p. 370), was about September 1694. Genest (II, 57-58), in his discussion of Ravenscroft's plagiarism, suggests that the play may have been acted in May of that year because the contract between Buffler and Furr in III. iv is dated the 3rd of May.

Ravenscroft uses farcical elements from all of his sources and adds enough horseplay to make a fair theatrical success. Usually he expands what he borrows, rarely copying a line or two without some verbal changes. A desire to avoid the rhythm of blank verse would account for this in the use of Massingerian material. Ravenscroft has no desire to improve on his sources and certainly no idea of purifying them. What he wants is a swiftly moving farce with plenty of surefire hits, and he comes near writing one. But the play met with little favor and does not seem to have been revived.

There is some reason for thinking that Ravenscroft made the acquaintance of a number of Massinger's plays long before 1694. Durzo, for instance, comes to *The Canterbury Guests* from *King Edgar and Alfreda,* but the name sounds like Durazzo in Massinger's *The Guardian;* it is sufficiently out of the ordinary to require some explanation. The name Lovell is found frequently in literature of this period, and it is probably only coincidence that Lord Lovel is one of the characters in *A New Way* and that Mr. Lovell is in *The Careless Lovers.* Again, Muchworth, the old alderman of the latter play, has a common enough name, and it is not necessary to believe that it was suggested by the name Alworth in *A New Way.* Finally, the portion of *The Careless Lovers* (Act IV) which confronts Lord DeBoastado with Mrs. Breedwel and Mrs. Clappam, while undoubtedly based on Molière's *Pourceaugnac* (II. ix, x), may well owe something to Massinger's *Unnatural Combat,* IV. ii. In this scene, a bawd and two wenches with two children set upon Belgardo and charge that he is the father of the children. Each of these points of resemblance is in itself trivial; taken together, they may have some cumulative value.

In *The Canterbury Guests,* Ravenscroft borrows from *A New Way* Justice Greedy, a suggestion of the Innkeepers, of Jack Sawce (called Order by Massinger), and of Dash, who is given the comic lines of Massinger's Marrall, as well as scenes in which these characters appear. The play derives its alternate title from a speech of Sir Giles Overreach (*A New Way,* III. ii. 217-18, ed. Cruickshank):

Mum, villaine, vanish: shall we breake a bargaine almost made up.

The play is in prose, except for couplets at the end of I. viii, III. v, V. vi, viii, and in the middle of IV. ix. The French practice of beginning a scene with the entrance of each new character is followed in this play but not in *The Careless Lovers* or *King Edgar and Alfreda.*

One of the most amusing incidents in this play, and also in *The Careless Lovers,* is the "proviso" scene in which Careless and Hillaria agree to wed. The possible origin of such scenes has been traced by Miss Lynch through Dryden to D'Urfé and in another branch ultimately to Massinger's *The City Madam,* II. ii.[48] There can be little doubt that Ravenscroft borrowed from Dryden's *The Wild Gallant* III. i in writing *The Careless Lovers* and retained the scene in *The Canterbury Guests.*

Three more plays before 1700 must be referred to. The first of these, Thomas Dilke's *The City Lady* (Lincoln's Inn Fields, *c.* January 1696/97), does not resemble Massinger's *The City Madam* in diction or plot but has enough similarities in characters to convince Kirk that Dilke must have had Massinger's play in mind.[49] The second, the anonymous *Timoleon; or, The Revolution* (quarto 1697), has the same source as Massinger's *The Bondman* and seems to Spencer to have been slightly influenced by the older play.[50] The last play of all to be mentioned is Congreve's *The Way of the World* (Lincoln's Inn Fields, March 1699-1700). This famous play contains a proviso scene which may be traceable to Massinger's *City Madam,* II. ii. There are even verbal similarities in several lines. Did Congreve merely follow in the tradition of Ravenscroft and Dryden, or did he remember the old play?

The period 1660-1700 ends just before Rowe's famous *The Fair Penitent* (1703; based on Massinger and Field's *The Fatal Dowry*); not many years later Benjamin Griffin produced and published an adaptation of *The Virgin Martyr* under the title, *Injured Virtue; or, The Virgin Martyr* (1715); four years after this appeared an anonymous adaptation of *The Bondman* (1719), and three years later an anony-

[48] "Durfé's *L'Astrée* and the 'Proviso' Scenes in Dryden's Comedy," *PQ,* IV (1925), 302-8.

[49] Rudolf Kirk, ed., *The City Madam* (Princeton University Press, 1934), pp. 40-41.

[50] B. T. Spencer, ed., *The Bondman* (Princeton University Press, 1932), pp. 258-59. Nicoll, 2nd ed., p. 351, notes that the play was probably unacted and that the Bodleian copy is attributed in a manuscript note to Southby.

mous version of *The Roman Actor* (1722). Throughout the whole Restoration period and well into the next century, then, Massinger's plays were read and acted. Less frequently performed and adapted than those of Shakespeare and of Beaumont and Fletcher, his plays must nevertheless have exerted a very considerable influence on playwrights and audiences.

Thomas Dekker: Further Textual Notes

[1938]

EADERS of Dr. Fredson Bowers's recent observations on *The Roaring Girle* in the December 1937 issue of *The Library* (pp. 338-40) may be inclined to accept his conclusion that the Dyce copy of the play contains the later state of the inner forme of sheet I. Certain additional evidence has come to light, however, which must reverse that conclusion.[1]

If the seven settings of the running-title be designated by the letters A to G, the variations A, B, C, and D will be found once in each forme of sheets B to E (none is found, of course, on B1^r, the first page of the text) and in the inner forme of sheet F. Variety E replaces B, as Mr. Bowers points out to me, in the outer forme of sheet F. In sheets G and H, varieties A, C, D, and E occur once in each forme. In sheet I, where Mr. Bowers found evidence of resetting of the text in the inner forme, the Folger and Pforzheimer copies (and presumably

---

[1] The problem came to my attention when Mr. Bowers wrote, pointing out that two settings of the running-title might be identified in *The Roaring Girle,* and asked my opinion about the order in which certain formes of the play had been printed. My reply took, in part, the form of a dummy of the quarto on which I noted the occurrence on each page of one of the seven varieties of the running-title, which I described. In a day or two he sent me a discarded proof of his article referred to above and questioned my identification of the settings of the running-title on I1^v and I4. With his table of variants before me, I reexamined the Folger quarto and the Farmer facsimile of the British Museum copy (which suffers from cropping) and formed the opinions to be given below. These I forwarded at once to Mr. Bowers, but since *The Library* was already in the mails he could not modify his printed conclusions. He in turn loaned me his photostat of part of the Huntington copy and gave me a report of his examination of the copy owned by Mr. Carl Pforzheimer of New York City.

The Library, 4th ser., XIX (1938-39), 176-79.

the Dyce[2] copy also) have settings A, C, D, and E on leaves I4, I1^v, I3^v, and I2, respectively; but the outer forme has settings D, E, F, and G on leaves I2^v, I3, I1,[3] and I4^v. In the British Museum, Bodleian, and Huntington Library copies the running-titles of the outer forme are exactly like those of the Folger and Pforzheimer copies (and Dyce?). The inner forme, however, has no trace of settings A and C of the running-title, but in their place settings F and G. And in the later sheets, only settings D, E, F, and G are to be found. What happened, obviously, is that in the course of printing sheet I there was some mishap to the inner forme which necessitated the replacement of the running-titles of leaves I1^v and I4. The new settings, F and G, appear in due course in the outer forme of the sheet and continue to appear regularly to the end of the play. Any copy of the quarto which has the original settings A and C of the running-title on leaves I1^v and I4 must contain the first state of this forme; any copy which has settings F and G of the running-title on these leaves must contain the later state.[4] That is, the Folger, Pforzheimer, and Dyce copies represent the text as originally set; the British Museum, Bodleian, and Huntington copies contain the text as set up after the mishap (an eighth copy is reported to be in the Boston Public Library, but I have no information about it).

An examination of the variants recorded by Mr. Bowers will now be profitable. When the accident to the inner forme of sheet I occurred, the chase was tilted in such a way that pages I1^v and I4 were right side up and pages I2 and I3^v were in an inverted position. The loosening of the type in the upper half of the chase permitted the period after the speech-tag *Lax.* in line 3 of I2 to slip down almost on a line with the period after the speech-tag *Lax.* at the beginning of line 2, forcing the period originally set there away from the letter *x*. In leaf

[2] The Wise copy, Dr. W. W. Greg informs me, is like the Dyce copy. It should be included in later enumerations.

[3] Mr. Bowers questions my identification of the setting of the running-title on I1. He suggests that after the printing of I(i), the running-title (setting A) which had been used for I4 was accidentally pied. To take its place, a new setting, which might be designated A', was prepared and used in the outer forme on I1. This new running-title, he thinks, was pied after quire I had been perfected, necessitating the preparation of still another setting—the one I have designated as F—which appears in the later quires. It is my opinion that what he would call setting A' is really a faulty impression of F.

[4] These running-titles may be identified readily. Setting A occurs on B1^v, B2^v, C1^v, C2^v, D3, D4, E3, E4, F3, F4, G3, G4, H3, H4; setting C, on B3^v, B4^v, C3^v, C4^v, D1^v, D2^v, E1^v, E2^v, F1^v, F2^v, G1^v, G2^v, H1^v, H2^v; setting F, on K1, K2, L1, L2, M1, M1^v; setting G, on K3^v, K4^v, L2^v, L3^v.

I3^v, the "e" of "moone" in line 11 dropped out entirely, as did the final "s" of "besides" in line 7; at the same time the letters of "makes" and "peticote" in line 7 began to work apart, as indicated by Mr. Bowers.

In the lower half of the chase the damage was more extensive, as Mr. Bowers has recorded. He has since noted another variant: on I4, line 5, the British Museum, Bodleian, and Huntington copies have "try", while Pforzheimer and Dyce (and Folger, of course) read "try,". I shall add only one particular. In line 7 of leaf I4, the British Museum, Bodleian, and Huntington Library copies read "'twas" where Folger and Pforzheimer (and presumably Dyce) have "t'was". Incidentally, as Dr. Greg points out to me, Mr. Bowers was ill advised to offer as bibliographical evidence the use in the Dyce copy of a long dash in line 26 of I4 where the British Museum copy has a series of four hyphens, for throughout the play the long dash and the series of from two to seven hyphens are employed indiscriminately, not to mention the occasional appearance of two short dashes and of a combination of hyphens with a dash.

The results are instructive, for most textual editors would feel justified in describing no fewer than a dozen of the differences between copies as press-corrections to be found in the Folger, Dyce, and Pforzheimer copies, while only seven readings are definitely "better" in the other three copies. Actually we know that the Folger, Dyce, and Pforzheimer copies have the text as set from the manuscript by the compositor, while the other state gives an attempted reconstruction of the text. This is a case in which "literary" evidence must be rejected in favor of the bibliographical evidence of the running-titles.

The "Lost" Canto of *Gondibert*

[1940]

N *GONDIBERT,* his major contribution to nondramatic poetry, Sir William Davenant planned a poem in five books, somewhat like the five acts of a play. The first two books, as is well known, were written in France and carried to sea in manuscript on the author's ill-starred venture to America. At Cowes Castle six cantos of the third book were committed to paper, and, after his removal to the Tower, Davenant arranged for the publication of his unfinished poem. But as one of Davenant's recent biographers puts it, "Whether there is war between Brescia and Bergamo, whether the machinations of Hermegild succeed, whether he wins Gartha, Hurgonil weds Orna, Tybalt wins Laura, Hubert wins Rhodalind, or Gondibert weds Bertha, we shall never know."[1] The inclusion of two small fragments of the poem in the folio edition of his *Works* (1673, pp. 326-35),[2] is proof that Davenant did not forget his ambitious project, but these fragments give no clue to the resolution of the plots. Bibliographers have discovered another possible source of information, without, however, enabling scholars to investigate it. As Professor A. H. Nethercot puts it,[3] "another full canto was ap-

[1] Alfred Harbage, *Sir William Davenant: Poet Venturer, 1606-1668* (University of Pennsylvania Press, 1935), p. 183.

[2] Herringman, the publisher, states in his address to the reader that the first of these, "The Philosophers Disquisition directed to the Dying Christian," had been intended by the author as a part of *Gondibert.* The second, "The Christians Reply to the Phylosopher," "is evidently a piece of the same stuff" (C. M. Dowlin, *Sir William Davenant's Gondibert, its Preface, and Hobbes's Answer: A Study in English Neo-Classicism,* Philadelphia, 1934, p. 7). These fragments do not find a place in *The Seventh Canto;* they must have been intended for Book Four or Book Five.

[3] *Sir William D'avenant: Poet Laureate and Playwright Manager* (University of Chicago Press, 1938), p. 270 and n. 10.

Modern Language Quarterly, I (1940), 63-78.

parently printed in 1685; but this mysterious continuation, seemingly no longer extant, was probably the compliment of some anonymous admirer and imitator. . . . On the SR, 1640-1708, III, 266, appears this entry for December 16, 1684: 'Master Wm. Miller. Entred . . . booke or coppy entituled *The seaventh and last canto of the third booke of Gondibert,* never before printed. By Sr Wm Davenant'; and *The Term Catalogues, 1668-1709 A.D.* . . , ed. Edward Arber (London, 1903), II, 114, state that it was printed in February, 1684/5. Wood, III, 808, lists: *'The seventh or last Canto of the third Book of Gondibert.* Lond. 1685. oct. never before printed.' W. C. Hazlitt, *Hand-Book to the* . . . *Literature of Great Britain* . . . (London, 1867), has added: 'By Another Hand.' Later bibliographers and critics have simply echoed these last two references."

Hazlitt's observation about the authorship of the *Seventh and Last Canto,* unless it was pure guesswork, could have been based on no more than a casual examination of a copy of it in circulation in the latter part of the last century. Actually two copies still exist, and it is the purpose of this article to make the text of the *Canto* available to scholars.

The copy in the Folger Shakespeare Library is a small octavo, bound up with a copy of the octavo edition of *Gondibert* (1651), in old brown calf, blind tooled.[4] The book is signed A-C^8, with pages numbered at the top center in parentheses (5)–(45). Page (5), Dedication, is misnumbered (4), and there are three unnumbered pages following the text. The contents are as follows: A1, Title-page; A1^v, blank; A2$^{r \text{ and } v}$, [Address to the Reader]; A3-4, [Commendatory Verses]; A4^v, [General Notice of books sold at the Gilded Acorn in St. Paul's Church-Yard]; A5-C7, Text; C7^v-8^v, *Books Printed for, and Sold by* William Miller, *at the* Gilded Acorn *in Saint* Paul's *Church-yard near the little* North-Door. Inside the front cover of the volume is the Jacobean armorial bookplate of Samuel Chandler, Gent. (Franks Collection 5562), and, pasted on it, the label of M. J. Naylor, D. D.

The question naturally arises: is the *Canto* spurious, as Hazlitt stated? To this, the first reply is the publisher's or editor's note: "This Seventh and Last Canto of the Third Book of Gondibert, having layn

---

[4] Through the kindness of Mr. Donald G. Wing of the Yale University Library, I have been able to locate a second copy. This book, bearing several signatures of Richard Cullen and the date, 6 August 1734, was presented to Wellesley College in 1923 by George H. Palmer. Miss Lilla Weed, Associate Librarian, has generously sent me a description of it and collated its text with a typescript of the Folger copy. I cannot adequately express my appreciation of her assistance.

long Buried in obscurity, came not to Light till after the Impression of
Sir William Davenant's Works: That this only Remain of that unparallel'd Heroick Poem might not be lost, it was thought fit to be Published,
as well to Assert its true Genuine Birth, as also to show it Self not not
[*sic*] to be Inferiour to the best of the other Canto's." This might be
dismissed merely as a publisher's statement of questionable authority,
were it not for the presence on the next three pages of a seven-stanza
poem written by Charles Cotton the Younger "in Answer to the Seventh
Canto . . . ," which had been dedicated to his father. These verses
are likewise to be found with slightly different text in the posthumous
volume of Cotton's *Poems* (1689). In the latter volume, they are printed
together with seven stanzas entitled "Sir William Davenant to Mr.
Cotton."[5] The association of Davenant with the Cottons, father and son,
must have been very close. In 1651 Davenant presented a copy of the
handsome quarto of *Gondibert* to the father.[6] At some later date
(possibly in 1652—see note 5) he dedicated his unpublished *Seventh
Canto* to him. In 1685 Charles Cotton the Younger assisted in the
publication of the manuscript and wrote a poem to his dead friend to
be prefixed to the *Canto*. Still later, the publisher of the pirated edition
of Cotton's *Works* (1689) took liberties with the texts of Cotton's seven
stanzas and seven of Davenant's.[7]

[5] So far from being an independent poem, the lines are actually stanzas 1-4 and 7-9 of
The Seventh and Last Canto. The omitted stanzas 5 and 6 are a eulogy of Charles II.
The publisher of the *Works*, a pirated volume, was probably misled by the name "Charles"
in stanza 4 into thinking that Charles Cotton was the subject, though the last line should
have saved him the error by its reference to "Monarchs." Recent scholars have perpetuated
the error; cf. C. J. Sembower, *The Life and the Poetry of Charles Cotton* (University of
Pennsylvania Press, 1911), p. 6. Also John Beresford, *Poems of Charles Cotton 1630-1687*
(London, 1923), pp. 16-17, 412. Both of these scholars accept as authoritative the notice in
Cotton's works that *The Seventh . . . Canto* was "Written by Sir William, when Prisoner
in the Tower, 1652." Beresford remarks that "It appears [Davenant] got no further with
his seventh Canto of Book III of Gondibert than this charming dedication to the elder
Cotton, unless there are still in MS. further portions of that immensely lengthy poem."

[6] See *A Book Hunter's Treasury* (The Rosenbach Company, 1940), Item 117. The in-
scription in Davenant's own hand is there given as follows: "For the much Honourd
Charles Cotton esquire from Sir Your most faythfull thankefull and humble servant
Will: Davenant. Tower: Decemb: 19th 1651." For this important item, I am indebted to
Dr. Joseph Q. Adams, who on numerous other points has generously given me the benefit
of his counsel.

[7] [Alvin I. Dust, "*The Seventh and Last Canto of Gondibert* and Two Dedicatory
Poems," *JEGP*, LX (1961), 282-85, points out that a then (1961) recently discovered
manuscript in the Derby Borough Library contains a large number of poems by the
younger Cotton, arranged in roughly chronological order, and that the poem "in Answer
to the Seventh Canto" follows one dated "Christmas Day 1659." The "Answer," then, was

One more bit of contemporary evidence may be adduced. A blank
leaf inserted between *Gondibert* and *The Seventh . . . Canto* bears the
following manuscript memorandum to Charles Cotton the Younger:
"Sir | I find that in (seuen of) | the seuen staⁿzas wherein | you have
made Sr William | liue, the printer is not | to be pardoned, no more |
then in seuenteene stanzas | wch I have marked in | the Poem: wherein
sir | in some places he hath | printed noncense." These lines of apology
must have been penned by the editor or one of the publishers of the
Canto in lieu of an errata list. Obviously they accompanied a copy of
the book which was supplied to Cotton, the author of the commendatory
poem in question, and he preserved them. The leaf of paper on which the
note is written is, curiously enough, just the size of an octavo leaf, and
the paper resembles very closely that found in the last gathering of
Gondibert (1651). Until the publication of Professor Dowlin's proof that
leaf V8 of *Gondibert* is never a blank,[8] I had supposed the leaf bearing
the manuscript apology to Cotton to be blank leaf V8. The Folger copy
is so tightly bound that I cannot satisfy myself on this point. More than
likely, however, the manuscript apology was inserted between the two
books by order of Charles Cotton the Younger.

The writer of the manuscript apology mentions seventeen typographical errors in the *Canto* which he has marked. These marks appear to
have been lost when the binder trimmed the margins very closely. At
any rate, they are not to be found at the present time.[9] I have, accordingly,
ignored obvious errors in punctuation and have even retained turned
letters and obvious misspellings (inserting *sic* as a guide to the reader).
[Some half a dozen irregularities of spacing have been corrected silently.]
The Wellesley Library copy is identical with that in the Folger. It

---

probably written in 1659 or 1660. Since the elder Cotton died in 1658, we may infer that
The Seventh . . . Canto and its dedicatory poem to him must have been written not later
than 1658. Dust thinks that upon the death of the elder Cotton his son felt it incumbent
upon himself to reply to Davenant's poem.

Dust's study of variant readings in the Derby Manuscript, *The Seventh . . . Canto,* and
the surreptitious collection of 1689 leads him to believe that the version in *The Seventh
. . . Canto* represents the earliest state and that the manuscript and 1689 contain later revisions, in that order.]

[8] C. M. Dowlin, "The First Edition of *Gondibert:* Quarto or Octavo?" *The Library,*
4th ser., XX (1939), 178-79.

[9] The ink used to note the errors in Cotton's poem is brown, while that of the manuscript apology is black. Perhaps the Folger copy of *The Seventh . . . Canto* is not after all
the one marked by the author of the apology—this would account for the absence of the
"seventeen" marks—but rather another copy belonging to Cotton and checked by him.

supplies one letter, one comma, and one period which have been trimmed from the Folger copy.

The stanza numbers have been removed from a central position and placed in the margin in order to save space. The publishers' notices have been omitted for the same reason. The passages checked in Cotton's poem, four in number, are indicated in this reprint as in the original by a large X in the margin.

[The Seventh . . . Canto . . . of Gondibert]

THE | SEVENTH | And Last | CANTO | OF THE | THIRD BOOK | OF | GONDIBERT, | Never yet Printed. | [rule] | By Sir *William Davenant.* | [rule] | *LONDON,* | Printed for *William Miller* and *Joseph Watts* at the | *Gilded Acorn* in St. *Paul*'s Church-Yard, over | against the little North Door, 1685.

THis Seventh and Last Canto *of the Third Book of* Gondibert, *having layn long Buried in obscurity, came not to Light till after the Impression of* Sir William Davenant's *Works: That this only Remain of that unparallel'd Heroick Poem might not be lost, it was thought fit to be Published, as well to Assert its true Genuine Birth, as also to show it Self not not* [*sic*] *to be Inferiour to the best of the other* Canto's.

TO | Sir WILLIAM DAVENANT, | IN | ANSWER | TO THE | Seventh Canto | OF THE | THIRD BOOK | OF HIS | GONDIBERT, | Dedicated to my Father.

O Happy Fire, whose Heat can thus controul
The Rust of Age, & thaw the Frost of Death;
That renders Man immortal, as his Soul.
And swells his Fame with everlasting Breath.

Happy that hand, that unto Honours climb;   X
Can lift the Subject of his living Praise;
That rescues Frailty from the Scyth of Time,
And equals Glory to the length of Days.

Such, Sir, in you, who uncontroul'd, as Fate   X
In the Black Bosom of Oblivions Night;
Can Suns of Immortality create,
To dazle Envy with prevailing Light.

In vain they strive your glorious Lamp to hide
In this dark Lanthorn, to all Noble Minds;   X
Which through the smallest cranny is descry'd,
Whose Force united, no resistance finds.

Blest be my Father, who has found his Name   X
Among the Heroes, by your Pen reviv'd;
By Running in Times Wheel, his thriving Fame
Shall still more youthful grow, and longer liv'd.

Had *Alexander*'s Trophies thus been rear'd,
And in the Circle of your Story come;
The spacious Orb full well he might have spar'd,
And reapt his distant Victories at home.

Let men of greater Wealth than Merit, cast
Medals of Gold for their succeeding part;
That Paper Monument shall longer last,
Than all the Rubbish of decaying Art.

THE | Seventh Canto | OF THE | THIRD BOOK | Dedicated to |
CHARLES COTTON Esq;

The ARGUMENT.

Wakt by the Duke's Adoption, Hubert *brings*
Borgio *beneath the shade of Nights black Wings,*
To dark Verona: Orna *is betray'd,*
And Hurgonil, *not Jealous, but dismay'd.*
The Chiefs *their Passions vent to* Hermegild,
But soon to Gartha's *braver Passion yield.*

1. UNlucky Fire, which tho from Heaven deriv'd,
    Is brought too late like Cordials to the Dead,
    When all are of their Sovereign sence depriv'd,
    And Honour which my rage should warm is fled.

2. Dead to Heroick Song this Isle appears,
    The ancient Musick of Victorious Verse:
    They tast no more, than he his Dirges hears,
    Whose useless Mourners sing about his Herse.

3. Yet shall this Sacred Lamp in Prison burn,
   And through the darksom Ages hence invade
   The wondring World, like that in *Tullie*'s Urn,
   Which tho by time conceal'd, was not decay'd.

4. And *Charles* in that more civil Century,
   When this shall wholly fill the Voyce of Fame,
   The busie Antiquaries then will try
   To find amongst their Monarchs Coins thy Name.

5. They will admire thy force 'gainst *Gothick* rage,
   Thy Head of *Athens,* and thy Woman breast,
   Which rescu'd these Records in a rude Age,
   When the free Arts were frighted, and opprest.

6. If they who read thy Victories, thus confest,
   Find not thy wreathed Image, their blind Skill
   In gath'ring Monarchs Medals, they'll detest,
   And think they made their long Collections ill.

7. They'll highly bless thy Vertue, by whose Fire
   I keep my Lawrel warm, which else would fade,
   And thus enclos'd, think me of Nature's Quire
   The chief, who still sing sweetest in the shade.

8. To Fame who rules the World, I lead thee now,
   Whose solid Power the thoughtful understand,
   Whom tho too late, weak Princes to her Bow,
   The People serve, and Poets can command.

9. And Fame the only Guide to Empires past,
   Shall to *Verona* lead thy Fancie's Eyes,
   When Night so black a Robe on Nature cast,
   As Nature seem'd afraid of her Disguise.

10. Ambitious *Hubert* to *Verona* came
    In the dark Reign of Universal Sleep;
    And means no Tears shall quench his Angers flame,
    Tho all the Dwellers must be wak'd to weep.

11. Till Fame had made the Duke's Adoption known,
    He painfully supprest this raging Fire:
    But now it was above his Conduct grown,
    And *Borgio* thus provok'd it to aspire.

12. Thy Wealth, thou painted City, who shall save?
    Black art thou now, and sleep thy business seems;
    Each dark abode is silent as the Grave,
    Thy sleep were perfect Death if Death had Dreams

13. Thou civil Crowd of soft Inhabitants,
    Sleep and forget thy Crimes; may *Adice*
    No more relieve thy thirsty Medows wants,
    But swelling here, thy drowning *Lethe* be.

14. Wake but to kindle lust, and boldly think
    Heaven has no Eyes, but the departed Sun;
    May thy new marri'd at Adult'ries wink,
    Both soon seek Strangers, and each other shun.

15. Sleep you who Ruin States by Trades Encrease,
    Rich Traffickers who fetch those Toyes from far,
    Which soften us at home, you plead for Peace,
    Because our Luxuries we quit in War.

16. Sleep as securely as your Carricks steer,
    When in deep Seas your Gale is from the East,
    You and Your Pilots want the Art to fear
    The suddain Tempest breeding in my Breast.

17. You Statesmen sleep, who States tame Lyons be,
    For you and Lyons sleep with open Eyes,
    And shut 'em when you wake, you seem to see
    Through darkness, and with Wink your sight disguise.

18. Sleep you Oppressors, Monsters quickly bred,
    When private Will is joyn'd to publick Power,
    Like Bears in Winter long by slumber fed,
    You wake with Hunger, that would Herds devour.

19. Sleep all, till waking each with ravisht Mind,
    Shall the strange Glory of new Light admire,
    And thinking 'tis the Morn, Curse when ye find,
    Your City is become your Funeral Fire.

20. *Borgio* did *Hubert*'s Fury thus excite,
    Which from his darkn'd thoughts breaks through his Eyes
    As suddainly as Morning breaks from Night,
    Or glorious *Chiefs* from sleep to Battle rise.

21. And now the Morn in suddain Glory rose,
    And to salute the World, shifts from his Face
    Night's Veil, as fast as Brides unmask to those
    Whom they saluting, would with kindness Grace.

22. To restless *Hubert, Borgio* leads the way,
    Near *Orna*'s Window *Hurgonil* he spies,
    Who there with Musick welcomes Break of Day,
    And as the Lark the East salutes her Eyes.

23. For there at ev'ry dawn with Lovers layes,
    Till this sweet Moon shall end their nuptial Rites,
    And Joyes begin, he love *Reveillees* payes,
    Which made their morning sweet as Lovers nights,

24. Such Aires the untun'd *Borgio* ill abides,
    For Musick which is so the Soul of Love,
    As Love is of our Life, his Soul derides,
    Whom only Drums ambitions Noice could move.

25. He oft sends back, as he does forward pass,
    His fatal Looks, which did the Count less awe
    Than did that Amorous, but more dreadful Face,
    Which he too soon in *Orna*'s window saw,

26. For there appear'd, tho but obliquely plac'd,
    As shrunk behind the Glass, a Youth, who seem'd
    Repleat with all those Graces, which have grac'd
    Great Courts, or greater Love has e'er esteem'd.

27. Such seem'd this Amorous Youth, who soon withdrew
    His Looks, and shut the Casement hastily,
    As if he only watch'd to scape from view,
    By stealth would see, and to be seen was shy.

28. A Youth, who thus his Beauty seems to hide,
    So guiltlessly in a suspicious time,
    And in the Chamber of a plighted Bride,
    Might blot the whitest Vertue with a Crime.

29. Yet this as Loves false Fire, the Count did scorn.
    Grave *Tybalt,* who these Rites attended, seems
    So lost in Sleep, as if not yet the Morn
    Were broke, and ranks his Vision with his Dreams.

30. Yet Jealousie, which does by Thoughts subsist,
    As Life by Air; grew stronger by their pause;
    For they their Musick silently dismist,
    And fearing ill Effects, must doubt the Cause.

31. Musick which here at *Orna*'s dawn had sung,
    For Love's Morn breaks not in a common Sky;
    But now their Lutes did seem on Willows hung,
    Where near some murmuring Brook dead Lovers lye.

32. Vain Jealousie, thou fruitful little Seed,
    Tho single, and as small as Atoms sown,
    Yet faster riseth than a forward Weed,
    In many Stems soon great and fully blown.

33. 'Tis Love's Alarm [*sic*] Bell too often hung
    Near Lover's Beds, and keeps 'em still awake;
    Yet Noble *Hurgonil,* when first it rung,
    Scarce seem'd to start, and now thus calmly spake.

34. Since Love the valiant Aids I must not dread
    A Shadows force, and I should vain appear,
    To let my Eyes be by a Vision led
    From Her whose Image in my Heart I wear.

35. Such Maiden Stratagems each plighted Bride,
    Rul'd by her Virgin Counsel does devise;
    And thus my Faith in *Orna* must be tri'd,
    Faith's Fort is best attempted by Surprise.

36. She as betroath'd does till this Moon be past,
    And Marriage Laws begin by Custom Sway,
    And now she tempts my Jealousie to taste
    How I will Reign, when she must long obey.

37. That Youth her near Ally, such harmless Art
    Assists, which may to Country Eyes seem bold;
    But Courts *Elixir* Vertue does convert
    The worst and most suspected Coyn to Gold.

38. *Tybalt* repli'd, this Tryal, *Hurgonil*,
    Exalts you both, it proves your love not light,
    And shews that she wants guilt to give her Skill,
    Where to direct her Jealous Tryals right.

39. Your solid healthful Love sweats not away
    At the faint Heat of Jealousies pale Flame,
    Nor even in Death will more than Souls decay,
    Which dye not, but return from whence they came.

40. And since her Tryal is so useless made,
    Her Errour does her Innocence proclaim;
    For as we trace strange Thieves by known Thieve[s][10]aid[,][10]
    So our own Guilt lights us to others Shame.

41. The Guilty often wake, when Jealous grown,
    To watch Love's Treasons in another's Bed;
    Yet after foul Adulteries in their own,
    Sleep as secure from Terrors as the Dead.

42. Thus as they homeward move, they timely draw
    Discretion's Curtain o'r each others Eyes,
    And would not see, what they with Sorrow saw,
    Truth oft more modest seems in a Disguise.

---

[10] Supplied from the Wellesley Library copy. [Both the *s* and the comma were lost as a result of trimming the Folger copy, the reading "aid," being a turnover in O 1651.]

43. Wise Nature does reprove our Jealousie,
    'Tis Fear, and Fear none willingly express,
    The Jealous shrink like Spies from every Spy,
    Aud [*sic*] what they find with Honours less confess.

44. But why (misterious Love) to blemish Truth
    In truest Lovers hast thou Art devis'd?
    Even in the Artless Sex, for that fair Youth
    Was *Gartha* in a manly shape disguis'd.

45. Whose Beauty stoop'd to *Hermegild*'s advice,
    And she of *Ulpha, Orna*'s Woman bought
    The Jewel Honour at a common price,
    And was by stealth to *Orna*'s Chamber brought.

46. There she in Night's black Bosom lay,
    As in dark Lanthorns Light for Treason lyes,
    And so when she peep'd forth, 'twas to betray,
    As those were made to shine for a Surprise.

47. Calm *Orna* fearless slept, since free from Sin,
    And little did her Womans duty doubt,
    Nor heard when she had took the Traytors in,
    Who through her Windows let her Honour out.

48. And still she slept with as becalm'd a Breast,
    As thoughtless Martyrs in a Monument,
    Whilst *Gartha* (whose Success her Cares encreas'd)
    Shifts her Disguise, and to her Palace went.

49. Where *Hubert* longingly expects that she
    The reason of her Absence should unfold,
    Who big with Plot longs for delivery,
    And thinks Successes lost that are not told.

50. With *Hermegild* she hastily arrives,
    Where when she *Hubert* and Bold *Borgio* spi'd,
    Her Anger seem'd to threaten Lovers Lives,
    And at her Frowns has many a Lover dy'd.

51. The two fierce Leaders gravely thoughtful grow
     Like scar'd Astrologers, as griev'd to take
     From this new Comet in her threatening Brow,
     The Empires Doom, and thus her Passion spake.

52. Wild Rumour, which from Court to *Brescia* fled,
     Has brought you here bright in your Angers Flame,
     You, *Hubert,* who in War have others led,
     Now for your own chief Guide chuse common Fame.

53. At *Gondibert*'s Success, and new Renown
     Your sick Ambition in a Fever seems;
     Which from the Camp so drives you to the Town,
     As fev'rish men shift Beds to change their Dreams.

54. Back to your Camp, and come not here to boast
     Of numerous Ensigns, which but seldom are
     By Valour gain'd, tho oft by Cowards lost,
     Rags which the Beggar Honour wears in War.

55. Dull force cannot wise Courts with threatnings fright,
     Who breed strong not in Helmets but in Heads,
     Those Battles which you know not why you fight,
     And whilst you frown in Fields, smile in their Beds.

56. More had she said, but studious *Hermegild*
     Begg'd with his Looks, grown pale with Lovers Cares,
     That her bold Passion would to Prudence yield,
     And thus to *Hubert* he his Mind declares.

57. Think not great Prince, that our Designs are slow,
     But think your Courage makes a dang'rous hast;
     The Cures of Inward Wounds then doubtful grow
     To Art, when outwardly they heal too fast.

58. The Duke's Adoption is a tender Wound,
     Which cannot rough and hasty hands endure,
     By gentle search are narrow Arteries found,
     Where we the Spirits closer Walks secure.

59. Think not the Wounds ill searcht, which Artists close,
    Whilst you to open it grow rashly bold;
    As men ill cur'd haste desp'ratly to Blows,
    Because new Wounds may launce and cure the old.

60. Your Station is on Hills, your Glories all
    Watch as a Beacon, that does bid 'em Arm,
    And here your Name but whisper'd, serves to call
    The sleeping Faction like a new Alarm.

61. Retire, tho like the Sun declin'd you keep
    Your Circle still, and give to others Light,
    Since we must wish your Enemies a-sleep,
    Give us betimes the benefit of Night.

62. Preserve your Camp, no Force but of the Mind
    Can make our way, and when such Force you doubt,
    Think then that Giants, loth to die, can bind
    And master Souls with Limbs from going out.

63. *Hubert*'s lost Patience, he did thus restore,
    Then *Gartha* with such Reverence he did chide,
    As Indian Priests in Storms check and adore
    Their Idols Rage, but *Hubert* thus repli'd.

64. Who doubts your Wisdom, *Hermegild,* which long
    Has led fierce Armies, and calm Councils taught,
    Must the worlds Mistress, grave Experience wrong,
    As if she wanted Worth, which all have sought.

65. Such who play with Truth, are punisht by
    Derided Anguish, till they serious turn,
    As wanton Scepticks, who Effects deny
    Of Fire, see others smiling whilst they burn.

66. Your Faith to me, your love of *Gartha* binds,
    Which doubting, I her force of Beauty doubt
    A Light held up, when Courts tempestuous Winds
    Threaten to blow Heavens Lamps, the Planets out.

67. Think my Impatience is the Armies Sin,
    And if when *Gartha* with my wrong's is warm'd,
    Your Power can hardly keep her Passions in,
    How should I stop three angry Legions arm'd?

68. Her Anger Heavenly is, for as kind Heaven
    Grieves that our own advantage we decline
    By doing ill; so her Rebukes are given,
    Because she suffers when the Loss is mine.

69. Victorious Maid, I find deep Wounds of Cares
    On your fair Brow; but so by Beauty shown,
    As youthful Victors wear their boasted Scars,
    To make their Vertue more than Beauty known.

70. Tell me the Empire's safe, and tell me where
    You and your Faction have so early met;
    To humble those who are so proud to fear,
    That at your Dawn their Sun must ever set.

71. *Gartha* from each to all now shifts her Eyes,
    As if too wild, and proud to be confin'd,
    So proud with Praise, that she does Praise despise,
    And spreads like Sails swell'd with a prosp'rous Wind.

72. Her Words abound,, [*sic*] as Maids first Stories flow,
    When to stoln Lovers they from Parents scape,
    And fast she speaks, as Scouts chas'd by the Foe
    Declare their Number, and their Battles shape.

73. She tells how scarce from man she knew,
    When so audacious made by her Disguise,
    How soon her treble Voyce a Tenour grew,
    Her bashful Looks, bolder than Eagles Eyes.

74. She makes her secret Progress fully known,
    And how false *Ulpha* aided the Success;
    Whose Treason though she scorn'd, she grac'd her own,
    As Traytors Greatness makes their Treason less.

75. Whilst thus her mourning Conquest she reports,
    Their forward hopes shrunk back & seem'd dismaid
    To be instead of Sovereign Gold, with Courts
    Small Plots (the common Coyn of Statesmen) paid.

76. Then thus spake *Hermegild* to highest Heights,
    The lowest Steps must be the first Degrees,
    The strongest stoop to carry greater Weights,
    And from conceal'd small Roots, spring lofty Trees.

77. Nature disguis'd, does oft from Lowness rise,
    To high Effects; so does her Servant Art,
    Courts which by Art subsist, and low Disguise
    Oft dress a King to play a Subject's part.

78. These Clouds which threaten *Hurgonil,* e'r long
    Shall o'r the sleeping Duke a Tempest breed;
    As weaker Winds may suddainly grow strong,
    And split a Mast, which first scarce shook a Reed.

79. The World is not subdu'd by Victories,
    Nor by the Voyce of Publick Councils sway'd,
    'Tis being wild best conquer'd by Surprise,
    And easi'st rul'd, when to the Yoke betray'd.

80. Wise Courts for Man have many a little Snare
    In Cities (now grown wild as Forrests) spread
    To take the useful Beast alive, whom War
    Destroyes, tho he be useless being dead.

81. Now *Borgio,* who with Hopes swell'd Sails had steer'd,
    Grows troublesom, as Sails then strong winds change
    Like Sails he slackn'd, when his Hope laveer'd,
    And seem'd as much a storm, as storms seem strange.

82. Invite, said he, State Student to your Feast
    Of Ruling Councils, an insipid Food.
    When *Canibal* Ambition is your Guest,
    Who is not fed with Percepts, but with Blood.

83. Poorly you make us fall from publick Heights,
    To private Depths; and all your great Designs,
    Are subt'ly shrunk to Lovers little Slights,
    Your *Indian* Voyage was to Copper Mines.

84. The Duke's Adoption by the King is seal'd,
    The Count by Marriage plight to *Orna* ti'd,
    Fast by Confederate the Crown is held,
    And we watch hard to scare a sleeping Bride.

85. Accurs'd be Courts where you, wise Statesmen, make
    Your selves, and not your Master great, you keep
    Your Watch with false Alarms, and only wake
    To breed those Fears, which hinder others sleep.

86. Falshood condemn'd you free from publick good,
    Bind Truth to the Authority of Schools,
    Least in your Priests you should be understood,
    Priests you make false, and they confirm you Fools.

87. Tho humbly first you low as Serpents crawl,
    Yet soon you show your power, which is your Sting.
    Wildly you catch at him, when you must fall
    Who by your Weights grows weak, your govern'd King.

88. Greedy [*sic*] as Lyons o'r your trembling Prey
    Rowling your Eyes about with Jealous Care,
    For fear some other strong Devourer may
    In what you long have hunted, quickly share.

89. You sell the Peace that with your Blood you bought,
    Then in your Clossets other Quarrels feign
    To break that Peace, for which like Fools we fought
    And make the People purchase it again.

90. At this old *Hermegild* renounc'd his Age,
    For heat of Anger made his Visage young,
    And soon in Words he would let loose his Rage,
    But *Gartha* sooner thus prevents his Tongue.

91. Is this your Lyon *Hubert,* whom you bring
    In terrour from his Canvas Cage, your Tent,
    That by instinct he may to free the King
    Roar, if he find him not of Kings Descent.

92. Or would he cure Courts tame Civility?
    Or must the Ladies yield to him for fear?
    Soon a dispis'd dead Lyon shall he be,
    If he pronounce his Savage Doctrine here.

93. Rebels to Courts, the Force of useful Power,
    Where Statesmen should be safe tho vext with Cares,
    To rescue whom your Fury would devour,
    They breed not War for you, but you for Wars.

94. Courts form'd not War to keep the World alarm'd,
    Or vex the Quiet, but to tame the Rude,
    To Right whom Tumults wrongfully have harm'd,
    And Conquer those who have the good subdu'd.

95. Courts your wise Masters, did invent the odds
    Of Camps o'r Crowds, you muster'd by your wills,
    Would now like Ruffian Giants brave your Gods,
    Who smile in Clouds to see you heave at Hills.

96. How wildly would the World be Rul'd, if left
    By Civil Courts to your uncivil Sway?
    Justice would hardly dare to blush at Theft,
    Nor Priests to sigh, when Priests become their Prey.

97. What are your Battles where Ambition tries
    Those Titles which avoid the Test of Law,
    Battles, the Worlds confused Lotteries,
    Where for the Prize thousands together draw.

98. Like mighty Murtherers you Honour boast,
    Ofener [*sic*] by Chance than Valour give Defeats;
    Vainly like Gamesters count not what you lost,
    But what you won, hiding your base Retreats.

99. By wretched Rapine urg'd to bold Attacks,
    And when a City even by Treaty yields,
    You oft out-do the Fame of *Gothick* Sacks,
    And where they City's left, leave desart Fields.

100. And when your conquering Train comes home quite tir'd
     With emptying Cities, and with filling Graves,
     Your Foreign Vices are at first admir'd,
     'Till low you fall in Riots as your Slaves.

101. Now *Hubert* did arrest her pleading hand,
     Which earnest grew, & did her Tongue out-plead,
     His Looks did *Borgio*'s Silence soon command,
     And on her Hand he Tears of kindness shed.

102. And that sweet Pledge with fervent Kisses held,
     As fast as Lovers then that fair Hand hold,
     Which has the long sought Promise newly seal'd,
     Whē Rivals hopes grow warm, & theirs grow cold[.][11]

103. He said she was Heavens private Mirrour wrought,
     For Kings that they might secret Truths discern;
     He prais'd the Court, that her such greatness taught
     As only Courts can teach, and Princes learn.

104. Now with one Mind to several Cares they hie;
     She hastes to Court to hasten *Orna*'s shame:
     And both the Chiefs disguis'd to *Brescia* fly,
     Thro Mists returning as in Crowds they came.

105. *Hubert* will wait till her Designs appear
     In larger Growth, for He was bred to sow
     Courts little Fields, and well he knew that there
     Small Rivals oft to mighty Mischiefs grow.

106. They look but wrong on Courts who can derive
     No great Effects from outward Littleness;
     Thro Foolish Scorn they turn the Prospective,
     And so contract Courts little things to less.

[11] Supplied from the Wellesley Library copy.

107. Man's little Heart in narrow space does hide
      Great Thoughts, such as have spacious Empire sway'd
      The little Needle does vast Carricks guide,
      And of small Atoms were the Mountains made.

FINIS.

VARIANT READINGS[12]

"To Sir William Davenant"

    1.1 O] Oh
    2.1 Happy] Happy's
         climb] clime
    3.1 in you] is yours
      2 Oblivions] o'er shading
      3 Suns] sons
    5.1 be] is
         who] that
      2 Among] Amongst

"To Mr. Cotton"

    4.4 Coins] coin
    7.1 They'll highly] Much they will
      2 I] I'll
      4 The chief, who still sing] Which still sings
    9.1 Guide to Empires] judge of Empire

The story of *Gondibert* remains a riddle still. Indeed, the long-lost *Canto* has added to the complications by the introduction of a scheme to defame Orna that derives from the plot against Hero in *Much Ado*. Unlike the Hero story and its sources and analogues, this one has for its villain a woman. The detailed resemblances to Shakespeare will be left to other commentators to point out.

[12] These are collected from John Beresford's text, pp. 272-74. Only verbal differences are recorded, for Beresford normalizes capitals, italics, and, apparently, punctuation.

Latin Title-Page Mottoes as a Clue to Dramatic Authorship

[1945]

THE POSSIBLE significance of Latin mottoes on the title-pages of Tudor and Stuart plays first claimed my attention in the course of a study of the anonymous manuscript play entitled *Dick of Devonshire*. This play, which is bound second in the collection known as B.M. MS. Egerton 1994, is a journalistic treatment of the heroic exploit of Richard Peek (or Pike) of Tavistock, Devonshire, who in 1625 sailed aboard the *Convertine* in the fleet commanded by Edward Cecil, Viscount Wimbledon, on the expedition to Cadiz. Peek, who had the misfortune to be captured by the Spaniards, was taken to Xerex for trial and afterwards challenged by the Duke of Medina to fight with dagger and rapier against a Spanish soldier, whom he easily disarmed. Provoked to a second combat, Peek provided himself with an irontipped quarterstaff and expressed his readiness to meet as many as six Spaniards at once. Three fully armed soldiers set upon him. One of these he killed outright, and the other two he put to flight. The Duke of Medina Sidonia was so much pleased by Peek's bravery and skill that he gave him protection and ultimately arranged his return to England. As a man who had won honor in an otherwise inglorious expedition, Peek was received at Court and acclaimed by the public, to whom he gave a full account of his exploit in a rare little pamphlet entitled *Three to One. Being, An English Spanish Combat* (1626).[1] An unknown playwright took advan-

[1] *STC* 19529. I have used the British Museum copy in connection with research made possible by a grant-in-aid from the American Council of Learned Societies. The pamphlet relates that Peek landed at Fowey on 23 April and that King Charles had "bene gratiously pleased, both to let [his] poore Soldier and Subject, behold [his] Royall Person, and to heare him speake in his rude Language."

The Library, 4th ser., XXVI (1945-46), 28-36.

tage of the public interest in the story and combined a romantic plot with Peek's narrative to create a play entitled *Dick of Devonshire*.

Unless the playwright obtained Peek's story from his own lips, it is unlikely that he wrote *Dick of Devonshire* earlier than 18 July 1626, the date of the pamphlet's entry in the Register of the Stationers' Company, but it is probable that the play was in being by the end of the year. It does not appear in our dramatic records, possibly because it was never acted, but perhaps because the extant entries from Sir Henry Herbert's office book are very scanty for the years 1626 and 1627.[2]

The later history of *Dick of Devonshire* may be found in the second volume of A. H. Bullen's *Collection of Old English Plays* (1883) and in Frederick S. Boas's accounts.[3] The manuscript possesses a title-page but lacks any preliminary material that might identify the author or the company for which the play was written. It is listed by W. W. Greg as B7 in his *Dramatic Documents from the Elizabethan Playhouses* (1931), *i.e.,* as a text similar to a promptbook but lacking positive evidence of theatrical use. It is, as he says, "carefully written in a small, very neat, and somewhat ornamental hand, of rather mixed character, with practically no attempt at distinction of script." He adds that "the general effect is scribal; on the other hand, what little alteration and correction there is rather suggests the author. . . ." With this statement I am in only partial agreement, and with a subsequent one I differ wholly. "The leaves," writes Dr. Greg, "have not been folded for margins, and these are rather narrow. There is no indication of playhouse use, nor even of the manuscript having been prepared with a view to production, while the Latin motto on the fly-leaf and the continuous writing strongly suggest a purely literary intention."[4]

I concur in the belief that the manuscript is in a scribal hand, not

[2] Malone's transcripts preserve one entry for January 1626, two for February, one for October, and one for November; for the following year one entry has been recovered for January, a second for June, and a third for July. This paucity of records is not connected with any recrudescence of the plague, for G. E. Bentley's *Jacobean and Caroline Stage* (1941) lists no orders for closing the theaters between 1625 and 1630. Obviously more plays were licensed than are thus represented. The fact appears to be that Malone, whose interest was in Shakespeare and his major contemporaries, would have found little of value to his studies in an entry of *Dick of Devonshire*, even if Herbert's book had contained one.

[3] See "A Seventeenth-Century Theatrical Repertoire," *The Library*, 3rd ser., VIII (1917), 225-39, and relevant chapters in *Shakespeare and the Universities* (1923).

[4] [Sir Walter's final decision about *Dick of Devonshire* is: "A fair copy, possibly the author's, designed for use as a prompt-book. Company unknown" (*The Shakespeare First Folio*, Oxford, 1955, p. 162, Note A). The play was published by the Malone Society in 1955 under the editorship of James G. and Mary Ruthven McManaway.]

only because of its fluency and regularity, but also because it has been my good fortune to come upon another dramatic manuscript in the same hand. The Folger copy of the quarto of Middleton's *Blurt, Master Constable* lacks its last two leaves, H2 and H3, but the missing portion of the text is supplied in manuscript. The handwriting is recognizable at a glance as being identical with that of *Dick of Devonshire*.[5] In both the text is written continuously; speech-tags, when in the middle of a line, are surrounded by rules; important stage directions are centered and enclosed in brackets and rules; speech-rules are placed below the line in which the speech ends; and the plays end with a horizontal rule followed by "finis" and several penwork spirals.

Since *Blurt, Master Constable* was printed only once—in the quarto of 1602—it is pertinent to inquire the nature of the text to be found in the transcript. It is not a line-for-line, word-for-word, point-for-point copy of the printed text. The transcriber, all of whose characteristics label him a professional scribe, supplies needed pointing in some places and omits it in others; he substitutes pairs of commas for parentheses; he introduces contractions to improve the meter, but expands a few others, to its detriment; he alters the word-order several times, but never, I think, capriciously, and omits one redundant marginal stage direction; he corrects "your" to "our" at one place and gives one correct reading, "signe", for a possible printinghouse misreading, "figure"; but, most important, he changes enough words, eliminates enough actors' gags, and exhibits enough independence in his treatment of lineation[6] to persuade me that he had access to a manuscript source, in all likelihood the prompt copy.[7]

[5] See Plates 1 and 2.
[6] See Plates 2 and 3.
[7] Omitting variations in spelling and punctuation, and contractions of indifferent value, there are seventeen readings to be compared. References are to the quarto, with manuscript readings on the right.

1. H2, line	5	with	by
2.	8	bright beauty, is a bright	bright Beauty, is a
3.	12	Law' [*sic*] giue me law.	Give me the Law.
4.	19	must now beare it off	must beare it off now
5.	29	your	our
6. H2ᵛ line	1	(to you all)	to all
7.	6	Alacke	alas
8.	7	This	It
9. Marginal S.D.		*Kisse*	*omitted*
10.	20	figure	signe
11.	22	thine	thy

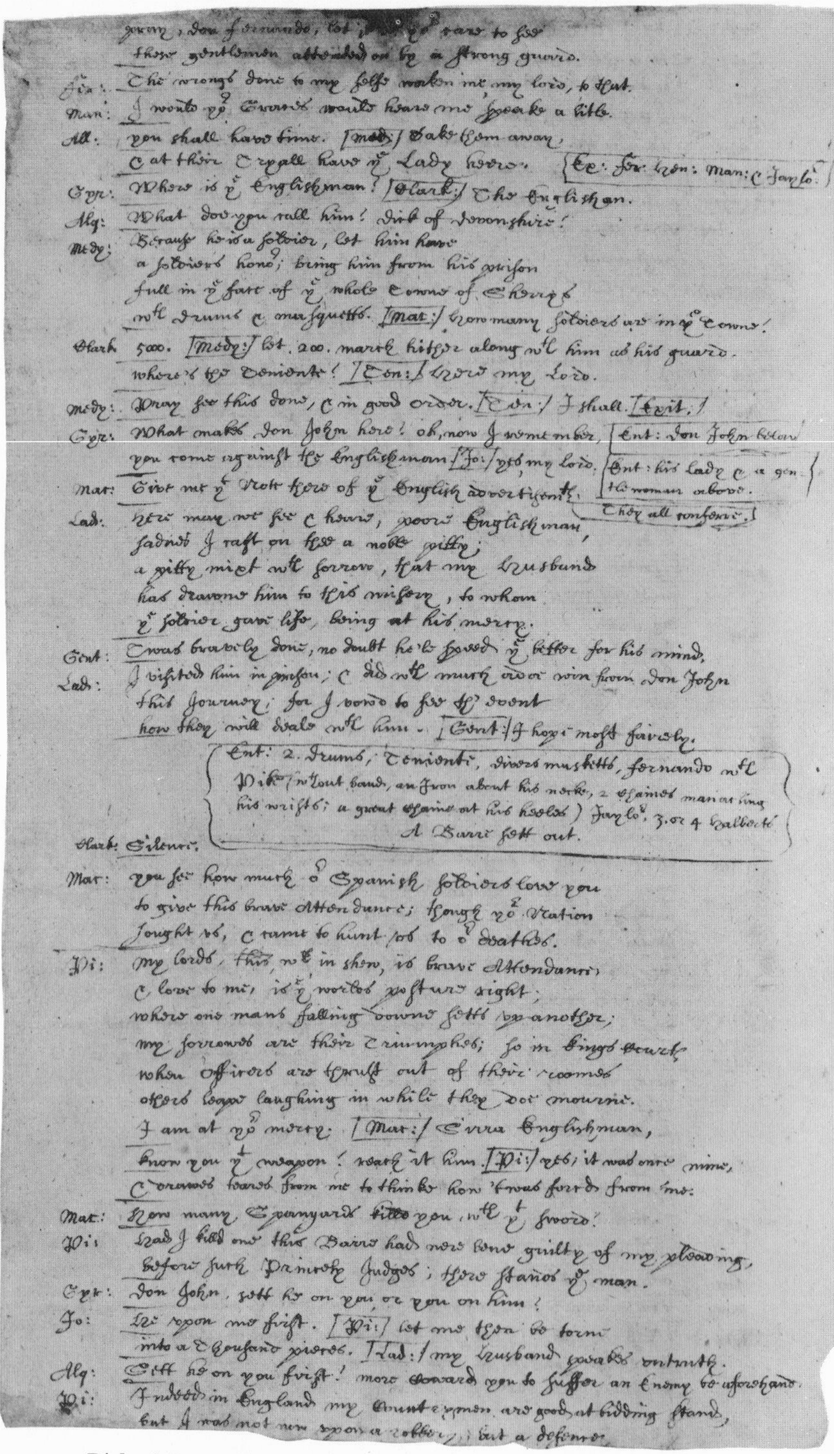

PLATE 1. *Dick of Devonshire*, part of fol. 46(16)ᵛ, British Museum MS. Egerton 1994.

Cam: Frenshman, thou art indebted to our Duke.

font: for what? /Cam:/ thy life, for, but for him, thy soule
had long ere this hung trembling in ye ayre,
being frighted from thy Bosome by our swords.

font: I doe not thanke ye Duke, yet, if you will,
turne bloudy exicutioners: who dyes
for so bright Beauty, is a Sacrifice.

Du: The Beauty you adore so is prophane,
the breach of wedlocke, by our Law, is death.

font: Give me the Law. /Du:/ With all severity.

font: In my Loves eyes imortall Joyes doe dwell,
she is my heaven, she from me, I'me in hell.
therefore ye Law, ye Law /Du:/ Make way, she comes.

Ent: Blurt, leading Imperia: Watch wth
Violetta maskd.

Imp: fye fye fye. /Blu:/ ye fye fye fye, nor ye foh foh foh ta
serve ye turnes; you must beare it off now wth heade shoul

Du: Now fetch Curvetto & ye Spanyard hither,
their punishmente shall lye under one doome;
what, is she maskd?

Blu: A punrke too? follow, fellowes; Slubber, afore.

Dio: She that is maskd is leader of this masque;
whats here? Sowes, Bills, & Guns? noble Camillo
I'me sure you are Lord of all this Misrule: I pray,
for whose sake doe you make this swaggering fray?

Cam: For yours, & for our owne; we come resolv'd
to murther him that poysons ye chast Bed;
to take revenge on you, for your false heart,
and, wanton Dame, our wrath here must not sleepe,
your sin being deepest, your share shalbe most deepe.

Dio: With pardon of ye Eares, my selfe to all
at your owne weapons thus doe answer all.
for paying away my heart, that was my owne,
fight not to win that, in good troth he's gone.

Unless we are to assume that the playwright who wrote *Dick of Devonshire* was also the original owner of the Folger quarto of *Blurt, Master Constable,* into which he himself had copied the four pages of missing text, it is clear that late in 1626 or early in 1627, before the public forgot the adventures of Richard Peek, there was in London a professional scribe who was available and competent to transcribe an author's manuscript play (or prompt copy) and who had access to theatrical manuscripts, *i.e.,* there was a playhouse scribe whose handiwork has not hitherto been recognized.

This inference is strengthened by the fact that that portion of Dr. Greg's description of the manuscript (see above) is erroneous which states that the leaves "have not been folded for margins." It is true that even in bright sunlight the paper shows no signs of creasing; but a lens sees in this case what eludes the eye, for photostats show clearly that the leaves have been folded in the manner usual in the preparation of theatrical manuscripts of this period.[8]

At least one other sign of possible playhouse use of the manuscript may be cited. On folio 46 (16)[a] the following boxed stage direction occurs in the left margin[9] five or six lines from the end of Act IV, Scene ii: "*A Table out, | sword & papers.*" The next scene begins with a centered stage direction, as follows: "*Ent: fernando bareheaded, talking wth ye Duke of Macada. | Duke Gyron, Medyna, Marquesse d' Alquevezzes, 2 gent^l: one wth Pikes sword. wch is laid on a Table, Iaylo^r, Teniente, Clarke wth papers.*" The warning to have properties ready may be the only surviving vestige of a prompter's notes in the source-manuscript,

12. H3 line	18 ere I marry with	I'll nere marry
13.	26 two and thirtie shillings	32s
14.	28 before	ere
15.	30 great Duke	Duke
16. H3^v line	3 did ever lye	co[? uld]
17.	*Exeunt*	Exeunt omnes.

MS. variants Nos. 2, 5, and 10 are positive corrections; Nos. 3, 6, and 12 are preferable readings. No. 16 seems preferable, as avoiding repetition, but the end of the line is trimmed off and possibly the MS. read "could lie". While some of the variants might be dismissed as obvious corrections or scribal errors, many others are not to be so explained. In any case, the total number of variants of all kinds is extremely high for a professional scribe (as I take the copyist to be) whose MSS. are so neat.

[8] In the illustration (Plate 1), a photograph of a photostat, the lines of broken fibers are unfortunately not visible. I have used both the original manuscript and a photostat.

[9] See Bullen's ed., pp. 72 and 73, and Greg, *op. cit.,* p. 331. I give the foliation as in *Dramatic Documents,* in which Dr. Greg notes that there is no room in the right margin for the direction.

Blurt Master Conſtable.

Cam. Frenchman, thou art indebted to our Duke.

Font. For what?

Cam. Thy life, for (but for him) thy ſoule
Had long ere this hung trembling in the ayre,
Being frighted from thy boſome with our ſwoords.

Font. I doe not thanke your Duke; yet (if you will)
Turne bloudie Executioners: who dyes
For ſo bright beauty, is a bright Sacrifice.

Duk. The beautie you adore ſo, is prophane,
The breach of wedlocke (by our law) is death.

Font. Law giue me law.

Duk. With all ſeueritie.

Font. In my Loues eyes immortall ioyes doe dwell,
She is my heauen; ſhe from me, I am in hell:
Therefore your Law, your Law:

Duk. Make way, ſhe comes.

Enter Blurt *leading* Imperia, *watch with* Violetta *maskt.*

Imp. Fye, Fye, Fye.

Blu. Your fye, fye, fye, nor your foh, foh, foh, cannot ſerue
your turne; ou muſt now beare it off with head and ſhoulders.

Duk. Now fetch *Curuetto,* and the *Spaniard* heather,
Their puniſhments ſhall lye vnder one doome,
What is ſhe maskt?

Blu. A puncke too; follow fellows, *Slubber* afore: *Exeunt.*

Vio. Shee that is maskt, is leader of this Maske,
What's heere? Bowes, Billes and Gunnes? noble *Camillo,*
I am ſure you are Lord of all this miſ-rule: I pray
For whoſe ſake doe you make this ſwaggering fray?

Cam. For yours, and for your owne, we come reſolu'd,
To murther him, that poiſons your chaſte bed;
To take reuenge on you, for your falſe heart:
And (wanton Dame) our wrath heere muſt not ſleepe,
Your ſinne being deep'it, your ſhare ſhall be moſt deepe.

H 2   *Vio.* With

PLATE 3. *Blurt, Master Constable,* 1602 quarto, sig. H2 (Huntington Library copy).

but, as Dr. Greg has noted, several other brief stage directions also occur in left margins, despite the fact that there is ample space at the right.

The identity of handwriting in the two manuscripts suggests that possibly *Dick of Devonshire* was the property of the company of players which about 1626-27 owned the manuscript of *Blurt, Master Constable*. Middleton's play was entered in S.R. on 7 June 1602 to Edward Allde[10] and was printed in the same year for Henry Rocket with the statement on the title-page that it had "bin sundry times priuately acted by the Children of Paules." This was a company which experienced a recrudescence of activity about 1600.[11] In the next few years it enjoyed the services of a group of vigorous young writers, including Chapman, Heywood, Middleton, and Marston, and won such a following that Shakespeare in *Hamlet* referred to the "little eyases." Contrary to the practices of other companies, the best plays of the Children of Paul's were put almost at once into print, and *Blurt, Master Constable* was performed, registered, and published in 1602.

What effect immediate publication had on the later fortunes of the plays is impossible to determine. They may have become common property at once, or they may have remained the exclusive possession of the Children of Paul's until they ceased to act—their last recorded performance was of *The Abuses,* a lost play, on 30 July 1606. There are several possibilities: (1) at the breakup of the company, the manuscripts and acting rights may have been purchased by the King's Man[12] or some other company;[13] (2) the playwrights may have received one or more of their manuscripts at the cessation of acting by the company as part

---

[10] Arber's reprint, III, 207.

[11] Cf. E. K. Chambers, *The Elizabethan Stage* (1923), II, 19 and n.

[12] Chapman's *Bussy d'Ambois,* one of their plays, appears more than once in the lists of plays performed at Court by the King's; cf. G. E. Bentley, *The Jacobean and Caroline Stage,* I, 118, *etc.* Another play, *The Woman Hater,* names "his Majesties Servants" on the title-page of the third edition (1648), though the manuscript was registered on 6 August 1607 and the first two editions (1607) name the Children of Paul's. More significant, possibly, is the history of *Satiromastix,* which appeared in print in 1602 with the statement that it had been acted privately by the Children of Paul's and publicly by the King's Men, as if there had been a working agreement of some sort between the two companies.

[13] *A Mad World my Masters* appears later, according to the title-page of the quarto of 1640, to have been in the possession of Queen Henrietta's Men at the private house in Salisbury Court. Many of the plays of this company seem to have been owned or controlled by Christopher Beeston, who began to acquire dramatic manuscripts as early as 1621-22. *A Trick to Catch the Old One* passed at once to the Children of Blackfriars, as we know from the second edition of 1608 (=1609; the first edition was in 1608).

compensation and subsequently sold them to other companies; and (3) Edward Pearce (or Piers), the Master of the Children, may have retained the authorized manuscripts against the day when he hoped to resume performances.[14]

Since *Blurt, Master Constable* does not reappear in the dramatic records, it is impossible to trace the ownership of the manuscript(s) of the play from 1601-2 until 1626-27, when *Dick of Devonshire* must have been written. It is equally impossible to trace the manuscript of the latter play from 1626-27 to the time when it became a part of MS. Egerton 1994. It may be remarked, however, that Robert Davenport, to whom some scholars have attributed *Dick of Devonshire,* was writing for Queen Henrietta's Company about this time, that *A Mad World my Masters* passed from the Children of Paul's to Queen Henrietta's, and that William Cartwright the Younger[15] was, according to James Wright's *Historia Histrionica,* once a member of Queen Henrietta's. The only other author to whom *Dick of Devonshire* has been attributed is Thomas Heywood. It is not known what company he was writing for about 1626-27, or whether he was composing plays at all at that time, but the fact must not be overlooked that MS. Egerton 1994 contains two holograph plays by Heywood: *The Captives,* a prompt copy, Greg A11, and *The Escapes of Jupiter,* which seems to have been intended for theatrical use, Greg B4.

The circumstances which brought together the manuscripts of *Blurt* and *Dick* so that a scribe could copy them are yet to seek, as is the identity of the author of the latter play. Perhaps a nearer approach to the solution of the second problem, the authorship of *Dick of Devonshire,* may be made by an examination of the Latin motto on the title-page of the manuscript, the starting-point of this investigation, which, as noted above, Dr. Greg interprets as a sign of literary rather than theatrical intention. An examination of the early plays with Latin mottoes on their title-pages reveals that Maurice Kyffin's translation of *Andria,*

---

[14] If so, the rival companies may have utilized copies of the printed texts. Pearce and his group of children remained a potential competitor to the other companies, as we know from the record of offers to him of a "dead rent" of £20 to abstain from performing plays; cf. *The Elizabethan Stage,* II, 22 and n.

[15] See Professor Boas's discussions of MS. Egerton 1994 for almost certain proof that William Cartwright was the original owner of this manuscript. Boas attempts to trace the early histories of the various plays there bound together and points out that Cartwright may have acquired some of them with a view to publication after 1642. Perhaps in this latter group would be the plays that Dr. Greg, *op. cit.,* has described as literary rather than theatrical.

published in 1588, was a closet drama, as were Samuel Daniel's *Cleopatra* (1594) and Samuel Brandon's *Vertuous Octavia* (1598); but Thomas Lodge's *Wounds of Civil War,* a play of the Admiral's Men in 1594, was published with a Latin title-page motto; Greene's *Scottish History of James the Fourth* appeared in 1598 with a Latin motto on the title-page; and after Ben Jonson's *Every Man out of his Humour* was printed with a Latin motto in 1600, the practice was adopted by numerous other popular playwrights, including Heywood, Middleton, Dekker, Daborn, Marston, Field, and Webster. It is worthy of note that Chapman and Shakespeare seem not to have adopted the practice; and some of the playwrights above named were infrequent in their use of mottoes, if we can rely on the only evidence we have—the title-pages of the printed quartos. Jonson's plays and masques, however, always have title-page mottoes, as do most of the plays and pageants of Thomas Heywood.

The case of Jonson is worth considering, for his interest in the publication of good texts is well known, and we shall not go far afield if we assume that for each of his plays the author's manuscript or a satisfactory transcript was used by the printer. Jonson's mottoes vary with the subject matter of the play. With Heywood, the case is different.

According to the printed bibliography of Heywood, his first publication to have a title-page motto was *Two Most Notable Histories,* a nondramatic translation that appeared in 1608. In the following year his *Troia Britanica,* likewise nondramatic, was published with the motto, "*Et prodesse solent, & delectare poetae.*" Three years later, in 1612, Heywood published his *Apology for Actors,* the title-page of which boldly proclaims, "*Et prodesse solent, & delectare,*" and thereafter all of his plays which have mottoes repeat this one or a variant thereof. His pageants almost uniformly have a motto, and it is always the same: "*Redeunt spectacula.*"

Enough evidence has been cited, I believe, for us to dismiss the surmise that *Dick of Devonshire* is probably a literary rather than a theatrical manuscript. This same evidence suggests that a number of authors, Heywood among them, habitually put a motto on the title-page of their dramatic manuscripts. For Heywood we have no absolute proof, for the manuscript of his *Captives,* though holograph, lacks a title-page, as does his holograph *Escapes of Jupiter.* But surely we have no reason to suspect that industrious printers or publishers of the

Heywood quartos supplied mottoes to otherwise unadorned manuscript title-pages.

If it be true, then, that after 1612 Heywood almost always provided his plays with Latin mottoes, and if the only motto to appear in the resultant printed copies is some variant of "*Et prodesse solent et delectare*," there is strong reason for questioning Arthur M. Clark's confident ascription to Heywood of *Dick of Devonshire*, since the Latin motto on this manuscript play is "*Hector adest; secumque deos in praelia ducit*."

It may be more than coincidence that this same motto occurs on the title-page of the anonymous play, *The Bloody Banquet,* printed in 1639, with attribution on the title-page to "T. D." These initials are frequently thought to belong to Thomas Drew, though others have ascribed the play to Robert Davenport on the strength of the fact that its title follows those of several of Davenport's plays reserved by the Lord Chamberlain in 1639 for the use of Beeston's Boys.[16] It is not my purpose at this time to enter into a discussion of the authorship of *The Bloody Banquet,* though I may say in passing that I find considerable internal evidence that it and *Dick of Devonshire* are from the same pen, and that the writer was indeed Robert Davenport. Internal evidence is the less satisfactory, however, for the reason that *The Bloody Banquet* has survived in a badly marred text. The play is fewer than 2,000 printed lines in length—nearer 1,900 lines of verse; and this fact alone is enough to make us suspect that its printed form is a bad quarto.

The problem has its paradoxical aspects. The plays of Jonson, Dekker, and others, and particularly of Heywood, that have Latin mottoes on their title-pages are good texts, printed from author's manuscripts or legitimate transcripts. The presence of a Latin motto on the title-page of *The Scottish History of James the Fourth* (1594), one used by Greene in other of his works, was considered sufficient evidence by A. E. H. Swaen for suggesting "that the manuscript may have been in some manner prepared for the press before [Greene's] death in 1592."[17] And the motto of Jasper Mayne's *Amorous War* (1649) suggested to another scholar that that play was printed from "authorized copy."[18] Yet here is a play, *The Bloody Banquet,* that has not one

---

[16] See *Malone Society Collections,* II, 389-90.

[17] Malone Society Reprint, pp. v-vi.

[18] W. W. Greg, "The Printing of Mayne's Plays," *Oxford Bibliographical Society Proceedings and Papers,* I (1922-26), 256 .

motto, but two: *"Hector adest; secumque deos in praelia ducit,"* and
"Nos haec novimus esse nihil." (The second motto has not come to
my attention on any other title-page of the period.) And normally
we should expect a good, full-length text. Instead, the play is nearly
500 lines shorter than Alfred Hart[19] has called the average length of a play
of this period. Perhaps it will be possible some day to explain how an
authorized manuscript, to borrow W. W. Greg's adjective, came to be so
drastically shortened.

The evidence presented above points out a possible clue to the
authorship of the two anonymous plays, *Dick of Devonshire* and
The Bloody Banquet, brings to light a hitherto unnoticed fragment of
a dramatic manuscript of the early 17th century, and identifies the
hand of a hitherto unnoted playhouse scribe.

Is it possible to go further and to form any general conclusions
that may be of value to students in this field? If we may take Heywood as an example, it is, I believe, safe to suggest that a first edition
of one of Heywood's plays dated later than 1612 and bearing his
motto may be supposed to derive from the author's manuscript or
a legitimate copy; conversely, one lacking the motto may, in the absence
of dedication or address to the reader, be suspected of being "stolne and
surreptitious." Corollary hypotheses are (1) that anonymous plays
lacking Heywood's motto are probably "bad" quartos or else the product of a different author, and (2) that if two or more anonymous
plays of this period have stylistic or other important points of resemblance and also bear the same Latin motto on their title-pages, they may
with reasonable confidence be attributed to the same author.

[19] [*Shakespeare and the Homilies* (Melbourne University Press, 1934), p. 119.]

The Cancel in the Quarto of 2 *Henry IV*

[1946]

HE FIRST and only quarto of 2 *Henry IV*[1] is known in two issues which differ essentially only in quire E. The first issue has a normal gathering of four leaves in sheet E; in the second issue, the original leaves E3 and E4 "are cancelled and replaced by a complete sheet of four leaves (of which the first three are signed 'E3' 'E4' 'E5') making good the omission of a passage corresponding to III. i of the text as printed in [the First Folio]."[2] The first issue, which will be called Qa for convenience, is signed A-K⁴ L²; the second, Qb, is signed A-D⁴ E⁶ F-K⁴ L². The comprehensive account of scholarly opinions on the two issues given by Professor M. A. Shaaber in his Variorum edition of the play indicates, in the words of Professor Alfred Hart (*Variorum*, p. 474), that almost all editors and commentators have assumed that the "scene [III. i] was inserted in Qb either while Qa was being printed or almost immediately after the discovery of the omission."

"This statement or assumption," Professor Hart continues, "is neither necessarily nor even probably correct." But like other scholars he is unable to contribute more to the discussion than unsupported conjectures about censorship, the popularity of the play, and the trade practices of the publishers. Since the cancel leaves contain the first printing

---

[1] The Second part of Henrie the fourth, continuing to his death, and coronation of Henrie the fifth. With the humours of sir Iohn Falstaffe, and swaggering Pistoll. As it hath been sundrie times publikely acted by the right honourable, the Lord Chamberlaine his seruants. Written by William Shakespeare. London Printed by V. S. for Andrew Wise, and William Aspley. 1600.

[2] W. W. Greg, *A Bibliography of the English Printed Drama to the Restoration* (London, 1939), I, 273.

Studies in Honor of A. H. R. Fairchild, ed. C. T. Prouty (University of Missouri Press, 1946), pp. 69–80.

of a famous scene of a Shakespearian play, any material evidence that would assist in determining the date of the cancel should be welcome. Such evidence it is my purpose to present.

The omission of III. i was noted as early as 1768[3] but provoked little comment until 1843, when J. P. Collier[4] remarked that the play was "produced from the press in haste." His description of the precise method by which III. i was inserted is somewhat confusing. A conjecture that the omission was caused by haste is followed by the statement that "the stationer must have discovered the error after the publication, and sheet E was accordingly reprinted" to supply the defect; but later he asserts (p. 393) that the omission "was discovered before the quarto impressions were all struck off." The first conjecture carries the implication that the type for Sheet E was wholly reset[5] at some time after the completion of presswork on the final quire L; the second is ambiguous, leaving it impossible for us to determine whether Collier was aware that leaves E1 and E2 are from the same setting of type in both Qa and Qb, but suggesting that the printing of the later quires may have been delayed to permit the running off of the cancel.[6]

Collier's account seems to have satisfied commentators until 1920, when the Reverend Mr. Bayfield[7] postulated that the compositor "must have set up a good deal, if not the whole, of sheet F before discovering his mistake," and that he then "decided to break up the type of his last 50 lines of II. iv and the first 100 of III. ii and to set these again, inserting III. i." It is interesting to note Mr. Bayfield's assumptions that the same compositor did the resetting; that he used the first setting as copy, ignoring the manuscript; and that he introduced variations in spelling and punctuation because of his indifference to such matters.

In the ensuing discussion in the columns of the *TLS*, Professor J. Dover Wilson (30 September, p. 636) expressed the opinion that the new sheet, E3-6, was set up by the same compositor who had set the canceled half-sheet and that most of the type of the canceled page E3ʳ

[3] Capell, ed. 1768, I, 12.

[4] Ed. 1842–4, IV, 339.

[5] Steevens, ed. 1793, IX, 110, thought, apparently, that all of gathering E in Qb was from a new setting of type: "Signature E consists of six leaves. Four of these, exclusive of the two additional ones, were reprinted to make room for the omission."

[6] Collier's knowledge of printinghouse practices was so vague that he may well have believed the printer kept his type-pages tied up for indefinite periods of time to permit the printing of successive impressions of the book and that III. i was printed for insertion in one of these later issues.

[7] *TLS*, 23 September 1920, pp. 618-19.

was transferred bodily to the new forme. In a rejoinder, Mr. Bayfield insisted (14 October, pp. 667-68) that the type on E3^r was "if not absolutely, yet to all intents and purposes, set up afresh." It was his belief that the cancel was printed "within a couple of days" after the original composition of sheet E.

At this point A. W. Pollard contributed (21 October, p. 680) the suggestion that the compositor "made large use of the original set-up, only changing some stops. . . . He also replaced some types which fell out in the process by others." Then, after recording his "final impression from the spelling and typography . . . that the compositor of the second set-up was a different man from the compositor of the first, probably Sims himself," he gave an important new turn to the discussion by professing to find evidence that "two compositors were at work simultaneously over a large part of the edition": all italic *F*s and mixed roman and italic *F*s appear in alternating runs of three pages—triplets of pages. "I submit that these alternating triplets suggest that there was one compositor whose box was well supplied with italics and another who was running short of them." Since a triplet of printed pages runs to $3 \times 36 = 108$ lines, and since there are 54 lines to a page of manuscript in the "Shakespearian" portion of *Sir Thomas More*, Pollard inferred that the two compositors divided the manuscript of 2 *Henry IV* leaf by leaf, producing the alternating triplets. One of these leaves, containing the 108 lines of III. i, was, he assumed, lost or overlooked at the printing of Qa.[8]

There, to all intents and purposes, the matter rested until Professor Hart proposed an entirely different explanation. On the assumption that the censor of printed books in 1600 was responsible for the very considerable deletions throughout the text of the quarto, he argues that "even a press censor in 1600 might be excused for believing that in [one] passage[9] an almost direct allusion was made to court politics. Change

[8] [In *The Shakespeare First Folio* (Oxford, 1955), p. 266, Sir Walter Greg echoes Pollard's explanation of how the scene was omitted.]

[9] III. i. 41-47:

> *King.* Then you perceiue the body of our kingdome,
> How foule it is, what rancke diseases grow,
> And with what danger, neare the heart of it.
> *War.* It is but as a body, yet distempered,
> Which to his former strength may be restored,
> With good aduise and little medicine,
> My Lord Northumberland wil soone be coold.

See *Variorum,* pp. 475-76.

'King' to 'Queen,' 'Warwick' to 'Robert Cecil,' and 'Northumberland' to 'Essex,' and we might be listening to the conversation of Elizabeth with Cecil on the worst of her domestic troubles. . . . The censor would undoubtedly strike out such an ambiguous passage; if, as I think, he had decided to remove from the play all references to Richard II and Bolingbroke, he would also mark for omission lines [57-79] and [90-95]." Removal of these and certain consequential passages would, Professor Hart argues, rob the scene of dramatic vitality and leave it so anemic that Shakespeare himself might well have suggested its omission from the published version.

Although recent editors have suggested other explanations of the omission from the quarto of passages that are found in the folio text, none of these has displaced Professor Hart's hypothesis that this was the result of government censorship.[10] It is at least possible, however, that the deletions were made by a cautious bookseller, and so it becomes necessary to review Professor Hart's arguments, particularly those that relate to the probable date of printing the cancel quire E3-6.

After detailing the now familiar parallels between the careers of King Richard II and Queen Elizabeth and of Bolingbroke and Essex, and painting a lively picture of the unrest and suspicion in Court circles in 1599-1600, Professor Hart points out that a play which would have been readily allowable for performance in 1597 and 1598 might encounter serious criticism in official circles when offered for publication about 1600,[11] and that after the harrowing experience of Samuel Harsnett, who had licensed (entered in the Stationers' Register on 9 January 1599) for publication the manuscript of Sir John Hayward's *The first part of the life and raigne of King Henrie IIII,* the sharp interrogation and brief imprisonment of John Wolfe, who printed the book, the imprisonment of Sir John Hayward himself, and the calling in and burning of the book, the licensing authorities would have viewed with suspicion any references to Richard II, and with alarm any account of his deposition. Professors Schücking, Hart, and Shaaber are generally in agreement that many of the cuts in the quarto text cannot be con-

[10] Working independently, but along the same lines, Mr. L. L. Schücking published a discussion of the problem in the *TLS* (25 September 1930), at approximately the time that Professor Hart was expressing his opinions in lecture form. These were first published in *Shakespeare and the Homilies* (London, 1934). The two scholars are substantially in agreement.

[11] 2 *Henry IV* was entered in the Stationers' Register on 23 August 1600 by Wise and Aspley.

sidered theatrical (even though the play's text of some 3,000 lines must certainly have been curtailed for performance), because transitions are abrupt or are faulty in that matter is omitted which is later referred to or is essential to the development of the action; and it seems easily possible that Andrew Wise and William Aspley may, without the knowledge or consent of Shakespeare or his company, have arbitrarily instructed Valentine Simmes to omit dangerous or equivocal passages.[12] In this connection it appears not to have been previously noted that Wise was the publisher (and Valentine Simmes the printer) of the first quarto of *Richard II* (1597), and that he must have known of the suppression from this text of the great Deposition Scene, which in fact was not included in Q2 (1598) or Q3 (1598), both of which were printed by Simmes for Wise, but first appeared in print after Queen Elizabeth's death and after the transfer of copyright to Matthew Law (Q4, 1608). Any reluctance on Wise's part to have a hand in publishing *2 Henry IV*, III. i would be understandable.

This scene, the longest passage omitted from Qa, is also the passage with the most extended account of Bolingbroke's dealings with Richard II. If it were possible to determine whether the printing of Qa were interrupted, as some have thought, to permit the insertion of the cancel sheet E3-6, or otherwise to date the printing of this cancel, it might be easier to guess whether the omission of III. i was by accident or design, and to clear the way for the discussion of who occasioned it.

The printer of Qa was Valentine Simmes, who, as noted above, had printed three editions of *Richard II* for Andrew Wise, and who in this same year 1600 printed *Much Ado About Nothing*, "one of the few Shakespeare play books that was decently printed,"[13] for Wise and Aspley. Simmes, one of the less prosperous printers of his day, was in trouble with the authorities throughout most of his career, his press having been confiscated in 1597 and his type melted down. He is nowhere listed

[12] If the manuscript had been read by the censor before it left the possession of the Lord Chamberlain's Men, we should expect that some effort would have been made to patch up the text, but in fact no such polishing was done, as reference to the First Folio reveals. Once it was in the hands of Wise and Aspley, however, there would have been no one with sufficient interest in the quality of the text to bother with such details, no matter how drastically the censor might have cut and slashed. It is equally true, of course, that if Wise and Aspley indicated the omissions, there would have been no one with the incentive to repair the damage they did.

[13] R. B. McKerrow, *Dictionary of Printers and Booksellers, 1557-1640* (London, 1910), p. 246; adapted from H. R. Plomer, "The Printers of Shakespeare's Plays and Poems," *The Library*, 2nd ser., VII (1906), 154.

with the printers who had more than one press, and so it is unlikely that, if the omission of III. i was discovered while sheet E was going through the press (or, indeed, at any later time before the completion of the final half-sheet L), Simmes would have had a second press with which to print cancel sheet E3-6 simultaneously with his main job of printing of the quarto. Either he would have been compelled to defer the printing of the cancel until after machining the last half-sheet L, or he must have interrupted the work on the quarto and resumed it only after completion of the cancel sheet. There is, I believe, good reason to think that the quarto was printed from A through L without interruption, and that at some later time the omitted scene, III. i, was printed.

The evidence is to be found in the running-titles, a careful examination of which reveals that Simmes used two skeleton formes. In printing sheet A, he needed running-titles for only five pages, because $A1^r$ is the title-page, $A1^v$ is blank, and $A2^r$ has only a head-title. Beginning with sheet B, however, and continuing through sheet K, he used two sets of running-titles in regular sequence with no shifting of position. Thus in a copy of Qa, the running-title of B1, for example, recurs again on C1, D1, E1, F1, G1, H1, I1, and K1; and so with each of the other seven running-titles required to make up two quarto skeletons. In half-sheet L, in which L2 is a blank, $L1^v$ has no running-title, and that which appears on $L1^r$ was last used on $K2^r$. The procedure throughout is perfectly normal, and there is every reason, therefore, to believe that Simmes printed his copy from beginning to end without interruption.

Copies of Qb have running-titles exactly like those in Qa, with the exception of those on the four cancel leaves E3-6. In this sheet, eight wholly new running-titles make their appearance, and from this fact we may infer that type for the quarto had been completely distributed and that there was an interval of time between the printing of Qa and the printing of the cancel.

Determination of the length of this interval would be highly desirable, but the absence of direct evidence makes certainty impossible. Perhaps a guess may be based on the relative numbers of extant copies of Qa and Qb. Twenty-one complete or fragmentary copies of the quarto are recorded. Of these, one fragment, at the British Museum, consists of sheet E only, in its original state; and the Harvard copy lacks sheet E in any form. Of the nineteen remaining copies, nine are Qa and ten are

Qb. According to the law of averages, then, about half of the original edition was sold as printed; then, presumably after an interval, the remaining copies were offered for sale with the inserted cancel.[14] But since we do not know how rapidly copies were disposed of, and since there was no second printing in quarto form,[15] we still cannot fix a later limit for the printing of the cancel. It may be significant that on 25 June 1603 Wise transferred his "copies" (*i.e.*, copyrights) of *Richard II, Richard III,* and *1 Henry IV* to Matthew Law, and that thereafter he disappears from the Stationers' records. The lack of a reference to *2 Henry IV* in this entry or elsewhere is sufficient warrant for the assumption that by private arrangement it became the sole property of William Aspley and was still in his possession in 1623, when his name appears in the list of publishers of the First Folio. Valentine Simmes continued in business until 1622, and it was possible for him to have printed the cancel sheet of *2 Henry IV* for Wise and Aspley at any time between 1600 and 1603, or even between 1603 and 1622 for Aspley alone. For reasons to be stated later I favor an early date.

At this point consideration may well be given to Professor Hart's suggestion that the reprinting, and even the sale, of *2 Henry IV* may have been interdicted; there is no record of governmental action of this sort, and if the quarto *were* withdrawn from sale—for which there is no evidence—I think it more likely that Wise and Aspley made the decision. The problem is to explain why, in a period when there was so much official and popular interest in the historical parallels between Richard II and Elizabeth, the play-reading public suddenly appears to have lost its taste for three such plays as *Richard II* and Parts 1 and 2 of *Henry IV.*[16] Was the market glutted? Or did Wise (or Wise and Aspley together), taking warning from the experiences of Hayward, Harsnett, and Wolfe referred to above and of Augustine Phillips, a sharer in the Lord Chamberlain's Men who was interrogated on 18 February 1601 about his company's revival—by arrangement with, and at the

---

[14] It is entirely likely, as Dr. Joseph Q. Adams has suggested to me, that copies of the two issues were on sale in the same shop(s) at the same time.

[15] R. P. Cowl's suggestion, in his edition (1923), pp. xi ff., that other quarto editions of so popular a play must have been required by the public but are no longer extant, is not supported by a shred of evidence.

[16] It will be recalled that *2 Henry IV* was not republished until 1623; that *Richard II,* which went through three editions in 1597 and 1598, was not issued again until 1608, when the famous Deposition Scene was first included; and that *1 Henry IV,* after editions in 1598 and 1599, was not reprinted until 1604.

expense of, some adherents of the Earl of Essex—of *Richard II,* conclude that these plays were dangerous commodities which it became a loyal publisher to refrain from selling? Such a decision early in 1601—and I repeat that I have little confidence in this wholly unsupported conjecture—might well have resulted in keeping in stock enough copies of Qa, about half of the edition, to permit the printing and insertion of the cancel sheet even as late as 1603, after the death of Elizabeth.[17]

This explanation of the phenomena involved is, of course, at variance with one of Professor Hart's theses, which rests on the tacit assumption that the omission of III. i from Qa was a typographical accident such as that described by Pollard. "We are entitled to assume," writes Professor Hart,[18] "that Wise and Aspley printed the customary 1200 copies of 2 *Henry IV.* Perhaps 600 copies were ready for sale by November, 1600, the remainder being left in sheets till ordered. As Shakespeare apparently did not see any of his plays through the press, the absence of this scene, if it was accidental, would probably not be discovered till the play was put on the market. When the printers were informed of the defect, they would agree to rectify it; but in fairness to the booksellers who had bought copies of Qa, Wise and Aspley would probably not insert the omitted scene in the unbound remainder until all the copies of the first issue had been sold. . . . It may be that the second issue did not make its appearance for some months or even years after November 1600; if the sale was very slow, they might endeavor to quicken it by adding the missing scene." Serious objections may be offered to the acceptance of a number of the points in this argument. In the first place, there is no reason to think that in 1600 anyone paid very much attention to whether a copy of 2 *Henry IV* was Qa or Qb—after all, Shakespeare's editors gave little if any heed until 1768! Certainly there is no evidence that Wise and Aspley delayed the printing of the cancel out of consideration for the financial interests of booksellers who had unsold copies of Qa. Indeed, at no time did they advertise the fact that there were two issues of the play, and their silence on this subject is the best possible proof that they were not faced with the problem of quickening the sale of a slow-moving book. Nor did they, I think, first come into possession of the manuscript of III. i, or first find it permissible to print it, at any considerable time after the original publication of Qa, for in either

[17] Other considerations lead me to question whether the printing of the cancel was so long delayed.

[18] *Shakespeare and the Homilies,* pp. 176-77.

case they would have announced the fact on a cancel title-page, as Matthew Law did in the second issue of his 1608 edition of *Richard II,* the first printing of the Deposition Scene, confident that increased sales would recompense them for their extra charges.

For after all, the printing of a full-sheet cancel was not only troublesome but expensive, and we may well ask who had sufficient interest in the publication of a full text of the play to arrange it. The simplest possible explanation is that Simmes discovered his error and corrected it more or less automatically. On the other hand, Wise and Aspley may have noticed the accidental omission of III. i and forced Simmes to print the cancel in order that they might retain the good will of the actors who had favored them (or one of them) by releasing for publication no fewer than five of Shakespeare's plays within four years. A third possibility is that the Lord Chamberlain's Men, or Shakespeare himself, persuaded them to insert the cancel. Though he has frequently been charged with indifference to the fate of his plays, Shakespeare may have been more sensitive than has been realized. The case is put fairly in Dr. Joseph Q. Adams's discussion of Thomas Heywood's quarrel with William Jaggard about the injustice done him in the third edition of *The Passionate Pilgrim:* "In the later years of his life, the poet . . . could afford to be, and generally was, complacent about injuries done him by piratical stationers; but early in his career, when he was seeking recognition in the literary circles of London, and while he was basking in the applause evoked by his *Venus and Adonis,* his *Lucrece,* and his privately circulated cycle of sonnets, he seems to have been quite sensitive about his reputation—as witness his care, in 1598 and 1599, to replace corrupt editions of *Love's Labour's Lost* and *Romeo and Juliet* with correct versions. That in 1599 he had indeed been 'offended' at Jaggard, and had then taken occasion to protest at the attribution of *The Passionate Pilgrim* to him, is indicated by evidence already pointed out."[19] So it is not past belief that in 1600 Shakespeare noted the omission of III. i by Wise and Aspley and asked its insertion. The quarto, it is generally agreed, had been printed from Shakespeare's foul sheets with the full approval of Shakespeare's company,[20] and since his plays were at this time greatly in request,[21] the publishers might

[19] *The Passionate Pilgrim,* ed. J. Q. Adams (Folger Shakespeare Library Publications, 1939), p. xli.

[20] See W. W. Greg, *The Editorial Problem in Shakespeare* (London, 1942), p. 115; also J. Q. Adams, *Life of William Shakespeare* (Boston, 1923), pp. 518-19.

[21] Adams, *loc. cit.,* notes that despite the written order of the Wardens of the Stationers'

be expected to do anything within reason to retain the favor of the author and of his company. It may be assumed, then, that immediately upon receipt of notice, they not unwillingly incurred the expense of printing the cancel and inserting it silently in the copies then in stock. And if this be correct, it follows that the omission of III. i was an accident: either the leaf of manuscript failed to reach the printer or somehow it was overlooked.

It has never been questioned that the printer of the cancel sheet was Valentine Simmes, the printer of the rest of the quarto. Opinion has varied from Professor Wilson's assertion that most of the type of Qa, leaves E3 and E4, was retained for use in Qb, leaves E3 to E6, to Pollard's statement that the cancel was not set by the compositor of the original sheet E but probably by Simmes himself. The type used in printing the cancel is, then, at least of the same sort that Simmes used in 1600.

What of the paper used for the cancel? Unfortunately it has not been possible to secure a description of the paper in the nine English-owned copies of the quarto,[22] but I have examined or received reports on the twelve American copies.[23] The identification of the watermarks is rendered difficult by the fact that many of the copies contain re-margined leaves, and that in some varieties of paper the watermarks are very indistinct or are nonexistent. From the sketches I have made and those that have been supplied me, it appears that for Qa Simmes used a job lot of paper of seven or more varieties, including at least one that has no watermark. One watermark resembles Briquet 7140 (made at Bayonne, 1600); another is somewhat like Briquet 14051 (from Lucq, 1600); and still another may be Briquet 10818 (from Limoges, 1599). The report and the sketches from the Huntington Library indicate that the same watermark appears in all three copies of sheet E3-6 but nowhere else in Qb, nor is it found anywhere in the Huntington copy of Qa. This same watermark (or one almost identical with it) occurs, according to report, in the cancel sheets of the two Rosenbach copies of Qb but

Company to the effect "That no plays be printed except they be such as have authority," *Henry V,* a play that had been "stayed," was published in 1600 without any license at all.

[22] At the British Museum, 3; at Bodley, 2; at Trinity College, Cambridge, 1; at the Hunterian Museum, Glasgow, 1; the Crichton Stuart copy; and the Quaritch copy.

[23] For assistance in this important matter, I give thanks to Mr. Gilbert Troxall, Librarian of the Elizabethan Club, Yale University; Dr. William Van Lennep, Curator of the Harvard Theatre Collection; Mr. Edwin Wolf, II, assistant to Dr. A. S. W. Rosenbach; and Mr. Herman R. Mead, of the Henry E. Huntington Library.

not in any other sheet, nor in any sheet of the Rosenbach copy of Qa. In the Elizabethan Club copy of Qb, the cancel leaf has a watermark that looks like the sketches of that in the copies at the Huntington and at Rosenbach's, but it also resembles closely that in sheet F of the Elizabethan Club copy (? Briquet 14051). The Harvard copy, lacking sheet E, seems to contain no paper bearing a watermark like that found elsewhere in the cancel sheet. In the three Folger copies, one of Qa and two of Qb, the two examples of the cancel sheet have identical watermarks, the same mark reported or observed in the cancel sheets enumerated above. Two of the quartos, however, have a sheet F which, like that in the Elizabethan Club copy, bears a watermark much like that in the cancel sheets. If the English-owned copies should yield no discordant results, it would be safe to assume that Simmes printed the cancel while a supply was yet available of a single variety of paper closely resembling, or identical with, some of that used in Qa.

One further kind of evidence remains to be considered, the spelling habits of the compositor(s) of Qa and of the cancel sheet. Plomer paved the way for this part of the investigation by his remark that the omission of III. i "was discovered before the whole impression was printed, and the missing scene inserted on two new leaves. In order to do this the type of part of the preceding and subsequent leaves was distributed, so that there are two different impressions for the latter part of Act II and the beginning of Act III, Scene 2" (*op. cit.*, p. 154). Later expressions of opinion have been quoted above in another connection. Out of the controversy, two questions emerge. (1) Was part or all of the type used in printing leaves E3 and E4 of Qa left standing, and was it later used in printing this portion of the text of sheet E3-6 in Qb? And (2) was the same compositor engaged in both tasks? A careful comparison of the individual types and a measurement of the corresponding spaces in the corresponding passages of Qa and Qb reveal so many differences that we may dismiss once and for all the suggestion of Pollard and Professor Wilson that any part of the original setting of E3 and E4 was transferred to a different chase and used in printing portions of E3-6 of Qb. Whatever resemblances exist are to be accounted for by use of the same measure and the same font of type and to the fact that it was easier for the compositor of Qb to adopt in general the disposition of text and the spacing of the words of Qa, which he used as copy, than to set the text afresh from the manuscript copy—even if that were still available.

The number of compositors at work on the quarto is not readily determinable. Pollard, as we have noted, believed that two compositors worked on alternate leaves of the manuscript, from which each set three pages of text, but the evidence to support this hypothesis requires close examination. It is true that a substitution of roman for italic *F*s in speech-tags occurs at several places in the quarto, to wit in C2^v, C3, and C3^v, at D2^v and D3, at E1^v, E2, and E2^v, and at E4^v, F1 and F1^v, and that these pages seem to correspond roughly to Pollard's triplets of pages (though actually there are only three groups of three consecutive pages). Pollard overlooked the fact that the shortage of italic *F*s would most readily have occurred if one compositor, using two cases of types, had been forced to set an abnormal number of italic *F*s in the pages immediately preceding the groups just listed. In sheet B, for example, seventeen italic *F*s are needed, and the first two pages of sheet C require five more. Again, preceding the shortage in pages D2^v and D3, sixteen italic *F*s were used in sheet C; the shortage in E1^v, E2, and E2^v follows the use of eight italic *F*s in sheet D and fifteen more in the first three pages of sheet E; and, finally, the shortage in pages E4^v, F1, and F1^v is preceded by the correct use of a total of twenty-four italic *F*s in sheet E. Small wonder that substitution of roman for italic *F*s was necessary! Actually the phenomena point strongly to the fact that one compositor set most of the quarto.[24] Had Pollard examined the speech-tags and stage directions for the use of italic *S*s, he would have found a similar condition, produced by Shakespeare's employment of the names Slender, Silence, and Shallow for three of his characters. Again, however, a careful analysis of the statistics suggests the presence of one compositor rather than two.

Pollard did not inquire into the spelling habits of the compositor(s);

---

[24] The statistics are as follows. Italic *F*s used correctly in stage directions and speech-tags: B2, 1; B2^v, 4; B3, 10; B3^v, 1; B4^v, 1; C1^v, 1; C2, 4; C2^v, 2; C3, 6, at top of page; C3^v, 3, at bottom of page; D3, 1; D3^v, 3; D4, 2; D4^v, 2; E1, 6; E1^v, 4, at top of page; E2, 5, at top of page; E3, 4; E3^v, 1; E4^v, 4; F1^v, 3; F2, 6; F2^v, 8; F3, 4. The plight of the compositor would indeed have been desperate if Falstaff had not been called *Sir John* or *John* in many of the speech-tags. Figures for the remaining pages are irrelevant, since no substitutions occur after F1^v, chiefly because not more than eleven italic *F*s are required in any one sheet until sheet K is reached. It uses correctly twenty-two, but this was possible, I suggest, because only four were needed in Sheet I and only three in sheet H. Roman *F*s were substituted as follows: C2^v, 1; C3, 2, at bottom of page; C3^v, 3, at top of page; D2^v, 4; D3, 3; E1^v, 2, at bottom of page; E2, 2, at bottom of page; E2^v, 7; E4^v, 1; F1, 11; F1^v, 10, plus one roman *E*. The data for pages C3 and C3^v suggest that the shortage of italic *F*s at the bottom of C3 and top of C3^v was relieved by the distribution of type from sheet B in time for three italic *F*s to be used at the bottom of C3^v.

in fact, it was not until 1940 that Dr. Charlton Hinman formulated criteria for identifying the work of two compositors from their spelling habits.[25] Since the use of roman and italic *F*s points, as we have seen, to the probability that one compositor did much if not all of the work on the quarto, we may properly search for the peculiarities of his workmanship and for his spelling habits. The most noticeable of these is certainly the use of parentheses in constructions where commas usually appear. On thirty of Qa's eighty pages of text, words or phrases are punctuated with parentheses.[26] This fondness extends to the treatment of run-over lines, four of which are printed as in line 23 on B4:

> pinches the other, and so both degrees preuent my curses,
> *Boy* Sir.   (boy

Some of the parentheses were undoubtedly taken over from Shakespeare's manuscript, for as Professor Percy Simpson has pointed out, the use of parentheses is an important part of the "theatrical" system of punctuation. Many, I am persuaded, are to be traced to the preference of the compositor, for it will be seen later that when setting from printed copy in E3-6, the compositor frequently introduces parentheses on his own responsibility.

Another characteristic of the quarto is the use of initial lower-case letters in marginal stage directions. Directions so printed, mostly for exits or sound-effects, occur twenty-three times. Marginal stage directions begin with a capital letter only seven times, but in one of these the first word is a proper name, and all but one of the remaining six indicate entrances on pages crowded with text. The exception is a direction for a sound-effect, and it occurs on a page that has a marginal direction beginning with a lower-case letter. All the centered stage directions (for entrances) have initial capitals except one on D3 and another on G4^v. The absence of variant practices makes it difficult to postulate the continued presence of a second compositor.

A careful examination of the spelling variants yields much the same result. Nowhere is it possible to find two opposed sets of preferential spellings such as would identify the work of two compositors, and it seems necessary to discard Pollard's hypothesis, which has already been

[25] "Principles Governing the Use of Variant Spellings as Evidence of Alternate Setting by Two Compositors," *The Library*, 4th ser., XXI (1940-41), 78-94. I am indebted to Dr. Hinman for valuable suggestions about the spelling variants in 2 *Henry IV*.

[26] On D3^v there are five such constructions; on L1^v, four; and on seven other pages, two. The other occurrences are scattered throughout the play.

shaken by the study of the use of parentheses and the setting of the marginal stage directions. It is comforting to know, as a result of Dr. Hinman's study of *Othello*,[27] that one compositor could set type rapidly enough to keep one press busy in the production of a play-quarto in an edition of normal size, and that therefore there is no compulsion to seek traces of a second compositor.

When we turn to cancel-sheet E3-6, we find that the treatment of stage directions is identical with that employed elsewhere in the book. All entrances are centered, and each begins with a capital letter. All three of the exits, one centered and two in the margin, are in lower-case type. The preference for parentheses continues, even to the point of substituting them four times for a comma or a pair of commas in the portions of Qa that were reset; and the four pairs of parentheses in Qa are retained in Qb. There is no occasion in Qb for the use of a single parenthesis in printing the runover of a long line, for the major problem of the compositor was to space out a limited amount of text over eight pages. With no manuscript to influence him, he used the spellings "Silence" or "Silens" throughout, ignoring the printed copy spellings "Scilens" (twice) and "Sci." (once) on E4^v. In the spelling variants there is nothing to indicate the presence of two compositors, and the preference for parentheses and the use of initial lower-case letters in the marginal stage directions make it probable that the same compositor set the cancel and Qa (or the greater part of it).

From our examination of the paper, typography, and spelling variants of the quarto of 2 *Henry IV,* we may fairly conclude that the cancel sheet E3-6 was not printed until after the completion of the rest of the play; that it was printed, in all probability, in Simmes's shop within a short time after the original publication;[28] and that it was set by the compositor who set the rest of the quarto. The reason for the initial omission of III. i remains unknown, but it is as likely that the publishers omitted it through timidity as that the censor forbade its publication— and if the printer or the publishers did not voluntarily prepare the cancel, it is at least possible that Shakespeare or a representative of the Lord Chamberlain's Men procured its later insertion.

[27] "New Uses for Headlines as Bibliographical Evidence," *The English Institute Annual 1941* (New York, 1942), pp. 210-11, n.

[28] [John Hazel Smith, in "The Composition of the Quarto of *Much Ado About Nothing*," *Studies in Bibliography,* XVI (1963), 9-26, has argued that Simmes interrupted the printing of the quarto of *Much Ado About Nothing* after sheet G in order to print the cancel for 2 *Henry IV*.]

The First Five Bookes of Ovids Metamorphosis, 1621, Englished by Master George Sandys

[1948]

HE DISCOVERY[1] during the summer of 1947 of a copy of *The First Five Bookes of Ovids Metamorphosis*, "Imprinted for W: B: 1621," puts an end to many conjectures[2] about this mysterious and elusive little book; but not to all, for according to the title-page, it belongs to "edit: 2d." The copy, which was acquired for the Folger Shakespeare Library, may be the very one of which just 140 years ago Joseph Haslewood supplied to Sir Egerton Brydges the following account:

Art. IV. *The First Five Bookes of Ovid's Metamorphosis, Second Edition. Imprinted for W. B. 1621. 16mo pp. 141, besides Introduction.*

This edition of the translation of Ovid by Geo. Sandys, is unnoticed in all the lists of his works. The title is engraved on a curtain, supported by two flying Cupids; above the curtain, Venus lying on a couch of clouds, holding a burning heart, attended with doves and the god of love, and below a full assembly of the heathen deities. "Fr. Delaram, sculp."[3] A head of Ovid in an oval, with

[1] It is a pleasure to record my thanks to Mr. Lionel Robinson for putting me in touch with the owner, who had found the book in a barrow in front of an obscure bookshop.

[2] For an historical survey of the facts hitherto known to bibliographers and scholars, and of their hypotheses, see Richard Beale Davis, "Early Editions of George Sandys's 'Ovid': The Circumstances of Production," *PBSA*, XXXV (1941), 255-76.

[3] A comparison of this engraving with photostats from the University of Chicago Library and Harvard University Library indicates that Delaram copied in reverse the unsigned engraving which serves as the general title of a duodecimo edition published in Amsterdam in 1619 by Guilielmus Ianssonius with the title, *Pub: Ovidii Nasonis Opera* (another copy is credited to Mills College and a fourth to the Bibliothèque Nationale). The work also appears in a 1624 edition (cf. copies credited to the American Antiquarian Society and to the Bibliothèque Nationale), but Dr. Brigham writes me that the copy in the library of the American Antiquarian Society is not a Jansson publication. The title-page of this edition, which has no engraved general title, reads as follows: *"Publii Ovidii*

Papers of the Bibliographical Society, University of Virginia [*Studies in Bibliography*], I (1948-49), 71-82.

verses beneath, as in the folios. "Ovid defended," is the only article prefixed to this edition, which has a trifling variance from the subsequent ones, as giving "Ovid's selfe-censure," a translation of the concluding lines of lib. 15. . . . Of the edition, dated 1621, I have never seen any other copy than the one above described. The date of the first edition of the five books yet remains to be ascertained.[4]

More than once the failure of scholars to locate this or any other copy of the book—nowhere is the name of the owner of the copy in question stated—has led to speculation about the accuracy of Haslewood's description and even about his veracity.[5] The vindication of the antiquary, who suffered deeply from the scorn of some of his more genteel contemporaries, in this instance may help to validate his other contributions to bibliography.

The Folger copy of *The First Five Bookes*—which, until another comes to light, I shall call unique—corresponds in almost every detail to that described by Haslewood. The book, which measures 6.4 × 10.2 cm., is actually a duodecimo and not a sexagesimo. When purchased, it possessed only the rear cover and portions of the backstrip of 18th-century calf, and its condition was such that after a careful examination the book was taken apart and then rebound in green niger. On blank leaf ¶6ᵛ, written in a childish scrawl as part of a doggerel statement of ownership,

---

Nasonis Operum Tomus I. quo continentur Heroidum Epistola. Amorum Libri III. De arte Amandi Libri tres. De Remedio Amoris Libri II. Et alia, qua aversa pagella indicat. [cut of 2 globes] Amsterdami Apud Guilielmum Caesium Anno MDCXXiiii." The appearance of the name Caesium suggests that the copy listed in the catalogue of the Bibliothèque Nationale as by "G. Janss. Caesium" may be inaccurately described. In 1629 the Jansson edition was reprinted with a different title, *Pub: Ovidii Nas: Opera. Daniel Heinsius textum recensuit,* by Ioannes Ianssonus (I have used a photostat of the title-page of the Harvard copy; other copies of this edition are in the Boston Public Library, the Washington and Lee University Library, the British Museum, and the Bibliothèque Nationale). This 1629 edition has an engraved title-page, unsigned, that is closely copied from that of 1619. According to the catalogue of the Bibliothèque Nationale, later editions were published by J. Jansson in 1634 and 1647 and by J. Blaeu in 1649.

I am indebted to Dr. Fredson Bowers for directing my attention to the Dutch engraving and to F. C. Francis, Esq., Mr. William A. Jackson, Dr. Clarence S. Brigham, and Mr. P. G. Morrison for help in securing photostats and other information on the Jansson editions.

[4] *Censura Literaria* (1808), VI, 132-33, 135.

[5] It has been hinted that the entry in *Censura Literaria* is a fabrication of the sort frequently attributed to John Payne Collier—cf. Davis, *op. cit.,* pp. 261-62. [Through the kindness of Miss Katharine F. Pantzer, who is completing the revision of the *STC,* I learn that Harvard has secured a perfect copy of *The First Five Bookes,* "edit: 2d," and that there is a copy at Winchester with the wording "edit: 3d" on the engraved title-page.]

is the name of Thomas Hickman. The collation appears to be, ¶⁶ A-F¹²
(F12, possibly a blank, wanting). Leaves "¶1/6 were not conjugate,
each having been backed with heavy wove paper. For this reason the
collation . . . cannot be entirely certain; but the exact correspondence
of chainlines made it appear highly probable that these two leaves had
originally been conjugate. . . . All other pairs of leaves were normally
conjugate except F2/11, F3/10, of which there was every reason to
believe that they had originally been conjugate."⁶ Contents: ¶1ʳ, engraved title; ¶1ᵛ, blank; ¶2ʳ-6ʳ, "OVID DEFENDED"; ¶6ᵛ, blank;
A1ʳ-F11ʳ, the text; F11ᵛ, blank. Pp. [xii] + 141.

It will be noticed immediately that the Folger copy lacks a leaf
bearing the head of Ovid engraved in an oval, with verses beneath.
Probably this was a frontispiece which was lost at the time the little
book lost its front cover.⁷ The title-page is exactly as Haslewood described it, and the prefatory defense of Ovid begins, as Haslewood
said it did, with a translation from the concluding lines of Book XV
of the *Metamorphoses*. These points have been conjecturally called in
question, and it is doing simple justice to Haslewood to affirm his
accuracy. The first sentence of "Ovid Defended" is identical in the
editions of 1621 and 1626,⁸ except that the words "from detraction" have
been added in line 3 of the later edition. In the 12mo, the second
sentence is as follows:

And, in that the traduced may with modesty enough report their owne
merits, I will first begin with

a   OVID'S SELFE-CENSVRE.

Now haue I ended, what the Thunders rage,
Nor fire, nor steele shall raze, nor eating Age.
Come when it wil my death's vncertayn houre;
Which o're this body onely hath a powre
Yet shall my better part transcend the skie:
And my immortall Name shall neuer die

---

⁶ Quoted from the bibliographical note by my colleague, Dr. Giles E. Dawson, Curator
of Books and Manuscripts, which is inserted at the end of the volume. Similar signed
notes are placed in every old book which is rebound at the Folger. The old calf cover
is mounted inside the rear cover.

⁷ If the frontispiece was printed on leaf F12 which was then detached and prefixed
to the book, its loss would be readily accounted for.

⁸ Upon his return from Virginia in 1626, Sandys published in a small folio his translation of all fifteen books—see below. See further Davis, *op. cit.*, and also his "America
in George Sandys' 'Ovid,' " *The William and Mary Quarterly*, 3rd ser., IV (1947), 297-304.

> For, wheresoe're the Roman Egles spred
> Their conquering wings, I shall of all be read.
> And, if we Prophets true presages giue;
> I, in my fame, eternally shall liue.[9]

The reference "a" is identified on ¶6ʳ as "L. 15 in fin." The preface continues: "A prediction already confirmed by many lustres of Ages. Heare we now that accurate Orator, MARCUS ANNÆVS SENECA." The section continues as in *1626* until ERASMUS is reached, where the earlier edition provides an ampler testimony. After STEPHANUS, *1626* inserts MARCUS ANTONIUS TRITONIUS and BERNARDUS MARTINUS. There are occasional variations in the wording of the transitional sentences.

Though the book was originally entered in the registers of the Company of Stationers to Matthew Lownes and William Barrett on 27 April 1621,[10] the engraved title-page of the second edition names only W[illiam B[arrett].[11] The printer of this edition is unknown, and no

---

[9] Readers may wish to compare this 1621 version with the translation that appears at the end of the folio of 1626:

> And now the Work is ended, which, *Ioue's* rage,
> Nor Fire, nor Sword shall raze, nor eating Age.
> Come when it will my deaths vncertain howre;
> Which onely of my body hath a powre:
> Yet shall my better Part transcend the skie;
> And my immortall name shall neuer die.
> For, where-so-ere the *Roman* Eagles spread
> Their conquering wings, I shall of all be read:
> And, if we Prophets truly can diuine,
> I, in my liuing Fame, shall euer shine.

[10] Arber's reprint, IV, 53. (If Haslewood had had access to the Stationers' Registers, he might have guessed that the first edition was almost certainly dated 1621.) This is the first entry of Sandys's translation. The compilers of the *STC* err, as pointed out by Russell H. Barker, *TLS,* 27 September 1934, p. 655, and again by R. B. Davis, "Early Editions," p. 259, n. 14, in identifying Sandys's work with the one entered to Jonas Man on 23 February 1617/18. The earlier book, "Ouids metamorphosis gramaticallie translated by John Bringsley" is in fact *STC* 18963, of which two copies (British Museum and Folger) are extant. Printed by Humphrey Lownes for Thomas Man in 1618, it is a textbook translation of *Metamorphoses,* Bk. I, by the celebrated teacher and Puritan divine, John Brinsley.

Davis, *loc. cit.,* mistakenly credits the entry of 23 February 1617/18 to "master Lownes"; instead the entry was to Jonas Man "vnder the handes of Master *Lownes* senior warden."

[11] Until a copy of the first edition of 1621 is discovered, it cannot be known whether the words "edit: 2d." were added to the plate at the time the book was reprinted, or even whether the first edition had an engraved title. But certain minor differences in the formation of the letters suggest the possibility that "edit: 2d." is an addition. If so, the insertion did not crowd the adjacent lines unpleasantly, but it should be noted that the absence of "edit: 2d." would not spoil the appearance of the page.

guesses as to his identity can be hazarded because the book contains no printer's devices, no ornaments, and no initial letters. From the date of the second edition, it is obvious that the book was popular, for a reprint was called for within twelve months of the date of entry.

The relationship between the second edition of 1621 and the folio of 1626 is very close. In the preliminaries, for example, the edition of 1626 has on the verso of the leaf of dedication an engraving that has for its central feature the head of Ovid in an oval, with verses beneath; this corresponds to the engraving described by Haslewood but now wanting in the Folger copy of the 1621 edition. Each edition has an engraved title-page, but these differ radically. And each edition has a section entitled, "Ovid Defended."[12] It is in the texts of the translation that the editions most closely resemble each other. These may be minutely collated for page after page without discovery of even a literal difference. From time to time, the compositors of the 1621 edition were forced by the length of a line to use an ampersand or to indicate the omission of "n" or "m" by printing a vowel with a tilde.[13] Occasionally *1626* corrects a typographical error in *1621*[14] or introduces one.[15] Sandys devoted much attention to smoothing the meter of the lines in the edition of 1626, frequently altering the spelling of a dissyllabic word to insure that it should be pronounced as a monosyllable and eliding *es* and *os* before vowels or the letter *h.*[16] Otherwise, except for verbal changes or alterations in

---

[12] See n. 9 above for detailed comparison. I wish to record my indebtedness to my colleague, Dr. E. E. Willoughby, for several suggestions, and to my son, James G. McManaway, Jr., for valuable assistance.

[13] Cf. *1621*, p. 20, line 27:

      To streams, & gentle Nymphs that streams frequēt.

and *1626*, p. 15, line 32:

      To streams, and gentle Nymphs that streams frequent.

[14] Cf. *1621*, p. 8, line 10:

      Nor rhine, for Thee, lesse thought, *Augustus*, tooke,

with *1626*, p. 6, line 13:

      Nor thine, for Thee, less thought, *Augustus*, tooke, . . .

[15] Cf. *1621*, p. 6, line 4:

      An other part on hissing Embers broyles.

with *1626*, p. 6, line 39:

      An other patt on hissing Embers broyles; . . .

[16] Cf. *1621*, p. 40, l. 17:

      Nor lesse the *Heliades* lament; who shead

with *1626*, p. 30, l. 19:

      Nor lesse th' *Heliades* lament; who shead . . .

the translation, which will be discussed together in another connection, the text of the first five books of the 1626 edition agrees to a remarkable degree with that of the edition of 1621. Only in the reprinting of Bibles, I think, will such literal correspondence be found in other 17th-century books.

If this be true, it follows that a corrected copy of the second edition of 1621 must have been supplied to the printer in 1626 for the use of his compositors,[17] and the accuracy of the reprint suggests that Sandys read the proofs zealously. Now if a copy of the second edition of 1621 was used as printer's copy in 1626, it is a safe presumption not only that this second edition was an exceptionally faithful reprint of the first edition of 1621 but that the latter was printed from a manuscript supplied by Sandys himself. It would follow that Sandys planned the book and its engravings in conjunction with his publishers, William Barrett and Matthew Lownes.[18]

While Sandys was in Virginia, William Barrett died, and on 3 April 1626, his relict, Mistress Barrett, conveyed to John Parker her rights in a number of books, including Sandys's *Ovid*.[19] Then, a little more than one month later, William Stansby entered "*A booke Called Ovids Metamorphosis XV bookes, in English verse* by George Sandes."[20] Although the imprint on the engraved title-page names neither printer nor publisher and the colophon reads "Printed by William Stansby 1626," it may be presumed that Stansby served as publisher of this edition, for in 1626 Sandys expected to return shortly to Virginia. He probably assumed that his rights in the book were fully protected by the pregnant words "Cum Priuilegio" engraved on the title-page. This phrase alludes

---

or *1621*, p. 67, l. 10:

To his Browe th' antlers of long-liuing Harts:

with *1626*, p. 50, l. 20:

T' his Browe th' antlers of long-liuing Harts: . . .

[17] It is possible that *1626* was set from a copy of the lost first edition. If so, the printer of the second edition must have worked with remarkable accuracy, for the close correspondence observable between the editions of 1621 and 1626 is rarely found in two independent printings of a copy-text.

[18] The fact that one of the publishers, Lownes, to whom the first edition of 1621 was entered, was a warden of the Company lends additional weight to my belief that the 1621 venture was not piratical, as has been more than once suggested.

[19] Arber, IV, 157-58.

[20] 7 May 1626. See Arber, IV, 160.

to letters patent granted by King Charles to Sandys on 24 April 1626[21] that gave him exclusive publishing rights for twenty-one years.[22] These rights he had to assert within two years, for Robert Young published an octavo reprint of the complete translation early in 1628.

The details of the transaction by which Young became possessed of rights in the book are obscure. Matthew Lownes was dead before 10 April 1627, for on that date many of his titles were transferred to his son Thomas,[23] but not the *Ovid*. Soon after, Thomas Lownes conveyed a large group of books to Humphrey Lownes and Robert Young,[24] but again the *Ovid* is not named. Yet the minutes of Court Book C are explicit in their statement that "the assignm^t to Robt Younge . . . shalbe . . . Crost out of the Regester Booke of the Company." It must be assumed that in a private and unrecorded transaction[25] Matthew Lownes had before his death transferred to Young his interest in *The First Five Bookes,* as recorded long before on 27 April 1621, and that Young had, somewhat unethically perhaps, taken advantage of this right in five books to reprint the complete translation of fifteen books.

The wording of the minute in the Court Book suggests that, though he had provided Stansby with a copy of the 1621 edition to print from in 1626, Sandys considered his Fifteen Books an independent publication and that he gave no compensation to John Parker, who had acquired William Barrett's rights in *The First Five Bookes,* or to Matthew Lownes, who had transferred his rights in the duodecimo to Robert Young.[26] It is my belief, as stated above, that William Stansby, printer of the folio of 1626, probably served only as Sandys's agent. But the outraged poet took no chances when he made his demands upon the Company of Stationers: the minute records that

[21] A typographical error in *DNB* causes Sir Sidney Lee to seem to date this grant 1621, to the confusion of scholarship.

[22] Noted by Alexander Brown, *Genesis of the U. S.* (1840), II, 994; Davis cites the edition of 1880.

[23] Arber, IV, 176.

[24] On 30 May 1627; cf. Arber, IV, 180.

[25] For a preliminary discussion of this and other interesting points of copyright practice, see Giles E. Dawson, "The Copyright of Shakespeare's Dramatic Works," in *Studies in Honor of A. H. R. Fairchild,* ed. C. T. Prouty (University of Missouri Press, 1946), pp. 12-14. The subject is treated at greater length in his forthcoming essay, "Copyright of Plays in the Early Seventeenth Century," in *English Institute Annual 1947* (Columbia University Press, 1948).

[26] It is possible, of course, that Young acquired these rights prior to Sandys's return to London in 1626 and that some arrangement should have been made with him instead of with Lownes.

Mr Sandes Patent for the sole printing of the 15. bookes of Ovides Metamorphosis by him translated into English verse was openlye reade in the hall this quarter day. And it is ordered that th' entrance of Mr Barret and Mr Lownes deceased of the first five books and the assignm^t to Robt Younge, and the Entrance of the whole 15. bookes to mr Stansby shalbe all Crost out of the Regester Booke of the Company for that noe man shall laye anie claime to the printing of the same or any pte thereof.[27]

And so it was done, but the transfer of Mistress Barrett's rights to Parker was somehow overlooked.

Between the years 1621 and 1626 Sandys made a number of revisions of his translation of the first five books of the *Metamorphoses*. Some of these appear to have been introduced for the purpose of improving the accuracy of the translation. Thus the reading of *1621* (p. 9, line 24), "Or must th' Earth be by saluages possest?" is changed in *1626* to "Must Earth be onely by wild beasts possest?" (*Met.* I, 249, ferisne paret populandas tradere terras). Again, "trembling" (*1621*, p. 80, line 28) is corrected to "wrathfull" (cf. *Met.* III, 577, ira tremendos), and "Epogus" (*1621*, p. 82, line 13) to "Epopeus" (cf. *Met.* III, 619).

More frequently Sandys amended his translation to improve the Latin pronunciation of proper names. In *1621* (p. 23, line 31), Pleias is trisyllabic, with the accent indicated on the second syllable:

> But, calls his sonne, of bright *Pleïas* bred;

in *1626* both syllabification and indication of accent are changed:

> But, calls his sonne, of fulgent *Pleias* bred . . .

(*Met.* I, 670, Pleias enixa est letoque det imperat Argum). In one case at least, Sandys corrected the pronunciation of one name at the expense of another. In *1621* (p. 36, line 13), he was not satisfied with his rendition of "Citheron":

> Mycale, with the sacred *Citheron:*

so he revised it to

> High *Mycale*, diuine *Cithaeron*, wast . . .

(cf. *Met.* II, 223, Dindymaque et Mycale natusque ad sacra Cithaeron), thus doing violence to the pronunciation of "Mycale."

Some of the revisions entail the rewriting of a complete line or even

---

[27] See Davis, "Early Editions," pp. 270-71, for this text and an account of later troubles that beset Sandys.

a couplet. The ravishment of Io (*Met.* I, 599-600) is rendered thus in *1621* (p. 21, lines 21-22):

> With darknesse he the Earth inveloped;
> And catching her, inforc't her Maiden-head.

In *1626*, the couplet is changed to read:

> He in the Aire a sable cloud displai'd,
> Caught, and devirginat's the strugling Maid.

The account of Phaeton's conversation with Apollo (*Met.* II, 33-34) appears in *1621* (p. 29, lines 27-28) as follows:

> What brought thee hither, *Phaeton,* said hee,
> My dearest sonne? well worthy so to bee.

In *1626*, the passage is altered thus:

> Who said, What hether drew thee *Phaeton,*
> Who art, and worthily my dearest Son?

Once Sandys rewrites a passage (*Met.* III, 185-88) to secure greater precision and compression. In *1621* (p. 66, line 31–p. 67, line 3), five lines are required:

> When from her aged Love shee takes her flight:
> Such was *Diana's,* taken in that plight.
> Although inuiron'd by her Virgin trayne,
> Shee side-long turneth, casting with disdayne
> A killing looke; and wisht her deadly Bowe: . . .

Three lines suffice in *1626:*

> Such flusht in *Dians* cheeks, being naked tane.
> And though inuiron'd by her Virgin trayne,
> Shee side-long turnes, looks back, and wisht her bow: . . .

The later version profits by the removal of the couplet that elaborates the reference in the preceding line to "rosie Morn," and in this revision Elizabethan exuberance can be seen yielding to classical correctness. Other examples might be cited of Sandys's efforts to polish his lines, but these indicate the care he expended on the translation.

Now that the finding of a copy of the second edition of *The First Five Bookes of Ovids Metamorphosis* has cleared Joseph Haslewood of charges of inaccuracy (or worse) and thrown new light on the history of Sandys's famous translation, it remains to inquire once again whether this book in the edition of 1626 may be considered the first published verse in the English language which was written on the mainland of North America.[28] The answer must be given in the negative. Another "American" poem preceded it by fully three years. In *Catalogue 77, A Selection of Extremely Rare and Important Printed Books and Ancient Manuscripts,* issued early in 1948 by the London firm of William H. Robinson, Ltd., item 98 is a broadside ballad entitled, "Good Newes from Virginia . . . ."[29] This was published without date in London "for John Trundle," but the title informs us that the poem was "Sent from *Iames* his Towne this present moneth of March, 1623 by a Gentleman in that Country." Since the ballad gives a highly circumstantial account of the Indian massacre of 1622, the date is probably accurate and the attribution of authorship correct. The author may have been "a Gentleman," but surely his literary attainments were of the slightest, if the ballad is a fair measure. The first stanza is typical:

> No English heart, but heard with griefe
> the massacre here done:
> And how by sauage trecheries,
> full many a mothers sonne:
> But God that gaue them power and leaue,
> their cruelties to vse.
> Hath giuen them vp into our hands,
> who English did abuse.

There is no need to detail the evidence of the author's firsthand knowledge of events. The ballad may be read in the facsimile provided in the bookseller's catalogue. It has, moreover, been available to scholars and historians in another form for eight years, having been reproduced as Number 105 in "Photostat Americana, Second Series" in May 1940 from the copy in the Public Record Office in London.[30]

[28] Professor Davis has demonstrated that although Books VI-XV were translated on the voyage to America or while Sandys was in residence in Virginia, the first explicit references to the American scene occur in the commentary of the edition of 1632—cf. his "America in George Sandys' 'Ovid'," cited above.

[29] The ballad is to be sung to the tune of "All those that be good fellowes." It consists of two parts, the first of eight stanzas and the second of fourteen stanzas. Below the title are a woodcut of a ship and another of an armed man surveying the corpses that lie at his feet.

[30] Reproductions are available in the fifteen American libraries that subscribe to "Photostat Americana." The stanza quoted below is printed by Davis, "Early Editions," p. 265, from E. D. Neill, *Virginia vetusta* (1885), pp. 147-48.

Appropriately enough, this rare ballad, generally overlooked by literary historians, includes a fine tribute to George Sandys:

> Stout Master George Sands vpon a night,
>   did brauely venture forth:
> And mong'st the sauage murtherers,
>   did forme a deed of worth.
> For finding many by a fire,
>   to death their liues they pay:
> Set fire of a Towne of theires,
>   and brauely came away.

The Two Earliest Prompt Books
of *Hamlet*

[1949]

I

ONE of the joys of watching a performance of a good play is the recollection of other performances, and so when I first saw the Laurence Olivier picturization of *Hamlet* it was natural that I should call to mind not only the stage productions I have seen but also those I have read about. The cuts and transpositions made by Olivier's textual editor reminded me of the fact that Shakespeare had required over 4000 lines to give full artistic expression to his concept of the tragic story, and that the first edition of the play seems to show that from the outset the acting versions had an abbreviated text with possibly some irregularities in the order of the scenes. As a matter of fact, Shakespeare must have known well enough that some 1500 lines would have to be slashed ruthlessly before his play could go into production. What and where to prune must have been a serious problem for the Lord Chamberlain's Men about 1601; certainly it has been for producers ever since.

How the text was altered in Shakespeare's lifetime remains a matter for speculation, but we are not entirely without grounds upon which to base conjecture. *Hamlet* has always been a popular play, and its acting traditions and stage business have been more faithfully preserved than those of any other play of its antiquity. According to John Downes, who prompted at the Duke's Theatre in 1662 and continued in this capacity at one house or another for nearly fifty years, Thomas Betterton was a peerless Hamlet for upwards of half a century, having been trained in the interpretation of the role by Shakespeare's godson, Sir William

Papers of the Bibliographical Society of America, XLIII (1949), 288-320. Read in abbreviated form at the meeting of the Society at Princeton, New Jersey, 4 June 1949.

Davenant. Furthermore, Davenant had learned from Taylor, who had carried on the tradition established in Shakespeare's lifetime by the great Richard Burbage. These are not exactly the words used by Downes in *Roscius Anglicanus* (1708), but they convey his meaning, and they seem to tell us of an unbroken tradition of *Hamlet* performances from about 1601 to 1709.

Now since the stage business and the interpretation of the characters are intimately bound up in the stage version of the text, it would seem reasonable to assume that, if Downes was not misinformed, the Restoration *Hamlet* is in essence the Elizabethan *Hamlet*.

Fortunately we know a great deal about the Restoration *Hamlet*. Its text is preserved in the playhouse quartos of the period. All these derive ultimately from the last pre-Wars quarto of 1637, but they differ from it in many respects, for the publishers took the trouble to consult the prompter's book in the theater and to indicate differences between the literary and the stage texts. All the Restoration quartos of *Hamlet,* beginning with that of 1676, contain the following address to the reader:

This Play being too long to be conveniently Acted, such places as might be least prejudicial to the Plot or Sense, are left out upon the Stage: but that we may no way wrong the incomparable Author, are here inserted according to the Original Copy with this Mark. "

But the differences between the Restoration stage versions and the literary text as represented by Q 1637 are not limited to the passages marked by a pair of inverted commas. Scores of minor modifications were made to conform to the promptbook.[1]

The Restoration quartos demonstrate, as does the "bad" first quarto of *Hamlet,* that what audiences wanted and what producers gave them from Elizabeth's time to Garrick's, and even later, was action. As Don Marquis so acutely has the manager say in his poem, "Pete the Parrot and Shakespeare," "give them a good ghost . . . and not too much of your damned poetry." In the Restoration quartos, several hundred lines of "damned poetry" are marked for omission, two or three lines at a time. The twenty-odd major cuts, ranging from nine lines in length to eighty, and totaling nearly 600 lines, include such favorite passages as Horatio's account of the prodigies before Julius Caesar's death,

---

[1] See Hazelton Spencer, *Shakespeare Improved* (Harvard University Press, 1927), for a detailed account and analysis of the changes.

Marcellus's legend of the cock crowing at Christmas, Claudius's reproaches of Hamlet for excessive grief, Laertes' reasons for thinking Hamlet a dangerous suitor to Ophelia, the maxims of Polonius and his reasons for breaking off the love affair between Ophelia and Hamlet, Hamlet's comments on drunkenness in Denmark and his apostrophe to the Ghost, much of the dialogue about Priam and of the Player's speech, Hamlet's self-reproaches that follow, his comments on the art of acting, and the portions of the Closet Scene that contain Hamlet's graphic instructions to his Mother about her future marital relations with Claudius. The omission of these and of the whole of the story of Fortinbras, save for his appearance after the death of Hamlet, not only speeds the action but reduces markedly the amplitude of the fable and simplifies the characters of Hamlet and Claudius. Gone are most of the lines in which Hamlet reproaches himself, and gone too are most of the speculations about the honesty of the Ghost. The spectator who saw a performance of this Restoration version would never question the valor of the Prince or suspect that he was tardy in driving to his revenge.

Modern audiences that have come to expect the golden lines, the arias of the play, and that tend to judge every actor by his rendition of the familiar soliloquies, would be shocked at their abridgement or omission. Yet there is good reason to believe that, in Shakespeare's lifetime and for over a hundred years after his death, the *Hamlet* that was acted on the stage was close indeed to what has lately been put on the silver screen. It is a meager play in comparison with the God's plenty of the full *Hamlet* text, but it is still exciting entertainment.

These are the thoughts that brought to my memory the two earliest promptbooks of *Hamlet* that are extant. A still earlier promptbook was once known, part of a copy of the Third Folio which was used in the Smock Alley Theatre in Dublin as early as about 1680. J. O. Halliwell-Phillipps broke up the Folio and had the plays bound separately; several of these have come to the Folger Shakespeare Library, but the *Hamlet* is untraceable.[2] Unless it can be found, the two earliest surviving promptbooks are (1) a copy of the quarto of 1676 with the four-line imprint and (2) a copy of the 1683 quarto. The first was at my instigation purchased many years ago by the Friends of the Johns Hopkins Library

[2] See R. C. Bald, "Shakespeare on the Stage in Restoration Dublin," *PMLA*, LVI (1941), 369 ff. [Since this article was written, the Smock Alley *Hamlet* has been located; see G. Blakemore Evans, ed., *The Smock Alley Hamlet* (Shakespearian Promptbooks, Vol. IV), Bibliographical Society of the University of Virginia, 1966.]

and deposited in the Tudor and Stuart Club at the Hopkins; the other I found more recently in the Folger Library, to which it had come by way of Halliwell-Phillipps and Marsden J. Perry. These two books contain hitherto unknown information about how *Hamlet* was performed in England during a good part of the 18th century and may even throw light on the Restoration performances and ultimately on the Shakespearian *Hamlet* itself.

II

The two promptbooks were prepared by and for the use of the same man, and it has been my good fortune to identify him. His handwriting occurs sporadically in a notebook containing the player's part of Gomez in Dryden's *Spanish Fryar,* a Heber-Dobell-Folger item. It is found, too, in a letter of 1748 addressed to the Reverend Joseph Greene, master of the free school in Stratford, and on several scraps bearing theatrical data, also procured by the Folger from Mr. Dobell. The writer's name is John Ward. He has not the prominence of an article in the *DNB*; as a matter of fact, he is more famous in his grandchildren, Sarah Siddons and John Philip Kemble, than in his own right, and yet, as we shall see, he has a perpetual if modest claim on Shakespearians.

A great deal of nonsense has been written about John Ward. It has been stated more than once, for example, that when young he acted with Thomas Betterton.[3] This would be exciting, if true, for it would strengthen the probability that John Ward's *Hamlet,* as revealed in his promptbooks, continued the Bettertonian (*i.e.,* Shakespeare-Davenant) tradition. But, as we shall discover from the inscription on Ward's gravestone, he died in 1773 at the age of 69. Now Betterton, who died in 1710, retired from the stage in the spring of 1709 when John Ward was an infant of five years, and the story that Ward acted with Betterton must be rejected with regret.

Ward's antecedents are doubtful. "In the irresponsible stage histories of his day," writes Mrs. Parsons (pp. 6-7), "he is termed an Irishman—for no reason the present investigator can discover beyond the facts that

---

[3] Cf. Yvonne Ffrench, *Mrs. Siddons: Tragic Actress* (London, 1936), p. 14: "John Ward, sometimes, though inaccurately, described as an Irishman, late of the Aungier Street theatre, had been Betterton's contemporary and a capable actor." Cf. also the more conservative statement of Mrs. Clement Parsons, *The Incomparable Siddons* (London, 1909), p. 6: "Ward, who had as a child, played under Betterton . . . ."

he once acted (with Miss Peg Woffington) at the Aungier Street Theatre, Dublin, and that his daughter was born at Clonmel. Actually, he and his family were well known locally as 'the Wards of Leominster,' at Leominster they were married and buried. . . . Close by his [Ward's] are the graves of his near relatives, Thomas and Humphrey Ward." Of the stories of John Ward's Irish origins I am as dubious as Mrs. Parsons. She is correct in her statements that he acted in Dublin and that his daughter Sarah was born in Clonmel. It remains for some future investigator to prove whether he was born and married in Leominster.

On one of the scraps of paper in Ward's handwriting in the collection known as Folger MS. 6643 are the following notations:

> 1733 Died Mr Charles Snell, an eminent
> writing Master Jan^ry 9th—In Foster Lane—
> of whom I learnt

> 1733 Feby 17th Died Mr Whadcock Surgeon in
> Bread Street—who set my leg when broke

These entries suggest a youth spent in London, unless we are to assume that both Snell and Whadcock migrated from Leominster to London.[4]

A strong element of mystery is introduced by the history of the Kemble family penned apparently for John Payne Collier by Anne Kemble Curtis Hatton, sister of Mrs. Siddons, and better known as Anne of Swansea, the author of a great many bad romances. According to Anne,[5] who was the black sheep of the family and whose statements may be tinged not only with malice but also with romantic imagination, the Kembles "had reason for believing" that John Ward was "the off-spring of a man of high Rank by a distant relation of his own, who

---

[4] It is tempting to assume that the leg was broken in boyhood, but of course Ward may have "learnt" of Snell before the latter established a London residence; and he may have broken his leg during the later years when he was a resident in London and Middlesex—see below.

[5] Her history is cited and quoted from by Herschel Baker, *John Philip Kemble: The Actor in His Theatre* (Harvard University Press, 1942), *passim,* who discovered the manuscript in the Folger Library. I am limited to the data gleaned by Professor Baker, for the item has been mis-shelved since the Folger treasures returned from wartime storage and is not available for further study. [The manuscript has long since been found; it is catalogued as Y.c. 423 (3a, b). According to Anne Hatton, John Ward's father was "an Irishman"; she does not name the place of John's birth or tell where the boy's "father . . . provided liberally for [his] support and education." One is left to speculate whether John bore his father's or his mother's surname—as Anne Hatton expresses it, to John "there is attached a certain degree of romance and mystery."]

did not outlive the infancy of her child." This is a curious story, for the activities of the Wards and Kembles centered about Leominster for many years, and if John Ward were derived from a family that had long been in residence there, as Mrs. Parsons maintains, the truth should have been readily ascertainable.

Mrs. Hatton's account goes on to say that "the boy was raised 'liberally,' being at length placed in the army with a commission. Ward was sent to Cork and there married a milliner who 'without any extraordinary talent for the profession, had imbibed a strong desire to quit her humble occupation, and figure a heroine on the Stage.' By his marriage Ward lost his father's assistance; he was forced to sell his commission and assume 'the management of an itinerant company of comedians,' of which he shortly became the 'grand attraction and support.' "[6]

I cannot avoid the suspicion that Anne has combined fact from her grandfather Ward's career with tradition about her father Roger Kemble's origin and humble calling (hairdresser), and decorated everything with the trappings of Gothic romance.

We come to provable fact in 1723, when Ward at the age of eighteen or nineteen played the part of Hazeroth, a young lord, in the initial performance of Elijah Fenton's *Mariamne* on Friday, 22 February, at Lincoln's Inn Fields. A general statement to this effect is made by several of the stage historians (*e.g.*, Genest, III, 121); it is corroborated by the printed cast in the first edition of the play and is given further confirmation by the Winston Manuscript in the Folger Library. From this same manuscript I have discovered for the first time that Ward joined the company that season and that his first role was Ascanio in *The Spanish Curate* on Saturday, 17 November 1722. This play was repeated three times before the end of the season, and *Mariamne* was given a total of eighteen times, presumably with Ward in the cast each time. It may be significant that the play chosen to be given at the joint benefit of Ward, Chapman, and Mackenzie was *Julius Caesar*. Ward's first Shakespearian role is not recorded.

Ward continued to act at Lincoln's Inn Fields throughout the seasons of 1723-24, 1724-25, and 1725-26, appearing again in *Mariamne* and also in *Titus Andronicus, The Spanish Fryar, Henry IV, The Island Princess, The Royal Merchant, The Old Batchelor, The Beaux' Stratagem, Love's Last Shift,* and *Hamlet.*

[6] Baker, p. 9.

Equally interesting as these items is another entry by Winston, and likewise hitherto overlooked: a Mrs. Ward played in *The Country Wife* on Wednesday, 5 October 1725. Genest gives the additional information that she played Mrs. Dainty Fidget and that the play was acted eight times. Curiously enough, Winston does not include Mrs. Ward in the list of actresses who were first employed at Lincoln's Inn Fields in 1725-26; nor does her name appear in any of his earlier lists (Winston gives only surnames). I suspect, therefore, that she had been engaged by the company before her marriage to Ward, but although I know from other sources that her baptismal name was Sarah I am unable to discover her maiden name.[7]

After 1726 there is a gap in the records of the Wards for three years, but a document of 1746 to be cited later indicates that they maintained a London connection. They next appear in their first engagement at the Smock Alley Theatre, Dublin, with Elrington's Company, where on 19 March 1730 *Hamlet* was performed for Mrs. Ward's benefit.[8] In their second season, 1730-31, Ward and his wife played Gloucester and Queen Elizabeth in *Richard III* for their benefit. "Sometime during the following month the Wards separated themselves from the S. A. company and set up an insurgent young troupe 'at the great Booth in Dames's Street.' Faulkner's *Dublin Journal* of May 2 advertises for May 5 a benefit performance of *The Double Dealer* ('never acted in this Kingdom') on behalf of the Wards.[9] They seem to have taken their troupe on tour during the summer and are reported by the *Dublin Intelligencer* of September 22 as acting in Chester."[10] According to Augustin Daly,[11] Ward had some authority in the Smock Alley company after the death of Elrington in

[7] In the *Catalogue of Dramatic Portraits in the Theatre Collection of Harvard College Library*, pp. 232-33, Mrs. Hall suggests that her full name was Sarah Hoare Ward. I cannot verify the statement, but I am of the opinion that all of the engravings there listed depict an entirely different, and a younger, Mrs. Ward, who played for Garrick many years after Mrs. Sarah Ward left London (cf. *The Thespian Dictionary*, 2nd ed., 1805, p. 212). I doubt that Sarah Ward's maiden name was Hoare. [From an unpublished source I now learn (1968) that the maiden name of Mrs. John Ward was Butcher.]

[8] For this and several other important details I am indebted to Professor W. S. Clark, who kindly gleaned them from the manuscripts relating to the Irish stage collected by the late W. J. Lawrence and now in the library of the University of Cincinnati.

[9] Cf. Robert Hitchcock, *An Historical View of the Irish Stage* (Dublin, 1788), I, 53 ff., where it is said that the booth is in Fownes's-Court, lately occupied by Madam Violante, and that a few months put a period to the insurrection.

[10] Quoted from Professor Clark's letter.

[11] *Woffington*, p. 14.

1732—but whether in the old or the new theater is not stated. The next recorded performance is on 11 December 1735, the opening night of the new Smock Alley Theatre, when the Wards played Don Carlos and Louisa in *Love Makes a Man*.[12]

Meanwhile, on 2 September 1735, at Clonmel, Mrs. Ward had given birth to a daughter, Sarah, the future wife of Roger Kemble and mother of Sarah Kemble Siddons.

In 1736-37, the Wards became regular members of the Aungier Street Company. "Ward played First Manager in *The Rival Theatres* . . . on January 10, 1737. He and his wife acted the same parts in *Richard III* as in 1731, at their benefit on February 10. Then, more importantly, on February 12 he was Hamlet to Peg Woffington's Ophelia at a benefit for the Mercer's Charitable Hospital. The Wards continued at A. S. in the following season. Mr. Ward's benefit on March 16, 1738, is of considerable interest because 'at the Lord Lieutenant's Command' *Measure for Measure* was given its first production on the Irish stage.[13] Mrs. Ward had her benefit on April 27 with Lee's *Lucius Junius Brutus*. There is no evidence to show that the Wards were at A. S. in 1738-1739, but they appeared again there for the 1739-1740 season. *King Lear* was acted on February 25, 1740, for Mrs. Ward's benefit. Then her husband's benefit on April 25 occasioned the famous première of Peg Woffington as Sir Harry Wildair in *The Constant Couple*."[14]

This is a good point at which to bring together some of the careless and at times irresponsible statements that have been made about John Ward and Peg Woffington. Daly states that Ward was "an overbearing and peevish old gentleman," who over a trifle quarreled with the youthful Woffington. Fitzgerald adds that Peg played once for Ward's benefit, "but it was said that [his] roughness drove her from the theatre." Nina A. Kennard[15] varies the story and contributes a new ingredient: "Peg Woffington, when only fifteen, played at [Ward's] theatre in Auniger [*sic*] Street, until Mr. Ward's strait-laced severity drove the wild young Irish girl away. The Wards seem, indeed, to have been almost Methodistical in their strict religious views." Miss Ffrench (p. 14; if she has other authority for her positive assertion, she does not cite it)

---

[12] Hitchcock, pp. 94 ff., and W. R. Chetwood, *General History of the Stage*, p. 74.

[13] The revival of the play at Smock Alley about 1670-80 had evidently been forgotten; cf. my forthcoming account in *MLR* [XLV (1950), 64-65] of several hitherto unknown Smock Alley prompt-books.

[14] Quoted from Professor Clark's letter.

[15] *Mrs. Siddons* (Boston, 1887), p. 8.

seizes upon "almost Methodistical" and phrases her version as follows:

He was a Methodist and he applied his principles both in and out of school with regularity. In former years his harshness had caused the flight of Peg Woffington from the Dublin theatre which he managed and where, as a girl of sixteen, she had already begun to captivate her audiences. But unable to endure his rigid discipline she had been frightened away to pleasanter surroundings.

Thus legends grow.

A legend in a different vein is to the effect that it was not by Ward's roughness but by Love that Peg was erept the stage (to borrow the quaint phrase that Downes used to describe some of the equally fair and frail ladies of the Restoration stage), for if we may believe some of her biographers[16] she eloped to London. There she is found on 6 November 1740 performing in *The Recruiting Officer* at Covent Garden.

After a quarrel with the management, Peg Woffington moved over to Drury Lane in May 1741, and there, at the beginning of the following season, she was joined by John and Sarah Ward. This second London engagement of the Wards, recorded in the Winston Manuscript at Folger, has also been previously overlooked by stage historians. Ward played Laertes in *Hamlet* in his first appearance (on 19 September 1741). I do not find the Wards at Drury Lane after the season of 1742, but it may be noted by way of summary that Ward had now played in *Hamlet* at Lincoln's Inn Fields, Smock Alley, and Drury Lane, and that his future production of the play may be expected to combine and carry on the traditions of those three theaters.

Before detailing the later career of the Wards, we may pause a moment to contribute a final episode to the Woffington story. On 5 April 1746, according to the parish register of Oswestry, was baptized Margaret Woffington Ward, "d. of John & Sarah Ward, of the Comedian Band, of St. Austin parish, Mdx."[17] This item not only gives us a happy ending to the story, as far as the Wards are concerned, but forecasts the future of the Wards. Apparently they had been unable or unwilling to meet the competition in the London theaters, and had decided to enjoy the independence and risk the hazards of the road.

[16] The biographers differ, too, about Woffington's age. According to some, she was 15 or 16, but others are quite as positive that she was 25 or 26. Ward, who had been born in 1704, was only about 35 or 36 at the time.

[17] According to Baker, p. 9, the Wards returned to England some time in the 'forties with Sarah and two sons; the names of the two boys are as yet unknown to me. [Anne Hatton gives their names as William and Stephen, adding that they "had no theatrical talent."]

The details that I shall next summarize are drawn partly from Mr. Cecil Price's article, "John Ward, Stroller," in *Theatre Notebook,* I (1946-47), 10-12, and his book entitled *The English Theatre in Wales,*[18] and partly from hitherto unused abstracts, made at my request by Dr. William Van Lennep, from the manuscript of Winston's "Theatric Tourist" in the Theatre Collection at Harvard. Dr. Van Lennep states that all the notes on Ward and his son-in-law, Roger Kemble, were copied by Winston from a manuscript (now lost?) called "Jones' Book," Jones having been a leading actor in Ward's company.

How, where, and when John Ward recruited his first English company of strolling players is not yet known. The Oswestry register quoted above refers to it as a going concern in the spring of 1746. From a letter of the Reverend Joseph Greene of Stratford, we learn that Ward's company played there from May to September of 1746:

A Company of Strolling-Players (much ye best Set I have seen out of London, & in which opinion I am far from being singular,) came here in May last, & continued wth a little intermission till September. . . . Ward, prevail'd with [Greene's] father Bartlett ye present Mayor, to lend him our Spatious Townhall, wherein to erect his Theatre for ye term aforemention'd; on ye previous condition of depositing in his hands five guineas for ye Use of ye Poor of Stratford . . . . [This sum was duly paid as proposed.] Y^e Actors met with much encouragement, even beyond what they themselves cou'd have expected.[19]

At that time the London theaters were active in raising funds to erect a monument of Shakespeare in Westminster Abbey. And in Stratford the Reverend Mr. Greene was distressed by the public neglect of the memorial bust in Holy Trinity Church and perturbed at its sad state of disrepair. John Ward, who seems to have maintained a lively interest in the theatrical affairs of London[20] and knew of the proposed Westminster monument, shared Greene's perturbation. He decided upon a course of action which Greene's letter describes as follows (see Plate 4):

Mr Ward to express his Gratitude, voluntarily made another generous proposal of Acting a Play of Shakespeare, the Profits arising from which, he declar'd

[18] University of Wales Press, 1948.

[19] I quote from the original letter, collected by Halliwell-Phillipps, in the Folger Library. It is addressed to Greene's brother Richard, an apothecary in Lichfield, and is now used, I think, for the first time.

[20] See the items in Folger MS. 6643, among which are Ward's transcripts of famous London prologues and epilogues, of epitaphs of actors and actresses, and also of news items relating to litigation with respect to some of the London playhouses.

1746.

AS the generous proposals of the Proprietors of the two greatest Play-Houses in this Kingdom, were kindly accepted and encourag'd, in relation to each of them Acting a PLAY, for the Sole purpose of erecting a New Monument to the Memory of SHAKESPEARE, in *Westminster-Abbey*: And as the Curious Original Monument and Bust of that incomparable Poet, erected above the Tomb that enshrines his Dust, in the Church of *Stratford* upon *Avon Warwickshire*, Is through length of Years and other accidents become much impair'd and decay'd; An offer has been kindly made by the Judicious and much Esteem'd Mr. JOHN WARD, and his Company, To Act one of SHAKESPEARE'S PLAYS, *Viz.*

Othello, or the Moor of Venice.
in the Town-Hall 1746.

At *Stratford*, on *Tuesday* the *Ninth* of this instant *September*: The Receipts arising from which Representation are to be Solely Appropriated to the Repairing the Original Monument aforesaid.

The part of Othello, to be perform'd by Mr WARD,

[handwritten box at left:] See an Explanation of y Beauties of this Play in y Guardian Vol. y M. No. 37.

Jago,		Mr. *Elrington*,	*a young man acts well.*
Cassio,		Mr. *Redman*,	*a middle-ag'd man. too indifferent in Action.*
Brabantio,	by	Mr. *Woodward*,	*an elderly man. Somethings well, others unworthy.*
Montano,		Mr. *Butler*, —	*an old man. Comic parts pretty well*
Roderigo,		Mr. *Butcher*,	*a young man. low humour pretty well.*
Gratiano,		Mr. *Bourne*,	*an Elderly man. low humour very well.*
Doge of Venice	by	Do	

Desdemona,	by	Mrs. *Elrington*,	*a 2nd wife, but young. a very agreeable actress.*
Emilia,		Mrs. *Ward*,	*a middle-ag'd Woman. a good Actress.*

[handwritten left margin:] Mrs Elrington's voice is rather more agreeable than miss Wilsons, but miss Wilson has most judgment in Musick.

With several Entertainments of SINGING, between the ACTs. by Mrs. Elrington. and Mrs. †Wilson.

[handwritten right margin:] †mrs Wilson since married to Mr Butcher Plays very well & generally on y Violin.

To begin punctually at 6 o'Clock. Pit, 2 s. 6 d. Gallery, 1 s.

It is therefore humbly wish'd, that such Persons as have a taste for the Inimitable Thoughts, the Sublime Expressions, the Natural and lively Descriptions and Characters of that Great Genius, and Consequently a Value for his Memory, will Encourage the propos'd method of perpetuating it, by attending the PLAY, at that juncture, for the laudable purpose of re-beautifying his Venerable Monument and Effigies.

N. B. The Money receiv'd on this Occasion, is to be Deposited in the Hands of the Church-Wardens.

PLATE 4. Playbill of the performance of *Othello* by John Ward's company to raise funds for repairing the bust of Shakespeare in Holy Trinity Church, Stratford-upon-Avon. Reproduced from the copy of the original in the Folger Shakespeare Library.

shou'd be Solely appropriated . . . to the repairing yᵉ Original Monument of yᵉ Poet; very genteely refusing to apply a Shilling of the Money to his Own Use: Printed Bills were therefore given out for this Purpose; and on yᵉ Ninth of this instant Septᵉʳ, about 16 or 17 pounds were receiv'd from yᵉ Spectators of yᵉ Play of Othello then Acted in yᵉ Town-hall, yᵉ Characters of which play, (except that of Brabantio,) were well personated, & the whole Conducted with much decorum, & its Consequence, Applause.

Mr. Greene honored the performance by contributing a Prologue,

Spoken by yᵉ ingenious Mʳ Ward; who enter'd fully into my Sentiments, & express'd every Sentence as I cou'd wish, wᵗʰ yᵉ justest Emphasis & most exact propriety, notwithstanding he had had the Composition but a very Short time in his Possession.

This from a schoolmaster is praise indeed. Obviously John Ward was as competent and willing as the First Player in *Hamlet* to study for a need a speech of some dozen or sixteen lines. The autograph copy of Greene's 45-line Prologue—"Which, pardon me, I do not mean to [reprint]"—is another item collected by Halliwell-Phillipps and now in the Folger Library, along with Greene's annotated copy of the playbill —one of two extant copies.[21] In justice to Ward it should be stated that he had nothing to do with the selection of the artist who restored the monument—or with the squabbles in Stratford about the administration of the fund. In fact, when Greene wrote him two years later about the state of affairs, Ward replied as follows from Hereford on 3 December 1748 (Folger MS. cs. 448):

I Rec'd the favour of yours, and am sensible of the honor you and the Gentlemen do me in appealing to my Iudgment with regard to the monument of

---

[21] See Plate 4. The playbill is particularly valuable for naming nine members of Ward's company at this early date. The cast is as follows:

Othello	Mr. Ward	Roderigo	Mr. Butcher
Jago	Mr. Elrington	Gratiano	Mr. Bourne
Cassio	Mr. Redman	Desdemona	Mrs. Elrington
Brabantio	Mr. Woodward	Emilia	Mrs. Ward
Montano	Mr. Butler		

With several Entertainments of Singing, between the Acts,
by Mrs. Elrington and Mrs. Wilson

Greene's comments on their abilities are likewise valuable. Woodward is possibly the actor who was at Lincoln's Inn Fields with Ward in the early 'twenties, and Elrington I take to be a relative of the erstwhile manager at Smock Alley. [The other copy of the playbill is in the library of the Shakespeare Research Centre, Stratford-upon-Avon.]

Shakespeare; I am ignorant of any disputes that may have happen'd on the Acct, but own I was surpriz'd when I heard nothing had been done in the affair —I entirely submit to the opinions of the Gentlemen, who so generously contributed to the play, in every respect; and as I intend paying a visit to Stratford, next summer, hope to have the pleasure of seeing the monum^t of our Immortal Bard, compleatly finish'd; and will readily come into any proposal to make good the sum for the use intended, if what is already in the Church warden's hands, should prove deficient.

Ward's conduct was generous and disinterested throughout, and though harsh words were written then and later about the manner in which the bust was restored, Ward is free from responsibility for such errors as may have been committed.[22]

In April 1747 Ward's company appeared in Ludlow, where they played in the guildhall during the races and the subsequent five weeks, presenting *Henry VIII,* for example, with new robes, armor, and decorations.

In December of the following year, Ward was as we have seen at Hereford, where performances were given at the Swan and Falcon at 6 P.M. on Mondays, Tuesdays, Wednesdays, and Fridays.

The company was back in Ludlow in August 1751. It seems also to have performed at Birmingham, for William Hutton[23] records that "in 1751 a company arrived who announced themselves as 'His Majesty's Servants' from the Theatres Royal in London." That this was Ward's company is rendered probable by the fact that it is known to have played there the following year, 1752. In March, Ward gave *Henry VIII* at Ledbury, intending to go on to Bromyard and thence to Leominster on Easter Monday. For theatrical history, however, the engagement at Birmingham overshadows everything else in 1752, because it was at this time that John Ward placed the advertisement in the London papers for "capital performers"[24] that lured Roger Kemble thither. In a short time Kemble's inamorata, Fanny Furnivall, was forgotten and he was paying court to Sarah, his manager's daughter and "the 'main prop' of her

[22] *The Victoria History of Warwickshire* (London, 1945), III, 245, errs in calling the actor *James* Ward. It refers to Saunders MS. 96, fol. 906, and adds that Roger Kemble's company played at Stratford between 1761 and 1782, both at the Town Hall and at "the Theatre," the location of the latter being unknown.

[23] *History of Birmingham* (1781), quoted in a memorandum by Mr. D. M. Norris of the Birmingham Public Library, which was written for me at the behest of F. J. Patrick, Esq., City Librarian.

[24] Baker, pp. 7 ff.

father's troop in the 'comic province.' " Though Sarah could not have been more than sixteen, the two eloped in 1753 and were married at Cirencester on 6 June—"Roger Kemble of Hereford & Sarah Ward of Gloucester."[25] The bride must have been as beautiful as she was head-strong, for according to Baker's sources (p. 10) there had already been "a young nobleman who loved her 'not wisely but unhappily too well' for ... it is said ... that he died for the love of Sarah Ward."

This elopement has provided the biographers of Mrs. Siddons with another occasion for letting the imagination run riot at the expense of John Ward's reputation. When Roger asked permission to marry Sarah, writes Miss Ffrench, the parents objected, for "knowing their profes-sional world, [they] had other views for their Sally. An actor's existence was the last into which they wished her to drift." After the marriage,

John Ward wriggled out of his defeat with as much dignity as he could com-mand and a side-thrust at his new son-in-law's professional competence. He re-sorted to casuistry hardly in accordance with Methodistical tenets: "I forbade you," he remarked to his daughter, "to marry an actor. You have not disobeyed me since the man you have married neither is nor ever can be an actor." Having evaded this matrimonial issue, the Wards magnanimously presented the young couple with their theatrical company and so pass out of the story.

Anne Hatton, writing of the emotions of the Wards, tells of the tempest of rage this dereliction of duty on the part of their daughter, a girl not yet sixteen, raised in their hearts—a hurricane not at all appeased by the convic-tion, that Roger Kemble's person was his only recommendation, it was obvious to them he had no talent for the Stage his education had been circumscribed, he had a good understanding but no genius.[26]

Baker carries on the story, apparently from Mrs. Hatton:

The truants were soon back in Ward's company—the wrath had subsided—and before long the old people retired to Leominster in Herefordshire, after a hectic life, living peacefully enough on an annuity from their son-in-law for the use of their theatrical properties and wardrobes.

But we shall see that the young couple did not come at once into ownership of the company—according to report they were so little affluent that Roger was his wife's only attendant when their daughter Sarah was ushered into the world on 5 July 1755—and that "the old

---

[25] The page of the parish register containing the entry is reproduced opposite p. 71 of Theodore Hannam-Clark's *Drama in Gloucestershire* (London, 1928).

[26] Quoted by Baker, p. 10. According to Anne Hatton, Roger's wife thought him the "only *gentleman* Falstaff" she had ever seen.

people" continued their strolling for another thirteen years before reluctantly turning the management over to Roger and Sarah Kemble.

An idea of the repertory of Ward's company and the elaborateness of their productions can be gained from their announced offerings at Hereford in 1753. On 6 February they presented *Romeo and Juliet* with the "Grand Funeral Procession and Solemn Dirge set to Music by Signor Pasqualli." And their programs were a judicious combination of the classics and the spectacular attractions, with pantomime, music, and dancing, so popular at the time in London. Shakespeare, Dryden, Rowe, Lee, Congreve, Vanbrugh, and Steele were their authors, and *Harlequin Ranger* and its like, with new scenery and machinery, dazzled those whose minds were less sober. Ward knew how to take advantage of popular interest in public events, as when at the end of a performance of *Lear* he recited Milton's lines on Shakespeare and appeared as the statue of Shakespeare recently erected in Westminster Abbey.

In October 1754 the company was at Ledbury, from which it moved to Hereford for a three months' stay. In May 1755 it opened at Brecon, from which it moved to the new Welsh spa, Llandrindod, for Race Week, in early July. Little has been discovered about 1756 beyond the fact that a performance of Lee's *Theodosius* was given.

From Winston's transcript of "Jones' Book," cited above, we learn that "in November 1757 Ward set up a sharing company to act 4 nights a week—on a circuit, beginning at Shrewsbury. On December 24, 1757, Roger Kemble joined the company at Leominster." During the following year, 1758, the company made its circuit of Brecon, Hay, Presteigne (4 weeks), Newtown, and Ludlow (23 weeks). In 1759 it opened in Coventry in January for a stay of 22 weeks (with Mr. and Mrs. Stanton in the Company, and also Bensley and Robertson), moving to Stratford in July for 5 weeks, thence to Shrewsbury for another 5 weeks, from there to Leominster, and then on to Brecon in November for 20 weeks.

The 1760 season began with performances at Brecon and continued with 5 weeks at The Hay and 9 weeks at Newtown, then 3 weeks at Stratford, where they played at the Races morning and night; in August Ward was back at Stratford for 6 weeks. There is not much variation in the records for 1761:[27] Leominster for 15 weeks, beginning on March

---

[27] Price, *English Theatre*, pp. 41-42, says that the Kembles split away in 1761 and did not return until 1763. Roger Kemble was not in the cast of *The Beggar's Opera* at Leominster in April.

19; Solihull for 4 weeks; Abergavenny for 10 weeks, beginning in July; Ross for 3 weeks, beginning in October; and Hereford for 13 weeks, to close the season.

In 1762 the season appears to have opened at Worcester on 18 February for a run of 20 weeks; the year closed with a stay of 7 weeks at Stratford. I find notes on a visit to Kidderminster of 17 weeks in February and one of 18 weeks to Stourbridge in July 1763. At this place on 9 September, "Money Box stole from Door—man committed to Gaol—M^r and Mrs Robson in comp^y—Sally Kemble Ben^t with Mr Robson."[28] In October the company moved to Worcester for a stay of 33 weeks.

For 1764 there are records of 17 weeks spent at Brecon, beginning in August, and 25 weeks at Hereford, beginning in December.[29] Apparently the company was so popular and prosperous that it was no longer necessary, as in the early years, to take to the road every week or two.

The earliest engagement I find in 1765 is in June at Ludlow, where Ward remained for 11 weeks. He opened in September in Worcester, but playing there was stopped on 3 October by the new mayor, Mr. Withers, and Ward moved on at once to Leominster for a stay of 18 weeks.

In the spring of 1766, after some twenty-five years of strolling in Hereford, Warwickshire, Gloucester, Shropshire, Radnor, Monmouthshire, and Brecknock, John Ward decided to retire. His well-regulated company had entertained the nobility and gentry with a judicious mixture of serious drama and spectacle and had prospered. He offered the management first to Jones and, when he declined, to his son-in-law, Roger Kemble, whom he disliked. And so on 24 May Kemble took over the company. John Ward was 62 or 63 years old, and Sarah was 55. Whether they retired on a pension, I am unable to say. Ward seems to have turned his attention to collecting materials for a stage history, if we may judge by the memoranda of theatrical interest that he recorded in 1767 and 1768 (among Folger MSS. 6643). The next and final record is found on a gravestone in Leominster:

> Here waiting for the Savior's great Assize,
> And hoping thro' his merits there to rise

---

[28] Transcribed by Dr. Van Lennep from Winston's manuscript at Harvard.

[29] Mr. Norris writes that there are advertisements of an unnamed company in 1764-65 in Aris's *Birmingham Gazette* and in the *Birmingham Weekly*.

In glorious mode in this dark closet lies
John Ward, Gent.
Who died Oct. 30, 1773, aged 69.
Also Sarah his wife, who died Jan. 30, 1786,
aged 75 years.

John did not live to see his granddaughter, the divine Siddons, at the height of her fame, but that pleasure was accorded Sarah. It would probably give them both quiet satisfaction to read the verdict of posterity as phrased by Joseph Knight in his *DNB* article about Roger Kemble: John Ward was "a noteworthy man and an actor of some merit, from whom, rather than from Kemble, it is probable that what was remarkable in the Kemble strain was derived."[30]

III

And now what about Ward's *Hamlet,* as revealed in his two promptbooks? Unfortunately Ward does not name the cast in either book or give any dates, but the handwriting in them is so much firmer than in the memoranda which he wrote about 1768 that it is safe to assign early dates to the promptbooks—I hazard the guess that they were prepared shortly after 1740.[31] Early dates are confirmed by the manner in which the promptbooks were prepared. They are much more closely akin to the promptbooks of the 17th century than to those of the 18th century. Thus the entrances are written in the outside margins some thirty to forty lines before the point of entrance. This method of writing warning entries had been employed on the Elizabethan and Jacobean stages, but it fell gradually into disuse, so that by 1700 one rarely finds an example from the London theaters. Opposite the text where a character is supposed to come on stage is a horizontal line crossed by from four to six vertical strokes.[32] These entrances are numbered, with a

[30] A portrait of "—— Ward . . . the grandfather of Mr. Kemble [and] Mrs. Siddons" was No. 255 in the *Catalogue raisonnée of Mr. Mathew's gallery of theatrical portraits now exhibited for the first time, and forming a nearly complete dramatic record from the year 1659 down to the present time. Queen's Bazaar, Oxford Street* (London, 1833), but I have not yet discovered who is its present owner. [This is one of two portraits of John Ward now hanging in the Garrick Club in London. They are Nos. 268 and 417 in *A Catalogue of the Pictures in the Garrick Club* (London, 1936), pp. 85, 125.]

[31] [Price conjectures (p. 39) that the Wards had recently quitted London, because the entry of Margaret Woffington Ward's baptism at Oswestry on 5 April 1746 identifies her parents as "of the Comedian band of St Austin Parish, Middlesex."]

[32] Bald notes the occurrence of this mark in some of the Smock Alley promptbooks abstracted from a Third Folio of Shakespeare.

new series for each act. There is only one of the O.P.'s and P.S.'s that are sprinkled throughout 18th-century promptbooks. It occurs in the form of *"Enter Hamlet. M: D: O: P."* late in Act II in the quarto of 1676, and I am confident that the letters M.D.O.P. are additions in a later hand.[33]

All such properties as were used in the performance are also noted in the margins. Thus in Q 1676 the third warning entrance in Act II reads: *"Polonius. A letter w^r[it]"*; the fourth, in the same act: *"Hamlet. a book."* Sound-effects are likewise noted in the margins. The fifth stage direction in Act I of Q 1676 is *"One to crow,"* and some thirty lines later the printed direction *"The Cock crows"* is emphasized by a large ×. With one exception, Act IV in Q 1676, there is a direction, *"Ring,"* before the end of each act. The warning is intended for the musicians to play between the acts, for in Q 1683 the note near the end of Act I is *"Ring for Musick."*

A careful comparison of the two books reveals that they were prepared to regulate somewhat similar but not identical performances. The stages on which the productions were to be given were probably alike in essentials, with two or more trap-doors and an inner stage. There is no indication that there was a front curtain or an upper stage, and I suspect that for most performances Ward had the equivalent of a pre-Wars platform stage, little influenced by the architecture of the pretentious London theaters. The locus of action is stated once in each book. In Q 1683 Ward has inserted at the head of Act I the words, *"a platform,"* which is of course amply warranted by the text. The corresponding notation in the other book is *"Town."* Perhaps we may infer that Ward used from time to time painted backdrops in imitation of the perspectives that came into fashion on the Restoration stage. Once in each book occurs the circle with a dot which means, "Blow whistle for change of scene."[34] In Q 1676 it stands opposite the long preparatory stage direction for the first court scene; in Q 1683, it is opposite the direction for the second scene on the Platform, where Hamlet meets the Ghost. There is no indication, unfortunately, of how the scene was to be changed.

[33] The ink is paler than that used elsewhere; and though the *M* is not dissimilar to Ward's the *P* is unlike the first letter in "Polonius" as Ward writes the word. [The abbreviations are of *Opposite Prompt, Prompt Side,* and *Middle Door, Opposite Prompt.*]

[34] W. J. Lawrence and Montague Summers (see the latter's *Essays in Petto,* London, 1928, pp. 103-10) are of the opinion that the symbol has this meaning, but Bald doubts that it always does in the Smock Alley promptbooks. The mark on p. 5 of Q 1676 is in fainter ink than that used in the other directions. May it be a late addition?

There is a curious difference between the two books in the staging of court scenes. While Q 1683 provides specifically that the Court shall be "*Discover'd*" at I. ii, there is no such notation in Q 1676. But in the Mouse Trap Scene and again in the scene of the Fencing Match Q 1683 is silent, whereas Q 1676 specifies that the Court shall be "*discover'd*." In I. ii the stage is empty, and the device of discovering the court by opening the curtain to the inner stage is employed to facilitate the placing of cumbersome properties on a stage that has no front curtain. In both the later scenes, Hamlet and Horatio are in conversation on the front stage, so that each time the curtain to the inner stage must be drawn to reveal the King and Queen and their attendants. The management of these three scenes at this late date should affect decisively the controversy whether thrones of state were kept as standing properties against the back wall of the main stage in Elizabethan times. Clearly the practice was to seat courts in the inner stage.

In the production represented by Q 1676, Ward introduces a piece of business in the Closet Scene that, I am happy to say, is not called for in Q 1683. It will be remembered that Polonius has concealed himself so that he may overhear the Queen's reproof of Hamlet—Ward's notation is, "*Polonius retires behind the arras*." At the point where Gertrude cries out to Hamlet, "What wilt thou do? thou wilt not murder me? Help ho," Ward inserts the direction, "*Enter Polonius*." This is all wrong. For Polonius to be seen even momentarily before the Prince runs his victim through is to destroy the dramatic value of Hamlet's "Nay I know not; is it the King?" when for one glorious moment he believes that his vengeance is complete and that Claudius has been slain in the midst of an action "that has no relish of salvation in it."

One major difference introduced by Ward is the omission of the Dumb Show. It had been retained by Davenant and Betterton—and, curiously enough, Olivier retains it, while canceling the Mouse Trap Play itself.

Another major difference is in the treatment of the conclusion of the final scene of the play, where Ward is more drastic even than Davenant. It will be remembered that earlier in the play both had eliminated the passages about Norway and young Fortinbras, and also the discussion between Hamlet and the Captain who is taking him captive to England about the sharked-up troop of lawless resolutes who are following Fortinbras in his harebrained enterprise. Davenant, being of the old school, brings on Prince Fortinbras in the final scene so that Hamlet may prophesy his choice as the next King of Denmark and so that a person of royal blood may be on hand to continue orderly government. Unmoved by these considerations, Ward eliminates Fortinbras from this scene, too, and rearranges the lines so that after Horatio's "Good night, sweet prince, / And Choirs of Angels sing thee to thy rest," he may end the play with what had been Fortinbras's final couplet:

> Take up the bodies; such a sight as this
> Becomes the Field, but here shows much amiss.

It would be interesting to discover how Sir Laurence Olivier and his textual editor, Alan Dent, hit upon precisely this arrangement.

Ward's versions are two or three hundred lines shorter than the Restoration *Hamlet*. On rare occasions he modernizes a word or debases a line, but surprisingly enough he restores many words and some phrases in both quartos that he could have found only in Q2 of 1604/5 or one of the early Folios, unless indeed he took the trouble to consult one of the 18th-century literary texts. As a matter of fact, Ward must have done one of these three things in the preparation of Q 1676, for time and again he restores words, phrases, and whole lines, changes the word order, and alters the punctuation to recapture the genuine Shakespearian text. It is amazing that an actor should have had such regard for the purity of text of his favorite dramatist. Thus quarto's "She used to hang on him" is restored to "Why she would hang on him." Again, "Wee'l teach you here to drink" is corrected to "Wee'l teach you to drink deep." At one place there are two stages of correction: Q prints, "But what make you from Wittenberg?"; the metrical deficiency is first supplied by the addition in manuscript of "Horatio"; and then the speech is restored to the pristine, "But what in faith make you from Wittenberg?" And when Hamlet is mocking Polonius at the entrance of the traveling actors, Ward inserts from an outside source two whole speeches about Jephtha and his daughter. These corrections do not affect the business of the play, and Ward could have made them only because at some time he had memorized the authentic lines or because a sensitive ear and a tender literary conscience moved him to restore Shakespeare's text.

The two promptbooks of *Hamlet,* then, carry on the early tradition of *Hamlet* for nearly three-quarters of a century and show surprising likenesses to certain modern productions. They disclose that John Ward was in many respects a greater purist than even David Garrick, the great Restorer of Shakespeare. No liberty he took with the text was so great as Garrick's practical elimination of the fifth act of the play.

IV

Ward's promptbooks provide information about the method of staging three scenes in the play that have been the subject of a great deal of argument. The first two are I. i, in which the Ghost appears to Horatio, and I. iv, where it is first seen by Hamlet; the third, the Closet Scene, in which the Ghost makes its last appearance and Hamlet compares the portraits of his father and his uncle. The problem of the Ghost is the same in the three scenes: how to get it on and off the stage. W. J. Lawrence is categorical in his statement that in the original production the Ghost entered and disappeared through a trap in I. i and I. iv.[35] In his reconstruction of the business in I. i he has Horatio, Marcellus, and Bernardo seat themselves on stools near the front of the stage (from which position "they cannot perceive the three entrance ways which are situated behind them"); then, "on the clock striking one," the appearance of the Ghost interrupts the narrative. "It is obvious," he continues, "that there was absolutely no other way by which the Ghost could suddenly make itself visible to the three save by emerging *in front of them* through a trap" (italics added).

This would indeed be a spectacular effect, but I am persuaded that what happened at the Globe was even more electrifying. Bernardo, telling how "last night of all, | When yond same Star . . . | Had made his course to enlighten that part of Heaven | Where now it burns," points his finger towards the zenith. Horatio and Marcellus follow his gesture, and every eye in the theater turns upward. At that instant, in my opinion, *"the Bell then beating one"* to signal the actor beneath the stage, the Ghost should rise through a trap at the rear of the stage and move quietly forward. The thrill that would go through the audience from the first appearance of the specter until it comes into the range of vision of Marcellus must have sent shivers up and down the spine.

Offended by Horatio's challenge, the Ghost then "stalks away," only to reappear in the same manner through the trap after the three watchers have resumed their seats. At the cock's crow, the Ghost moves as to

[35] "The Staging of Hamlet," in *Pre-Restoration Stage Studies* (Harvard University Press, 1927), pp. 102-21.

depart. Marcellus, trying to stay it, swings his partisan, which the Ghost avoids by dropping unharmed through a trap-door—to the delight of the groundlings. As the three men rush to where it was last seen, the Ghost rises through another trap. They rush at it, as Horatio cries, "'Tis here," only to have it vanish again through a trap. And after searching frantically, Marcellus concludes, "'Tis gone."

This is what I believe happened in the Elizabethan performances of *Hamlet* I. i. In I. iv, too, I think the Ghost entered and departed through a trap. But I am forced to admit that my reconstruction of the stage business is conjectural.

If the Smock Alley promptbook of *Hamlet* could be recovered,[36] we might discover how the business was managed in the Restoration period. The promptbooks of John Ward continue the story in the next century and provide detailed information about several of the points in question but are tantalizingly silent about others. There are, for example, no manuscript directions to show how the Ghost enters or exits in I. i. In I. iv the Ghost enters nine lines after the offstage *"Flourish of Trumpets and Guns"* that signals the King's carouse. There is nothing to indicate that the Ghost rises from below the stage, but it may be noted that if a trap were used, the sound-effect could easily take the place of a marginal stage direction, since the actor and the necessary stage hands could easily be in readiness together beneath the stage awaiting their cue. It is dangerous, however, to argue from silence, and I cannot insist that in this scene the Ghost used a trap to enter.

There can be no question of how the Ghost made his final departure in I. iv. Just as he is saying, "methinks I scent the morning air," Ward has written, *"Ring for Trap to be Ready"* (Q 1683); and opposite the Ghost's line, "Farewel, remember me," is the manuscript direction, *"Sink"* (Qq 1676, 1683). This corresponds exactly with Lawrence's conjecture (p. 110). Almost at once comes the prompt note, *"Ghost Ready below"* (Q 1683; in Q 1676, *"Ghost under the stage"*). And when Hamlet is enjoining his friends to secrecy, three times Ward has written, *"Ring,"* and each time the Ghost in the cellarage cries, "Swear" (Q 1683). In Ward's touring company about the middle of the 18th century, then, the stage business of the Ghost in one scene is very much as I conjecture it to have been nearly a century and a half earlier.

In the Closet Scene, "I am open to conviction," writes Professor Sprague, "as to how the Ghost should enter." He adds that since the

[36] [See n. 2 above.]

Pol. What hoe help.

Ham. How now, a Rat, dead for a Ducket, dead.

Pol. O I am flain. ————— *Dyes*

Qu. O me, what haft thou done?

Ham. Nay I know not; is it the King?

Qu. O what a rafh and bloody deed is this!

Ham. A bloody deed; almoft as bad good mother,

As kill a King, and marry with his brother.

Qu As kill a King.

Ham. I Lady, It was my word.

Thou wretched, rafh, intruding fool, farewel,

I took thee for thy betters, take thy fortune;

Thou findeft to be too bufie is fome danger.

Leave wringing of your hands; peace, fit you down,

And let me wring your heart; for fo I fhall,

If it be made of penetrable ftuff;

" If damned cuftom have not braz'd it fo,

" That it be proof and bulwark againft fenfe,

Qu, What have I done that thou dar'ft wag thy tongue

In noife fo rude againft me?

Ham. Such an act,

That blurs the grace and blufh of modefty;

Calls vertue hypocrite; takes off the Rofe

From the fair forehead of an innocent love,

And fets a blifter there; makes marriage vows

As falfe as Dicers oaths : oh fuch a deed

As from the body of contraction plucks

The very foul, and fweet Religion makes

A rapfody of words, " Heavens face does glow

" Yea this folidity and compound mafs

" With heated vifage as againft the doom,

" Is thought fick at the act.

Ah me that act

Qu. Ay me, what act?

Ham. That roars fo loud, and thunders in the Index;

Look here upon this picture, and on this,

The counterfeit prefentment of two brothers;

See what a grace was feated on this brow;

Hiperions curls; the front of *Jove* himfelf;

An eye like *Mars* to threaten and command;

" A ftation like the Herald Mercury

" New lighted on a heaven kiffing hill,

A combination, and form indeed;

Where every god did feem to fet his feal,

　　　　　　　　H 3　　　　　　　　　　　**To**

(20)
Ghoft
Ready at
Long trap

PLATE 5. P. 53 of Ward's promptbook of *Hamlet*. Ward's note 20 warns the Ghost to be ready below the stage.

Ghost does not wear full armor but presents a changed appearance, being "in his habit as he liv'd," Lawrence thinks the trap-door should be used.[37] This conjecture is supported by the fact that in Ward's production the warning entry reads, "*Ghost Ready at long trap*" (Q 1676; see Plate 5). (Q 1683 reads, "*Ghost Ready at great Trap*," followed by a second direction, "*Ring Ghost up.*") There is no room for uncertainty about the manner of entrance; nor is there about the Ghost's departure, for where Ward's printed text reads, "look how it steals away," he has changed the word to "stalks" in both quartos (cf. I. i, "See, it stalks away").

The really controversial piece of stage business in this scene is, however, the problem of the pictures. Lawrence accepts the suggestion of R. W. Lowe[38] and argues that the famous engraving in Rowe's edition of 1709 depicts the current stage usage, citing *Der bestrafte Brudermord* and Q1 in support of the practice of having two large portraits hanging on the walls of the stage.[39] This hypothesis has been attacked vigorously by Hazelton Spencer, who examined all the illustrations in Rowe's edition and found serious discrepancies in several.[40] There are, he reminds us, a number of solutions:

Should there be two portraits on the wall; or should there be two miniatures, one hanging from the Queen's neck and the other from Hamlet's; or should Hamlet take two miniatures from his pocket; or should there be one wall portrait and one miniature; or should the pictures be located in a supposed gallery off stage, invisible to the audience, and merely be pointed at by Hamlet; or

[37] Arthur Colby Sprague, *Shakespeare and the Actors* (Harvard University Press, 1944), p. 164; Lawrence, p. 111, who buttresses his argument by citing Q1 and *Der bestrafte Brudermord*, in which the Prince locks all the doors.

[38] "How the Old Actors dressed 'Shakespere'—II," in *The Illustrated London News*, 18 February 1893.

[39] Lawrence admits that the use of two half-length portraits from the period of the Restoration may not have been "precisely the original method." He adds that Rowe's illustration is defective in that it fails to show the curtains that habitually covered oil paintings in Elizabethan times.

[40] "How Shakespeare Staged his Plays," *The Johns Hopkins Alumni Magazine*, XX (1932), 205-21. Spencer was anticipated at several points by letters in the *Times Literary Supplement*. Miss Edith E. McCarthy objected (30 August 1928, p. 617) that portraits could not be conveniently hung on the rear walls of the stage, for Polonius has to hide behind the arras, *i.e.*, the curtain of the inner stage. To this Lawrence replied (6 September, p. 632) impatiently that his meaning had been mistaken: the action occurred on the front stage and the portraits hung "on the back part of the scene." William Poel, listing four different solutions to the problem, says (20 September, p. 667) that any is good which is emotionally convincing but that he prefers to have Hamlet point offstage, where the portraits would hang unseen by the audience.

O my offence is rank, it smells to heaven,
It hath the eldest curse upon't ;
A brothers murder : pray I cannot,
Though inclination be as sharp as will,
My stronger guilt defeats my strong intent ;
And like a man to double business bound,
I stand in pause where I shall first begin,
And both neglect : what if this cursed hand
Were thicker than it self with brothers blood ?
Is there not rain enough in the sweet heavens
To wash it white as snow ? whereto serves mercy,
But to confront the visage of offence ?
And what's in prayer, but this twofold force,
To be forestalled e're we come to fall,
Or pardon'd being down ? then I'll look up :
My fault is past : but oh ! what form of prayer
Can serve my turn? forgive me my soul murther ?
That cannot be, since I am still possest
Of those effects for which I did the murther,
My Crown, mine own ambition, and my Queen :
May one be pardoned and retain th' offence?
" In the corrupted currents of this world
" Offences guilded hand may shew by justice,
And oft 'tis seen the wicked prize it self
Buyes out the Law ; but 'tis not so above,
There is no shuffling, there the action lies
In his true nature, and we our selves compell'd
Even to the teeth and forehead of our faults
To give in evidence : what then? what rests ?
Try what repentance can ; what can it not ?
Yet what can it when one cannot repent ?
O wretched state ! O bosom black as death !
O limed soul ! that struggling to be free,
Art more ingaged ! help Angels, make assay,
Bow stubborn knees, and heart with strings of steel
Be soft as sinews of the new-born babe,
All may be well.   [*Enter* Hamlet.
    Ham. Where is this murderer? he kneels and prays,
And now I'll do't, and so he goes to heaven,
And so am I reveng'd ? that would be scann'd ;
He kill'd my father; and for that,
I his sole son send him
To heaven.
Why this is reward, & not revenge :
                    H 2   He

should they be placed, still invisibly, on the fourth wall, which, convention dictates, separates the modern stage from the audience; or should we not assume their physical presence at all but take them merely as word paintings by the Prince? (p. 208)

And although Spencer is insistent that "it is the passionate torrent of the actor's words that will arouse the right emotional response in the audience, not the presence or absence of glowering canvases or jeweled miniatures" (p. 209), he concedes that "if we must have the pictures physically present (and I think they were) and fix their form and location, the best guess is that Shakespeare planned to use miniatures worn by Hamlet and his mother" (p. 213).

This is the business I myself should prefer, but it looks as if Ward did not use it. His directions for this scene are unusually numerous. The first warning in preparation for the scene is "(17) *Queen Polonius 2 Chairs on*" (see Plate 6). This is followed (Plate 7) by "(18) *Hamlet 2 pictures,*" the direction appearing just opposite the couplet with which Claudius concludes his scene. Then, in the outside margin, opposite the centered direction printed in the Quarto, "*Enter Queen and* Polonius," is the bold mark which Ward uses to indicate entrances; and in the inside margin, another manuscript note that echoes and amplifies No. 17: "*Two Chairs on below yᵉ long trap.*" Opposite the printed direction "*Enter* Hamlet" is Ward's symbol for an entrance; and then, as Gertrude says "Withdraw, I hear him coming," we find the manuscript direction, "*Polonius retires behind the arras.*"

Several points are worth noting. In the first place, two chairs are to be got ready for use in the scene. This confirms the stage tradition as depicted in Rowe's engraving, where Hamlet stands beside an overturned chair and Gertrude sits in another.[41] The chairs are brought on at the time Gertrude and Polonius enter and placed "*below yᵉ long trap,*"[42] so that the Ghost may rise behind them.[43]

The next point of importance is that there is no reference to pictures until Hamlet is warned to be ready for his entrance. There is no alterna-

[41] See the interesting account of the overturned chair in Sprague, pp. 164-65.

[42] That is, the large platform trap, not the smaller grave trap in the floor of the inner stage.

[43] This is where the Ghost ought, in my opinion, to rise also in I. i and I. iv, and it troubles me that Ward, who is so specific at this juncture, is silent earlier. Was the business so clearly understood at the beginning of the play that detailed instructions were not required? Or did he consider that I. i and I. iv had enough thrills without a Ghost's rising from the depths and so reserve this piece of business for the present scene?

He took my father grofly, full of bread,
With all his crimes broad blown as fluſh as May,
And how his audit ſtands, who knows ſave heaven,
But in our circumſtance and courſe of thought,
'Tis heavy with him; and am I then reveng'd,
To take him in the purging of his ſoul,
When he is fit and ſeaſoned for his paſſage?
No,
Up ſword, and know thou a more horrid time;
When he is drunk, aſleep, or in his rage,
Or in th' inceſtuous pleaſures of his bed,
~~At game, a ſwearing,~~ or about ſome act
That has no relliſh of ſalvation in t,
" ~~Then trip him that his heels may kick at heaven,~~
" ~~And that his ſoul may be as damn'd and black~~,
" ~~As hell whereto it goes:~~ " my mother ſtays,
This Phyſick but prolongs thy ſickly days.　　　　　[Exit.

King. My words flie up, my thoughts remain below,
Words without thoughts never to heaven go.　　　[Exit.

　　　　　　　Enter Queen and Polonius.

Pol. He will come ſtrait, look you lay home to him,
Tell him his pranks have been too broad to bear with,
And that your grace hath ſtood between
Much heat and him. I'll here conceal my ſelf,
Pray you be round.　　　　　　　　　[Enter Hamlet.
Qu. I'll warrant you, fear me not,
Withdraw, I hear him coming.
Ham. Now, mother, what's the matter?
Qu. Hamlet thou haſt thy father much offended.
Ham. Mother, you have my father much offended.
Qu. Come, come, you anſwer with an idle tongue.
Ham. Go, go, you queſtion with a wicked tongue.
Qu. Why how now Hamlet?
Ham. What's the matter now?
Qu. Have you forgot me?
Ham. No by the Rood not ſo,
You are the Queen, your husbands brothers wife,
And would it were not ſo, you are my mother.
Qu. Nay then I'll ſet thoſe to you that can ſpeak,
Ham. Come, come, and fit down, ~~you ſhall not budge~~,
You go not, till I ſet you up a glaſs,
Where you may ſee the utmoſt part of you.
Qu. What wilt thou do? thou wilt not murder me?
Help ho.　　　Enter polonius　　　　　Pol. What

Handwritten marginal annotations:
(18) Hamlet 2 pictures
Two chairs on belon 14 long trap
Polonius returns behind the arras
(19) Polonius
4th

PLATE 7. P. 52 of John Ward's promptbook of *Hamlet*. The printed direction for the entrance of the Queen and Polonius follows forty lines after Ward's marginal note 17 on p. 51. Note 18 calls for a picture to be ready when Hamlet enters eight lines later.

tive to believing that Hamlet brought the pictures on with him, miniatures, of the kind he had mentioned shortly before in conversation with Rosencrantz and Guildenstern—"my Uncle is King of Denmark; and those that would make mouths at him while my father lived, give twenty, forty, fifty, nay, a hundred duckets apiece for his picture in little." It is characteristic of Shakespeare that a detail mentioned so casually in the early part of a play should now be turned to spectacular account, as Hamlet confronts his mother with the two likenesses.

The wearing of miniatures about the neck seems to have fallen out of fashion among gentlemen in the late 17th century. Perhaps this is why it was thought best for Hamlet to carry the miniatures, whereas in Elizabethan times he might have worn one and found the other hanging on Gertrude's bosom. In any case, it is clear that in Ward's production, Hamlet carried the two miniatures.[44] It is interesting that John Philip Kemble, Ward's grandson, introduced, as one of his innovations,[45] the use of two miniatures (Baker, p. 84). In all probability he had grown up with this piece of business in the provinces, and using it on the London stage was a simple act of piety.

[44] This confirms the statement of Tom Davies, who wrote in 1784 that it had been "the constant practice of the Stage, ever since the Restoration, in this scene, to produce from [Hamlet's] pocket two pictures in little"; cited by Miss McCarthy, Spencer, and Sprague.

[45] Another of Kremble's innovations was the omission of Hamlet's discourse on the art of acting. Kemble professed to be governed by the dictates of modesty, but it should be remembered that Ward, and before him Betterton, had omitted the speech.

King James Takes A Collection

[1951]

HE EFFORTS made during the later years of the reign of King James I to strengthen the English colony in Newfoundland illustrate vividly the mixed motives which to a greater or less degree inspired all the proponents of colonial expansion. Richard Whitbourne, whose publications in support of the venture are the starting-point of this investigation, was seeking to relieve his momentary impoverishment; but at the same time he was scornful of the unbusinesslike methods then being practiced in the colony—methods both amateurish and irresolute—and sought to amend them. He likewise burned with patriotic zeal for the advancement of English interests in this area of the New World, where there were profits to be gained by the adventurous in an enterprise that would win honor for the nation and at the same time relieve the conditions of poverty and overpopulation in England by the threefold expedient of providing new lands for occupation, new employment in outfitting and sustaining the colony and its industries, and a new food supply from the inexhaustible riches of the Grand Banks fisheries. To crown all this, Whitbourne was genuinely concerned about the lost condition of the souls of the natives, and he sought to lay the burden of responsibility for their continuing risk of damnation upon the conscience of his countrymen. For purse, for country, and for God, or, in Whitbourne's own words, "Religion, Honour, Empire, and Profit."

The monarch to whom Whitbourne turned for succor and encouragement was the sort of man whom all of these motives would strongly move. James I had not known affluence before he came to the throne

Essays Honoring Lawrence C. Wroth, ed. Frederick R. Goff (Portland, Maine, 1951), pp. 223-33.

vacated by Elizabeth, and though his affairs improved financially he never commanded wealth that seemed commensurate with his great office. The prospect of acquiring new lands peaceably and at the same time giving employment to restless, hungry citizens while increasing their food supply appealed to him mightily.

Yet since the King had no funds with which to recompense Whitbourne for his losses or to supply backing for the colonial project, he had to resort to an extraordinary device for raising money. I say extraordinary, for that is precisely the word used by the bishops to describe it: "in an extraordinary manner." The direct appeal by the head of a government for popular contributions is familiar enough today. After every great disaster there are nationwide collections by the Red Cross for the relief of suffering: starving refugees in the Near East were given succor after World War I; Liberty Loan and War Bond campaigns come readily to mind. Whether the idea originated with King James, I do not know. He must have been acquainted with the medieval devices for gaining financial support of the crusades, and he had firsthand knowledge of the legal fiction that underlay the royal subsidies granted him by Parliament from time to time. Perhaps the combination of personal, national, and religious motives in the Newfoundland project prompted him to make his appeal to England through the parish churches.[1] In doing so, he illustrated a quality that was possessed also by Richard Whitbourne.

Resourcefulness is a prominent characteristic of colonizers and missionaries, and likewise of adventurers who need to recoup their fortunes. Captain, later Sir, Richard Whitbourne was all three of these,

---

[1] On more than one occasion James granted to individuals the privilege of collecting funds for their personal relief; see *STC* 8651, 8652, 8653, 8654, and 8656, proclamations issued between 19 January and 13 February 1621 for the benefit of a helpless man, a widow, a vicar who suffered loss in a fire, a mariner, and a husbandman who was victimized by fire. *STC* 8601, of 18 February 1619, authorizes a collection to be taken over a period of a year for the repair of the bridge at Staines; and *STC* 8602, of the same date, relates to a collection for cleansing the river Fosse in Lincolnshire. Though interesting, these acts of compassion are not positively constructive in the sense that the grant to Whitbourne is—even the assistance granted Staines and Lincolnshire is little other than a substitute for taxation. Relief in an emergency was granted Stratford-upon-Avon in 1616 after the fire that destroyed fifty-four houses, at which time James named the bailiff and burgesses and three private citizens to make a collection; see *STC* 8521. A closer parallel to the Whitbourne incident is referred to by A. L. Rowse in *The England of Elizabeth* (London, 1951), p. 51; here he states, without giving details, that in 1594 Lord Burghley asked voluntary contributions from the gentry towards the payment of John Norden's expenses in collecting data for his description of Middlesex.

and he possessed resourcefulness in a high degree. After "nearly forty
years" spent in voyages and discovery, he had in 1616 suffered the misfortune of having his ship of one hundred tons fall into the company of
a French pirate, Daniel Tibolo, to whom he had lost more than £860
(nearly a quarter of a million dollars), but his zeal for colonizing and
evangelizing Newfoundland, building the English merchant fleet, and
relieving the wants of unemployed Englishmen was not abated, and
the low state of his fortunes drove him to renewed effort.

From "The Epistle Dedicatory" to King James of Whitbourne's *A
Discourse and Discouery of New-found-land* (1620), we learn that he
had presented a manuscript of that work to the King at Huntingdon
in October 1619 which so much pleased his Majesty that the Lords of
the Privy Council in session at Whitehall on 24 July 1620 were induced
to order that the book should be printed[2] and to recommend to the
Lord Archbishop of Canterbury and the other Lords Bishops that it
be distributed to the several parishes of the kingdom "for the better
incouragement of such as shall be willing to assist that Plantation,
either in their persons or otherwise." In little more than a month
arrangements for publication were completed, and soon the book appeared, printed by Felix Kingston for William Barrett, with the notation
that it was "published by Authority."

No manuscript or printed order of the Privy Council can be traced,
but Whitbourne's account of the proceedings may, I think, be accepted
at face value, for this first book was shortly followed by another from
the same pen. Again the author gives a circumstantial account (in the
Epistle Dedicatory addressed to "Henry Lord Cary, Viscount of Faulk-
land, Controller of his Maiesties household, and one of his Maiesties most
Honourable privie Councell"), but this time, to omit nothing that
might impress his readers and further his project, he prints a "Copy
of a Reference from the Kings most Excellent Maiesty: As also a Letter
from the Right Honourable Lords of his Maiesties most Honourable
Priuy Councell, to the Most Reuerend Fathers in God, the Lords Arch-
Bishops of Canterbury and Yorke their Graces."

The "Letter" of the Privy Council, which is dated 30 June 1621, from

---

[2] It was entered to Master Barrett in the Stationers' Register on 26 August 1620, under
the hands of Master Doctor Goade and Master Lownes as written by Captain Richard
Whitmore; the spelling "Whitmore" persists in the entry of 3 April 1626, by which
Mistress Barrett assigned the title to Master Parker.

Whitehall, informs their Graces of Canterbury and York that Whitbourne

hath set downe in wryting diuers good obseruations and notes touching the state and condition of [New-found-land], and the plantation there, which being by order from vs now printed: It is desired to be published throughout the Kingdome. . . .

It becomes apparent that Whitbourne's *Discourse and Discouery* of 1620 won the support of several of the nobility and a number of wealthy men and enterprising groups but that interest is flagging; so he has produced a second book. This also has gained the approval of James and his Privy Council. This, too, has been authorized for publication. The language of the Privy Council letter implies that the second book existed in manuscript at the end of June 1621, and we may suppose that arrangements were made for printing it; but the affair progressed tardily, and Whitbourne seems to have invoked the royal authority a second time, for on 12 April 1622 James addressed a message (the "Reference" named above) "to the most Reuerend Fathers in God, the Lords Arch-Bishops of Canterbury and Yorke their Graces." Its purport is that "His Maiesty is graciously pleased, That the Lords Archbishops . . . doe . . . proceed according to the Letters of the Lords of the Councell, bearing date the last of June 1621."

Whitbourne's second book, *A Discourse Containing a Louing Inuitation,* bearing Felix Kingston's imprint and the date 1622, may already have been printed before James applied pressure to the archbishops; if not, it was shortly put in print. There is no entry in the Stationers' Register, for the reason, probably, that the book needed no "copyright" protection, the "Reference" having concluded with the statement of "his Maiesties pleasure . . . that the said Captaine Whitbourne shall haue the sole printing of his booke for one and twenty yeares."

The exact date of publication is not known, but it must have been before 16 September, for on that date George Montaigne, Bishop of London, addressed a letter to "all and singuler Archdeacons, Deanes, and their Officials, Parsons, Vicars, Curates, Churchwardens; and to all other Ecclesiasticall Officers and Ministers within [his] Diocesse," pursuant to the instructions he had received by way of the Privy Council and the Archbishop of Canterbury from his friend and benefactor King James. Several copies of this letter have survived, bound with the preliminaries or at the end of copies of Whitbourne's *Discourse Containing a Louing Inuitation*. The letter is printed on one side of a small folio leaf. There is no imprint, but the initials at the top of the page are from an alphabet like that used by Kingston, and since copies of the letter were to accompany the book there would be many advantages in having Kingston print both. At this time, Whitbourne was occupying a "Chamber at the signe of the gilded Cocke in *Paternoster-Row*,"[3] where Kingston had his shop, and we shall later discover that Kingston was authorized to receive funds that should be collected for Whitbourne. It may be safely assumed, therefore, that Kingston was the printer of the Bishop's letter.

Although the Bishop's letter is a bibliographically independent unit and is mentioned in the *Dictionary of National Biography* account of Whitbourne and again by Cole,[4] it has never been adequately described, and it is not listed in the *Short-Title Catalogue of English Books* (1926). The letters measure about $6\frac{3}{8}''$ to $7\frac{1}{4}''$ in width and $11\frac{3}{4}''$ to $12\frac{1}{8}''$ in height in the copies I have examined. The lines of text are $5\frac{13}{16}''$ long. In the shortest form of the letter there are forty-three lines of text plus the signature; in the longest, forty-seven lines plus the signature plus four additional lines of postscript.

Before giving attention to the minutiae in which these surviving copies differ, it is worth while to consider the general intention of the letter. Addressed by the bishops to the local church officials in their respective dioceses, the letter rehearses the directions of King James, the instructions of the Privy Council, and the injunctions of the Archbishop of Canterbury. It describes the "extraordinary manner" by which Whitbourne is to be assisted: a copy of his book, accompanied by the letter, is to be distributed to each parish church, where "in the time of Diuine Service" on a Sunday when no other offering is being received, the proper church official is to present the project to the congregation and "seriously stir vp and exhort them to extend their bountifull liberality herein," and the churchwardens shall take a collection in the "vsuall manner from seate to seate"; then the total shall be endorsed

---

[3] See *A Discourse Containing a Louing Inuitation,* sig. ¶2ᵛ.

[4] George Watson Cole, *A Catalogue of Books Relating to the Discovery and Early History of North and South America Forming a Part of the Library of E. D. Church* (New York, 1907), II, 913. Cole cites the catalogue of the Hoe Library, V, 110-11, which describes a copy of *The Discourse Containing an Inuitation* that had bound in at the end a folded "License by the Bp. of London," bearing "the autograph of Whitbourne, dated Septemb. 16, 1622." Cole notes that there are two printings of the letter.

on the letters and certified, and the proceeds, together with the letter, shall be forwarded more or less directly to Captain Whitbourne. Furthermore, "such of the Parishioners as shall be then absent" are to be visited by the churchwardens "at their houses" "to collect their gratuities" thereunto. Nothing was left to chance. And all this was to be done "within one Moneth next after the said Captaine Whitbourne's Booke, with this my Letter, which I doe allow to be Printed, shall be by him, his Assignee or Assignes brought vnto any of you." After heartbreaking delays, Whitbourne was to see tangible results. The proceeds are for Whitbourne's "use and behoofe" "towards his great trauels, charge, and expence of time, with seuerall Commissions [that are nowhere detailed!], and otherwise in this businesse; and towards the Printing and free distributing his Bookes, and his seuerall great losses received at Sea by Pirats and otherwise, in aduenturing to further the said Plantation. . . ."

If Toby Matthew, the Archbishop of York, and the other bishops complied with the royal injunctions as promptly and loyally as did the Archbishop of Canterbury and the several bishops to be named below, the letter addressed to the parish clergy should exist in many variant forms. No letter has yet been located that was sent out at the behest of the Archbishop of York. This is not stated to his prejudice, for it is mere chance that any copy of the letter has survived.

At least four bishops are known to have complied with the request of George Abbot, Archbiship of Canterbury, for copies of their letters have been preserved, one of them in two different printings. These bishops are George Montaigne, Bishop of London; Rowland Searchfield, Bishop of Bristol; Samuel Harsnett, Bishop of Norwich; and Nicholas Felton, Bishop of Ely. And their letters bear dates from 16 September 1622 to 2 June 1623. For reasons of economy and speed, the printer kept the type standing and made as few changes as possible from one letter to the next, as will be indicated in detail, and his failure to alter the name of the diocese at its second occurrence in the earlier setting of the Bishop of London's letter affords proof of the obedience of a fifth bishop. Line 4 of this was negligently permitted to continue reading "my diocesse of *Winton*," where "*London*" is required; so we know that Lancelot Andrewes, Bishop of Winchester, sent out a letter even earlier than that of the Bishop of London.

Except for variations in the permissive phrase in line 1, which appears as "by the diuine prouidence," "by God's prouidence," and, more modestly, "by the diuine permission," the text of the letters is generally uniform up to the point where directions are given for forwarding the money collected to Richard Whitbourne. The letters agree in cautioning that "the Churchwardens are . . . ioyntly with the Minister [to] endorse the summe and place where it is collected, in letters, and not in figures, vpon these Letters." Then the Bishop of London names "M^r. *Robert Christian*,[5] Gent. at his house in Knightrider-street, neere the Cathedrall Church of S. *Paul* in *London,* whom the said Captaine *Whitbourne* hath intreated to receiue the same to his vse." This arrangement was modified for at least one unnamed church, probably in the archdeaconry of St. Albans (which was included in the diocese of London after 1550), as we learn from a manuscript note added below the Bishop of London's signature on the Hoe-Huntington copy. It reads as follows:

I pray what shall bee freely | geven & collected where | this aboue sayd łre & boke | shallbe presented to retour- | ne the same vnto Mr Rolf[6] | Officiall to the Archdeacon | of S^t. allbons to bee | by him retourned as | aboue sayd for mee | Richard Whitbourne[.]

The note is in a secretarial hand; the signature, in an italic hand.

Rowland Searchfield, Bishop of Bristol, arranged that the receipts and the letters "within the Citty and Deanery of *Bristoll*" should be delivered to his "seruant *Samuel Gulliford*,[7] at my Palace in *Bristoll*" but that "all such money as shall be collected in my Diocesse within the County of *Dorcet,* the same forthwith to be paid ouer vnto Master *William Orchard*,[7] Gentleman, deputy Register, at his house in *Blandfordforum* in the said County."

The Bishop of Norwich, Samuel Harsnett, gave instructions that the collections were to be returned to the local "Archdeacons Registers, by

[5] Possibly this is the man who was a scholar at Westminster School in 1587 from co. Herts., pleb. Christ Church, Oxford, matriculated 29 November 1588, aged nineteen; B.A., 9 June 1591, M.A., 13 May 1594—see Joseph Foster, *Alumni Oxonienses* (Oxford, 1891), I, 275.

[6] James Rolfe (Roffe), admitted pensioner (age seventeen) at Caius, 20 April 1582; the son of William Rolfe, burgess (and mayor) of St. Albans. He was baptized at the Abbey 1 November 1565; attended St. Albans school. Scholar at Caius, 1582-89; B.A., 1585-86; M.A., 1589. Official of the archdeaconry of St. Albans. Later, Commissary of the archdeaconry of Huntingdon; Master in Chancery. Married Grace, the daughter of John Robotham of St. Albans. Died 27 October 1630, aged sixty-five (J. and J. A. Venn, *Alumni Cantabrigienses, Pt. 1, to 1751* (Cambridge, 1922-27), III, 482.

[7] Samuel Gulliford's name does not appear in the *Dictionary of National Biography* or in the registers of Oxford or Cambridge; nor does that of William Orchard.

a trusty friend, who may speedily returne all such Letters and moneies so paid ouer vnto either of them, vnto my Chancelor in *Norwich,*" who would repay the same to Mr. Robert Christian, Gentleman, the same man whose name appears in the Bishop of London's letter.

Norwich's letter, for the first time, has a postscript of four lines:

Any Parator or other person that shall bring this Letter with the Booke vnto any Parish, is agreed withall for his paines therein beforehand, that none such shall receiue any of the money that shalbe collected, as abouesaid.

This I take to be an indication that some person or persons unknown had been engaged in the Elizabethan equivalent of what is now called chiseling. The practice must have been widespread, for this same postscript appears at the end of the second printing of the Bishop of London's letter. Whitbourne, however, kept himself informed and took the necessary steps to eliminate the graft.

Just why the Bishop of London should have issued a second letter is not easy to discover, unless it was for the sake of adding the four-line postscript. The text agrees in the main, not with his first letter, but with that of the Bishop of Norwich of 2 December 1622, even to the naming of the local "Archdeacons Registers," who will transmit money received to Mr. Robert Christian. Its printed date, 16 September 1622, is then not the actual date of publication, which must have been after 2 December 1622, but merely a repetition of the original date of utterance.

The latest letter which has survived is that of Nicholas Felton, Bishop of Ely. It names "my Register Master *Iohn Poole,*[8] Gentleman, at his house in Cambridge," to receive the funds to be collected and "also to see what charges shall be deducted from the same by such as shall take paines therein; whereby the remainder thereof and the Letters may be carefully returned to the foresaid Captaine *Whitbourne* . . . or vnto Master *Felix Kyngston,* at his house in *Pater-noster-row,* at the Signe of the Golden Cocke, in *London,* Printer, to the vse of the said Captaine *Whitbourne.*" This letter has no postscript, for the good Bishop had taken note of the chiseling and appointed his register to adjudicate claims. The concluding sentence has additional importance, for it is strengthens the assumption that Felix Kingston printed not only Whitbourne's two books but also the bishops' letters. Furthermore, it gives Kingston's

---

[8] John Poole's name has not been found in the *Dictionary of National Biography* or in the registers of Oxford or Cambridge.

place of residence twenty-two years earlier than that mentioned in Plomer's *Dictionary,* where it is stated that he was at the sign of the Gilded Cock in Pater-Noster Row in the year 1644.

Perhaps the publication of this account of King James's efforts to relieve the distress of Captain Richard Whitbourne will awaken interest in a neglected figure. It was an ingenious scheme, in the working out of which human nature is revealed to be changeless. Against the apathy and inertia of officialdom, the King and his doughty captain struggled for their project, only to have the proceeds trickle away into the pockets of petty officials. It is to be wished that a sheaf of the letters, duly certified as to the amounts collected and the congregations which donated them, might now be recovered, but probably they perished with Captain Richard Whitbourne or in the shop of Felix Kingston at the sign of the Gilded Cock.

Finding List[9]

Bishop	*Diocese*	*Date*
George Montaigne	London	16 September 1622

43 lines of text, printed as two paragraphs and signed "*Geo. London,*" without postscript. In line 1, "by the diuine prouidence." Reads "Diocesse of *Winton.*" [*rectius, London*] in line 4 but "*London*" correctly in line 29. Copies: British Museum (278. c. 31), Folger Shakespeare Library, Henry E. Huntington Library (Hoe copy, with postscript signed by Richard Whitbourne), New York Public Library (Lenox copy).

Rowland Searchfield	Bristol	5 October 1622

45 lines of text, printed as two paragraphs and signed "*Rou. Bristoll,*" without postscript. Corrects "possible" to "possibly" in line 32. Printed from the same setting of type as "London" (except for changes in the name of the bishop and the diocese) through "money and Letters" in line 39. Probably the same type was used to print identical phrases in the concluding lines, especially the words

[9] For assistance in compiling this finding list I am indebted to many unnamed librarians who perforce gave negative replies to my inquiries and to the following for their assistance and their courtesy in granting permission to use photostats of copies that lie in their custody: F. C. Francis, British Museum; Herman R. Mead, Henry E. Huntington Library; Stephen T. Riley, Massachusetts Historical Society; Lewis M. Stark, New York Public Library; and, not least, Lawrence C. Wroth, John Carter Brown Library.

"redeliuered . . . *Palace at.*" Copies: John Carter Brown Library, New York Public Library.

Samuel Harsnett   Norwich   2 December 1622

47 lines of text, printed as three paragraphs and signed "*Samuel Norwich*," with 4-line postscript. In line 1, "by Gods prouidence." Lines 2 through 27 (with the necessary change in the names of the diocese) printed from the same setting of type as "Bristol" but with different lineation in lines 4-5. A new paragraph begins with the words, "These are therefore." Lines 28-30 at least partly reset; lines 31-36 probably from the original setting. Copies: British Museum (G. 2907), Massachusetts Historical Society.

George   Montaigne   London   16 September 1622 [*sic*]

44 lines of text, printed as three paragraphs and signed "*George London*," with 4-line postscript. In line 1, "by the diuine prouidence." In lines 4 and 29 "*London*" correctly. Lines 2-40 (except for necessary changes in proper names) through the words "speedily returne" printed from the same setting of type as "Norwich." Copy: Henry E. Huntington Library (Lefferts-Church copy).

Nicholas Felton   Ely   2 June 1623

45 lines of text, printed as three paragraphs and signed "*Nicholas Elie*," without postscript. In line 1, "by the diuine permission." In line 2, "singuler" becomes "singular," and there is a change in the lineation of lines 4-5. Lines 2-27 (except for the necessary change in proper name) printed from the same setting of type as the second issue of "London." The words "pray &" are omitted in line 29; a period is improperly substituted for a semicolon after "*Elie*" in line 30; "his Maiestie's pleasure herein, as also the Lords of the most Honorable priuie Councels order, and" is inserted before "this my Letter" in lines 34-35; "and the scope" becomes "as also the scope" in line 36. Copy: New York Public Library.

Songs and Masques in The Tempest

[1953]

INTRODUCTION

THE DISCOVERY in the Folger Shakespeare Library of two copies of *Songs and Masques in the Tempest*, previously unknown to scholars,[1] calls attention to what is perhaps the earliest English libretto. The leaflet preserves certain details about the first performances of the operatic version of *The Tempest*, raises once more the question of Thomas Shadwell's participation in the redaction, and leads to a more precise dating of *The Ariels Songs in the Play call'd the Tempest*.

I

Songs and Masques is printed on a single sheet of paper in quarto format, the first two leaves being signed A and A2. The pages are numbered from 1 to 8 in arabic numerals, which are enclosed in parentheses and centered at the tops of the pages. There is neither title-page nor colophon, page 1 being headed, *Songs and Masques* | IN | THE | TEMPEST. | [rule]. Copy 1, unbound and with untrimmed fore-edges, measures 175 × 219 mm. It seems to have been abstracted from a collection, for the number 25 has been written in ink in an early hand just below the printed page number 1, and the number 24 in the lower right-hand corner. The source of the leaflet is unknown, but presumably Mr. Folger purchased it from an English dealer, for "1/10/-" is penciled in the upper right corner of the first page. In the same hand is the notation "*c.* 1690" below the catchword.

---

[1] It is recorded as item 327a in Gertrude L. Woodward and James G. McManaway, *A Check List of English Plays 1641-1700* (Chicago, 1945), p. 150.

Theatre Miscellany, Luttrell Society Reprints, No. 14 (Oxford, 1953), 69-96.

Copy 2, bound in three-quarter red morocco, is somewhat smaller. Folger acquired it in the last year of his life by private negotiation.[2]

The last page of each copy is discolored where the leaflet has been thrice folded. The first fold is along a horizontal line midway of the page. The second and third folds, along vertical lines, reduce the leaflet to one-eighth of its original area, producing a size and shape convenient for insertion in a pocket.[3]

In the absence of imprint and colophon, it is impossible to identify the printer or publisher with certainty, but in all likelihood the publisher was Henry Herringman, who published the 1670, 1674, 1676, and certain other Restoration editions of *The Tempest*.[4] The printer was probably J[ohn] M[acocke], who printed the quartos of 1670, 1676, and 1690, or T[homas] N[ewcombe], to whom Herringman entrusted the printing of the quarto of 1674. Both men were regularly employed by Herringman to print plays. No help is afforded by the small (*c.* 30 × 40 mm.) watermark in *Songs and Masques,* a fleur-de-lys surmounting the initials F G which is unlike anything in the quartos of 1674 or 1676. The probability that Macocke was the printer is increased by the fact that an unusual three-line bracket appears three times in Masque II in *Songs and Masques,* at lines 29-31, 37-39, and 69-71, and also in corresponding places in Q 1674. Q 1674 uses the bracket a fourth time in a three-line stage direction at lines 29-31, where *Songs and Masques* has only a one-line stage direction.

II

All the evidence suggests that *Songs and Masques* was intended for use in the theater. Texts of the two masques which the operatic version featured and of the favorite songs, old and new, were provided so that members of the audience might follow the performance or recall it later. These, with the head-title, occupy seven and one-third pages, leaving no room for a title-page to advertise the leaflet; but there is ample space

[2] See item 254 in J. Pearson and Co.'s *Catalogue of Armorial Bindings, Books, Autograph Letters & Manuscripts* (1929), where it is tentatively identified as the 1669 edition of *The Tempest* listed (erroneously) by Lowndes, and is priced at £250.

[3] One is reminded of the way Abraham Hill folded some of the paper he used for listing plays. See n. 1 on p. 76 of Joseph Q. Adams, "Hill's List of Early Plays in Manuscript," *The Library,* 4th ser., XX (1939-40), 71-99. The manuscripts are identified as B.M. Add. MSS. 2891-2901.

[4] See Hugh Macdonald, *John Dryden: A Bibliography* (Oxford, 1939), pp. 101-4, and Woodward and McManaway, *A Check List,* items 328-35. Two editions falsely dated 1676 may be piracies.

for a colophon, which a publisher or bookseller might have been expected to provide if the item were intended for sale anywhere but at or in Dorset Garden Theatre. The presence in Masque I of the printed explanation, *"Here they are interrupted by the Speakers,"* at the three points in the text where the dialogue of the play breaks into the performance of the masque is confirmatory evidence that the leaflet was prepared for the benefit of the audience rather than the reading public.

No similar publication is known in the Restoration period, or earlier in England.[5] Perhaps the idea of printing a sort of libretto originated in such publications as Thomas Dekker's *The Magnificent Entertainment: Giuen to King Iames, Queene Anne his Wife, and Henry Frederick the Prince, vpon the day of his Maiesties Tryumphant Passage (from the Tower) through his Honourable Citie (and Chamber) of London, being the 15. of March. 1603,* which was rushed through the press while excitement was still at the highest pitch. There was equal haste in printing certain court masques, as Sir Walter Greg has demonstrated in the case of James Shirley's *The Triumph of Peace* (1633),[6] which created a sensation in London.

A closer prototype is found in the group of court masques by Ben Jonson which were issued between 1617 and 1624 in quarto format without imprint. It is generally agreed that *Lovers Made Men, The Masque of Augurs, Time Vindicated, Neptune's Triumph,* and *The Fortunate Isles* were printed for private distribution by the author among his patrons and friends and perhaps for use by the noble participants in the performances.[7] The paucity of surviving copies of these quartos and

[5] [Immediately after the publication of *Theatre Miscellany*, Professor Charles Haywood found in the Henry E. Huntington Library the only surviving copy of *The Songs and Masques in the New Tempest*, the libretto of Thomas Duffet's *The Mock Tempest: or, The Enchanted Castle*, a foul burlesque performed by the King's Company and published early in 1675. The text is reprinted in Haywood's article, "The Songs & Masques in the New Tempest: An Incident in the Battle of the Two Theaters, 1674," *HLQ*, XIX (1955-56), 39-56. Before the end of the 17th century there were other and more elaborate librettos such as *The Musical Entertainments in the Tragedy of Rinaldo and Armida*, written by John Dennis and set to music by John Eccles. The text of the unique copy in the library of Worcester College, Oxford, is reprinted by Herbert Davis in *Theatre Miscellany*, pp. 97-118.]

[6] "*The Triumph of Peace:* A Bibliographer's Nightmare," *The Library*, 5th ser., I (1946-47), 113-22.

[7] Perhaps *News from the New World* should also be included. See, for example, *The Carl H. Pforzheimer Library, English Literature, 1475-1700* (New York, 1940), II, 569; Sir Walter Greg, *A Bibliography of the English Printed Drama to the Restoration* (London, 1951), II, item 350 (a); also items 381 (a), 385 (a), 407 (a), 411 (a), and 610 (a);

the absence of imprint and colophon suggest strongly that no public sale was intended and that the audience in general did not have opportunity to acquire them.[8]

A note by J. O. Halliwell-Phillipps on John Crowne's play, *Justice Busy; or, The Gentleman-Quack,* may be interpreted as meaning that another Restoration libretto exists: "Not printed, but the songs introduced into it were published separately with the music."[9] The play, performed at Lincoln's Inn Fields *c.* 1699, is not extant, nor is any collection of its songs now traceable. Two songs have been preserved, as Mr. G. R. Noyes pointed out several years ago:[10] (1) "A Song in the Comedy call'd *Justice Buisy,* or the *Gentleman Quack*; Set by Mr. John Eccles, Sung by Mrs. Bracegirdle; and exactly engrav'd by Tho: Cross," beginning, "I'll hurry, hurry, hurry, hurry thee"; and (2) "A Song in the Comedy call'd (Justice Buisy, or the Gentleman-Quack;) Sett by Mr. John Eccles, Sung by Mrs. Bracegirdle," beginning, "No, no ev'ry Morning My Beauties renew."[11] The wording of the title of the first song indicates that it was issued for sale as a single sheet and not as part of a collection. If a book of songs from *Justice Busy* was ever seen by Halliwell-Phillipps, it has disappeared or perished. Unless a copy of such a collection comes to light and proves to have been intended for sale in the theater rather than in music and book shops, *Songs and Masques* may be considered the first and only Restoration libretto.

---

and C. H. Herford and Percy and Evelyn Simpson, *Ben Jonson* (Oxford, 1925, *etc.*), X, 566 ("This [*Lovers Made Men*] was the first English opera"), 567, 647, 658; also IX, 9-10.

[8] No copy of *News from the New World* is known; *Lovers Made Men* and *Time Vindicated* have survived in unique copies; there are three copies each of *Neptune's Triumph* and *Masque of Augurs,* and eight of *Fortunate Isles,* the latest of the six masques.

[9] *A Dictionary of Old English Plays* (1860), p. 136. See also G. P. Winship, *A Bibliography of the Restoration Dramatist John Crowne* (Harvard University Press, 1922), p. 16.

[10] "Mrs. Bracegirdle's Acting in Crowne's *Justice Busy,*" MLN, XLIII (1928), 390-91. I am indebted to Dr. William Van Lennep, Curator of the Harvard Theatre Collection, for this reference.

[11] The first, as noted by Noyes, is to be found in a collection of songs in the British Museum, k. 7. i. 2 (49), catalogued under John Eccles: "I'll hurry thee hence, in the comedy *Justice Buisy*" (London, 1700), p. 63; the second was printed in *Wit and Mirth; or Pills to Purge Melancholy,* IV (1706), 107. See notes in Day and Murrie, *English Song-Books 1651-1702* (London, 1940 for 1937), item 2320 in the Index of First Lines, which refers also to *The Compleat Academy of Complements* (1705).

III

The songs of the playhouses were immensely popular, and the music publishers found it profitable to issue them singly and to include them in their song-books. The earliest collection of theatrical songs listed in Day and Murrie's *English Song-Books* is No. 35, John Playford's *Choice Songs and Ayres for One Voyce . . . Being Most of the Newest Songs sung at Court, and at the Publick Theatres* (1673). In the following year, Playford published Thomas Jordan's *The Goldsmiths Jubile; or Londons Triumphs . . .* , containing the music for one song. It is apparently the first edition of a play or pageant to include musical notation.[12]

These were followed in 1675 by the second edition of Playford's *Choice Ayres, Songs, & Dialogues* with a great many theatrical songs. In four copies of this book is an inserted sheet signed Vv and paged 77-80, which is headed, "The Ariels Songs in the Play call'd the Tempest."[13] The exact date of publication of *Choice Ayres* (1675) is not known, for, it being a second edition, Playford had no need to enter it in the Stationers' Register; but the book is mentioned in the *Term Catalogues* (ed. Arber, I, 200) among "Books Reprinted" in Hilary Term, 15 February 1674/75.

There is ample evidence that Playford did not decide to include *The Ariels Songs* until after the rest of the book was in print. This may now be considered. *Choice Ayres* (1675) is a folio signed [A]² B-Z². *The Ariels Songs* could not well be added at the end of the book, for the last page, Z2ᵛ, contains advertisements; so the sheet was assigned the arbitrary signature Vv and the pages were numbered 77-80, as an indication that the insert was to come between V2ᵛ (page 76) and X1 (page 77). The unavoidable duplication of page numbers was ignored.[14] The irregular signature of the quire and the duplicated pagination are not the only proofs that *The Ariels Songs* is an insert. In "An Alphabetical Table of the [ninety-seven] Songs and Dialogues

---

[12] [Music for five songs was printed in *The Masque at Lord Hay's Marriage* (1607; Greg, *Bibliography of the English Printed Drama,* No. 238.]

[13] Day and Murrie list *Choice Ayres* (1675) as No. 40 and record that "Another Issue" contains the insert. Copies of this second issue are at the British Museum, the Royal College of Music (London), the Watson Music Library (Manchester), and the Folger Shakespeare Library.

[14] That the new quire was intended as an insert and not a cancel of quire X is proved by the fact that the song which begins on X2ᵛ (the original page numbered 80) continues to Y1ᵛ (p. 87).

in this Book," Playford advertises the fact that thirty-five are "added in this Edition" by marking the new items with an asterisk. The "Alphabetical Table" and the announcement about new songs appear on the last page, [A2ᵛ], of the preliminary quire. Whether the introductory material was printed earlier or later than the text (quires B–Z), it was certainly done before Playford arranged to include the six songs from *The Tempest,* which are not listed in the "Alphabetical Table." Furthermore, all the songs and dialogues in the other quires, with the exception of the song, "If languishing Eyes," on Vıᵛ, begin with large ornamental initials, while in quire Vv small display capitals are used. The reason for the change is that it was barely possible for William Godbid, Playford's printer, to set the six songs from *The Tempest* in four pages; to do so he had to sacrifice beauty by substituting display caps. for initials; he had also to increase the length of the type-page on both the recto and verso of Vv2, even omitting the signature which he customarily put on the second leaf of each quire; and even so it was necessary to omit the second and third stanzas of "Dorinda Lamenting the loss of her Amintas."

The discovery in the British Museum of a copy of *The Ariels Songs*[15] which lacks signature and pagination led Day and Murrie to the conclusion that Playford had the quire printed in this form for sale as an independent item, as well as in the form described above, for insertion in *Choice Ayres.*[16] They list it as No. 39 in their *Bibliography* and describe it as follows: "2°. No signatures. 2 leaves, unpaged." At my request, Mr. F. C. Francis examined the item and compared it with

[15] W. Barclay Squire is not alone in referring to this publication as *The Ariels Songs.* There is only one Ariel in *The Tempest,* it is true, but at the end of the last act this long stage direction occurs: *"Scene changes to the Rising Sun, and a number of Aerial Spirits in the Air, Ariel flying from the Sun, advances towards the Pit."* A few lines later, *"Ariel and the rest sing the following Song. | Where the Bee sucks,"* etc. Playford may have been misled by this scene or by something which John Downes records in *Roscius Anglicanus* (ed. Summers, p. 34): "Particularly, one Scene Painted with Myriads of Ariel Spirits."

[16] Perhaps they were influenced by the discussion of *The Ariels Songs* by W. Barclay Squire, "The Music of Shadwell's *Tempest,*" *Musical Quarterly,* VII (1921), 565-78. He expressed the opinion that there were two editions, the first of which lacked signature and pagination; these were added when the item was printed for insertion in *Choice Ayres.* Squire seems to have been confused by the bibliographical problems, and he does not use terms precisely, but he raises a pertinent question about the omission of *The Ariels Songs* from Playford's *Choice Ayres* (1676). Only one in six of *The Ariels Songs* is included, "Adieu to the pleasures and follies of love" (p. 73), and it is not identified as from *The Tempest.* In *Choice Ayres* (1676), a second and third stanza are added to the one printed in *The Ariels Songs.*

the signed and paged copy inserted in *Choice Ayres* in the Royal College of Music. He writes me that the two are identical, except that "the top of each leaf and the bottom of the first leaf" have been trimmed off the British Museum copy; "the cuts have been skilfully disguised and both leaves have been carefully mounted to size." Since the only other separate copy of *The Ariels Songs,* that in the Folger Library, is signed and paged, it is safe to assume that *The Ariels Songs* was not published in two states. This is not to say that Playford had the whole edition bound up as part of *Choice Ayres;* on the contrary, the prominent head-title, *The Ariels Songs in the Play call'd the Tempest,* suggests that he took every advantage of the popularity of the opera and also offered *The Ariels Songs* for sale as sheet music.

It has been shown above that the second edition of *Choice Ayres* was in print at least as early as 15 February 1675. There is good reason for believing that it appeared considerably earlier. At the end of page B4ᵛ of Thomas Jordan's *The Goldsmiths Jubile,* printed by William Godbid for John Playford, the publisher advertises his *Choice Ayres and Dialogues,* "to which in this new Edition are added many more new Songs, and also those Songs sung in the famous Play call'd the *Tempest,*" which "is newly Reprinted."[17] Although Day and Murrie (p. 44) state that *The Goldsmiths Jubile* was not entered in the Stationers' Register or the Term Catalogues, it was in fact entered in the Register by Playford on 26 October 1674, three days before its performance, and he doubtless published it at once, for such a book is most in request on the day of the event and immediately thereafter. Playford's assertion that *Choice Ayres* "is Newly Reprinted" probably means no more than that the book was at press, since the title-page is dated 1675. It is evident, however, that as early as 26 October Playford intended the inclusion of *The Ariels Songs,* and that even at this date it was too late to list its song titles in the "Alphabetical Table" or assign normal signatures and pagination to the quire.

IV

For nearly half a century the authorship of the operatic version of *The Tempest* and the date of its first performance have been in dispute. Henry Herringman, the publisher of the Davenant-Dryden version of Q 1670 and also the operatic version of Q 1674, might have spared scholars a world of trouble by stating exactly who prepared the opera;

[17] From a photostat of the Huntington Library copy.

instead, he reprinted the 1670 Prologue and Epilogue in Q 1674, as well
as Dryden's Preface. There is no allusion to Thomas Shadwell in it.
A reasonable summary of scholarly arguments is given by Mr. William
M. Milton,[18] who thinks it improper to speak of the authorship of a work
in which there were so many hands. The Shakespearian play was first
altered for performance in 1667 by Sir William Davenant assisted by
John Dryden, who in his 1669 Preface to the quarto of 1670 describes
their collaboration in terms that are something less than precise. This
version already contained operatic features such as dances and songs,
including "Go thy way," the Echo Song, which on 7 May 1668 Samuel
Pepys requested the composer John Banister to note down for him, and
also Pelham Humphrey's setting of "Where the bee sucks."[19] That the
words of at least one song, "Arise ye subterranean winds," were contributed to the operatic *Tempest* by Thomas Shadwell is proved by its
ascription to him in *Songs Set by Signior Pietro Reggio* (1680), pt. II,
pp. 12-13, a volume which contains not only commendatory verses by
Shadwell but also Reggio's sonnet in Italian addressed to Shadwell.
Both Charles E. Ward and William M. Milton recognize that Thomas

---

[18] *"Tempest* in a Teapot," *ELH*, XIV (1947), 207-18. For the principal discussions, see
W. J. Lawrence, "Did Thomas Shadwell Write an Opera on the *Tempest?*" *Anglia*, XXVII
(1904), 205-17; W. Barclay Squire, "Purcell's Dramatic Music," *Sammelbände der Inter-
nationalen Musik-Gesellschaft*, V (1904), 489-564; Sir Ernest Clarke, "*The Tempest* as an
Opera," *Athenaeum*, 25 August 1906, p. 222; W. J. Lawrence, *The Elizabethan Playhouse
and Other Studies*, 1st ser. (Stratford-upon-Avon, 1912), pp. 191-206; E. J. Dent, Preface
to *The Tempest*, in *Works of Henry Purcell*, XIX (1912); M. L. Pereyra, "La Musique
écrite sur *La Tempête* d'après Shakespeare par Pelham Humfrey," *Bulletin de la Société
Française de Musicologie*, II (1920), 75-85; W. B. Squire, "The Music of Shadwell's
Tempest," *Musical Quarterly*, VII (1921), 565-78; Montague Summers, ed., *Shakespeare
Adaptations* (Boston, 1922), pp. xl-lix; George Thorn-Drury, "Some Notes on Dryden,"
RES, I (1925), 324-30; D. M. Walmsley, "Shadwell and the Operatic *Tempest*," *RES*, II
(1926), 463-66; G. Thorn-Drury, "Shadwell and the Operatic *Tempest*," *RES*, III (1927),
204-8; Hazelton Spencer, *Shakespeare Improved* (Harvard University Press, 1927), pp.
192-210; Montague Summers, ed., *The Works of Thomas Shadwell* (London, 1927),
I, civ-cx; Cyrus L. Day, *The Songs of John Dryden* (Harvard University Press, 1932);
Willard Thorp, *Songs from the Restoration Theater* (Princeton University Press,
1934); J. A. Westrup, *Purcell* (London, 1937), pp. 93-94, 295; R. G. Noyes, "Contemporary
Musical Settings of the Songs in Restoration Dramatic Operas," *Harvard Studies and
Notes in Philology and Literature*, XX (1938), 99-121; Helene M. Hooker, "Dryden's and
Shadwell's *Tempest*," *HLQ*, VI (1942-43), 224-28; and Charles E. Ward, "*The Tempest*:
a Restoration Opera Problem," *ELH*, XIII (1946), 119-30.

[19] Willard Thorp, *Songs*, p. 85, n. 1; he points out that Barclay Squire overlooked
this fact when arguing that all the songs in *The Ariels Songs* were new in the operatic
Tempest. W. M. Milton follows Barclay Squire in questioning whether Humphrey returned from France early enough in 1667 to compose the music for "Where the bee sucks."

Betterton, as co-manager of Dorset Garden Theatre, played an important part in the production. John Downes, of course, calls the opera the
work of Thomas Shadwell without qualification.[20] It may be truly
said of the operatic *Tempest* that, like Topsy, it "just growed." The
fourth song included in *The Ariels Songs* is headed, "Dorinda Lamenting
the loss of her Amintas." One stanza, beginning "Adieu to the Pleasures
and Follies of Love," is in *The Ariels Songs;* two more stanzas were
added in *Choice Ayres* (1676). But the text is not found in any of the
quartos of *The Tempest,* as Barclay Squire points out. Furthermore,
there is no Amintas among the dramatis personae. Squire is surely right
in his conjecture that James Hart's song was interpolated at some time
after the original performance at the point in IV. iii where Dorinda
is told that Hippolito is dead.[21] What he does not comment on is the
fact that the courtly-pastoral verses are wholly unsuited to the unsophis-
ticated Dorinda. In a word, the Duke's Company retained all the popular features of the Davenant-Dryden version and added others from
time to time. The text remained fluid; songs were interpolated. Alterations were even made in the choreography, as Matthew Locke discloses,
who in publishing his instrumental music for *The Tempest* in *The
English Opera* (1675) omitted "the Tunes of the Entries and Dances
in the *Tempest* (the dancers being chang'd)" "by the consent of their
Author, Seignior Gio. Baptista Draghi." When the texts of *Songs and
Masques, The Ariels Songs,* and the quarto editions of *The Tempest*
are compared, it will be found that differences in speech-tags reflect
other changes in the personnel of the Dorset Garden cast. And before
the century ended, Henry Purcell provided many new musical settings,
one of which, "Dear pretty Youth," displaced James Hart's song for
Dorinda lamenting the supposed death of Hippolito. The operatic *Tempest* had much in common with a modern musical show.

V

All discussions of the date of the first performance of the operatic
Tempest begin with the account of John Downes in *Roscius Anglicanus*
(ed. Summers, 1928, pp. 34-35):

[20] *Roscius Anglicanus,* ed. Montague Summers (London, 1928), pp. 34-35.
[21] Since Hart was on loan from the Chapel Royal, the song may have been omitted
from performance when his services were no longer available—*i.e.,* at some date later
than 16 May 1674 (see footnote 23 below).

The Year after in 1673. The Tempest, or the Inchanted Island, made into an Opera by Mr. *Shadwell,* having all New in it; as Scenes, Machines; particularly, one Scene Painted and *Myriads* of *Ariel* spirits; and another flying away, with a Table Furnisht out with Fruits, Sweetmeats and all sorts of Viands; just when Duke *Trinculo* and his Companions were going to Dinner; all things perform'd in it so Admirably well, that not any succeeding Opera got more money.

Lawrence's argument that the aged Downes suffered a lapse in memory has been generally accepted, and a date of "*c.* 30 April 1674" has been assigned. This may be the closest possible approximation, especially if Lawrence is correct in his interpretation of the lines with which Dryden concludes his "Prologue . . . at the Opening of the New House"[22] on 26 March 1674. On this date the King's Company, for which Dryden was contracted to write plays and in which he had a share, opened the new theater Wren had designed to replace the building destroyed by fire in January 1672. After apologizing for the plainness of the building, as compared with sumptuous Dorset Garden, and girding at the folly of raising a stately pile "Whilst Scenes, Machines, and empty *Opera*'s reign," Dryden closes with these lines:

> I wou'd not prophesie our Houses Fate:
> But while vain Shows and Scenes you over-rate,
> 'Tis to be feared—
> That as a Fire the former House o'rethrew,
> Machines and Tempests will destroy the new.

A variant reading of the last line has been discovered by Dr. Helene M. Hooker in Huntington Library MS. EL 8923: "Tempests and Operas will destroy ye New." Lawrence insists that the last line does not refer to the operatic *Tempest* but to the recently performed operatic version of *Macbeth.* His opinion is buttressed by the manuscript prologue and epilogue to *The Tempest* contained in British Museum MS. Egerton 2623, which he demonstrates to be a point-by-point reply to Dryden. Now if Dryden is hitting at the operatic *Macbeth* or at an operatic *Tempest* then known to be in rehearsal, the pedestrian verses in MS. Egerton 2623 may indeed have been intended (by Shadwell or another) for recitation at Dorset Garden; but until it can be shown that they were used in that theater, their value as evidence is dubious. It is not

---

[22] *Miscellany Poems* (1684), pp. 286-89. This is item 42 a 1 in Hugh Macdonald's *John Dryden: A Bibliography* (Oxford, 1939).

unknown for friends of a playwright or a playhouse to contribute un-
solicited prologues and epilogues, and not all of these have been accepted
and spoken on the stage. No one knows who wrote the pair in Egerton
2623, or whether they ever came to the attention of a Dorset Garden
audience; they were not printed until Lawrence brought them to light
in 1912.

The King's Company were in a difficult position. Impoverished,
they were opening their new house with a revival of a Jacobean play,
Beggars' Bush, in competition with the extravagant productions of the
Duke's Theatre. Dryden's own predicament was even worse. A play
which he and Davenant had altered with conspicuous success seven
years earlier (the Court patronized no fewer than five performances in its
first season) was either in rehearsal or actually in performance at the
rival house. True, it had been refurbished and elaborated, but essentially
it was his and Davenant's "improvement" of the Shakespearian *Tempest.*
Preparations for the opera had been grandiose. Pelham Humphrey, Master of the Children of the Chapel Royal, John Banister, sometime leader
of the King's Band, Matthew Locke, Composer in Ordinary to the King,
Giovanni Baptista Draghi, organist to Queen Catherine, and the famous
Pietro Reggio had been employed to compose the music. Through the
favor of Charles II, William Turner and James Hart and others of
the Chapel Royal were permitted to sing in the first performances.[23]
This swelled the number of singers to thirty, according to the epilogue
in MS. Egerton 2623. And it is known from the initial stage direction
of Q 1674 that the orchestra was, contrary to custom, seated *"between the
Pit and the Stage,"* augmented for the occasion by 12 violins from the
King's Music, so that the Band consisted of *"24 Violins, with the
Harpsicals and Theorbo's"* to *"accompany the Voices."* Arrangements
such as these were not made in a corner. Dryden had good reason to
fear that "Machines or Tempests" or, as in the Huntington Library
Manuscript, "Tempests and Operas" would destroy the King's Company's new house.

[23] "It is his Maties pleasure that Mr Turner & Mr Hart or any other Men or Boyes
belonging to His Maties Chappell Royall that sing in ye Tempest at His Royall Highnesse
Theatre doe remaine in Towne all the Weeke (dureing his Maties absence from Whitehall) to performe that service, only Saterdayes to repaire to Windsor & to returne to London on Mundayes if there be occac͞on for them And that (they) also performe ye like
Service in ye Opera in ye said Theatre or any other thing in ye like Nature where their
helpe may be desired." (L.C. 5/15, p. 53, quoted by Allardyce Nicoll, *A History of Restoration Drama 1660-1700,* Cambridge University Press, 1928, p. 318.)

It is difficult to believe that Dryden is not alluding to the operatic *Tempest*. And it is equally difficult to understand why he should give such prominence to the opera unless it was already on the stage. It is one thing to attack as "empty Opera" a competing attraction that is playing to full houses; it is quite another to give such a production advance publicity. Is it not likely that on 26 March 1674 the operatic *Tempest* had already been performed more than once at Dorset Garden? If so, if even one of these performances came two days before Dryden's Prologue, then John Downes is not in error, for the date would have been 24 March 1673/74.[24]

VI

Although Draghi's incidental music and dances have not been preserved, practically all the rest of the music of the operatic *Tempest* has survived and, with one exception, has been printed. *The Ariels Songs* appeared in 1674 or very early in 1675; Locke's instrumental music[25] came out in *The English Opera* soon after the first performance of *Psyche* on 27 February 1674/75; Shadwell's song, "Arise, arise," was included in *Songs set by Signior Pietro Reggio* in 1680; and part of Pelham Humphrey's setting of the Fifth Act Masque was published by Barclay Squire.[26] The exception is, of course, "The Vocal Musick in *the Tempest* by Mr Pelham Humfrey," in the Libri Manuscript, which Mlle. Pereyra discovered in the Bibliothèque du Conservatoire de Paris in 1920, and which Squire reprinted only in part. The manuscript contains "The Song of the 3 Divells" (*i.e.,* the Masque in Act II); "My Lord great Neptune" (the Masque in Act V); and "Arise, arise" (after the conclusion of the Masque in Act II).[27] It bears no marks of theatrical use, however, and its separation of "Arise, arise" from the Masque which it follows, as well as its frequent lack of speech-tags, warrants the belief that it is a private transcript for such a lover of theatrical music as Samuel Pepys.

[24] This point would have less importance if some commentators had not used Downes's supposed error in the date as evidence of his lack of credibility in attributing the operatic redaction to Shadwell.

[25] Locke's "Lilk" was reprinted in John Stafford Smith's *Musica Antiqua* (1821), p. 68, and his "Curtain Tune" on pp. 68-69 (on p. 9 they are carelessly mis-identified as from *Psyche*). The "Lilk" and part of the "Curtain Tune" are also reprinted in *The Oxford History of Music* (London, 1901-5), III, 288-90.

[26] In "The Music of Shadwell's *Tempest*."

[27] This last is, of course, by Pietro Reggio, as Barclay Squire observed (*Musical Quarterly*, VII, 571); see above, Section IV.

VII

The text of *Songs and Masques* differs from corresponding passages in *The Ariels Songs, Songs by Reggio,* "The Vocal Musick in the Tempest," and the quarto editions of *The Tempest,* beginning with that of 1674, in details of spelling, punctuation, and capitalization; there are also differences in the use of contractions. These are unimportant, as is such a variant as that in the fourth line of Masque I, where *Songs and Masques* reads "must" and the quartos "does". In the song books, phrases are often repeated that are printed only once elsewhere. On the other hand, *Songs and Masques* twice repeats a passage in the form of a refrain that the quartos print only once, as at line 11, "*Chor. of all.* Who in earth all others, &c." Where the dialogue of the play intrudes and breaks off the action in Masque I, *Songs and Masques* indicates the omission of the dialogue by such a warning as, "*Here they are interrupted by the Speakers.*" Once *Songs and Masques* introduces a word as if to improve the meter, in line 16 of Masque I, "And their Crowns unjustly *would* get."

It is clear from a collation of *Songs and Masques* with the quartos that it was not printed from any of them or used in printing them. The speech-tags in Masque I provide sufficient evidence. *Songs and Masques* assigns the third speech (actually, the masque was sung) to "3. *Dev*[*il*]"; the quartos, to "1. Dev." The next speech in *Songs and Masques* is given to "4. *Dev.*"; in the quartos, to "3. Dev." Again, in line 9, "2. *Dev.*" sings, "Who in Earth," but in the quartos the line belongs to "3. Dev." The four-line passage beginning, "And barbarous monarchs" (lines 15-18), is divided equally in *Songs and Masques* between "2. *Dev.*" and "3. *Dev.*"; the quartos give it all to "2. Dev." And so throughout the masque. Curiously enough, however, there is close typographical resemblance in Masque II between *Songs and Masques* and Q 1674.[28] There is likewise a similarity in the spacing of the lines in the two books. The resemblances must be casual, however, for there is a verbal difference in line 9 (*Songs and Masques,* "Surges"; Q 1674, "bosome"), and there are numerous differences in spelling, punctuation, and capitalization. *Songs and Masques* must have been printed from an independent transcript of part of the theatrical manuscript. This conclusion is supported by a comparison of the stage directions. *Songs and Masques* and *The Ariels Songs* are likewise mutually independent.[29]

[28] See above, Section I.
[29] It has already been remarked that the Libri Manuscript of Pelham Humphrey's songs

Sources of the Words and Music in the Operatic *Tempest*

Music	Composer	Song	Author	Location
"The First Musick"	Locke			The English Opera
"Galliard"	,,			,,
"Gavot"	,,			,,
"The Second Musick"	,,			,,
"Lilk"	,,			,,
"Curtain Tune"	,,			,, *Mus. Antiqua*, Oxford [*Hist. Mus.*
"The First Act Tune"	,,			,, ,, ,, [*Hist. Mus.*
		I shall no more to Sea	Shakespeare (?)	Folios, Quartos
		The Master, the Swabber	Shakespeare (?)	,,
		No more Dams I'll make	Shakespeare	,,
Masque in Act II	Humphrey	Where does the black Fiend	Shadwell (?)	Words, *S. and M.*, Q 1674, *etc.*; Music, Libri MS.
	Reggio	Arise, arise!	Shadwell	Words, *S. and M.*; Music, *Songs by Reggio*, Libri MS. (where attrib. to Humphrey), B.M. Add. MS. 19759 (attrib. to Grabu), B.M. Add. MS. 29397 (to Reggio)
"The Second Act Tune"	Locke			The English Opera

Music	*Composer*	*Song*	*Author*	*Location*
	Banister	Come unto these yellow sands	Shakespeare	Words, Ff., Qq., S. *and* M.; music, *Ariels Songs*
	Banister	Full fathom five	Shakespeare	Words, Ff., Qq., S. *and* M.; music, *Ariels Songs*
	Banister	Dry those eyes	Dryden (?)	Words, Qq., S. *and* M.; music, *Ariels Songs*, B.M. Add. MS. 29396, f. 112v (C. L. Day, *The Songs of John Dryden*)
	Banister	Go thy way	Dryden (?)	Words, Qq., *Windsor Drollery* (1672), *teste* Day, S. *and* M.; music, *Ariels Songs*
"The Third Act Tune"	Locke			*The English Opera*
		We want Musick	Dryden (?)	Qq.
"Dorinda Lamenting"	Hart	Adieu to the Pleasures		Words, *A Perfect Collection of the Several Songs Now in Mode* (1675, two issues; a different version, *teste* Day and Murrie); music, *Ariels Songs*, *Choice Ayres* (1676), *Wit and Mirth* (1699, etc.), *Songs Compleat, Pleasant and Divertive* (1719), etc.
"The Fourth Act Tune"	Locke			*The English Opera*
Masque in Act V	Humphrey	My Lord: Great Neptune	Shadwell (?)	Words, S. *and* M., Q 1674, *etc.*; music, Libri MS.
	Humphrey	Where the bee sucks	Shakespeare	Ff., Qq., S. *and* M.; music, *Ariels Songs*
"The Conclusion"	Locke			*The English Opera*

If *Songs and Masques* was printed from an independent transcript of the playhouse manuscript, it may well represent the promptbook at the time of the first performance or soon afterward. At this time, it will be remembered, there were thirty singers, some of them regular members of the company, but others, and these the stellar performers, from the choir of the Chapel Royal. Now in Masque I, as printed in *Songs and Masques,* there are four singing Devils, as compared with only three in Q 1674. This difference is almost certainly not to be explained as an error by the transcriber or the printer, for although she gives no details Mlle. Pereyra notes that in the Libri Manuscript of this masque there are not only variants in the text but, even more important, "quelques différences de distribution parmi des interlocuteurs."[30] The redistribution of lines in Q 1674 is most easily explained as the result of a reduction of personnel, for although on 16 May Charles II was still directing that William Turner, James Hart, and other singers on loan from the Chapel Royal should remain in London to perform in *The Tempest,* this arrangement was to continue only for the period of "his Majesty's absence from Whitehall." The detail cited is not in itself important, but it testifies to the independence of *Songs and Masques* and its priority over Q 1674.

VIII

It may be noted that "*Song IV in Eccho. in Act IV*" is incorrectly attributed. It must be sung in III. iii (*sic*); see Q 1674, p. 42.

The two copies of *Songs and Masques* differ in line 9 of Masque I, where copy 1 fails to show the *r* in "torments", and in the two parts of the bottom rule on A4^v. In copy 2, the short segment is separated from the long by about 5 mm.

---

in *The Tempest* is not a theatrical manuscript. From Mlle. Pereyra's description it is evident that it is not even a transcript made in the theater—Reggio's setting of "Arise, arise" is out of place and seems to be attributed to Humphrey; there are obvious errors in the assignment of lines and numerous failures to identify the singers. Verbal differences between *Songs and Masques* and that portion of Masque II which Barclay Squire reprints may be ignored.

The source of the words printed in Reggio's *Songs* is unknown. They differ from those in *Songs and Masques* only in spelling, punctuation, capitalization, and contractions.

[30] The Libri Manuscript is not demonstrably reliable in its allocation of lines. In Masque II, for example, most of the singers are unidentified, but in several instances the identification is clearly erroneous, as when the passage beginning, "Great nephew Eolus," is indicated as a solo by Neptune instead of an "ensemble" with Amphitrite: the manuscript notation is, "*Verse for a bass alone.*" A more trustworthy detail is contained in the notation that the Chorus of Tritons and Nereides is "*à trois voix.*"

Songs and Masques

IN THE

TEMPEST.

Masque I. *in Act* II

1. *Dev.*   Where does the black Fiend, Ambition, reside,
          With the mischievous Devil of Pride?
2. *Dev.*   In the lowest and darkest Caverns of Hell,
          Both Pride and Ambition must dwell.
3. *Dev.*   Who are the chief Leaders of the damn'd Host?
4. *Dev.*   Proud Monarchs, who tyrannize most.
1. *Dev.*   Damned Princes there
          The worst of torments bear.
2. *Dev.*   Who in Earth all others in pleasures excell,
          Must feel the worst torments of Hell.
Chor. of all.   Who in earth all others, &c.
          Here they are interrupted by the Speakers.
1. *Dev.*   Tyrants by whom their Subjects bleed,
          Should in pains all others exceed.
2. *Dev.*   And barbarous Monarchs, who their Neighbours invade,
          And their Crowns unjustly would get:
3. *Dev.*   And such who their Brothers to death have betray'd,
          In Hell upon burning Thrones shall be set.
2. *Dev.*   In Hell, in Hell, with flames they shall reign,
      And for ever, for ever shall suffer the pain.
Chor. of all.   In Hell, in Hell, &c.
          Here they are interrupted again.
1. *Dev.*   Who are the Pillars of a Tyrants Court?
2. *Dev.*   Rapine and Murder his Crown must support.
          His cruelty does tread

On Orphans tender breaſts, and Brothers dead.

3. *Dev.*   Can Heav'n permit such Crimes shou'd be
　　　　　　Attended with felicity?

4. *Dev.*   No: Tyrants their Scepters uneasily bear,
　　　　　　In the midſt of their Guards they their consciences fear;
　　　　　　Care their minds when they wake unquiet will keep,
　　　　　　And we with dire Visions diſturb all their sleep.

Chor. of all.   Care their minds, &c.

　　　　　　　　　　　　　　　　Here they are interrupted again.

1. *Dev.*   Say, say, shall we bear these bold Mortals from hence.
2. *Dev.*   No, no, let us show their degrees of offence.
3. *Dev.*   Let's muſter their crimes up on every side,
　　　　　　And first let's discover their Pride.

Enter Pride.

Pride.   Lo here, here is pride, who firſt led them aſtray,
　　　　　And did to Ambition their minds then betray.

Enter Fraud.

Fraud.   And Fraud does next appear,
　　　　　　Their wandring ſteps who led,
　　　　　　When they from vertue fled,
　　　　　They in my crooked paths their course did ſteer.

Enter Rapine.

Rapine.   From Fraud to Force they soon arrive,
　　　　　　Where Rapine did their actions drive.

Enter Murder.

Murder.   There long they could not ſtay,
　　　　　　Down the ſteep Hill they run
　　　　　And to perfect the mischiefs which they had begun,
　　　　　　To murder they bent all their way.

Chorus of all.   Around, around we pace
　　　　　　About this cursed place;
　　　　　　While thus we circle in
　　　　　　These Mortals and their sin.

　　　　　　　　　　　　　　　　　　　　　　　[Exeunt.

Fifth Devil rises and sings.

5. *Dev.*   Arise, arise, ye subterranean Winds,
              More to diſtract their guilty minds;
          And all ye filthy Damps and Vapours rise,
      Which use t'infect the Earth, and trouble all the Skies.
              Rise you, from whom devouring Plagues have birth,
              You that i'th' vaſt and hollow womb of Earth;
              Engender Earthquakes, make whole Countries shake,
              And ſtately Cities into Desarts turn:
      And you who feed the flames by which Earths Entrals burn.
              Ye raging Winds, whose rapid force can make
              All but the fix'd and solid Centre shake.
              Come drive these Wretches to that part o'th' Isle,
                  Where Nature never yet did smile.
              Cause Fogs and Storms, Whirlwinds and Earthquakes there,
              There let 'em howl and languish in despair;
              Rise, and obey the powerful Prince o'th' Air.
                                          Dance of Winds.

                    Song I. *in Act* III.

              Come unto these yellow Sands,
                  And then take hands,
              Cursy'd when you have, and kiss'd;
                  The wild Waves whiſt.
              Foot it featly here and there,
                  And sweet Sprights the burthen bear.
              Hark! hark!
                  Bow waugh, the Watch-dogs bark.
              Bow waugh. Hark! hark! I hear
              The ſtrain of ſtrutting *Chanticleer*,
                  Cry, *Cock a doodle doo.*

                    Song II. *in Act* III.

              Full fathom five thy Father lies,
                  Of his Bones is Coral made:
              Those are Pearls that were his Eyes,
                  Nothing of him that does fade.
              But does suffer a Sea-change

Into something rich and ſtrange:
Sea-Nymphs hourly ring his Knell;
Hark! now I hear 'em, *Ding dong Bell.*

Song III. *in Act* III.

Dry those eyes which are o'rflowing,
    All your ſtorms are overblowing;
While you in this Isle are biding,
You shall Feaſt without providing:
Every Dainty you can think of,
Every Wine which you would drink of
Shall be yours: all want shall shun you,
Ceres blessing so light on you.

Song IV. *in Eccho. in Act* IV.

Ferdinand.   Go thy way.
Ariel.   Go thy way.
Ferd. Why shouldſt thou ſtay?
Ariel.   Why shouldſt thou ſtay?
Ferd. Where the Winds whiſtle, and where the Streams creep.
Ariel.   Where the Winds, &c.
Ferd. Under yonder Willow-tree fain would I sleep.
Ariel.   Under yonder Willow, &c.
Ferd. Then let me alone, for 'tis time to be gone.
Ariel.   Then let me alone, &c.
Ferd. What Cares or Pleasures can be in this Isle.
Ariel.   ·What Cares or, &c.
Ferd.   Within this desart place
            There lives no Humane Race.
Ariel.   Within this desart, &c.
Ferd. Fate cannot frown here, nor kind Fortune smile.
Ariel.   Kind Fortune smiles, and she
            Has yet in ſtore for thee
            Some ſtrange felicity.
    Follow me, follow me, and thou shalt see.

Masque II. *in Act* V.

Neptune *and* Amphitrite,⎱ *rise out of the Sea in a Chariot drawn with*
Oceanus *and* Tethys   ⎰ *Sea-horses: on each side of the Chariot,*
    Sea-gods and Goddesses, Tritons and Nereides.

Amph.	My Lord: Great *Neptune,* for my sake,
	Of these bright Beauties pity take:
	And to the reſt allow
	Your mercy too.
	Let this inraged Element be ſtill,
	Let *Eolus* obey my will:
	Let him his Boyſtrous Prisoners safely keep
	In their dark Caverns, and no more
	Let 'em diſturb the Surges of the Deep,
	Till these arrive upon their wish'd-for Shore.
Neptune.	So much my *Amphitrite'*s Love I prize,
	That no commands of hers I can despise.
	Tethys no furrows now shall wear,
	Oceanus no wrinkles on his brow,
	Let your sereneſt looks appear!
	Be calm and gentle now.
Nep. &	Be calm, ye great Parents of the Flouds and the Springs,
Amph.	While each *Nereide* and *Triton* Plays, Revels, and Sings.
Oceanus.	Confine the roaring Winds, and we
	Will soon obey you cheerfully.
Chorus of	Ty up the Winds, and we'l obey,
Tritons	Upon the Flouds we'l sing and play,
and Ner.	And celebrate a *Halcyon* day. [*Dance.*
Nept.	Great Nephew *Æolus* make no noise,
	Muzle your Roaring Boys. [*Æolus appears.*
Amph.	Let 'em not bluſter to disturb our ears,
	Or ſtrike these Noble Passengers with fears.
Nept.	Afford 'em onely such an easie Gale,
	As pleasantly may swell each Sail.
Amph.	While fell Sea-monsters cause intestine jars,
	This Empire you invade with forreign Warrs.
Nept.	But you shall now be still,
	And shall obey my *Amphitrites* will.
Æolus de-	You I'll obey, who at one stroke can make,
scends.	With your dread Trident the whole Earth to quake.
	Come down, my Bluſterers, swell no more,
	Your ſtormy rage give o'er } *Winds from*
	Let all black Tempeſts cease— } *the four Cor-*
	And let the troubled Ocean reſt: } *ners appear.*

Let all the Sea enjoy as calm a peace,
As where the *Halcyon* builds her quiet Neſt.
　　To your Prisons below,
　　Down, down you muſt go:
You in the Earths Entrals your Revels may keep;
But no more till I call shall you trouble the Deep.
　　　　　　　　　　　　　　　　[*Winds fly down.*
Now they are gone, all ſtormy Wars shall cease:
Then let your Trumpeters proclaim a Peace.

Amph.　　Let your *Tritons,* my Sons, your Trumpets sound,
And let the noise from Neighbouring Shores rebound.

Chorus. {
Sound a Calm.
Sound a Calm.
Sound a Calm.
　　　a Calm.
Sound a Calm.
}
　　　　　　　　　[*A short Symphony of soft Musick, like Trumpets.*

Nept.　　See, see, the Heavens smile, all your troubles are paſt,
Your joys by black Clowds shall no more be o'rcaſt.

Amph.　　On this barren Isle ye shall lose all your fears,
Leave behind all your sorrows, and banish your cares.

Both.　　And your Loves and your Lives shall in safety enjoy;
No influence of Stars shall your quiet deſtroy.

Chor. of　{ And your Loves, &c.
all.　　 { No influence, &c.

Oceanus.　We'l safely convey you to your own happy Shore,
And yours and your Countrey's soft peace we'l reſtore.

Tethys.　To treat you bleſt Lovers, as you sail on the Deep,
The *Trytons* and *Sea-Nymphs* their Revels shall keep.

Both.　{ On the swift Dolphins backs they shall sing and shall play;
　　 { They shall guard you by night, and delight you by day.

Chorus of　{ On the swift, &c.
all.　　 { And shall guard, &c.
　　　　　　　　　　　　　　　　　　　　　Dance.

Song V. *in Aɛt* V.

Where the Bee sucks, there suck I,
In a Cowslips Bell I lie;
There I cowch when Owls do cry,

On the Swallows wings I flie,
After Summer merrily:
Merrily, merrily shall I live now,
Under the Blossom that hangs on the Bough.

FINIS.

The Colophon of the Second
Folio of Shakespeare

[1954]

FOLLOWING the explicit of *Cymbeline* in the Second Folio, on the recto of leaf 3d4, are four horizontal rules, about 25 mm. apart, extending the width of the type-page. And between the third and fourth rules is the familiar two-line colophon: "Printed at London by *Thomas Cotes*, for *Iohn Smethwick, William Aspley, Richard Hawkins, Richard Meighen,* and *Robert Allot*, 1632."[1] One copy of the Second Folio is known that lacks the colophon. It was purchased by a Dr. Bulley on 25 March 1876 from Sotheran for £48, and it is now No. 34 in the Folger Shakespeare Library. Curiously enough, Dr. Bulley possessed another remarkable Second Folio (No. 35 in the Folger collection): in it the colophon appears twice, once in the normal position, and once on 3d2, where it is overprinted on the text. A careful comparison shows that the two impressions are from the same setting of type and that this setting was used to print the colophon in all the other copies examined (sixty-seven copies in the Folger Shakespeare Library and the Henry E. Huntington Library; unfortunately, not all sixty-seven copies have the last leaf, 3d4).[2]

There are several possible explanations of the absence of a colophon from Folger copy 34. Perhaps it was not the original intention to have a colophon, though this seems unlikely in view of the fact that there

[1] Explicit, rules, and colophon are, of course, within the four rules which enclose the area used for the letterpress.

[2] At some time during the printing of the colophon a lead was inserted after the first comma in the second line, or else the type separated. In two out of every five copies examined there is a narrow space between the comma and *"Richard Meighen"*; in three, a somewhat wider space.

The Library, 5th ser., IX (1954), 199-200.

is a colophon in F1 and that six different men were associated in publishing the reprint. Or, second, the omission may have been accidental. Or, third, the details of publication and distribution may not have been worked out when the printing of 3d4 and its conjugate was begun.[3]

In any case, since only one copy is known without a colophon, it is tempting to suppose that after a few copies of the forme in question had been printed, the presswork was interrupted so that the type of the colophon might be inserted, *i.e.,* the colophon was added by means of a routine stop-press correction. Such an explanation might be accepted readily without further consideration were it not for the other Bulley-Folger copy, in which the colophon is also printed over the text of 3d2.

It seems much more probable that the Second Folio, every copy of it, was first printed without a colophon. Then the type of the colophon was set, and the sheets containing 3d4 were run through the press a second time. By accident, one sheet was missed; later it was bound up in what is now the Bulley copy, Folger No. 34. Again by accident, a copy of the sheet containing 3d2 was run through the press a second time, with the result that the colophon is overprinted on the text; this sheet, too, was later bound up in the Bulley-Folger copy No. 35.

The insertion of the colophon in the manner described is proved almost beyond question by the fact that in the copies examined the two lines of type do not always appear in precisely the same position in relation to the vertical and horizontal rules that enclose them. Instead, they shift as much as two mm. to right or left, and up or down. The vertical movement is often like a see-saw, with first one end of the lines high and then the other.[4] Such displacements would scarcely be possible if the type of the colophon had been locked in the chase with the rules and the other letterpress on the page.

Memoranda reveal that Dr. Bulley was aware of the extraordinary nature of his Folio with no colophon. One can only marvel at his good fortune in obtaining a copy equally rare in having two colophons.

[3] Sir Walter Greg offers the plausible suggestion that a general colophon may have been omitted so that each publisher might insert one of his own to correspond to his imprint.

[4] In contrast, the word FINIS near the top of the page remains constant in its relation to the adjacent rules.

A Miscalculation in the Printing
of the Third Folio

[1954]

HE 1663 issue of the Third Folio edition of Shakespeare's plays, as William A. Jackson first pointed out,[1] was the work of three printers. To Roger Daniel are attributed quires A-E, I-Z, 2G-3A, and 3P-4E; quires 3B-3H are identified as by Alice Warren; and quires F-H, 2A-2F, and 3I-3O are by an unidentified printer.[2] It is not my purpose to question these attributions; there are many signs that the work was distributed as indicated.[3]

The accident—or miscalculation—to which attention is now directed occurred in connection with the printing of *Richard II* and *1 Henry IV*. The former begins on 2D6 and concludes on 2F5, falling wholly within the second section of the book set by the unknown printer. *1 Henry IV*, which follows on 2F5[v] and ends on 2H6, is thus the work of Roger

---

[1] *The Carl H. Pforzheimer Library, English Literature, 1475-1700* (New York, 1940), III, 939.

[2] There is some reason to think the third printer was Thomas Ratcliffe, but proof is lacking.

[3] Chief among these is the evidence of the head-ornaments. Each of the twenty-three plays in sections assigned to Roger Daniel has above its head-title a rectangular ornament measuring 101 × 28 mm., flanked by a rose and a thistle, each 10 × 24 mm. Alice Warren's four plays are alike in using as a head-ornament a rectangular piece about 136 × 20 mm. of conventional design. Instead of headpieces, the unidentified printer used rows of type-ornaments: in two plays, a double row of acorns; in two others, a double row of ornaments with a line of horizontal acorns between; in one play, two rows of the same ornaments without the acorns; in two plays, three rows of the same ornament; and in the last two plays, two rows of pineapple-like ornaments with a line of horizontal thistles in between. Slight variations in the arrangement show that the type-ornaments were set anew for almost every play. It may be noted that in the first setting of type-ornaments at the head of *1 Henry IV* the intermediate line of acorns was omitted—see copy 1 in the Folger Shakespeare Library; all other copies examined have the acorns.

The Library, 5th ser., IX (1954), 129-33.

Daniel (2G1-2H6), except for the first three pages (2F5ᵛ-6ᵛ) which were set by the unknown printer. It is not surprising, therefore, that the head-title of the play has above it two rows of type-ornaments with a line of horizontal acorns sandwiched between.[4]

One copy of the Third Folio has come to attention which, in addition to the normal leaves of quire 2F, has bound between 2F5 and 2F6 two leaves that appear to be unique. Through the courtesy of the owner, Mr. John Francis Neylan of San Francisco, I have been privileged to examine the Folio and describe it.[5] The peculiarities of the copy were referred to in the catalogue of the Jerome Kern sale in 1929,[6] but no explanation was attempted at that time or subsequently.

The two leaves, which may be designated X and Y, have every appearance of being conjugate, but the binding—crimson levant morocco by Rivière—is so tight that one cannot be positive. The chainlines in each are about 25 mm. apart, and the texture and color seem to be the same. The watermark in leaf Y—there is none in X—resembles, but does not exactly match, one[7] that occurs later in the volume (see, for example, leaf 3P4 in the Bridgewater-Huntington copy). It is a narrow shield, about 55×94 mm., with multiple fleurs-de-lis, not easy to trace because of the printed text, but resembling Heawood type 1753.

Leaf X has a blank recto, smudged in several places with ink; its verso bears the text of the first page of *1 Henry IV*. On leaf Y are the second and third pages of text of the play. The leaves are unsigned, but the printed pages are numbered correctly, 350, 351, and 352. Instead of the three lines of type-ornaments found in normal gatherings at the top of the first page of text, there is Roger Daniel's familiar ornament flanked by rose and thistle. The head-title, too, is different. Normally it runs as follows: "The First Part of Henry the Fourth, | with the Life and Death of HENRY | Sirnamed HOTSPURRE." On Xᵛ it is: "The first part of HENRY the Fourth: with the | Battel at *Shrewsbury,* between the King, and Lord *Henry* | *Piercy,* sirnamed HOTSPURRE."

---

[4] See n. 3 above for reference to a copy without the acorns.

[5] It is a pleasure to record my gratitude also to Mr. Warren Howell of San Francisco, who first brought the book to my attention and facilitated the examination of it.

[6] Part 2, J-Z: "Leaves Ff5 and Ff6 in duplicate, the two extra leaves being variants, differing somewhat in set-up, in the decorated chapter-headings, and with the recto of Ff5 blank instead of carrying the conclusion of *Richard the Second.*"

[7] There are half a dozen or more different watermarks in the mixed lot of paper used in printing the Folio. Their distribution in the copies examined suggests the possibility that all the presswork was done in one shop.

And the running-titles, which on the usual 2F6, recto and verso, are *"The Life and Death of* Henry *the Fourth."*, are on Y *"The first part of King Henry the Fourth."* As for the text, although the last lines in column two of X^v, Y^r, and Y^v agree respectively with those on 2F5^v, 2F6^r, and 2F6^v, it is obvious at a glance that there have been two completely different settings of type. The first line of text on 2F5^v begins with a factotum *S;* that on X^v with an ornamental initial.[8] The centered stage direction at the head of I. ii on 2F6 is *"Enter Henry Prince of Wales, Sir John Fal-* | *staffe, and Pointz."*, set on two lines; that on Y^r, *"Enter Prince of Wales, and Sir Iohn Falstaffe."*, set on one line.

Collation of the text verifies the first impression. At I. ii. 40 (using the numbering of Hemingway's New Variorum Edition), for example, the usual Third Folio reading, which for convenience will be identified as F3, is, "As is the honey"; in XY, "As the hony of *Hybla."* At I. ii. 85-86, F3: "Thou didst well: for no man regards it."; XY: "Thou didst well: for wisdome cries out in the streets, and no man regards it." In I. ii. 92, XY supply "By the Lord,", which is omitted from F3. And at I. ii. 147, XY omit "true,", which is present in F3. In these and other readings, F3 agrees with F2, which in turn follows F1, whereas XY agree with Qq 1622, 1632, and 1639. One line, I. i. 14, supplies the proof that XY were set from a copy of Q 1639: this reads "mutuall" in all the early editions except Q 1639, where "naturall" has been substituted. In XY the word is "natural".

Why should Daniel, whose compositors had already set eleven plays from F2 and were to set twelve more, suddenly abandon his folio copy and turn to the most recent quarto? Why, indeed, should Daniel's shop set any of the first three pages of text of *1 Henry IV,* when these comprised the last three pages of gathering 2F, part of the second batch of text allocated to the unknown printer? The answer, I suggest, is that the method of distributing the work among three shops[9] was to break up a copy of F2 and parcel it out, several quires in a batch. Thus Daniel received (or retained) quires A-E, comprising three complete plays,

[8] This initial *S* appears again on ¶ E2 in the first line of *The Yorkshire Tragedy,* one of the apocryphal plays, all printed by Daniel, that were added in the 1664 issue of the Third Folio. The only other initial *S* in the text of the Folio occurs on D2, at the beginning of *The Merry Wives of Windsor,* also printed by Daniel, but it is from a different alphabet.

[9] It is immaterial at the moment whether the publisher had an arrangement with only one printer, who in turn secured the assistance of two other shops, or whether the publisher dealt directly with all three printers.

The Tempest, The Two Gentlemen, and *Merry Wives.*[10] The second batch went to the unknown printer, quires F-H, containing *Measure for Measure* and all but the last four pages of *The Comedy of Errors.* The next eleven quires, with eight complete plays, were Daniel's, the last of them, *Twelfth Night,* ending on Z6^r and leaving Z6^v blank. The unknown printer received the next six quires, 2A-2F. What happened later in the Folio is not necessarily relevant, though Alice Warren's section does begin with the Prologue to *Troilus and Cressida* on 3B1.

It is helpful now to turn to *The Comedy of Errors,* where the text of a play was divided between two printers without, as far as is known, causing any complications. The unidentified printer of the major portion of the play used two settings of the running-title and two sets of rules throughout quire H (except, of course, on H1). Different rules and different settings of the running-titles appear, as might be expected, in the last four pages of text of *Errors, i.e.,* in I1^r-I2^v, set in Daniel's shop. There is another difference: the vertical rules which enclose the two columns of text are some 2 mm. closer together in Daniel's pages— *c.* 85 mm. as against *c.* 87 mm. The same difference in measurement is observable in all the work in this book done in the two shops.

To return to the problem raised by leaves X and Y, it appears that, when the compositors in the unidentified shop finished setting the text of *Richard II* on 2F5^r, they proceeded to complete the quire by setting also the text of the first three pages of *1 Henry IV.* Eventually the quire was printed as set. This is proved not only by the appearance of the three rows of type-ornaments above the head-title of *1 Henry IV* but by the distance between the vertical rules on 2F5^v-6^v, which is *c.* 87 mm.

It appears, further, that in Daniel's shop the compositors set the bulk of the text of *1 Henry IV* on 2G1^r-2H6^r, using as copy e1^r-f6^r of F2. Desiring to supply the missing portions, and lacking a copy of leaves d5-6 of F2, someone in the shop turned to a copy of Q 1639 and from it set the text of three folio pages. Daniel's headpiece was then inserted, a head-title was improvised from the title-page of Q 1639,[11] and running-

---

[10] The text of F3 is a page-for-page and, except at one point, a quire-for-quire reprint of F2. The signatures agree from A through 2A. Then F3 has 2B^8 instead of 2B^6 2C^2. Thereafter the signatures are entirely different. To avoid confusion I use here the signatures of F3.

[11] The relevant portion of the title-page of Q 1639 is given below, ignoring italics; words retained in Daniel's head-title are underscored: "The Historie of <u>Henry the Fourth</u>: with the Battell at Shrewsbury, betweene the King, and Lord <u>Henry Percy</u>, surnamed <u>Henry</u> <u>Hotspur</u> of the North."

titles were provided that agree in wording with those that had been used in quires 2G and 2H for the remainder of the play.[12] Then, it must be assumed, one or more trial pulls were taken,[13] using three pages of a sheet of paper and leaving the first recto blank to receive the last page of text of *Richard II* which was being set in the unidentified shop. The leaves X and Y in the Kern-Neylan Third Folio are the only known survivals. By accident a trial sheet must have become mixed with the other sheets of the book and eventually bound up and preserved, much as were three of the known proof-sheets of the First Folio.[14]

When the time came to print quire 2F, the setting of type of 2F5^v-6^v by the unknown printer was used and that by Daniel was rejected. This may have been done because the unknown printer stood upon his right to receive payment for setting all of quire 2F or, less likely, because a consistent reprint of the F2 text was preferred to the mixed text Daniel's setting of the first three pages would have produced. On the other hand, if the unidentified printer did the presswork on quire 2F, as well as the composition, the job might have been completed before Daniel's abortive setting of 2F5^v-6^v came to notice.

The retention of Daniel's setting of the first three pages of *1 Henry IV* in the Third Folio would have given a text somewhat closer to Shakespeare's intention than that now in F3, but it is amusing to speculate on how editors would have accounted for this unique departure from F2.

[12] The vertical rules in X and Y are *c.* 85 mm. distant, as in the other pages set by Daniel.

[13] Trial pulls because, of course, the text printed on X and Y would not normally appear on the same sheet of a folio in sixes. That on X^v corresponds to the letterpress of F5^v, a part of the outer forme of the middle sheet of the quire; that on Y, recto and verso, to a half, respectively, of the inner and outer formes of the outside sheet. It is difficult to imagine why these three pages of text should be imposed and printed on—presumably—a single sheet of paper except for purposes of proofing or as a matter of record.

[14] Whether leaves X and Y have always been a part of the Kern-Neylan copy or are a late insertion, it is impossible to say, for the history of the copy before the Kern sale is unknown.

Elizabeth, Essex, and James

[1959]

T does not seem to have been noticed that the device invented by the nobility of England to assure Queen Elizabeth the safe enjoyment of her crown was later adapted, with a minimum of variation, by James VI of Scotland to help assure his eventual succession to that crown. A series of events began in the 1580's that has a remarkable parallel in 1598. Philip II of Spain set a price on the head of William of Orange, and in March 1582 a fanatic shot and almost killed him. In the spring of 1583 it was learned in England that the murder of Elizabeth was being planned by the Duke of Guise. And in July 1584 a second fanatic shot William of Orange and succeeded in killing him. The alarm in England can be understood by those who remember the assassination of King Feisal of Iraq in July 1958 and President Nasser's denunciation by radio of King Hussein of Jordan that was followed by an attempt upon his life.

To English Protestants, whose sole shield was the life of their Queen, the assassination of William the Silent administered the severest shock they had yet received. The powers of darkness appeared to be concentrating against them: villainy without limit or scruple. And as though to emphasize the alarm and horror, a few weeks later, when the Jesuit Creighton was seized aboard a ship bound for Scotland, further details came to light of the wide-flung Catholic conspiracy.

The crisis called for new legislation. But as statesmen reflected on the situation, they decided that delay was dangerous. Something must be done at once. The outlook was indeed preposterous. If the Queen were slain before Parlia-

Elizabethan and Jacobean Studies Presented to Frank Percy Wilson, ed. Herbert Davis and Helen Gardner (Oxford, 1959), pp. 219-30.

ment met, there would be a constitutional vacuum in the land. Royal officials would immediately lose their positions and all authority derived from the Queen's commission would lapse. There would be no Privy Council, no judges, no Lords Lieutenant, no justices. With the government in eclipse, the way would be open for the organized forces of conspiracy, centered on the Catholic Mary Queen of Scots. It was an invitation to speedy murder.[1]

Within a few weeks, the Privy Council devised a Bond of Association that was circulated throughout the country, the signers of which pledged their lives, their fortunes, and their sacred honors to defend the Queen and to pursue implacably anyone who might attempt to assassinate Elizabeth or remotely benefit by such an attempt.

Put bluntly, this meant that should an attempt be made on Elizabeth's life, Mary Queen of Scots was to be destroyed, whether a party to the action or not. And not only Mary: though the wording may seem ambiguous, it was held to involve the destruction also of her son, certainly if he claimed the throne. The inclusion of James is sufficiently explained by his place in the scheme of the conspirators and by the distrust his actions bred in England. (Neale, p. 17)

A copy of the Bond dated 19 October at Hampton Court bears the signatures of thirteen members of the Privy Council, and many other manuscript copies are extant.[2] It appeared in print first in 1598 in the second part of *A Pithie Exhortation,* a posthumously published book by Peter Wentworth that will be discussed later. The Bond being informal and extra-legal, when Parliament met in November its gravest concern was for the drafting and adoption of legislation that would embody the main purposes of the Bond.[3] The bill provided, in effect, that any attempt upon the life of Elizabeth for the purpose of advancing the claims of Mary Stuart would disable the Queen of Scots and would authorize pursuit of her to the death, whether or not she were a party to the plot. It provided, further, that her heir, James VI, would be dis-

---

[1] J. E. Neale, *Elizabeth I and her Parliaments 1584-1601* (London, 1957), II, 15-16.

[2] C.S.P. Dom., Elizabeth, vol. CLXXIV, no. 1. See also nos. 2-18; vol. CLXXV, nos. 4 and 9, dated 6 and 20 November; vol. CLXXVI, no. 11, dated 15 January 1585; Addenda, vol. XXVIII, nos. 101, 102, and 108, of various dates. The original minute corrected by Walsingham is in vol. CLXXIII, no. 81; no. 82 is a revised draft; no. 83, with Walsingham's corrections, is described as the final version. Other copies are in no. 87. The reasons for revision are discussed by Neale, pp. 16-17. The copy among the Egerton papers, bearing the contemporaneous endorsement "Lincolnes Inne" is printed in vol. XII of the Camden Society Publications (1840), pp. 108-11. It is signed by Thomas Egerton and ninety-four others.

[3] See Neale, pp. 28 ff., for an account of the debates and a discussion of the statute as adopted.

abled in his claim, but it did not make his assassination mandatory—indeed, Elizabeth might in certain conditions restore his title.

It is not a little ironic that when Elizabeth's age and infirmity aroused the hopes of all pretenders to the succession, James VI should have turned to the English Bond of Association that touched him so nearly and should have fashioned from it an instrument to support his claim.

The similarity of the documents came to my attention when examining Folger MS. V. b. 214, a large folio compiled by someone deeply interested in the affairs of the Earl of Essex, perhaps by one of his clerks. Inserted after fol. 201, which has on its verso the conclusion of the Scottish Bond, is a fold of smaller paper bearing the text of the English Bond. The insert was whipstitched into the book at a very early date, for both bonds are listed on the contents leaf, the handwriting of which is largely the same as that of the document transcribed on fol. 214.[4] The volume contains transcripts in several hands. The first nine items listed in the table of contents are theological, relating chiefly to the Bishops' Articles. Then follow thirty-four other numbered items, most of which relate directly or indirectly to Robert Devereux, Earl of Essex. Among the exceptions are two sermons, an oration by the Queen, a letter from the Queen to Lady Norris, Sir Henry Savile's oration to the Queen, two memoranda by Thomas Digges, Spenser's *View of the Present State of Ireland* (which, it will be recalled, has a specific reference to Essex), and three letters of members of the Howard family. Following the items listed in the table are some twenty-five documents, many of them copies of letters from Essex to Elizabeth or the Privy Council, or from them to him about affairs in Ireland. One exception is a transcript of the instructions left by Philip II of Spain to his son, and another outlines a plan to permit Catholic worship in England. The volume concludes with a letter from Abdie Ashton, Essex's chaplain, to Sir Henry Wotton, dated from St. John's College on 3 June 1601.[5]

[4] The insert consists of a single sheet of paper, folded once. Each folio leaf measures about 200 × 275 mm. The paper, which has no watermark, is much lighter in weight than that of the book. Before being inserted, if one may judge by the darkening of the paper from wear and exposure, the document had existed independently for a considerable length of time. For convenience in filing or carrying about the person, it had been folded twice along the horizontal axis; then, at a later date, it was folded a third time, along the vertical axis. There is nothing to contradict the supposition that the transcript dates from 1584 or 1585.

[5] The volume is in the original calf binding, blind tooled on both covers. The paper is heavy and of uniform quality. The several watermarks are variants of Briquet's 11383 or 11387, a hand and flower *c.* 87 mm. tall, with a "3" at the base of the palm and below

Several names are scribbled inside the front cover, on the contents leaf, and on the otherwise blank verso of the last leaf, and inside the back cover: Thomas Scott (four times), G. Scott, Melton, Thomas Payne, Iacob Silver, and John Knatchbull. Some of the signatures are in italic, others in secretarial script. John Knatchbull's looks late enough to be the signature of Sir John Knatchbull (1636-96), but there is nothing to identify him. Of greater importance, it would seem, is the italic inscription at the top left corner of the front pastedown: *"Die Veneris Iulij 1° 1601 per me Richardũ Greeneũ."* It would simplify the story if this were the man named by the Earl of Essex in his letter of 11 July 1599 to the Privy Council: "In my last letter sent by Green from Wicklow, I gave an account of . . . my journey thro' Munster and Leinster. . . ."[6] But this Greene was probably the man mentioned in two letters from Essex's secretary, Henry Cuffe, to Edward Reynolds. In the first, dated 18 July 1599, Cuffe writes that, "In the last part of the journal sent unto you by Francis Greene, in setting down the skirmish near Arkloughe . . ."; and in the second, from Dublin on 4 August, he states that, "Since our last to you we have received from you two despatches, one from Fr. Greene, the other by Mr. Mynne's man." Though the wording is ambiguous in the letters of Essex and Cuffe, Francis Greene appears to have been only a messenger. Another man named Greene was also attached to Essex, as we learn from two other documents at Hatfield. On 26 February 1601 Captain Thomas Lee wrote to Sir Henry Lee, giving the names of participants in the conspiracy that were in durance, and among those "To be discharged without bonds, without indictment, arraignment, or fine" is one William Greene. He is referred to in more colorful detail, in a letter from William Reynolds to Sir Robert Cecil in February 1601, as follows:

There is one William Green, called Captain Green, in the Counter Poultry, who I hear was in the rebellious troop with the Earl of Essex; which Green (amongst divers of the Earl's men which have quarrelled with me) met me in

---

it the initials "PB" or "PR" (Neuberg, 1537; Hamburg, 1544-46; Coudenberg, Belgium, 1550). The first leaf contains an incomplete table of contents; the last leaf appears to be conjugate with the pastedown on the back cover. Leaves 1-3, 6, 110, 167, and 168 are wanting, as is a leaf between 198 and 199; the bottom of leaf 109 was torn away at an early date, but not before item 32, Sir Edward Dyer's letter to Sir Christopher Hatton, had been transcribed, for this title is listed in the table of contents and then marked through; what remains of the letter is likewise marked for cancellation.

[6] Thomas Birch, *Memoirs of the Reign of Queen Elizabeth* (London, 1754), II, 420.

Thames Street about two years ago, where he quarrelled with me. He is generally reported to be a cutpurse, picklock and thief, and lives by cosening shifts.[7]

It seems unlikely that the Richard Greene whose signature appears in the Folger manuscript is the Londoner who was the subject of two letters (7 and 17 October 1599) from Sir John Hart to Sir Robert Cecil; at some time prior to 7 October this man had been admitted to "our hospital," where he "uttered divers lewd speeches," in consequence of which he had been put in prison to await an expression of Cecil's pleasure.[8] No other man named Richard Greene has been traced in the records of the Earl of Essex or among the papers at Hatfield. The handwriting of the signature in the Folger manuscript occurs again in the italic heading of the Queen's letter to Essex on fol. 205^v. It is recognizable in several other places and, crucially, in the italic heading and in occasional italic words of the Scottish Bond. Since it may be presumed that the man who wrote the italic headings also transcribed the text of these documents in secretarial script, Greene's hand may be identified frequently in the latter part of the volume.

Is it stretching credibility too far to suggest that Essex had three different men named Greene in his employ and that this compilation, containing as it does so many letters to and from the Earl while he was in Ireland, besides numerous other documents that reflect his interests or relate to his activities, belonged to the unhappy favorite and was prepared by his agents?[9] The presence of Ashton's apologia to Wotton dated a little more than three months after the execution of Essex need not militate against such a supposition. Its inclusion may have been a last loyal gesture by a faithful servant. And the date of Richard Greene's signature inside the front cover, 1 July 1601, may be a record of the date when the volume came finally into his possession (though *per me* is not particularly appropriate if the phrase was intended to mean other than that Greene's name was written by himself).

It is well known that Essex had an active interest in the problem of the succession and dabbled in private diplomacy. As early as 1589 he sought to open a secret correspondence with James, but the attempt

[7] Historical Manuscripts Commission, Marquis of Salisbury, Hatfield, pt. IX, pp. 236 and 270; pt. XI, pp. 44, 87, and 93.

[8] *Hatfield Manuscripts,* IX, 367-73. The writer was almost certainly the Sir John Hart who was Lord Mayor of London in 1589 (Musgrave's *Obituary*).

[9] The frequent departure from chronological order of the Essex papers and the intermixture of extraneous documents are indications that the volume was not the Earl's official letter-book.

did not prosper. With the passage of years and the intensification of factional rivalries in England, James appears to have moved away from the Cecils and put more dependence in Essex. "By 1598," writes Helen Georgia Stafford, "their friendship had grown to such an extent that the French ambassador in London noticed how James entrusted to Essex all that he wished negotiated in the English court."[10] James could hardly forget the Earl's forthright avowal of friendship and loyalty:

such as I am, and all whatsoever I am (tho' perhaps a subject of small price) I consecrate unto your regal throne. . . . Neither do I doubt, that the minds of all my countrymen . . . will jointly unite their hopes in your majesty's noble person, as the only center, wherein our rest and happiness consist.[11]

Of all the Englishmen who favored the pretensions of James, the most outspoken was probably Peter Wentworth, stalwart advocate of the rights of Parliament and vigorous champion of a declaration in favor of James as heir to the crown. The first part of his *A Pithie Exhortation to her Maiestie for Establishing her Successor to the crowne. Whereunto is Added a Discourse containing the Authors opinion of the true and lawfull successor to her Maiestie* (STC 25245) was probably written in 1587. Copies were made surreptitiously and put into circulation, with the result that Wentworth was examined by the Privy Council in August 1591 and on the 15th of that month was imprisoned in the Gate House, where he remained until 11 February 1592. Wentworth was imprisoned again (25 February 1593) for his stubborn insistence upon a settlement of the succession and was still a prisoner nearly five years later (1597) when death came. It was during his imprisonment that he wrote the Discourse that forms Part II of *A Pithie Exhortation,* in answer to N. Doleman's (*i.e.,* the Jesuit Robert Parsons's) *A Conference about the Next Succession to the Crowne of Ingland* (1594).[12] Neale writes ("Wentworth," p. 182) that *A Pithie Exhortation* "was published surreptitiously by his friends in 1598, after his death." In the light of later investigations, this statement proves to be only partly accurate. The book was indeed printed first in 1598, but since the publication of Pollard

[10] *James VI of Scotland and the Throne of England* (New York, 1940), p. 203.

[11] Quoted by Stafford, p. 204, from Birch, *Memoirs,* I, 176. The letter, signed with the cipher "7," is dated from London, 17 May, with no indication of the year.

[12] J. E. Neale, "Peter Wentworth," *English Historical Review,* XXXIX (1924), 36-54, 175-205. He cites British Museum Add. MS. 24664, fol. 44ᵛ, for the date of Part I of *A Pithie Exhortation.* Neale seems not to have known that Doleman was a pseudonym used by Parsons.

and Redgrave's *Short-Title Catalogue* in 1926 it has been known that the place of publication was not London, as Neale seems to have assumed, but Edinburgh. This fact widens the field of conjecture. Wentworth's friends may have brought the manuscript to the attention of Robert Waldegrave, the putative printer,[13] or of James himself. Wentworth's ideas were well known, and a manuscript may have been picked up by one of the Scottish agents in London; Waldegrave may have had no other prompting than the desire for a book that would sell rapidly in Scotland. Or the Earl of Essex may have sent Wentworth's treatise to King James, for when it became impossible for Wentworth to present his treatise to the Queen during the sessions of Parliament in 1589, he considered asking the Earl of Essex to do this.[14] In any case, the book was a potent weapon of propaganda in James's active campaign to win the English crown.

Prompt reports went to London about the King's projects. Late in 1599, Cecil had a letter from George Nicolson in Edinburgh dated 27 November:

I hear, which I beseech your honor to keep close, that there is a general band, subscribed by many, and to be subscribed by all earls, lords, and barons: binding them, by solemn vow and oath, to serve the king with their lives, friends, heritages, goods, and gear; and to be ready in warlike furniture, for the same on all occasions, but especially for his claim to England.[15]

Nicolson's letter adds that a full convention of the Estates is to be held on 10 December to adopt a solid course intended to supply the King with money and to provide arms. As news of the Bond spread abroad, James appears to have tried dissimulation, for, in his report from Liège of 30 May–9 June 1600, J. B., alias John Petit, wrote to Peter Halins in London that "What I wrote you of the King of Scots is true . . . ; but whatsoever he says touching these practices, the association in Scotland . . . shows there is fire that will kindle at the first opportunity."[16] Copies

---

[13] Though students of Scottish printing accept the attribution to Waldegrave, it has not been possible for me to confirm the attribution, for the three ornamental initials, *G, M,* and *S,* that occur on sigs. A3, B1, and I8 of *A Pithie Exhortation* do not appear in any of Waldegrave's books available to me for examination.

[14] J. E. Neale, *Queen Elizabeth* (New York, 1934), p. 317.

[15] Quoted by Patrick Fraser Tytler, *History of Scotland* (3rd ed., Edinburgh, 1845), VII, 387-88, from a letter in the P.R.O.

[16] C.S.P. Dom., Elizabeth, vol. CCLXXIV, p. 439.

of the Bond were received in England,[17] and the transcript in the Folger Manuscript is proof that at least one copy was in private hands.[18]

James's Bond is certainly a document that the Earl of Essex would have wished to possess, and his agents would have been remiss had they failed to supply one. The presence of a transcript of the Scottish Bond (the Folger Manuscript) among documents relating to the Earl is highly significant. And the insertion of the old transcript of the English Bond suggests that the indebtedness of one to the other was recognized.

The Bond was something Essex had to take into account, whether he was a loyal supporter of James or his rival. In his colloquy with Ashton just before his execution, Essex touched on both these matters:

> For the crown, I never affected it. . . .
>
> . . . I knew myself to be bound in conscience, as a Christian, to prevent the subversion of religion, and as an Englishman to have regard to my native country. The only means left to turn away these evils was to procure my access to Her Majesty, with whom I assured myself to have had that gracious hearing, that might have tended to the infinite happiness of this state, . . . and in settling a succession for the Crown, to the preventing of Spanish servitude, and the saving of many thousand Englishmen's lives.[19]

Contemporaries had been somewhat less certain about the goal of Essex's ambition:

> . . . I think that unless some good order be taken, the King of Scots will win the game, if the Earl of Essex be not in his way, whom nevertheless the Scots take to be his greatest friend, but I think that they are deceived.[20]

Throughout the trial of Essex and Southampton, the references to Essex's dabbling in the matter of the succession were few and inconspicuous—presumably upon instructions from the Queen—and

---

[17] Stafford (p. 197) refers to State Papers, Scotland, vol. LXV, nos. 72-75.

[18] Through the kindness of H. N. Blakiston, Esq., it is possible to state that the Folger Manuscript was not copied from any of the four documents at the Record Office, though the text is essentially the same.

[19] Quoted by Walter B. Devereux, in *Lives and Letters of the Devereux, Earls of Essex* (London, 1853), II, 166, 167.

[20] Thomas Fitzherbert, writing on 1 March 1599 from Madrid to Sterrell in London, C.S.P. Dom., Elizabeth, vol. CCLXX, no. 47. See also Stafford, p. 205, n. 24, citing the warning of Ferdinand of Tuscany to James that Essex was the man most able to hinder a pretender. It is significant that Mountjoy felt it necessary in his letter to James in the summer of 1599 to reassure the latter that Essex was his supporter and not a rival for the crown (Birch, II, 470).

there is no trace of them in the official account (Stafford, pp. 210-24). The government could hardly have known how deeply Essex was involved, for his letter to James of 25 December 1600 (British Museum Add. MS. 31022, fols. 107-8) did not come to public attention until modern times. (Stafford, pp. 221-24). James's answer is reported to have been carried by the Earl in a little black bag that hung about his neck and was burned before his surrender.[21] Other documents, in a chest, are also reported to have been destroyed as soon as Essex returned from the disastrous ride through London.[22] Incriminating documents were hunted out systematically,[23] and it is remarkable that a volume with so much intimate information about Essex as that of Richard Greene escaped detection. Its contents would have confirmed many suspicions.

Peter Wentworth's name crops up once more before the story ends. On 11 March 1601 the Privy Council dispatched a letter to Mr. Gilpin in the Low Countries instructing him "to deale with the Estates" about the printing at Middleburgh of a great number of books in two treatises by Wentworth touching the succession, to the end that the printer might be identified and the books seized and suppressed. Arrangement for the publication had been made by "some Englishemen of factious humour," with intent to disperse the books "amongst such as are curious of noveltyes" (*cupidi alicuius novi,* as Cicero would have phrased it). There is no evidence to connect this printing of Wentworth's book with Essex, but it is of a piece with the conspirators' employment of the Lord Chamberlain's Men to perform *Richard II* for the instruction of Londoners in how to deal with a weak king; and no other group of Englishmen are known to which the project may be attributed. The letter of the Council does not indicate that any books had yet reached England; so it may be surmised that information about the edition came from one of the rebels. In this venture, as in his plot to have James send ambassadors to England by 1 February with demands for an immediate recognition of his rights to the succession, Essex's timing

[21] On 16 February 1601 the Privy Council instructed Sir John Peyton, Lieutenant of the Tower, to make an exhaustive search "in decent sorte" for "some paper in a blacke cover." Although several confessions mentioned it, Essex denied to the Lord Admiral that he had it; but the Council had testimony of its existence (*Acts of the Privy Council,* new ser., XXXI, 166).

[22] "All his papers, among which was one called a history of his troubles" (Devereux, II, 146).

[23] On 16 February the Council issued a warrant for the search of a trunk belonging to Anthony Rowse, a page to the Earl (*Acts of the Privy Council,* new ser., XXXI, 163).

would seem to have been fatally upset by the Council's request of 7 February that Essex appear before them.

There is insufficient evidence to prove Essex's complicity in the publication of Peter Wentworth's book in Edinburgh in 1598, in the planning of the Scottish Bond or the adaptation of it from the English document in 1599, or in the printing of Wentworth's book in Middleburgh in the winter of 1600-1. One or more of these ideas may have originated with James VI, or they may have occurred independently to persons unknown. They fall into such a neat pattern, however, that one is tempted to say that if Essex did not plot them he should have.

In putting the Scottish Bond into print for the first time, I have expanded the contractions within square brackets and (generally) put into roman type the names of persons and places and the Latin (and a few other) words that are in italic in the Folger Manuscript. To show the verbal indebtedness to the English Bond, words that are identical to (or substantially the same as) the text of the English Bond are printed in italics; those that are a close paraphrase of the text of the English Bond are printed in small capitals.

[The Scottish Bond]

A generall band made by the good subjects of the kings *Ma*[*iestie*] *for the preseruation of* his highnes *p*[*er*]*son,* [and] pursuit of his vndoubted right of the Crowne of England and Ireland. *made.* 1599.

ffor as much as the providence of *god hath* ESTABLISHED KINGDOMEES [*sic*] AND MONARCHIES, and hath APPOYNTED *kinges and princes* to beare *rule over the* same, rep[re]sentinge his devine power in administrac[ion] of Justice to ther *subiects,* and honouring him by establishing *true* and *Cristiane religion according to his word,* In contemplating of which benefits redounding to the people by the lawfull Authoritie of the prince, they are bound to *love, reverence and obaye ther* native *sou*[*er*]*aignes,* to p[ro]cure *to ther vttermost power* ther standing and aduancment, to resist and *withstand all* what soeu[er] practices or attempt[e]s which may be *hurtfull* to there *p*[*er*]*sones or states; therefore we* SUBSCRIBING (the *naturall* and loyall *borne subiect*[*e*]*s of this Realme*) calling to memorie and finding dayly before our eyes, the *greate felicitie* and *estimable comfort,* wher w[ith] all the most happie and *gracious* raigne of our soveraigne hath enriched vs: and the woonderfull QUIETNESSE, wherwith by gods p[ro]vidence, and his highness prudent *gover[n]ment* in soe vniu[er]sall troubles of all Europe, we have beene blissed: *acknowledging our selves* most *iustly bound w[ith] our bodie, lives, landes, goodes* and geare, *in* HIS *defence and safetie* against what *soeu[er]*, of *what nation degree* or QUALITIE *soeu[er] they be,* that would directlye or indirectly *attempte any* HARME against his most sacred *person,* or estate. Therefore *we and every of vs* CONIUNCTLIE *and severally,* in p[re]sence of the *almightie* POWER, by whome princes rule, whome we call vpon not onely as a Judge, but as a full revenger of suche (as shall violat and contradict or with stand these p[re]sent[e]s) of OUR OWNE FRE MOTIVE, AND WILL, *bindes* and obliges *our selves* MUTUALLYE EACH ONE OF VS TO OTHER, in *firme bond* and whole *societye,* wherby we solemnelye VOWE AND *p[ro]mise before the* GREAT *god with our whole powers, bodies, lives, land[e]s, goodes, children and servantes* and all that is vnder our com[m]andement, truly and *faithfully to serve, and humblye obey our saide soueraigne against all estates, dignities, and earthlie* PRINCES, *whatsoeuer,* invade or *pursewe by all* manner of hostilitie *as well by force of armes as by all other meanes, all* SORTES *of p[er]sones ther* COMPLICES assistant[e]s and p[er]takers, as *shall attempte* or vndertake by DEEDE, *counsell,* or concealment, *to any* PRACTISE *that* may in any respect *tend to the harme of* HIS *Ma[iesties]* most *Royall p[er]son,* honour estate or dignitie. *And shall neur* [*sic*] *desiste frome* ANY *manner of* hostilitie, *pursuits of such* traiterouse tyrant[e]s, till *ther counsellers,* LEADERS, AND PERTAKERS BE VTTERLIE ROOTED OUT, to the example of others vpon the hope of impunitie to attempt the like. And by cause almightie god amongst diuers his inestimable blessinges which he multiplies vpon our said soveraigne Lord to his glorie [and] our great comfort, hath established the vndoubted right of the Crownes of England [and] Ireland in his most royall p[er]son, next to his dear sister Elizabeth nowe Queene of England, which not withstanding diu[er]se p[er]sons, vpon friuolouse and imp[er]tinent p[re]tences, would goe aboute to impugne, contrarye to his birthright, and the most aunctent and allowed lawes of both the Realmes. Wherfore we vpon our bounden dueties to our native soveraigne, and moved in conscience to aduance the righteous successor, solemnly swear and protest by the name of the great god, onely to [the] vttermost of our power [and] strengthe, to mantaine [and] defend or [*sic*] soveraigne in his vndoubted right and title to the crowne of England and Ireland against all other p[re]tenders what soeuer, but like wise shall readilie with out any further drifte or excuse, vpon whatsoeue[r] p[re]text, bestowe our selves, our lives, children, servantes [*sic*] frends good[e]s and geare, what soeue[r] else in the *persuite* there of against what soeuer p[er]son, that shall after the death of the Queene of England, hinder impugn or with stand his Ma[iesties] heires or successors, in the peaceable getting and enioying, or possessing of the said crownes of England and Ireland. And shall by forceable meanes take the *vttermost revenge* vpon them, ther leaders *Counsellers* PERTAKERS AND ASSISTANT[E]s, that *by anie meanes possible we or any of vs cane* excogitat or *devise:* and *neuer desist* till we haue established our dearest sou[er]aigne (or in case of his decease *which god forbid*) his heires and successors, in the Royall Kingdome of England and Ireland, and peaceable fruition of the same, without p[re]iudice All wayes to his Ma[iesties] dearest sister Queene Elizabeth, during all the dayes of hir life tyme. *And* FOR THE MORE SURE *corroboration of this o*[*ur*] VOLUNTARIE *bond* ['and] entrie in to soe whole and lawfull a SOCIETIE, *we* and eu[er]ye of vs subscribing *confirme the whole content*[*e*]*s* THEROF *by our* solemne and great *othes, taken vpon the holie* SCRIPTURES, *with this expresse condic*[*ion*] [*that*] *none of vs shall* VPON *anye respect of p*[*er*]*sones, or cause of feare* or daunger, *or* hope of *reward, separate our selues frome this* CONDIC[ION], NOR *fayle* in any p[ar]te the p[re]misses *during o*[*ur*] *liues.* And if we doe to the contrary (as god forbid) [*that*] we by our most graciouse sou[er]aigne [and] his heires and the rest of o[ur] societie, be not onely reputed *as p*[*er*]*iurd p*[*er*]*sons,* but also to be *p*[*er*]*secuted* as vnworthie to BEARE OFFICE *in any christian Realme, or civill* COM[M]ON WEALTH. And also to be *p*[*ro*]*secuted* as most vile and destestable Traytours, *and publique enimies to god o*[*ur*] SOU[ER]AIGNE *and native Country. To the which paine and punishment we doe voluntarilie submit o*[*ur*] *selves and every one of vs,* without appellac[ion] reclamation [*sic*]: which as we are contented that these p[re]sent[e]s be ratified by the states in the nex [*sic*] parliament, and p[re]sentlie inserted and registred in the booke of counsells in futura[m] rei memoriam: And that executors may be secreated ther vpon in firme effect. *In witnesse* whereof to this p[re]sent bond subscribed with *our handes, and seales* of armes affixed, the yeare of god. 1599 and the 34 yeare of his Maiestie reigne.

The Authorship of Shakespeare

[1962]

Hamlet. Why look you there. . . . My father in his habit as he lived.

VERY writer who wishes to write about the man William Shakespeare longs, but longs in vain, to see him "in his habit as he lived," to tell his story with the wealth of intimate detail that is expected in the biographies of famous men. Nowadays literary men and people of the theater are idolized. Their voices are on the radio, their faces on television and in the movies. Their goings and comings are reported as news, and the public knows, or thinks it knows, their tastes in breakfast food, beverages, cigarettes, and women (or men, as the case may be). They are public characters, lionized and, on occasion, mobbed by ecstatic admirers.

To imagine a society in which there were no actresses, in which actors were scarcely respectable, and in which literary men were for the most part either wealthy amateurs or impoverished professionals—to imagine, in a word, the kind of society in which Shakespeare lived—is difficult indeed.

For a playwright of his time, Shakespeare's life is well documented. He was christened on 26 April 1564 in Holy Trinity Church, Stratford-upon-Avon, the eldest son to John and Mary (Arden) Shakespeare; he died on 23 April 1616 and was interred in the chancel of Holy Trinity Church. We know his wife's name and origin, the dates of christening and burial of their three children, as well as many facts of their later lives. The elder daughter married the well-known Dr. John Hall and in 1643

The Authorship of Shakespeare, Folger Booklets on Tudor and Stuart Civilization, The Folger Shakespeare Library, Washington, D. C., 1962.

was hostess to the Queen of England, who spent two nights and parts of three days at New Place, which Susanna Hall had inherited from her father. Susanna's daughter, Elizabeth, took for her second husband John Bernard, who was knighted by Charles II in 1661.

From the time that he began to enjoy prosperity—about 1596—William Shakespeare's financial dealings are recorded in some detail. He bought and restored New Place, the imposing house built about 1483 by Sir Hugh Clopton, mayor of Stratford. With his son's support, John Shakespeare secured the grant of arms for which application had been made earlier; thenceforth, each was *generosus,* a propertied gentleman. There were purchases of real estate in and about Stratford and, in 1613, in London. The London property was the Blackfriars Gatehouse, a logical purchase for a man whose company of actors had been performing in an adjacent Blackfriars building since 1609.

William Shakespeare, gent., of Stratford-upon-Avon, gave a deposition in a suit brought in 1612 by Stephen Belott to gain possession of the dowry promised Belott's wife, Mary Mountjoy, at the time of their marriage about 1603, when Shakespeare was lodging with the Mountjoys. His signature identifies him with the purchaser of the Blackfriars Gatehouse (two related documents bear his signature) and with the man who in the spring of 1616 signed the three pages of his will, bequeathing, among other things, twenty-six shillings and eightpence to his "fellows" Richard Burbage, John Heminges, and Henry Condell to buy memorial rings. These men had been his fellow actors and friends since about 1594, and in 1623 Heminges and Condell brought out the First Folio edition of his plays, "without ambition either of self-profit, or fame; only to keep the memory of so worthy a friend, and fellow alive, as was our Shakespeare."

Men of Shakespeare's age had a very different set of values from our own. Plays written for the public stage were not considered to be literature. *Nos haec novimus esse nihil:* "We know these things to be nothing" appears on the title-page of one play-quarto. The Latin motto expresses the opinion of many of the playwrights, who turned out scripts to be used by actors in the entertainment of a not always discriminating public.

The actors themselves led a precarious existence. A few gifted players who had business ability and prudence managed to become sharers in the ownership or operation of a playhouse and thus to acquire property and recognition as substantial citizens. Edward Alleyn, the great tragic actor of the Lord Admiral's Men, became wealthy enough to found Dulwich College. Heminges and Condell were churchwardens of St. Mary Aldermanbury in London. There is probably envy of their economic success mixed with scorn of their aspirations to gentility in the words that, about 1600, Ben Jonson puts into the mouth of one of his characters: "They [the actors] forget they are i' the statute, the rascals, they are blazoned there, there they are tricked, they and their pedigrees; they need no other heralds, I wis" (Tucca, in *Poetaster,* I. ii. 53 ff.). The statute is that of 39 Elizabeth (1597-98), ch. 4, where it is required that

[2] All fencers, bearwards, common players of interludes, and minstrels wandering abroad (other than players of interludes belonging to any baron of this realm, or any other honorable personage of greater degree, to be authorized to play, under the hand and seal of arms of such baron or personage) . . . shall be taken, adjudged, and deemed rogues, vagabonds, and sturdy beggars, and shall sustain such pain and punishment as by this Act is in that behalf appointed.

The initial punishment was that the culprit be

[3] stripped naked from the middle upwards and shall be openly whipped until his or her body be bloody.[1]

Prosperity among actors was the exception. From the earliest times, minstrels, jugglers, and such entertainers of the public had been very low in the social scale, and it was with difficulty that they managed to rise in public esteem. A forceful character like Edward Alleyn or Richard Burbage might be sought after by certain of the young gentlemen of the Inns of Court and celebrated in verse at his death. But their Bohemian way of life, the uncertainty of regular employment that was not lessened by frequent recurrences of the plague, which closed all places of entertainment, and the discomforts of taking to the road kept most actors outside the pale of respectability. This state of affairs continued until David Garrick proved later, in the 18th century, that an actor could live on terms of intimate friendship with the nobility. In the reigns of Elizabeth and James no one thought actors worthy of biographical notice.

Poets fared little better. Edmund Spenser, recognized by his contemporaries as the greatest nondramatic poet since Chaucer, writes that London was his "most kindly nurse," but the year of his birth is unknown, and although he claimed kinship with the great Spencer family of Althorpe, no one has discovered the nature of the relationship. His father's baptismal name is unknown; his mother's name is known only because the poet's praise of his second (or perhaps third) wife, Elizabeth Boyle,

---

[1] Sir Edmund Chambers, *The Elizabethan Stage* (Oxford, 1923), IV, 324.

mentions the fact that Queen, mother, and wife shared the one name. There is no absolute certainty about the identity of Spenser's first wife. His early love, "Rosalind," is a mystery. There is only conjecture about what dashed his hopes of quasi-diplomatic service on the Continent. In Ireland, to which he seems to have been rusticated, he acquired property and became Clerk of the Council of Munster; but in 1581 he is also, mysteriously, prebendary of Effin. As clerk to Lord Grey, and in other official capacities, Spenser wrote many letters and documents, at least fifty-nine of which have been identified. They are written in three distinct hands: two for English (secretary and italic) and one for Latin. No personal letter to or from him has come to light and not one line of poetry in his handwriting.

John Milton, who was born in 1608 a few years before Shakespeare's death and who lived till 1674, was famous as a poet and political writer. He was the first great English poet to have his biography written by his contemporaries, but the first life of Milton to appear independently was composed by one of his adopted nephews (Edward Phillips), not because Milton was a poet but because he had written a violent political book while serving as Latin Secretary during the Commonwealth period. Yet with all the autobiographical publicity that accompanied Milton's bitter pamphlet-war with foreign critics of England, the cause of his rustication from Cambridge is unknown, and the facts of his unhappy first marriage are still a mystery. It was to be expected that Milton would lose his life, along with the regicides, when Charles II came to the throne in 1660; but while his friends spirited the blind poet away from London, Andrew Marvell interceded for him in Parliament, and the Royalist Sir William Davenant (whom Milton is reported to have saved from execution about 1651) obtained his release. "The details," writes a recent biographer, "remain obscure."

It is instructive to note that in William Winstanley's *England's Worthies* (1660) the two Elizabethan poets, Sir Philip Sidney and John Donne, are included because the first was the flower of chivalry (there is a brief reference to the *Arcadia* and to the *Astrophel and Stella*) and the second was Dean of St. Paul's (there is one reference to a religious poem).

That blazing star, Sir Walter Raleigh, illustrates well the indifference of his age to biography and to literary manuscripts. A well-known editor of his poems writes of him:

Raleigh was born about 1552, at Hayes Barton in Devonshire. . . . Some time in his teens he went up to Oriel College, Oxford, where it is not recorded that he took a degree. . . . Of the next ten years, the formative years of his life, we know very little beyond the fact that he fought in the French Wars of Religion and in the Irish campaigns of Lord Grey. . . . There is more than one story that professes to account for his sudden rise to favour, but they are fairy-tale chances and lean on the logic of day-dreams.[2]

The date of his birth is uncertain; the name of the school he attended is unknown. There is a decade of which research has discovered almost nothing. This is the man who for ten years was a reigning favorite at Court, a great sea-captain, the adventurer who sank £40,000 of his private fortune in attempts to colonize Virginia, the man who is credited with introducing tobacco into England and the potato into Ireland. He was envied and hated by the greatest in England. His *History of the World,* written while he was a prisoner in the Tower, went through ten editions between 1611 and 1700. Some autograph letters survive, but not one manuscript page of *The History of the World.* Of his poetical works, a fragment of *Cynthia,* 522 lines in his handwriting, is among the Cecil Papers at Hatfield House, and the late W. A. White is reported to have owned a two-page autograph manuscript of "The Lie." No one troubled to preserve the original manuscripts of anything else that he is known to have written.

The author of the Jacobean tragedies that rank nearest to Shakespeare's was John Webster. Here is a biographical note about him published in 1941:

Of the Elizabethan dramatists there is not one concerning whose life we know less than John Webster's. Hitherto antiquarian research has failed to bring to light any biographic data of any consequence. We do not know when or where he was born or died, who his parents were, what sort of education he received, whether he really was a tailor by trade, whether he was married, how he earned his living, and so forth.[3]

The other playwrights of the time are little better known to us, with the exception of Christopher Marlowe and Ben Jonson, and there are special reasons why so much is recorded about them. The parish registers and school records of Canterbury, where Marlowe, the son of a shoemaker, was born, have been preserved. He won a scholarship and matriculated at Corpus Christi College, Cambridge, from which he received the degree of Master of Arts in mysterious circumstances. Something of his

---

[2] Agnes M. C. Latham, ed., *The Poems of Sir Walter Raleigh* (London, 1951), p. xv.
[3] S. A. Tannenbaum, *John Webster: A Concise Bibliography* (New York, 1941), p. vii.

later life is recorded because of a killing in which he became involved, because of his outspoken, unorthodox opinions about religion, but most of all because of his violent death. About Jonson, whose stepfather was a bricklayer, considerably more is known, but even of this pugnacious man's biography many details are in question. He was born in 1572, possibly on 11 June. His father was probably a clergyman, but his baptismal name is unknown; neither the baptismal name nor the surname of the mother is recorded. In 1589 Jonson was withdrawn from Westminster School, to which he had been sent by "a friend," and "put to another craft." And in July 1597 "he makes his sudden appearance in Henslowe's employ." In the "lost years" he had service (dates unknown) in the wars in the Low Countries, where he won a duel and stripped his dead foe. Of his long-suffering wife, the one recorded fact is that she and her husband were subject to "correction" in 1606 for habitually absenting themselves from service and communion in the parish church. The couple had at least two children, Mary, who lived only six months, and Ben, who died in 1603 at the age of seven. Jonson fought another duel, with a fellow actor, and escaped execution only by pleading benefit of clergy. (In medieval times the clergy were permitted to plead exemption from sentence for having committed certain felonies; later, this privilege—not abolished until 1827—was extended to any first offender who could read. The test passage, often called the "neck verse," was usually a Latin version of Psalm 51, printed in black letter.) Most of the known details of his later life have been preserved because of his irregularity in religion, his association with the nobility while writing court masques, and his aggressiveness in every relationship. His part in writing a play, *The Isle of Dogs,* landed him in prison in 1597, and he was in prison again in 1604 for his part in *Eastward Ho.* Jonson was at the center of the War of the Theaters in 1599-1602; he quarreled with Inigo Jones about court masques; and he was contemptuous in criticism of contemporary writers and dictatorial in stating his own literary theories. In short, Marlowe and Jonson had color; they made news. Their lives were filled with actions that brought them in conflict with authority and thus into the kinds of official records that have been preserved.

The other playwrights of the time led less violent lives and, consequently, are shadowy figures. Of John Lyly, Thomas Lodge, George Peele, Thomas Dekker, Robert Greene, Samuel Daniel, George Chapman, and Thomas Heywood, for example, the year of birth can only be guessed. No autograph of Robert Greene has been discovered. Of the others named, there are a few signatures, an autograph letter or two, but no literary autographs except a scrap from Marlowe, a fragment of a poem of Daniel's, an autograph poem by Peele, lines in *Sir Thomas More* in Dekker's hand, [and two plays in Heywood's autograph—*The Captives* and *The Escapes of Jupiter*]. These men are better known to us than Webster, less known than Marlowe and Jonson.

Shakespeare lived quietly, unobtrusively, for the most part—there are many contemporary references to "gentle" Shakespeare. He fought no duels, had no religious difficulties, served no time in jail for debt or violence, avoided dogmatism in literary matters, wrote no court masques. He did not make news or get into official records in the same way that Marlowe and Jonson did.

The first English playwright to have a formal biography written to be published with his *Works* was William Shakespeare. For his edition of the plays in 1709, the first modern edition of an English playwright, Nicholas Rowe collected what data he could in London and then sent the famous Shakespearian actor Thomas Betterton (1635?-1710) to Stratford to look at records there, such as the parish registers, and to collect local traditions of Shakespeare. Betterton began acting *Hamlet* in 1660 and continued to play the title-role and other Shakespearian roles until 1709. His career began while William Beeston and the younger William Cartwright were still active in the theaters. Pepys saw Cartwright play Falstaff in 1667. Both Beeston and Cartwright had been actors before the Puritans closed the playhouses in 1642. The elder William Cartwright was an actor with the Lord Admiral's Men, chief rivals to Shakespeare's company; and Beeston's father Christopher was a fellow member of Shakespeare's company in 1598. They knew Shakespeare, and their sons knew of him. About 1681 or so William Beeston told John Aubrey, among other things, that Shakespeare had been a schoolmaster. He was also Aubrey's authority for the statement that Shakespeare was "the more to be admired *quia* [because] he was not a company keeper; lived in Shoreditch; wouldn't be debauched. And if invited to, wrote [that] he was in pain." In other words, Shakespeare did not care for drunken riots and, if invited, pleaded a headache. He could put into Falstaff's mouth the praise of sherry sack, but his own opinion seems to have been more like that of Cassio: "O God, that men should put an enemy in their mouths to steal away their brains! That we should, with joy, pleasance, revel, and applause, transform ourselves into beasts!"

Another man from whom Betterton learned about Shakespeare was

Sir William Davenant (1606-68), who was writing plays in 1634 and managed the Duke's Company after 1660. He it was who instructed Betterton
in how Shakespeare had taught Burbage to play Prince Hamlet. Davenant
was godson to Shakespeare and, in his cups, suggested that the relationship might be closer. His elder brother, Robert, who became an eminent
divine, said in Aubrey's hearing that when he was a small boy (he was
born in 1603) Shakespeare "gave him a hundred kisses." For a hundred
years after Shakespeare's death there was an unbroken tradition among
playwrights and theater people, who knew him "indirectly, and directly
too." These were the people in the best position to know the facts, and
they accepted without question the fact that Shakespeare the actor was
the poet and playwright.

Against this background of Shakespeare's biography and reputation it
is desirable now to place some of the particular details of his life, beginning with his education and following with some of the recorded facts of
his life in London and of his literary career.

The law of the universe seems to be that everything changes. Men establish new forms of government—republics instead of absolute monarchies; scientists prove that the earth moves around the sun and then relate
our galaxy to the countless other galaxies in space; biologists and psychol-
ogists discover some of the marvels of the human body and mind; and the
new learning displaces the old. Systems of education are revolutionized.
Latin, the universal language, once the most important subject for study
from primary school to the university, is now read with pleasure by very
few people, and spoken by still fewer. Literary classics written in former
times seem difficult and a little strange. The plays of Shakespeare have suffered this fate. The ideas about physiology and psychology current in his
day seem quaint. Stories that he borrowed from Ovid, his references to
characters in classical myth, give his lines now an appearance of erudition.
How amazed he would be to hear a modern ten-year-old prattle about jet
propulsion and trips to the moon! Other times, other customs; the com-
monplaces of one age are marvels to another.

What appears to modern readers as great learning in Shakespeare was
more justly appraised by his contemporaries and by those in succeeding
generations who attended similar grammar schools and had, besides, the
advantages of university education. In *The Progress to Parnassus* (Plate 8),
written by Cambridge students about 1601, the character called "Kemp"
(after Will Kemp, the comic actor in Shakespeare's company) says to
"Burbage": "Few of the university men pen plays well, they smell too

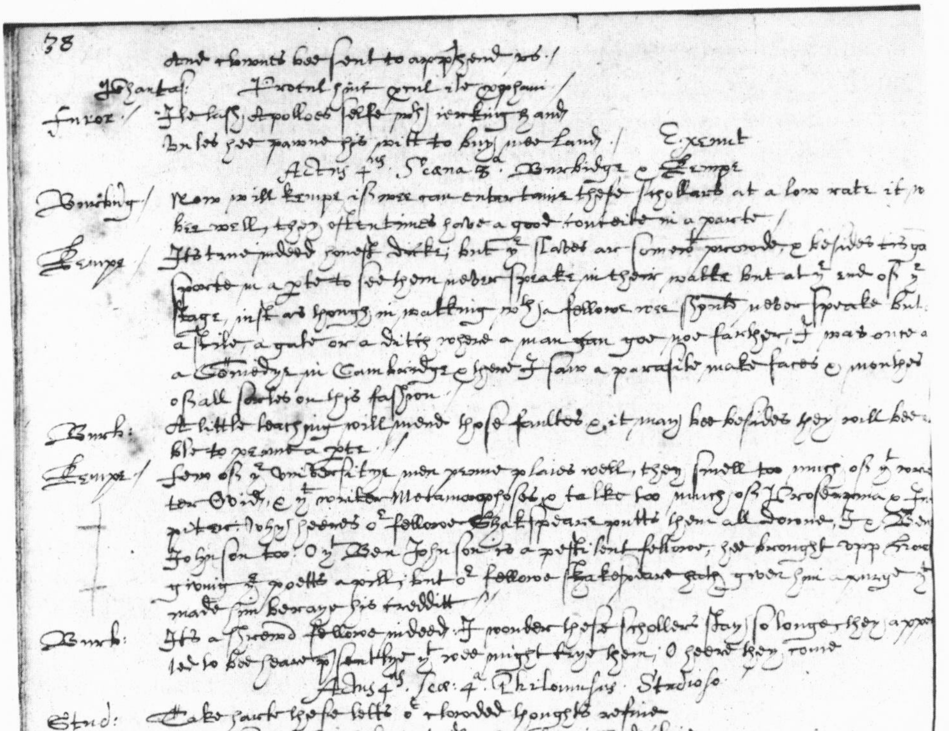

78

PLATE 8. A page of *The Progress to Parnassus,* "as it was acted in St. John's College in Cambridge, Anno 1601." An anonymous play, written and performed by students at Cambridge. Folger MS. V.a.355. The cross in the margin is opposite the reference to Shakespeare quoted on page 182.

much of that writer Ovid, and that writer Metamorphoses, and talk too much of Proserpina and Jupiter. Why here's our fellow Shakespeare puts them all down, aye and Ben Jonson too." Ben Jonson told the Scottish poet William Drummond that "Shakespeare wanted art." Francis Beaumont's poetical letter from the country to Jonson is more explicit:

> Here I would let slip
> (If I had any in me) scholarship,
> And from all learning keep these lines as clear
> As Shakespeare's best are, which our heirs shall hear
> Preachers apt to their auditors to show
> How far sometimes a mortal man may go
> By the dim light of Nature.

Thomas Fuller, in his *Worthies, Warwickshire* (1662), compares Shakespeare to Plautus, "who was an exact comedian, yet never any scholar," and adds boldly: "Indeed his [Shakespeare's] learning was very little." A paragraph in Nicholas Rowe's "Life" that prefaced his edition of Shakespeare in 1709 puts the matter admirably. Rowe was poet laureate, a writer of successful plays, a friend of Addison and Pope, and a beneficiary of the Prince of Wales's generosity. Among the bits of information he gleaned about Shakespeare, probably through Betterton's inquiries at Stratford, is a direct statement about Shakespeare's schooling.

His father, who was a considerable dealer in wool, had so large a family, ten children in all, that tho' he was his eldest son he could give him no better education than his own employment. He had bred him, 'tis true, for some time at a free school, where 'tis probable he acquired that little Latin he was master of; but the narrowness of his circumstances, and the want of his assistance at home, forc'd his father to withdraw him from thence, and unhappily prevented his further proficiency in that language. It is without controversy that he had no knowledge of the writings of the ancient poets, not only from this reason, but from his works themselves, where we find no traces of anything that looks like an imitation of 'em; the delicacy of his taste and the natural bent of his own great genius, equal, if not superior to some of the best of theirs, would certainly have led him to read and study 'em with so much pleasure that some of their fine images would naturally have insinuated themselves into and been mix'd with his own writings; so that his not copying at least something from them may be an argument of his never having read 'em. Whether his ignorance of the ancients were a disadvantage to him or no may admit of a dispute; for tho' the knowledge of 'em might have made him more correct, yet it is not improbable but that the regularity and deference for them which would have attended that correctness might have restrain'd some of that fire, impetuosity, and even beautiful extravagance which we admire in Shakespeare: and I believe we are better pleas'd with those thoughts, altogether new and uncommon, which his own imagination supplied him so abundantly with, than if he had given us the most beautiful passages out of the Greek and Latin poets, and that in the most agreeable manner that it was possible for a master of the English language to deliver 'em. Some Latin without question he did know, and one may see up and down in his plays how far his reading that way went. In *Love's Labour's Lost*, the pedant comes out with a verse of Mantuan, and in *Titus Andronicus*, one of the Gothic princes, upon reading

> *Integer vitae scelerisque purus*
> *Non eget Mauri jaculis nec arcu—*

says, "Tis a verse in Horace," but he remembers it out of his grammar, which, I suppose, was the author's case.

What is known of Shakespeare's education comes, then, largely from the poems and plays themselves. The Stratford of his boyhood was blessed with a good grammar school refounded under the charter of 1553 from Edward VI. Its master was paid £20 a year and provided with a house. This equaled the salary of the Master of Eton and enabled the borough to employ first-class men. Thomas Jenkins, for example, who was master from 1575 to 1579, the years when young William would have been in the upper school, was fellow or scholar of St. John's College, Oxford, B.A. 6 April 1566, M.A. 8 April 1570. A high-school principal of equivalent education today would be a Ph.D. of Harvard.

The registers of the school are not extant, but it is incredible that William Shakespeare was not one of the pupils. His father was an energetic and ambitious man. A relative newcomer to Stratford, he was chosen a member of the borough council in 1557. Five years later he served two years as one of the two chamberlains, and upon the expiration of his term he was charged with preparing the borough accounts during the two-year term of the men who followed him in office. In 1568 he was elected to the highest municipal office, that of high bailiff. His application for a grant of arms in 1576 shows his aspirations. Such a man would never deny his first-born son the privilege of schooling to which his father's position entitled him.

Passages in several of the plays show intimate knowledge of the books that were used in the lower and upper schools of England. The hornbook, from which the children learned their letters, is twice referred to (*Love's*

Labour's Lost, V. i. 48; *Richard III,* I. i. 54-57). Next came the *ABC with the Catechism,* alluded to in *King John,* "And then comes answer like an Absey book" (I. i. 196), and *The Two Gentlemen of Verona* (II. i. 22). There are frequent quotations from the Psalms, regularly in the version found in the Book of Common Prayer, which in some schools replaced the usual primer. From each of these, boys learned selections from the services of the church, certain prayers, and passages from the Scriptures. These books were the chief texts of the petty school; when committed to memory, as they had to be, they stored the pupils' minds with the best English prose, the great poetry of the Psalms, and the fundamentals of Anglican religion.

At the age of about six William would have entered grammar school, where he would have been expected to learn to read and write Latin easily, and to speak it. The important text was Lily's *A Short Introduction of Grammar,* printed largely in Latin. It is named in one of the earliest plays, *Titus Andronicus* (IV. ii. 20-23), where two lines are quoted from Horace. In the *Sententiae pueriles* of Culmannus and the *Disticha moralia* of Cato with notes by Erasmus a boy found moral maxims and explicit warnings against vice. Other maxims were committed to memory from the *Adagia* and *Apophthegmata,* in which were found many of the best lines from the Greek and Roman writers. *Æsop's Fables,* a play or two from Terence and Plautus, Mantuan's *Eclogues* (see reference in *Love's Labour's Lost,* IV. ii. 95-96), the *Zodiacus vitae* of Palingenius, and Nowell's *Catechism,* which was studied in English, Latin, and Greek, gave the grammar-school boys more and better Latin than all but a few college students now possess. And the intensive method of teaching fixed the religious and profane texts indelibly in young memories. The oral and written exercises imparted skill in rhetoric and stretched the imagination, for the boys practiced writing letters and delivering orations, taking care always to choose sentiments appropriate to the given situation and words suitable to the writer or speaker. Ovid, Virgil, Cicero, Horace, and Juvenal gave schoolboys a familiarity with classical mythology that in these days, when even the modern languages are studied with reluctance, would be expected only in college courses in Latin. The textbooks of the petty and the grammar school were the ones that Shakespeare knew. The curriculum of the universities was a closed book to him.

Shakespeare's education was one of the topics about which John Aubrey questioned William Beeston, and this is his memorandum: "Though as Ben Jonson says of him, that he had but little Latin and less Greek, he understood Latin pretty well: for he had been in his younger years a schoolmaster in the country." Such a youthful occupation is entirely compatible with scenes in several early plays. Holofernes in *Love's Labour's Lost* is described as a pedant who teaches the *ABC,* and there is much schoolboy punning on Latin words. In *The Taming of the Shrew* Lucentio disguises himself as a tutor so that he may court Bianca, and there is a short burlesque of a Latin lesson (III. i; Tranio has already quoted Lily's *Grammar* at I. ii. 167). Another tutor, Sir Hugh Evans, is introduced in *The Merry Wives of Windsor,* and when William recites his elementary Latin there is much laughter at Mistress Quickly's ignorance (IV. i). The good humor with which pedagogues are treated shows that though Shakespeare may have crept unwillingly to school he had vivid—and fond—recollections of his experiences there.

Once the limits of Shakespeare's formal education are recognized, it is easier to see the qualities that make his writings immortal. He read books in London, read them avidly and efficiently, taking from them stories for his plays and ideas for his characters, but he was not bookish. "Small have continual plodders ever won," says Biron in *Love's Labour's Lost,* "save base authority from others' books." A main part of Shakespeare's genius lay in his possession of a quality that his Julius Caesar attributes to Cassius: "He is a great observer, and he looks quite through the deeds of men." Not for him the simplicity of King Duncan, who reflects sadly, "There's no art to find the mind's construction in the face." Better than any other poet, Shakespeare could listen to a voice, regard a face, and, in imagination, conjure up the thoughts and emotions of all kinds of people, low and high. The other part of his genius was in his ear for the rhythms of speech and his matchless use of words.

The year of Shakespeare's arrival in London is unknown, as are the circumstances that brought him there. Whether he was a private tutor, as Beeston reported, or simply a young man with a family to support and the consciousness of a gift of poetry, he must shortly have become an actor and a playwright. For by 1592 he was vilified in a posthumous book by Robert Greene for his presumption in writing plays. When powerful friends came to his defense, Henry Chettle, Greene's literary executor, published an apology: "Myself have seen his demeanor no less civil than he excellent in the quality he professes. Besides, divers of worship have reported his uprightness of dealing which argues his honesty, and his facetious grace in writing, that approves his art." This means that Shakespeare was thus early a good actor ("the quality he professes") and a successful writer, that he conducted himself like a gentleman ("uprightness," "honesty"), and that he had won the favor and friendship of people of high station ("divers of worship").

When the plague closed the playhouses in 1592-94, he had time to write —or at least to publish—two narrative poems, *Venus and Adonis* (1593) and *The Rape of Lucrece* (1594), the only books he saw through the press. Each of these is dedicated to the young Earl of Southampton, who may plausibly be identified as one of the "divers of worship."

The popularity of Shakespeare's plays that made Greene envious led publishers to buy his play-manuscripts whenever they could. *Titus Andronicus* appeared in print in 1594. Unauthorized texts of *Henry VI Parts 2 and 3* were published in 1594 and 1595 as *The Contention betwixt the Two Famous Houses of York and Lancaster* and *The True Tragedy of Richard Duke of York*. By 1598 publishers began to put Shakespeare's name on the title-pages: *Richard II* (Quartos 2 and 3), *Love's Labour's Lost,* and *Richard III* (Quarto 2). Before this time the public had paid little attention to the authorship of plays.

In this same year, 1598, Londoners could read in *Palladis Tamia: Wits Treasury* a description of the state of English poetry. The author, Francis Meres, probably taking a hint from Richard Carew's *The Excellence of the English Tongue* (*c.* 1596), in which Shakespeare had been compared to Catullus, names the important English writers beginning with Chaucer and equates each with one of the classical authors. Meres's purpose was to proclaim that the English language was a suitable medium for good writing and that England had poets equal to the best of other lands. Incidentally, he names twelve plays by Shakespeare.

Meres lists Shakespeare as a distinguished writer of many kinds of literature. He names him along with Sidney and Spenser as an enricher of the English language; with Spenser and Daniel as a lyric poet; with Lord Buckhurst, Dr. Legge, Dr. Edes, and Marlowe as a writer of tragedies; with the Earl of Oxford, Dr. Gager, Rowley, and Lyly as a writer of comedies; and with the Earl of Surrey, Sir Thomas Wyatt, Sir Philip Sidney, Spenser, and Drayton as "the most passionate among us to bewail and bemoan the perplexities of love." "The Muses," he writes, "would speak with Shakespeare's fine filed phrase, if they would speak English." As for drama in general, "As Plautus and Seneca are accounted the best for Comedy and Tragedy among the Latins; so Shakespeare among the English is the most excellent in both kinds for the stage."

This testimony of Meres is invaluable, not only because it names twelve of Shakespeare's plays then in existence and mentions that his sonnets were circulating in manuscript among his private friends, but because it represents the knowledge of a hack writer familiar with all the gossip of literary London. A master of arts of both Universities, Meres came to London and began a literary career. Between 1595 and 1602 he published a sermon, translated a devotional book, and had a share in the production of a series of anthologies. In 1602 he was named rector of Wing in Rutland and removed from London.

Three things make Meres's record important: (1) he names the poets in each group in order of social rank: earls, barons, knights, doctors, gentlemen, common people; (2) writing while most of the men were still living, he mentions both the Earl of Oxford and Shakespeare in one group: "The best for Comedy amongst us be, Edward Earl of Oxford, Doctor Gager of Oxford, Master Rowley once a rare scholar of learned Pembroke Hall in Cambridge [of which Meres was B.A.], . . . Lodge, . . . Shakespeare . . ."; and (3) Meres moved in the same circles as many of the poets. Nicholas Ling, who collected the first volume of the series of anthologies to which Meres contributed the second, was the publisher of the first and second quartos of *Hamlet* (1603, 1604/5); and James Roberts, the printer of Volumes I and III of the series and also the first quarto of *The Merchant of Venice,* Quarto 2 of *Titus Andronicus,* and Quarto 2 of *Hamlet,* had a contract with the Lord Chamberlain's Men, Shakespeare's company, to print their playbills; he also made a series of staying entries for them in the Stationers' Register. Roberts, Ling, and, consequently, Meres were in a position to know Shakespeare personally, both as actor and playwright.

Shortly after his arrival in London to ascend the throne of England, King James took under his protection the Lord Chamberlain's Men, who were thenceforth known as the King's Men. The license, dated 19 May 1603, begins thus: "We . . . do license and authorize these our servants Lawrence Fletcher, William Shakespeare, Richard Burbage, Augustine Phillips, John Heminge, Henry Condell . . . to use and exercise the arts and faculty of playing comedies, tragedies, histories . . . during our pleasure." And pursuant to this appointment Shakespeare was one of those to whom four yards of red cloth were issued by the Master of the Great Wardrobe, to walk (or ride) in procession with the King through London on 15 March 1604. This is only one of the documents that link Shakespeare with Heminges and Condell.

The fortunate discovery in the Public Record Office of some of the documents in a suit brought in 1612 by Stephen Belott against his father-in-law, Christopher Mountjoy, a Huguenot refugee, provides a positive link between Stratford and London. The details of the suit are relevant only to the extent that they prove Shakespeare's acquaintance with the Mountjoy family in 1602 and his dwelling in their house, at least for a time, in 1604, where he might have improved his knowledge of French. One of the documents is a deposition by William Shakespeare of Stratford-upon-Avon, gentleman, of the age of forty-eight years or therabouts, the signature to which corresponds to those on Shakespeare's will (see Plate 9).

On 10 March 1613, Shakespeare bought of Henry Walker a house in Blackfriars known as the Gatehouse. The conveyance, bearing Shakespeare's signature, is in the Guildhall Library, London (see Plate 10); the counterpart, signed by Walker, is in the Folger Library. Shakespeare is identified as a gentleman of Stratford-upon-Avon. Associated with him in the transaction were John Heminges, gentleman, William Johnson, vintner, and John Jackson, gentleman, all of London. Heminges, Jackson, and Johnson were trustees for Shakespeare. The purchase price was £140. Heminges is the fellow actor named in the King's warrant of 1604 who would help bring out the Folio of 1623. William Johnson has been identified as the owner of the famous Mermaid Tavern in Bread Street. John Jackson, gentleman, was a well-to-do Londoner from Kingston-upon-Hull, who in 1599 had acted as a trustee for Shakespeare and the other members of his company in distributing the shares in the ground lease of the Globe. Another document relating to the property, a mortgage deed now in the British Museum, was executed on the following day. This, too, is signed by Shakespeare, Johnson, and Jackson. Heminges was again a participant. The mortgage was to ensure that Walker would receive a balance due of £60. (See Plate 11.) Without possibility of question, the actor at the Globe and the gentleman from Stratford were the same man.

Shakespeare's will provides still more links with London. Each page is signed by him, and in it he makes bequests to three of his long-time friends of the London stage: "to my fellows John Heminge, Richard Burbage and Henry Condell twenty-six shillings, eightpence apiece to buy them rings." To Thomas Russell, Esq., he bequeathed £5 and entreated and appointed him to be one of the "overseers" of the will. Russell was a gentleman of good estate, who had inherited manors at Alderminster and Broad Campden, both within a few miles of Stratford-upon-Avon. He married, as his second wife, the widow of the great and wealthy scientist Thomas Digges, whose fine house was in the parish of St. Mary Alder-

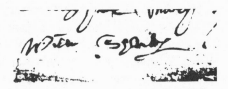

PLATE 9. Shakespeare's signature to his deposition of 11 May 1612 in the Belott-Mountjoy lawsuit. From the original in the Public Record Office, London.

PLATE 10. Shakespeare's signature to the conveyance of the Gatehouse in Blackfriars, 10 March 1613. From the original in the Guildhall Library, London.

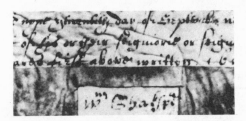

PLATE 11. Shakespeare's signature to the mortgage deed of the Gatehouse in Blackfriars, 11 March 1613. From the original in the British Museum.

manbury in London. John Heminges was a fellow parishioner and later a churchwarden of St. Mary's. Russell came of an ancient family and had important relatives and friends. The younger of his stepsons, Leonard Digges, an Oxford graduate and a poet, was often at Stratford. His two poems in praise of Shakespeare take on greater importance from having been written by a man with every opportunity to know the dramatist personally. The shorter one, printed in the First Folio, gives the earliest reference to the memorial bust of Shakespeare in Holy Trinity Church.

> To the Memory of the Deceased Author,
> Master William Shakespeare.
>
> Shakespeare, at length thy pious fellows give
> The world thy works: thy works, by which outlive
> Thy tomb thy name must; when that stone is rent,
> And time dissolves thy Stratford monument,
> Here we alive shall view thee still. This book,
> When brass and marble fade, shall make thee look
> Fresh to all ages.
>
> .   .   .   .   .
>
> Be sure, our Shakespeare, thou canst never die,
> But, crown'd with laurel, live eternally.
>
> L. Digges

The longer poem, which was first printed with Shakespeare's *Poems* (1640), gives additional proof of personal knowledge of "never-dying Shakespeare":

> First, that he was a poet none would doubt
> That heard the applause of what he sees set out
> Imprinted; . . .
> Next Nature only helped him; for look thorough
> This whole book, thou shalt find he doth not borrow
> One phrase from Greeks, nor Latins imitate,
> Nor once from vulgar languages translate,
> Nor plagiary-like from others glean,
> Nor begs he from each witty friend a scene
> To piece his acts with; all that he doth write
> Is pure his own. . . .

At Shakespeare's death it was thought that he should be buried in the Poets' Corner in Westminster Abbey alongside Chaucer, Spenser, and

Francis Beaumont. One of the widely circulated poems of the time begins thus:

On Mr. Wm. Shakespeare he died in April 1616

Renowned Spenser, lie a thought more nigh
To learned Chaucer, and rare Beaumont lie
A little nearer Spenser, to make room
For Shakespeare. . . .

William Basse

John Milton realized that burying Shakespeare in Westminster Abbey would not have increased his fame. His poem "W. Shakespeare" in the Second Folio (1632) opens with these lines:

What needs my Shakespeare for his honor'd bones,
The labor of an age, in piled stone . . . ?

.   .   .   .   .

Thou in our wonder and astonishment
Hast built thyself a lifelong monument.

Milton is echoing Jonson's poem in the First Folio:

I will not lodge thee by
Chaucer or Spenser, or bid Beaumont lie
A little farther, to make thee a room:
Thou art a monument, without a tomb,
And art alive still, while thy book doth live.

But the actual "monument," the portrait bust in the chancel of Holy Trinity, has great importance. Erected before 1623, it was executed by the younger Gerard Johnson, son of the Dutch immigrant Gheerart Janssen, who carried on his business in London. Below the bust an inscription names Shakespeare and praises his writings. Above the cornice is a square block bearing the arms of Shakespeare. The inscription on the monument, in Latin and English, is itself a positive identification of Shakespeare as a poet.

Iudicio Pylium, genio Socratem, arte Maronem:
Terra tegit, populus maeret, Olympus habet

Stay, Passenger, why goest thou so fast?
Read, if thou canst, whom envious Death hath plast [placed]
Within this monument; Shakespeare, with whom

> Quick nature died, whose name doth deck this tomb
> Far more than cost. Sith all that he hath writ
> Leaves living art but page to serve his wit
>
> *Obiit Anno Domini 1616*
> *Ætatis 53, Die 23 April.*

The Latin verses may be rendered thus: "Him who was a Nestor in wisdom, in intellect a Socrates, in art a Virgil, the earth encloses, the people mourn, and Olympus holds."

The arms on the monument are depicted according to the grant of arms issued on 20 October 1596 by the College of Heralds. William Dethick, Garter Principal King of Arms, drew up the document, of which two copies are in the official files of the College of Heralds. In the upper lefthand corner, opposite his first words, Dethick wrote Shakespeare's motto, *Non sanz droict,* and made a drawing of his arms (see Plate 12):

Gold, on a bend sables, a spear of the first steeled argent. And for his crest or cognizance a falcon, his wings displayed argent, standing on a wreath of his colors, supporting a spear gold, steeled as aforesaid, set upon a helmet with mantles and tassels as hath been accustomed and doth more plainly appear depicted on this margin.

The arms on the Stratford monument agree in every detail with Dethick's grant. They appear again on the seal of Susanna Hall. There is no possibility that the family of the actor-poet was not the recipient of the grant, because in the course of a quarrel in 1602 among the heralds a paper was written which names Shakespeare and gives a sketch of his arms; in the margin, apparently in the hand of Ralph Brooke, York Herald, are the words: "Shakespeare the player." Another officer of the College of Heralds, the learned William Camden, author of the *Britannia* (1586) and of the *Annals* (1615) of Queen Elizabeth, and Clarencieux King of Arms, wrote as follows:

These may suffice for some poetical descriptions of our ancient poets; if I would come to our time, what a world could I present to you out of Sir Philip Sidney, Ed. Spenser, Samuel Daniel, Hugh Holland, Ben Jonson, Th. Campion, Mich. Drayton, George Chapman, John Marston, William Shakespeare, & other most pregnant wits of these our times....[4]

Within a few years of his death Shakespeare was bringing fame to Stratford. The unknown author of *A Banquet of Jests, or Change of Cheer*

[4] "Poets," in *Remains* (1605).

PLATE 12. A sketch of the coat of arms of "Shakespeare the player" as granted by William Dethick, Garter King-of-Arms, in 1596. Probably in the hand of Ralph Brooke, York Herald, about 1602. Folger MS. V.a.156.

(1630) begins a mildly amusing joke with words that illustrate the growth of Shakespeare's reputation: "One traveling through Stratford-upon-Avon, a town most remarkable for the birth of famous William Shakespeare. . . ." A more detailed statement was written by a Lieutenant Hammond in 1634:

In that day's travel we came by Stratford-upon-Avon, where, in the Church in that town, there are some monuments; which Church was built by Archbishop Stratford; those worth observing and of which we took notice were these . . . a neat monument of that famous English poet, Mr. William Shakespeare, who was born here.[5]

In the year 1662 the Reverend Mr. John Ward, M.A. of Oxford in 1652, became rector of Holy Trinity Church. Upon leaving the university, Ward had taken lodgings in London near Barber-Surgeons' Hall so that he might attend lectures on anatomy, for he was almost equally interested in the cure of the body and the cure of souls. His notebooks, now in the Folger Shakespeare Library, are filled with memoranda about medicine and theology and contain many references to events in his life and to people he met or heard about. They show that upon his arrival in Stratford he did what every prudent, conscientious clergyman does: he inquired about the important parishioners. One family name would interest him, for whenever he went into the chancel of Holy Trinity Church there was the monument to William Shakespeare, and there were the burial places of Anne his wife, Susanna his elder daughter, and her husband the prominent physician Dr. John Hall.

Hall, the physician, a selection from whose casebooks had been translated into English and published in 1657, Ward would know about. Hall's daughter Elizabeth's first husband, Thomas Nash, was also buried in the chancel; she was in 1662 the wife of Sir John Bernard of Abingdon. Elizabeth had inherited New Place, one of the finest houses in Stratford, and, as all Stratford remembered, she and her mother had been hostesses in 1643 to Queen Henrietta Maria and her attendants when they occupied New Place en route from London to join King Charles in the North. Ward's notebooks contain four entries about Shakespeare and his family:[6]

[5] *A Relation of a Short Survey of 26 Counties . . . By a Captain, a Lieutenant, and an Ancient, All three of the Military Company of Norwich* (1634).

[6] [Two other entries demur at Peter Heylin's omission of Shakespeare's name from lists in his *Cosmographie* (1652; reprinted 1657, 1666, 1668-69, *etc.*) of the chief men of note in English history, including poets. See Laetitia Yeandle, "Shakespeare Allusions," *SQ*, XX (1969), 87-88.]

Shakespeare had but two daughters, one whereof Mr. Hall the physician married and by her had one daughter, to-wit the Lady Bernard of Abingdon: ...

I have heard that Mr. Shakespeare was a natural wit, without any art at all. He frequented the plays all his younger time, but in his elder days lived at Stratford; and supplied the stage with two plays every year, and for that had an allowance so large that he spent at the rate of a £1000 a year, as I have heard: ...

Remember to peruse Shakespeare's plays and be versed in them that I may not be ignorant in that matter: ...

Shakespeare, Drayton, and Ben Jonson had a merry meeting and it seems drank too hard, for Shakespeare died of a fever there contracted.[7]

The testimony of the Reverend Mr. John Ward is unimpeachable. The most famous names in recent Stratford history were Shakespeare and Hall. The most exciting event in recent memory was the visit of Queen Henrietta Maria. Shakespeare's granddaughter was now Lady Bernard, and the family home was one of the showplaces of the town. Of course the new rector must read Shakespeare's plays, so as not to show ignorance of them, for apparently they were part of the subject of conversation among the best people.

There are two authentic likenesses of Shakespeare. One of these is the engraving by Martin Droeshout, printed on the title-page of the First Folio (1623). Since the artist was only about twenty-two when the book came from the press, he must have worked from a portrait; at the age of fifteen, which he was when the poet died, he was too young to have formed a trustworthy impression. The identity of the portrait he copied is unknown. Possibly it was that now in the National Portrait Gallery in London. This has been attributed to Richard Burbage, who is known to have painted portraits; it has also been attributed to Joseph Taylor, an actor with the King's Men (or to John Taylor, a contemporary artist). According to early tradition, Taylor bequeathed it to Shakespeare's godson, Sir William Davenant. From him it passed to Thomas Betterton. From Betterton it went to his long-time associate on the stage, Mrs. Barry. The record of its ownership continues unbroken until it became the property of the Duke of Chandos, from whom it passed to the National Portrait Gallery. Whatever faults of execution Droeshout may have committed in his engraving, it is certain that Shakespeare's friends provided him with an authentic portrait to copy.

[7] It has been conjectured that he caught pneumonia, for drinking does not cause a fever.

The portrait bust in Stratford was erected in 1622. Gerard Johnson the Younger carved it, possibly from a life mask or a death mask. Its acceptance and erection in Holy Trinity Church are reasonable assurances that the family considered it a satisfactory likeness. About 1748 it required minor repairs and repainting. Later, in 1793, it was painted stone color to give it a classical appearance. And still later, in 1861, the original colors were restored as faithfully as might be. Because of differences in detail in the engraving printed in William Dugdale's *Warwickshire* (1656), there has been controversy about the reliability of the bust as it is now seen. This need not be taken seriously, for many of the monuments depicted by Dugdale, unchanged from his day to this, differ markedly from the engravings in *Warwickshire*. It may be remarked that Dugdale shows the arms of Shakespeare, as granted by Dethick in 1596, and the inscription below the bust which names the poet.

When interest in Shakespeare caused collectors to buy early quartos and folios at ever higher prices, it was natural that a search should be made for early portraits. Some of those brought to light may be genuine likenesses, painted in his lifetime, but not one has an unbroken pedigree, and so all are suspect. Others, when subjected to close study, have proved to be clumsy or skillful alterations of early portraits of subjects unknown. The market for Shakespeare portraits was brisk, buyers were not always critical, and false claims were made. This kind of shady business has nothing to do with the authorship of Shakespeare; it is simply proof that a painting called "Shakespeare" would fetch a higher price than a "portrait of a gentleman unknown."

The Elizabethan indifference to playwrights extended to their manuscripts. Manuscript plays had value only for actors, who might want to perform them, or publishers, who might want to have them printed. There were no Elizabethan collectors of literary autographs. When Francis Bacon arranged with Humfrey Hooper to publish his *Essays* in 1597, Hooper delivered the manuscript to John Windet the printer, and when the job was finished this manuscript was discarded. No one treasured it, not even the author. By 1625 the number of Bacon's essays had increased in successive editions from ten to fifty-eight. If Bacon had been a man of relatively small importance in 1597, he had risen meteorically under King James until he became Baron Verulam, Viscount St. Alban, and Lord Chancellor; then, meteorlike, he had fallen. Had Elizabethans been collectors of literary autographs, surely the manuscripts of the successive revisions of, and additions to, the *Essays* should have been a prize worth

striving for. But no one was interested, and in consequence Bacon's manuscripts of the *Essays* perished. In just the same way Shakespeare's holograph copies of *Venus and Adonis* and *The Rape of Lucrece* were discarded as waste paper as soon as Richard Field had set them in type.

As a matter of fact, paper was an expensive commodity and was seldom wasted. Almost all the paper was imported, and people used it until
it went to pieces. The bindings of Elizabethan books are filled with scraps
of manuscript and pieces of printed matter that accumulated in the shops
of printers and bookbinders. All that is left of the first edition of Shakespeare's *King Henry IV, Part 1,* is a single sheet, now in the Folger
Shakespeare Library, that someone used in making a binding for a copy
of Thomas's *Rules of the Italian Grammar* (1567). As late as 1700 a favorite way to insult a poet was to suggest that his verses would be good for
lighting a fire or wrapping a fish, or for some humbler use.

Very few of the plays written in Tudor and early Stuart times were
printed. The actors believed that popular plays should be kept out of
print, for if people could buy and read them they might be less eager to
pay to see performances in the theater. Another danger was that rival
companies of actors might use them for giving performances, for there
was no law to prevent such competition.

Then, as now, a playwright sold his new play to a producer, who was
in Shakespeare's age a company of actors. The modern playwright may, if
he wishes, retain publishing, radio, television, and moving-picture rights.
Not so in Elizabethan times. When a company of actors bought a play, it
acquired all rights. The company could perform the play as written or
employ someone to revise it; it could even lock up the play without performance; it could, at its discretion, sell the play to a publisher. The publisher, in turn, acquired absolute copyright to himself and his heirs forever.
When he had the play printed, it did not occur to him to ask or permit the
author to read proofs, for in selling his play to the actors the author had
disposed of all his rights in it. In Shakespeare's case he sold his plays, after
1594, to the company of which he was a sharer. The manuscripts went
into what may be called the company library, and there the licensed
promptbooks presumably remained until Parliament closed all playhouses
in 1642 and the King's Men distributed their assets among the then
sharers.

The other companies of actors may be presumed to have parceled out
their play-manuscripts in the same way in 1642. Several promptbooks,
such as Philip Massinger's *The City Madam,* were sold to publishers or

published by their unemployed actor-owners. By 1653 Humphrey Mose-
ley, the publisher, had bought up from the actors a quantity of manuscript plays that had never been printed and entered them in the Stationers' Register. Only a few of these were printed, because the London of the
Commonwealth period had little love for the stage; many of the manuscripts have disappeared. Probably the Great Fire of 1666 took a heavy toll
of unprinted plays as it swept through London and destroyed untold
quantities of bookshops and their contents. (Copies of the Third Folio of
Shakespeare of 1663-64 are scarce for the probable reason that many of the
unsold copies were burned.)

It was not until about 1660 that private collectors appear to have de-
veloped an interest in unprinted plays. A letter from the Lords Somerset,
Cavendish (later the Duke of Devonshire, builder of Chatsworth), Gerard, and Roscommon contains greetings to a wealthy fellow-collector,
Abraham Hill. Cavendish, along with the Earls of Oxford, Pembroke,
Winchelsea, and Sunderland, and others of lower station, made regular
Saturday excursions to the shops in quest of rare books and manuscripts.
And about 1678 Hill copied down the titles of more than fifty manuscript plays he had come upon. Only three plays are now extant in man-
uscript with titles corresponding to those in Hill's list; no manuscripts of
the other plays are traceable.

There is no reference to Shakespeare's play-manuscripts in his will for
the obvious reason that he no longer possessed them. As written, each
had been sold to the actors. (See Plate 13 and compare Plate 14.)

During Shakespeare's life approximately half of his plays were put into
print in one way or another; sometimes from unauthorized manuscripts,
as in the case of the first quartos of *Romeo and Juliet, Hamlet, Henry V,*
and others; sometimes from copies that seem to have been in Shakespeare's own handwriting, as *The Merchant of Venice* or the second
quarto of *Romeo and Juliet.* When the printer finished his job, the manuscripts were regarded as worthless. The same thing happened after Jaggard had finished printing the Folio of 1623; the printer's copy was
thrown away. This tossing out of printer's copy was not peculiar to Shakespeare. Of all the hundreds of plays put in print up to 1700, there is not
one surviving example of a manuscript that went through a print-shop.
Obviously the nonsurvival of Shakespearian literary manuscripts has no
bearing on the subject of authorship.

Letters and private papers, except the real-estate documents referred to
above, have all disappeared. At Shakespeare's death they would have re-

mained in New Place in the care of his widow Anne and his elder daughter Susanna Hall. After the death of the widow in 1623 Dr. John Hall and his wife remained at New Place. Hall's will, probated in 1636, provided that his "Study of Books" (these may or may not have included volumes belonging to Shakespeare) should be disposed of as his son-in-law Thomas Nash might wish: "As for my manuscripts . . . you may, son Nash, burn them or do with them what you please." In consequence of a lawsuit against Dr. Hall and his heirs, a charge was filed in 1637 by Susanna Hall, her daughter Elizabeth, and the latter's husband, Thomas Nash, that in August 1636 Baldwyn Brookes, mercer of Stratford, with the assistance of the undersheriff and some of the Stratford officers, broke into New Place and "there did take and seize upon the ready money, books, goods, and chattels of the said John Hall deceased . . . to the value of one thousand pounds at the least and have converted the same to their or some of their own uses without inventorying or appraising the same." No further documents in the suit have been discovered, and so it is not known whether Mistress Hall recovered anything.

At the death in 1670 of Shakespeare's last lineal descendant, his granddaughter Elizabeth, it may be supposed that any surviving books and papers remained at Abingdon, the residence of her second husband, Sir John Bernard.

There are several books in which Shakespeare's name is written. Some of the signatures may be genuine, but others are obvious forgeries.

As Shakespeare's plays gained ever wider popularity, some of their admirers expressed their admiration in extravagant terms. Idolaters professed to find technical knowledge about law, medicine, military science, and the like that is ordinarily possessed only by professionals, together with familiarity with foreign lands betokening wide travel, and erudition and elegance suitable to university-educated members of the nobility. No human ever possessed all the qualities that were in sum attributed to Shakespeare. In reaction against these absurdities, first one and then another writer began to point out the discrepancies between the biographical facts then known and the supposed accomplishments. The next stage was to propose that someone else wrote the plays.

Reduced to simplest terms, the process was as follows: The plays must have been written by a learned man, an intimate of the Court, who had traveled extensively. Who had these qualifications? The first name to be proposed was that of Francis Bacon, who in youth had "taken all knowledge to be [his] province." Other people, dissatisfied with this candidate,

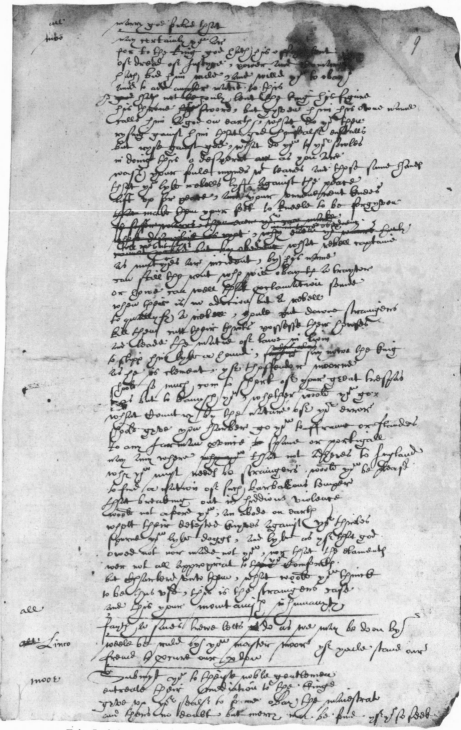

PLATE 13. Fol. 9ᵛ of the collaborative play *Sir Thomas More*. The text on this and the two preceding pages is thought by many scholars to be in the handwriting of William Shakespeare. From the original in the British Museum (Harl. MS. 7368).

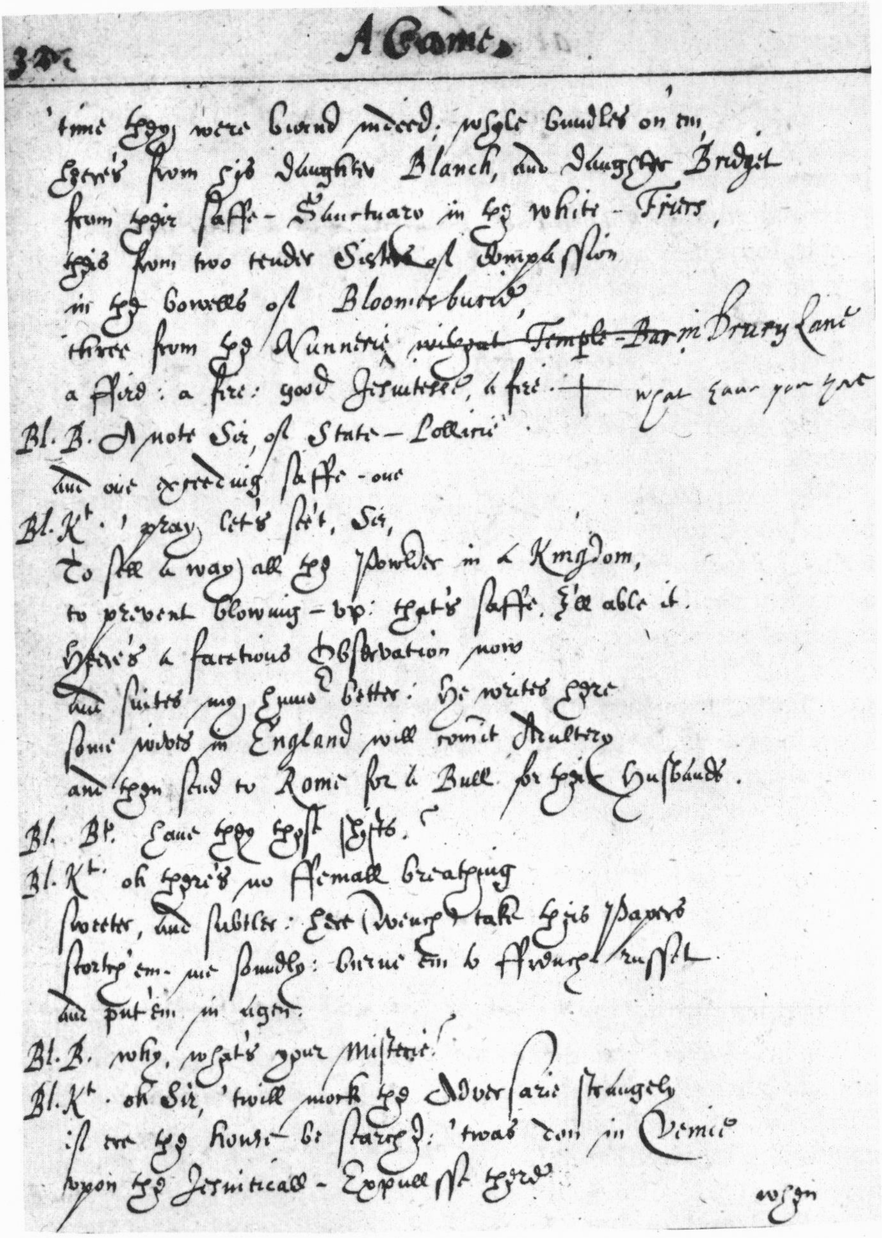

PLATE 14. A page of Thomas Middleton's *A Game at Chess* (1624), in the handwriting of Ralph Crane, who did professional copying for the King's Men. In lines 6 and 7 the author, a younger contemporary of Shakespeare, has made corrections in the text. Folger MS. V. a. 231.

suggested Edward de Vere, seventeenth Earl of Oxford, or Henry Wrio-
thesley, third Earl of Southampton, or William Stanley, sixth Earl of
Derby, until twenty or more rivals were in the field, including Queen
Elizabeth I and Anne Hathaway. When each of these in turn was proved
by opposed partisans to be ineligible, it was argued that a coterie wrote the
plays and poems or that the works had been parceled out to a number of
people. In no case has it been possible to produce a shred of evidence that
anyone in Shakespeare's day questioned his authorship. And not one
fact has been discovered to prove that anyone but Shakespeare was the
author.

It may be well to classify the objections to William Shakespeare and
consider them apart from the claims advanced for any of the proposed
authors.

The bitter attacks on Shakespeare often begin by calling Stratford-
upon-Avon a mean, dirty, bookless town, incapable of producing a great
man. The facts are that Stratford was a prosperous borough town with
an ancient charter, where citizens were not merely renters but were the
owners of their homes. The charge that Stratford was dirty proceeds out
of a single item in the borough accounts: the record of a fine levied upon
John Shakespeare for permitting a heap of refuse to collect before his
house in 1552. The commendable zeal of the authorities in enforcing their
regulations is the best evidence that Stratford had standards of sanitation
and took vigorous measures to uphold them. The grammar school had
been conducted for two hundred years before the Reformation and customarily employed Oxford and Cambridge graduates at high salaries.
This "proper little market town," as William Camden the historian described it, was capable of producing important men. John de Stratford,
who enlarged the parish church and founded a college of priests nearby,
rose to the Archbishopric of Canterbury in the reign of Edward III, and
his brother Robert became Bishop of Chichester and Chancellor of England. Another son of Stratford, Sir Hugh Clopton, was Lord Mayor of
London in the year Columbus discovered America. Sir Hugh built the
stone bridge that is still used by traffic crossing the Avon; he also built the
nave of the Guild Chapel, still a landmark in Stratford; and the house he
erected in 1483, New Place, became in due time the residence of William
Shakespeare. Clopton's will provided funds for what would now be called
five-year scholarships to six poor boys, three at Oxford and three at Cambridge.

The second charge brought against Shakespeare is ignorance. He has been called, among other things, "the mean, drunken, ignorant and absolutely unlettered rustic of Stratford," who could neither read nor write a line. Some people, after trying to decipher the signatures to Shakespeare's will and other legal documents have, in their own ignorance, called him illiterate. The usual hand written in England from about 1500 until long after Shakespeare's death bears the name of English or secretary. The "fine Italian hand" that Shakespeare mentions was introduced in the 16th century and by 1700 it had almost completely displaced the secretary hand. English or secretary letters resemble those used in German script, and most of them are totally different from the familiar italic letters of the modern cursive hand. Once the secretary forms are learned, Elizabethan manuscripts are no more or less difficult to read than modern hands. It is just as proper to call Goethe illiterate for writing German script as to say that Shakespeare was illiterate because he wrote English or secretary script.

The nature and extent of Shakespeare's schooling has already been described, as has the extent of formal education exhibited in the plays. The poet laureate John Dryden, a "learned" poet of the reign of Charles II, sums up the situation neatly in his *Of Dramatic Poesy, An Essay:*

To begin, then, with Shakespeare: he was the man who of all modern, and perhaps ancient poets, had the largest and most comprehensive soul. All the images of nature were still present to him, and he drew them not laboriously, but luckily: when he describes anything, you more than see it, you feel it too. Those who accuse him to have wanted learning, give him the greater commendation: he was naturally learn'd; he needed not the spectacles of books to read nature, he look'd inwards, and found her there.

A third objection to Shakespeare is that he could have had no opportunity to hear the conversation of royalty and nobility and, consequently, could not have written the dialogue of the plays. But just how did royalty and the nobility talk? Where are the transcripts of councils, private conversations, and amorous courtship? A modern poet (Don Marquis, in "Pete the Parrot and Shakespeare") has a manager hand Shakespeare a "mouldy old script" and demand that he prepare at once a manuscript filled with some of his usual hokum: fat men making love, "and kings talking like kings never had sense enough to talk." The fact is that Shakespeare's court scenes are psychologically convincing, and we assume that people in the Renaissance actually talked in this way. If it were true that only courtiers could write dialogue like that, John Webster, the son of a

London merchant tailor, must have been an Italian courtier to write the effective dialogue of his plays *The White Devil* and *The Duchess of Malfi.*

Several of Shakespeare's plays include details that have not yet been traced in source books and appear to suggest firsthand observation of foreign places and customs. Thus *Love's Labour's Lost* shows more than casual familiarity with French names. *The Two Gentlemen of Verona* has unusual geographic details. Some knowledge of Elsinore is supposed to be revealed in *Hamlet,* and possession of then unprinted historical details in *Macbeth.* Now Bacon or the Earl of Derby might be proposed as the authors of *Love's Labour's Lost* because of their travels in France. The Earl of Rutland had an embassage to Denmark, a fact not overlooked by those who would assign *Hamlet* to him. A reputed journey to Italy by the Earl of Southampton encourages some writers to think he wrote *The Two Gentlemen of Verona.* Plays have been attributed on similar grounds to the Earl of Essex, Sir Walter Raleigh, and others. Even if one single piece of evidence could be found to support any or all of these various ascriptions, the results would be chaotic, for it would be necessary to believe that a coterie composed of these, and perhaps other, people wrote the plays.

That is, of course, absurd. Some of these men were the bitterest rivals and at times deadly enemies. It is inconceivable that for a period of about twenty-five years (1588-1612) they could have collaborated to produce the plays at the dates they are known to have appeared on the stage. To hold such opinions is to shut one's eyes to the many sources of information open to a playwright. Even an island-bound poet could talk to travelers, who brought back stories from France and Italy and vivid accounts of their cities and customs. News pamphlets taught Londoners the names of the principal leaders in the French Wars, if only because English treasure was invested in the cause of Henry of Navarre and because the outcome of that religious struggle was of vital importance to every Englishman. English actors, reputed to be the best in Europe, performed frequently in Denmark, as well as in Germany and the Netherlands, and they reported their observations and experiences to all who would listen. Shakespeare's Romans are as truly Roman as his Renaissance Italians are Italian. No one, on this account, would suggest that the author of *Julius Caesar* must have lived in ancient Rome. The truth of the matter is that poetic genius overleaps both space and time.

The author of the plays was not a formally trained lawyer—or doctor, or soldier, or sailor—however vividly and appropriately technical terms are often used. Research has shown that Shakespeare uses legal terms and situations less frequently than some of the other playwrights, and often less accurately. It was a litigious age. People haled each other into court upon small provocation, and a certain number of legal terms made up a part of every man's vocabulary. So with war and navigation. A sword or dagger was never very far from an Elizabethan's hand. The citizenry were expected to know something of the use of weapons. And the average Londoner was much closer to the sea in those days of Drake and Hawkins and Frobisher than today. What a poet needed was a quick eye, a keen ear, a sensitive imagination, and a retentive memory—and, in Dryden's words, "the largest and most comprehensive soul of all modern, and perhaps ancient poets."

Most of the objections to Shakespeare as the author of the plays have originated in ignorance of theatrical conditions and of the records that have survived. Frequently it is stated, for example, that Shakespeare could not have been a playwright because his name does not appear in the records of Philip Henslowe. Henslowe was a London businessman with a variety of interests. He engaged in pawnbroking, invested in real estate, was active in bearbaiting, and held minor court appointments; but his name lives because of the contents of his theatrical account books. Between 1592 and his death in 1616 he owned or financed several playhouses (the Rose, the theater at Newington Butts, the Fortune, the Hope) and had financial dealings with, or was banker for, several companies of actors (chiefly the Admiral's Men, 1594-1604; then Worcester's, the Lady Elizabeth's, *etc.*). His *Diary* and *Papers,* as the account books are called, are among the most detailed and valuable records of the Elizabethan theater. They contain, among other matters, many entries of payments to Jonson, Dekker, Hathaway, Drayton, and others for writing plays (see Plates 15-16). Shakespeare is not mentioned. Why? The answer is easy. In the early 1590's the theater was in a turmoil. Acting companies formed, disintegrated, and reformed, with much shifting about of actors and sale and resale of promptbooks. The plague closed the playhouses for much of the time between 1592 and 1594, with occasional brief intervals of theatrical activity. Several titles of Shakespearian interest appear in Henslowe's business records for these years: *Henry VI, Titus Andronicus, The Taming of the Shrew, Hamlet.* But at this period Henslowe did not name the authors of plays, and so it is not possible to match plays and poets.

In the autumn of 1594 relief from the plague permitted the resumption

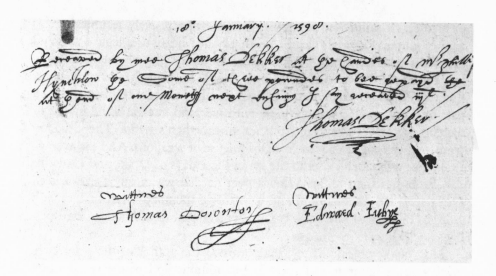

PLATE 15. A note, written and signed by Thomas Dekker, for £3 loaned to him by Philip Henslowe on 18 January 1598. Thomas Downton and Edward Juby, two actors, sign as witnesses. One side of Folger MS. X. d. 319.

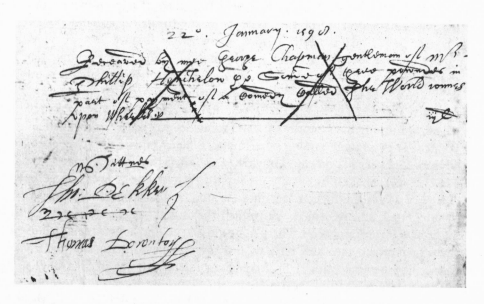

PLATE 16. A receipt written and signed by George Chapman on 22 January 1598, for £3 from Philip Henslowe, in part payment—in advance—for writing a play called *The World Runs upon Wheels*. Chapman's signature has been cut out by an autograph collector. Thomas Dekker and Thomas Downton sign as witnesses. The other side of Folger MS. X. d. 319.

of theatrical activity in London. And just at this time the Lord Chamberlain took under his protection a newly organized company of actors that included William Shakespeare. From 1594 until the playhouses were closed in 1642 this company had a continuous history, with a succession of noble patrons until 1603, when King James chose them to be the King's Men. During the long years from 1594 to 1642 this company was, almost without interruption, the strongest, best, and most successful in London, as the record of payments to them for performances at Court clearly demonstrates. Not once in these years did Shakespeare's company have any financial connections with Philip Henslowe or with any of the acting companies dependent upon him. Since after 1594 Shakespeare acted and wrote only for the company of which he had become a sharer, his name could not appear in Henslowe's records any more than the president of General Motors could be named on the payrolls of Chrysler or Ford.

Much ingenuity has been expended in the attempt to find in Shakespeare's works hidden messages about their authorship, and there is a voluminous literature on the subject. This has all been subjected to impartial scrutiny by two eminent cryptanalysts, William F. and Elizebeth S. Friedman, who in *The Shakespearean Ciphers Examined* (1957) prove conclusively that no crypto-system hitherto used by anti-Shakespearians meets the basic tests of cryptology. Determined to avoid partisanship, they refuse to make a search for codes or ciphers, but they give assurance that none of the supposed discoveries thus far reported has any validity.

Shakespeare's artistry, unique in its perfection, did not develop in a vacuum. The Shakespeare of the early plays sounds, for lines on end, like Marlowe or Greene or Kyd or Peele, because these men had slightly preceded him in the field and had something he could learn by imitation. Then Heywood and Middleton and a dozen others, slightly younger, began to learn from Shakespeare. Theatrical London of those years was an exciting, intoxicating little world, somewhat like New York and Hollywood in the early days of radio and television. Everyone tried to improve on everything that had succeeded for anyone else, and then to invent something new. Writers imitated, they borrowed, each man learning from the others and, with luck, doing something original that the rest would try to copy. At the same time they ridiculed and criticized each other, so that the exact date of a play can sometimes be arrived at by a study of the plays it imitates or borrows from and those that, in turn, imitate or satirize it. These things were true of diction and metrics, as well as of incident, character, and plot. So it is relatively easy to write the history of English drama from, say, 1585 to 1642. The events hang together, with a place for everyone and everyone in his place. In such a scheme the observed development of Shakespeare as theatrical writer and poet is credible and logical. The chronology of his works meshes perfectly with the chronology of the whole literature of the age.

There is no problem of authorship for those who have read Elizabethan drama in a setting of Elizabethan literature and history. Those who find difficulty do so because they attempt to treat Shakespeare as a special case, without proper reference to contemporary writers and the customs and attitudes of his age. Read Shakespeare's works in chronological order of composition, and it will be obvious that they are the product of a single intellect. Metrical devices, characteristics of expression, qualities of mind that are present in the earliest writings, are traceable throughout. But as the poet develops, his early exuberance changes to skillful mastery and ripens into mature profundity. The early comedies tinkle with rhyme and sparkle with wordplay as the poet revels in the discovery of his talent. The golden comedies and the late histories reveal a writer who has mastered his craft and is free to contemplate the vanities of "Man, proud Man." The next stage of development is to investigate some of the complexities of the human spirit and to grapple with the timeless problems of evil and death. At length come the romances, in which the poet is concerned with forgiveness and reconciliation and the renewal of life. Throughout, there is the same mind at work, revealing itself in the careful architecture of the plays. Throughout, there is the same sensitive spirit, able to enter perfectly into the mind and heart of every character in every situation. And throughout, there is the same incredible mastery of language, so that each character always has the right words to express his particular thought or emotion.

> Nature her selfe was proud of his designes,
>   And joy'd to weare the dressing of his lines! . . .
> Yet must I not giue Nature all: Thy Art,
>   My gentle Shakespeare, must enjoy a part.
> For though the Poet's matter, Nature be,
>   His Art doth giue the fashion. . . .
> For a good Poet's made, as well as borne.
>   And such wert thou.[8]

[8] Ben Jonson, "To the Memory of My Beloved, the Author Mr. William Shakespeare: and What He Hath Left Us," prefixed to the First Folio (1623).

Notes on Act V of *Antony and Cleopatra*

[1962]

THREE of Shakespeare's plays name two people in the title: *Romeo and Juliet, Troilus and Cressida,* and *Antony and Cleopatra.* The hapless young lovers of the first tragedy die by their own hands at the end of the play, each worthy of the other. In the Trojan story, both protagonists are alive at the close, though heartbroken Troilus would as lief be dead, for Cressida has proved a wanton, a daughter of the game. *Antony and Cleopatra* differs from both of these. In it, the hero dies a suicide at the end of Act IV, and all of the Fifth Act is concerned with the last hours of the heroine. This detail of the structure of the tragedy, unique in Shakespeare, has been mentioned in discussions of the theme of the play, but these references rarely go beyond noting the fact that Shakespeare is following the general chronology of his sources. The question may be asked, however, whether Shakespeare has not here turned historical fact to extraordinary dramatic account.

If it can be shown that other dramatists have sought to produce an unexpected emotional effect by the use of unconventional structure at the end of a play, it may be possible to come closer to Shakespeare's intention in *Antony and Cleopatra*. Two plays suggest themselves: Thornton Wilder's *Our Town* (1938) and Jean Anouilh's *The Lark* (1956). The later play will be considered first, not only because its historical fable imposes limits upon the author much as Shakespeare's sources did, but because the dramatist's purpose is single.

As *The Lark* draws to its close, Joan of Arc is forsaken by those she has befriended and overwhelmed by her enemies. She submits to judgment, renounces arms, and lets Ladvenu guide her hand in signing the

Shakespeare Studies (The Shakespeare Society of Japan), I (1962), 1-5.

confession. But as she begins her sentence of life imprisonment, her vital forces rally and she says to Warwick:

> Monseigneur, I have done wrong. And I don't know how or why I did it. (*Slowly, bitterly*) I swore against myself. That is a great sin, past all others— (*Desperately*) I still believe in all that I did, and yet I swore against it. God can't want that. . . .[1]

Life holds two alternatives for her: (1) if she be freed, the disgrace and contempt that fall on one who "ate the dirt of lies when she was faced with punishment"; or (2) "a prison dungeon, and filth and darkness." "What good is life either way?"

Then she *"calls out, speaking to the Voices,"* and audiences thrill as she cries to God, ". . . Forgive me and take me back for what I am. Call your soldiers, Warwick. I deny my confession." Instantly, the faggots that have been kept in readiness are heaped about her—off-stage—and the theater is lurid with the flames of Joan's execution

Within moments, spectators are on the verge of tears from beholding one so fine, so courageous, done to death in such a fashion, and by such people. This is sickening tragedy. It seems to say that there is no place in this world for virtue. But Anouilh is too fine an artist to stop at this point. La Hire, who had ridden knee to knee with Joan in battle, intervenes: "I knew the girl and I loved her. You can't let it end this way. If you do, it will not be the true story of Joan." "The true story of Joan is the story of her happiest day. . . . Go back and act it out." And so the Coronation of Charles in Rheims Cathedral is presented in dumb show. *"Joan stands clothed in a fine white robe, ornamented with a fleur-de-lis."* "Oh, Warwick," she says, "I wanted [Charlie] crowned because I wanted my country back. And God gave it to us on this Coronation Day. Let's end with it, please, if nobody would mind." The Chorus starts to sing the Gloria of the Mass, and the curtain falls. And the hearts of the audience lift again. They have seen History, the burning of Joan; but they leave the theater triumphant in the confidence that man's finest hour is well worth whatever it may cost.

The structure of *Our Town,* which also has a trick ending, is more complex, because Wilder has more purposes than one in writing his

---

[1] [I quote from Lillian Hellman's adaptation (New York, 1956), in which I saw Julie Harris play Joan in 1956. In Christopher Fry's translation (London, 1956), it is Baudricourt, not La Hire, who demands the Coronation Scene.]

final scene. One of these is to round off the life of young Emily, who dies giving birth to her second child (who also dies), and then to take her into the company of her mother and others who have gone before. Wilder's main purpose, however, is to impart a cosmic touch to the story, to illustrate what the Stage Manager asserts:

I don't care what they say with their mouths—everybody knows that *something* is eternal . . . and that something has to do with human beings.

"You know as well as I do," he continues—and this is Wilder's thesis to be illustrated at this point—

You know as well as I do that the dead don't stay interested in us living people for very long. Gradually, gradually, they let [? go their] hold of the earth . . . and the ambitions they had . . . and the pleasures they had . . . and the things they suffered . . . and the people they loved.

.   .   .   .

They're waitin'. They're waitin' for something that they feel is comin'. Something important and great. Aren't they waitin' for the eternal part in them to come out clean?

This cosmic theme concerns us only because Emily, newly joined to the Dead, has not yet lost her mortal yearnings. She wants to go back, and in the face of repeated warnings she does so. Her first impulse is to choose to relive a happy day, the day she first knew she loved George. "No," says Mrs. Gibbs. "At least, choose an unimportant day. Choose the least important day in your life."[2] What day she selects, and how she begins to see with the eyes of those long dead, is another story. The point of interest is that the playwright (in 1938) sends a dead person back into Time, somewhat as Anouilh would do (in 1956), in order to make a dramatic point and secure an emotional effect impossible of achievement by normal means.

Shakespeare, it seems to me, had a problem similar to that of Anouilh. His fable required that Antony should die, disgraced, defeated, tricked into suicide by the whim of the woman he had loved. A demigod, ruler of half the world, had let dominion and honor and life itself slip through his fingers. At his death, "Wither'd is the garland of the war. . . . And there is nothing left remarkable Beneath the visiting moon." Through four acts, the main concern of the play has been with Antony. Although

---

[2] Contrast this with the choice of Joan's happiest day. Wilder wishes to disillusion his heroine by letting her see—from the point of view of eternity—the triviality of life of purblind humans.

Cleopatra has her big scenes, these have had significance less for themselves than as pieces in the mosaic of Antony's story. In the struggle for
power, attention has been concentrated upon the mighty opposites:
Antony and Caesar, with Cleopatra moving occasionally into and then
out of the action.

The play might have stopped with Antony's death, and there Shakespeare could have ended it, had he chosen. But he was writing the tragedy
of Antony *and* Cleopatra. This man, this hero, with mastery of the world
at stake, why did he play it away? Shakespeare has written of him as he
was, extenuating nothing. Like Othello, Antony had "loved, not wisely,
but too well." And what had he loved? The Serpent of Old Nile, cunning past man's thought, a woman of infinite variety, who made hungry
where most she satisfied. But also the woman who had been a morsel
cold upon dead Caesar's trencher, a fragment of Cneius Pompey's; she
was the ribaudred nag of Egypt, who, in the midst of battle—the breeze
upon her, like a cow in June—hoisted sail and fled. Was Cleopatra no
more than this?

Perhaps it was to answer this question that Shakespeare devoted the
concluding act of the play to Cleopatra. She was entitled to at least a
brief study in her own right. If she had the capacity to learn from
Antony's life and death, what could she attain to? In Act V her moods
are various and her actions devious, perhaps surprising even herself. Not
Caesar himself can fathom her thoughts; and at the last, executing a
plan worked out in advance, she slips through the conqueror's fingers.
Instead of haling her in triumph through the streets of Rome, he finds
her regal and beautiful in death, looking like Sleep, "As she would catch
another Antony In her strong toil of grace." Learning finally the worth
of Antony's love, she has chosen the high Roman way. Only at the end
had she dared to call Antony husband. "Give me my robe, put on my
crown; I have immortal longings in me."

Does not a Cleopatra capable of such a finest hour deserve Shakespeare's final summing up of her worth?

Notes on Two Pre-Restoration
Stage Curtains

[1962]

NE of the fascinating problems in the study of English theatrical history is that of the shape, size, and appointments of the public and private theaters. The drawing of the Swan is well known, as are the engravings of stages in Alabaster's *Roxana* (1632), Richards's *Messallina* (1640), and Kirkman's *Wits* (1662). Unfortunately, the information they give is incomplete and unreliable. Any new pictorial material should, therefore, be welcome, and so I venture to put on record two engravings that are little known.

The first of these came to my attention several years ago. It illustrates Fable 55, "Of an Ægyptian King and his Apes," in John Ogilby's *The Fables of Æsop Paraphras'd in Verse, and Adorn'd with Sculpture* (London, 1651).[1] This fable is rarely found in editions of Aesop, and it is reasonable to suppose that Ogilby included it because his talents as a youthful dancing master had started him on his extraordinary career. In his own lively fashion, Ogilby tells the story of an Egyptian king whose greatest pleasure was in entertainment and princely feasts. When a courtier asked whether apes might be taught to dance, a mission was sent to fetch dancing-masters from France to make the experiment. The apes proved apt, and soon a performance was scheduled.

> Now Eastern *Apes* ply *Gallick* dancing Schools, . .
> The *Apes* were so refind,

[1] The engraving measures 93 × 143 mm. The only reproduction of it that I have found is without comment as one of numerous illustrations in a lively account of Ogilby's life and works by Marian Eames, "John Ogilby and his Æsop, The Fortunes and Fables of a Seventeenth-Century Virtuoso," *Bulletin of the New York Public Library*, LXV (1961), 73-88.

Philological Quarterly, XLI (1962), 270-74.

That all our *Allamodes* they far surpasse:
How they a Brawl, a Saraband would doe!
How stately move in a Coranto! who
From their great Masters, now, the cunning Scholler knew.

Oft for his Monsieur the King pleas'd to aske:
But when he heard they had perform'd their task,
He Solemn Order gave to have a stately mask.
And now th'expected night was come: when late
    Enters the joyfull King,
    And takes his lofty Chaire:
About him Peers and Princes of the State,
    And in a glorious Ring,
Sate Gypsie Ladies, there, accounted fair.
The Scean appears, the envious Curtain drawn
In Gold and Purple, tufted with pure lawn,
Beasts Frenchifi'd, shewd like the blushing dawn.

When from the Scean, a nimble *Hermes* springs,
With his *Caduceus,* golden Shoes, and Wings,
Conducting in a *Dynastie* of antient Kings: . . .
Each in his hand a mighty Scepter bears,
    And from their heads display
Twelve Silver rays, shot from a Golden Sun.
Like demie Gods the *Apes* began to move,
Semele saw, such a Majestick *Jove,*
The men admire, the taken Ladies fire, with love.

In the midst of the solemnity, a mischievous courtier tossed out a handful
of nuts, and the apes, reverting to type, fell into a mad scramble for them.

    Rich Cloaths, nor cost, nor education can
    Change nature, nor transforme an Ape into a Man.

Amusing as the fable is in its own right, with its gibes at impression-
able ladies and dancing Frenchmen, it is the illustration (Plate 17) that
claims attention. Ogilby's entertainment is a court masque, the setting
such a room as the theater at Whitehall. The king sits in his chair of state,
flanked by his courtiers and their ladies. Before them, on the same level,
are the apes, some still performing their courtly dance, the others fighting
for the nuts. A flight of steps leads to the center of the stage, on which
stand Hermes, the presenter, on one side, and three musicians on the
other. The backdrop, in perspective, shows Apollo in his chariot descending in a cloud. Between the audience and the steps hang two heavy cur-

tains, drawn back and up, to disclose the stage. With Ogilby's lines and illustration, compare a sentence from Ben Jonson's *The Masque of Queenes*, performed by Queen Anne and her Ladies at Whitehall on 2 February 1609:

> *First, then, his Ma.*tie *being set, and the Whole Company in full expectation, that w*c*h presented it selfe was an ougly* Hell . . . ;

and three introductory paragraphs from his *Chloridia*, performed by the Queen's Majesty and her Ladies at Shrovetide, 1630:

> *The Curtain being drawne up, the* Scene *is discouer'd, consisting of pleasant hills, planted with young trees. . . .*
>
> *Ouer all, a serene skie, with transparent cloudes, giuing a great lustre to the whole worke, which did imitate the pleasant* Spring.
>
> *When the Spectators had enough fed their eyes, with the delights of the* Scene, *in a part of the ayre, a bright cloud begins to breake forth; and in it, is sitting a plumpe Boy, in a changeable garment, richly adorn'd, representing the mild Zephyrus. . . .*

Ogilby is obviously using the technical language of the court masque, and his engraving depicts such a scene as delighted King James and King Charles. Well he might do so, for in 1638 Lord Wentworth, Lord Deputy of Ireland, had appointed him Master of the Revels in Ireland, and there he had built a little theater in Werburgh Street, where professional plays were performed in Ireland for the first time. Associated with him for a time was his close friend James Shirley, author of many plays and masques.

Ogilby's engraving is in some respects better evidence of what the curtains of the court masques looked like and how they were drawn up than some of the drawings of Inigo Jones, which show frontispieces with festoons of drapery, rather than curtains themselves.[2] The curtains in Ogilby are those that hung before the frontispiece,[3] like those referred to in the first stage direction in *The Tempest* (1674): ". . . *the Curtain rises,*

[2] See Plates X, XXI, and XLVIII in Percy Simpson and C. F. Bell, *Designs by Inigo Jones for Masques and Plays at Court* (Oxford, 1924).

[3] The use of a curtain to conceal the stage until the elaborate settings might be dramatically revealed did not, of course, originate in the English court masque. George R. Kernodle quotes from and discusses Filippo Pigafetta's account of the first performance of *Oedipus Rex* in the Teatro Olimpico in 1585, when a front curtain hid the entire stage until the fashionable audience were assembled and ready to give undivided attention to the spectacular stage setting (*From Art to Theatre: Form and Convention in the Renaissance*, University of Chicago Press, 1944, pp. 169-71).

55

PLATE 17. Engraved illustration of Fable 55, Of an Ægyptian King and his Apes, in *The Fables of Æsop Paraphras'd in Verse,* by John Ogilby (London, 1651).

PLATE 18. Engraved illustration by Ro. Stoop of Fable 55 for the second edition (1668) of Ogilby's *Fables of Æsop.*

PLATE 19. Engraved illustration of Fable 55 for the third edition (1673) of Ogilby's *Fables of Æsop.*

and discovers a new Frontispiece. . . ." A parallel more nearly contemporary with Ogilby is in Sir William Davenant's *The First Day's Entertainment at Rutland House* (performed in May 1656):

On each side of the platform was a rostrum decorated in purple and gilt,
And before it were curtains to be parted, also in cloth of gold and purple.

When Ogilby reprinted *The Fables* in a very handsome folio in 1668 (many of the engravings being done by Wenceslas Hollar), a new and larger plate (Plate 18) had to be provided.[4] King, Court, and curtains are essentially unchanged, except that the curtains are more obviously drawn up in a French valance.[5] Gone are the steps leading to the stage. Hermes has been eliminated, and there are now four musicians. Instead of a backdrop painted in perspective, a figured curtain some ten or twelve feet high hangs across the stage. Above this is what seems to be a curtain of different texture and pattern (masking, perhaps, the music-room or upper stage), and higher yet is a top border decorated along its lower third.

For the octavo-sized third edition of *The Fables,* a third, smaller plate (Plate 19) was required.[6] King, Court, apes, and curtains are little changed. Hermes and the steps to the stage are forgotten, and the musicians number three as in the first edition. A sort of tapestry curtain forms the background, with a curtain suspended above it, as in the second edition. At the next higher level is something that might be the grill before a music-room or an upper stage, and behind the grill is a surface extending upwards to the ceiling.

The second picture of a stage (Plate 20) to which I wish to call attention has been reproduced once without comment,[7] but since it appeared in

[4] It is 168 × 221 mm. and is signed by Ro. Stoop, probably the same man who executed the engraving of "Den Engelschen Koort-Dansser," a Dutch satire of 1653 on Oliver Cromwell, reproduced in Leslie Hotson, *The Commonwealth and Restoration Stage* (Harvard University Press, 1927), p. 146.

[5] For evidence that Ogilby did not abandon his interest in the theater, see Eames, p. 79 and notes. He calls himself "Master of His Majesties Revells in the Kingdom of Ireland" in the second and third editions of *The Fables.*

[6] This edition, in two volumes, was published by the author in 1673 (a variant title-page dated 1675 names T. Basset, R. Clavel, and R. Chiswel as the publishers and Samuel Keble as bookseller). The engraving is 93 × 143 mm.

[7] I am indebted to Dr. Robert W. Dent for the information that Kenneth Macgowan and William Melnitz reproduce the cut in *The Living Stage* (New York, 1955), p. 257, with the remark: ". . . this picture shows us one variety of stage and scenery in use on the Continent at the time of Cromwell's revolution."

CXXX.

Ludas Scenicus.

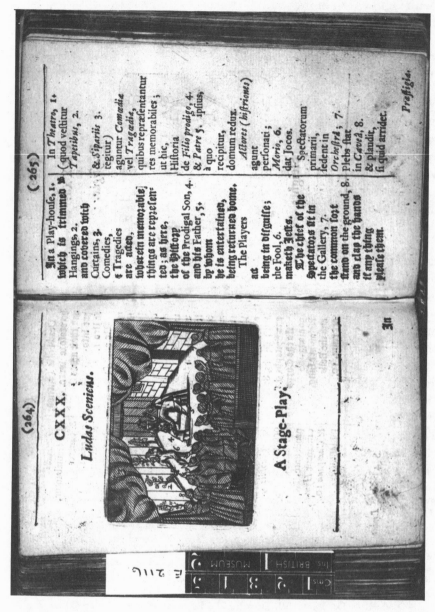

A Stage-Play.

In a Play-house, 1.
which is trimmed with
Hangings, 2.
and covered with
Curtains, 3.
Comedies,
& Tragedies
are acted,
wherein memorable
things are represen-
ted; as here,
the History
of the Prodigal Son, 4.
and his Father, 5.
by whom
he is entertained,
being returned home.
The Players
act
being in disguise;
the Fool, 6.
maketh jests.
The chief of the
Spectators sit in
the Gallery, 7.
the common sort
stand on the ground, 8.
and clap the hands
if any thing
please them.

In *Theatro*, 1.
(quod vestitur
Tapetibus, 2.
& *Sipariis* 3.
tegitur)
aguntur *Comediæ*
vel *Tragediæ*,
quibus repræsentantur
res memorabiles;
ut hic,
Historia
de *Filio prodigo*, 4.
& *Patre* 5. ipsius,
à quo
recipitur,
domum redux.
Actores (*histriones*)
agunt
personati;
Morio, 6.
dat Jocos.
Spectatorum
primarii,
sedent in
Orchestra, 7.
Plebs stat
in *Cavea*, 8.
& plaudit,
si quid arridet.

Præstigiæ.

In

PLATE 20. "Ludas [*sic*] Scenicus. A Stage-Play," in Jan Amos Komenski's *Orbis sensualium pictus* (London, 1659), translated by Charles Hoole. Reproduced by permission from the British Museum copy.

print in the same decade as Ogilby's in a book that was widely circulated and many times reprinted (there are four or more London editions by 1700; that of 1777 is called the twelfth), its influence must have been considerable. The book is the first English edition of Jan Amos Komenski's *Orbis sensualium pictus* (London, 1659), the first illustrated school-book in England, with Latin and English texts in parallel columns. It is derived from the first continental edition, printed in Nuremberg in 1658. Lesson CXXX is "Ludas [*sic*] Scenicus. A Stage-Play," illustrated by an engraving of a scene from a dramatization of the story of the Prodigal Son.[8] The engraving is a close copy of the woodcut used in the second Nuremberg edition of 1659.[9] It appeared again in Komenski's *Ars sensualium pictus* (London, 1664). By 1705, the original plate had been defaced or lost, and a new engraving was used in the edition of that year. It differs little from the original, except that there are unmistakable curtains before the inner stage, and the valance above them is a little clearer.

The important feature of the Komenski illustration, for our immediate purpose, is the pair of curtains at the front of the stage. These are raised in a French valance, as in the Ogilby engravings. Front curtains, it would appear, were a well known part of stages, both continental and English, and were used not only in court masques but in the performance of popular Biblical stories.

The English translation was made by the well-known educator, Charles Hoole, and his definitions are instructive. "In a Playhouse," he tells us, "which is trimmed wth Hangings, and covered with Curtains, Comedies & Tragedies are acted. . . . The chief of the Spectators sit in the Gallery, the common sort stand on the ground."[10] Perhaps "concealed" or "hidden" would have been a more accurate translation of *tegitur* than "covered." It may be supposed that Hoole, the pedagogue, would, how-

---

[8] The 1658 Nuremberg engraving is 78 × 58 mm. See Allardyce Nicoll, *Stuart Masques and the Renaissance Stage* (London, 1937), p. 153, for a reproduction.

[9] For information about this and Komenski's *Ars sensualium pictus*, I am indebted to Sir Frank C. Francis, who examined the British Museum copies of the second German and first London editions of *Orbis sensualium pictus*. I have been unable to secure a report on the first Nuremberg edition, but if the reproduction in C. W. Bardeen's reprint (*The Orbis Pictus of J. A. Comenius*, Syracuse, 1887) may be relied upon, the same woodcut was used in the first and second German editions.

[10] Interestingly enough, Komenski's word for curtain is *siparium*, which signifies the lesser curtains between scenes of a comedy, and not *aulaeum*, the main curtain. His name for the seats occupied by the *primarii* is *orchestra*, the same word used in the Swan drawing. The placing of the spectators, seated and standing, is not to be taken literally.

ever, choose his words with care and use terms that would be understood by his readers.[11]

If the engravings in Ogilby and Komenski do not add greatly to our knowledge of the English stage about the middle of the 17th century, they at least supplement the scanty pictorial evidence.[12]

[11] Stage curtains of some sort were well known by 1659, for in Matthew Locke's manuscript of the music for James Shirley's masque, *Cupid and Death,* the third movement of the introduction is designated as "For the Curtayne." Cf. the reproduction in E. J. Dent, ed., *Cupid and Death* (London, 1951), pp. 3, 78.

[12] It is tempting to comment on the side walls of the stage, that appear to converge upon the curtain at the rear. One of these has figured (tapestry?) hangings; the other looks like the exterior wall of a house with a window and a door.

The Renaissance Heritage of
English Staging (1642–1700)

[1964]

THE English stage flourished in a remarkable way under the first three Stuart monarchs. Anne of Denmark, Queen to King James I, delighted in theatrical festivities, and under her patronage began a series of elaborate court masques that became ever more splendid until Parliament put an end to them in 1642. From her, presumably, Charles I inherited the temperament that made him one of the foremost art collectors in Europe.[1] His French queen shared his and his mother's enjoyment of spectacle; and with their encouragement, aspiring courtiers, talented playwrights, and artist-architects competed and collaborated in the presentation of gorgeous entertainments. After the restoration of Charles II in 1660, England had a king in whom the love of music, masque, and the theater, honestly inherited from both his parents, suffered no diminution. It may even have been intensified, for during the humiliating years of expatriation he had tantalizing glimpses of the gaiety and brilliance of the French court, just enough to rouse his envy of his wealthy and powerful French cousin and to stimulate his own appetite for ballet and opera. Upon his accession to the English throne, Charles sought at once to duplicate in London what he had become acquainted with on the Continent, but never was he financially able to satisfy his artistic longings.

What was the state of theatrical development in England in 1642? From architectural sketches that have been discovered in Oxford and

---

[1] [See C. V. Wedgewood, "The Prince of Patrons," *Horizon*, III (1961), 78-95.]

"L'Héritage de la Renaissance dans la mise en scène en Angleterre (1642-1700)," in *Le Lieu théâtral à la Renaissance*, ed. Jean Jacquot, Paris, 1964, pp. 459-72. Read at the International Conference on Renaissance Theater sponsored by the Centre National de la Recherche Scientifique at Royaumont, March 1963.

London, and especially from the priceless Chatsworth drawings by Inigo Jones, it has been possible to trace the transformation of the English court masque from its relative simplicity in the early years of King James to the peak of its elaboration in such Caroline extravaganzas as Sir William Davenant's *Salmacida Spolia* of 1640.[2] (See Plates 21 and 22.)

From Italy, Jones had brought a firsthand knowledge of the theory and practice of theatrical architecture and stagecraft; and in the Palladian Banqueting House at Whitehall and the "Great new Masking Room" he introduced all the latest devices: scenes, machines, and lighting effects; frontispieces with curtains hanging before them, transparencies, relieves, wings, perspectives, mists, and clouds. The professional actors were not slow in borrowing many of these effects. Already they were reputed to be the most skilled performers in Europe, and their public and private theaters were admired extravagantly by visitors from abroad. At the Phoenix, a private house, changes of locale were effected in Nabbes's *Hannibal and Scipio* as early as 1635 by "translating" the scene "as the musick plays Betwixt the acts." The younger playwrights began to write plays in which the changing of scene was organic to the development of the fable and in which song, recitative, and variations in the structure of the verse approximated the texture of early opera.

In 1639, Sir William Davenant secured backing for what would today be called a cultural center, where a permanent company would "exercise action, musical instruments, scenes, dancing, and the like," and would also perform plays. The program seems to have included acrobatics, ballet, vocal and instrumental concerts, and also dramatic performances with scenery. An extant drawing by Inigo Jones corresponds rather closely to what Davenant had in mind, and it would be surprising if these two grand "projectors," who had already collaborated in two successful court masques, were not associated in the enterprise. That the project was blocked does not lessen its importance. The London stage was in process of transformation, and even in defeat Davenant focuses attention upon himself as one of the principal revolutionaries.

Between 1642 (when the playhouses were closed) and 1656, there is little to record. Drolls, a few surreptitious plays, jigs—some of which were a sort of rudimentary ballad opera—and a quite remarkable number of song-books kept alive the tradition of dance and song. And interest in

---

[2] [See *A Book of Masques in Honour of Allardyce Nicoll,* ed. T. J. B. Spencer and Stanley Wells, Cambridge University Press, 1967.]

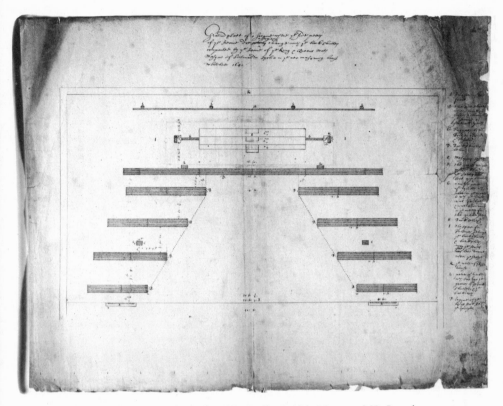

PLATE 21. Plan of the stage for *Salmacida Spolia*. British Museum MS. Lansdowne 1171.

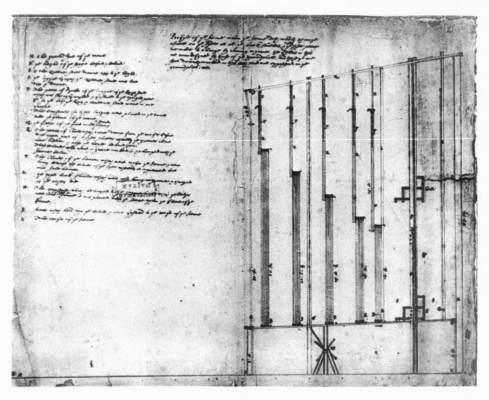

PLATE 22. Section of the stage for *Salmacida Spolia*. British Museum MS. Lansdowne 1171.

the theater was sustained by the news books, which have reports—not always satiric—of performances in Paris and Brussels, many of them attended by members of the exiled royalty and their attendants.

In the winter of 1656, Sir William Davenant, who this time appears to have forecast the political climate more accurately than in 1639, secured financial backing to build a theater "for representations and shows." He was not immediately successful but managed to give performances of some sort in a number of places. Then, for some reason, authority nodded, and Davenant posted bills announcing a performance at his private residence of "Moral Representations" in a series of "Entertainment[s] . . . By Declamations and Musick: After the manner of the Antients." *The First Day's Entertainment at Rutland House* had declamations, recitatives, and consort music, but no dancing; and the narrow room would not accommodate elaborate machinery. This was not yet opera, but Davenant, ever sanguine, had the Prologue assure the audience they were to "Think this your passage, and the narrow way To our Elysian Field, the Opera." It is typical of the promoter that the performers were not actors, who might have provoked government wrath, but former court musicians; typical, too, that one of the singers was a woman.

Growing bolder, Davenant offered *The Siege of Rhodes* (1658), "a Representation by the Art of Perspective in Scenes, And the Story sung in Recitative Musick." The painted scenes were in the latest continental fashion, with crowds of people, armies, and even spectacular action painted on the backcloths. John Webb, disciple of the now deceased Inigo Jones, set the stage, and his extant drawings show that he adapted the masque techniques of Jones to Davenant's residence. The author (? Settle) of *The Fairy-Queen* (1692) is representative of contemporary opinion in his emphatic assertion "That Sir William Davenant's *Siege of Rhodes* was the first Opera we ever had in England."

After the Restoration, Charles II issued a license to Giulio Gentileschi to build a theater for a band of Italian musicians, but he provided no money; so the project came to naught. He demonstrated his continuing interest in opera by paying £300 to Jean Channoveau in 1661 for a performance of (probably) Chapoton's *The Descent of Orpheus into Hell*, and it has been suggested that the machines used in this production were left behind in England when the actors returned to France. At Court, John Webb, probably the only living architect familiar with the pre-Wars masques, was commissioned to design and construct the new Hall Theater (1665) at Whitehall. Webb's plan and elevation show that this was essentially the court-masque stage of Jones. From the first, there were provisions to "take up and let downe the Curtaine," which is referred to in the Accounts as a "traverse." It was equipped with rings and pulleys for raising and lowering; but whether the curtain was in one piece or two cannot be decided from the wording of the documents. Provision was made for four pairs of wings and a pair of shutters, three relieves, and a backcloth. Corresponding to each section of wings and shutters were upper sections for clouds, later to be called borders. Back of the shutters, and above them, was a sloping platform for seats for the musicians. The stage was covered with green baize lined with canvas. There was no apron, nor were there proscenium doors. Troughs for footlights are first referred to in 1671.[3] There was a trap door in the floor of the stage, but there could have been very little machinery below, for the front edge of the stage was only five feet above the floor of the hall.

When John Crowne's *Calisto* was performed in 1675, the last great court masque, there were minor alterations to the stage and new scenes were prepared. The curtain was raised to disclose the prospect of Somerset House. When billowing clouds overhead were drawn, a Temple of Fame was revealed in the air. This was painted on silk-covered frames, behind which lights were set. Later, the Temple of Fame was replaced by an "open Heaven," in which four gods and goddesses sat, attended by airy spirits and a number of musicians. The back piece was a "glory," illuminated from the rear by lights arranged in frames. To judge by the carpenters' bills, the stage must have been a blaze of light, for all sorts of framework had been set up behind the clouds and elsewhere for candlesticks and sconces.

These details are worth mentioning because they are documented in the Works Accounts. Had the account books of the public theaters survived, they could doubtless give similar information. Lacking them, we are limited to the descriptive stage directions in some of the play-quartos, to the promptbooks, to the diarists Pepys and Evelyn, and to the visitors from abroad.

Unable to have a great court theater or opera house, Charles was forced to rely on the public theaters for much of his entertainment, and to these we must turn to information about the important developments in scenery and staging.

---

[3] [Although, as pointed out below, footlights themselves are recorded in the *Wits* engraving of 1662.]

Two royal companies had been set up in 1660, the King's, under the control of Thomas Killigrew, and the Duke of York's, assigned to Sir William Davenant. Like his rival, Killigrew was a pre-Wars playwright; he served Charles in France and Italy during the interregnum, and his enthusiasm for music, opera, spectacle, was hardly less than Davenant's. Davenant opened a new playhouse in Lincoln's Inn Fields in 1661, featuring actresses, costumes, and painted scenes. During the next ten years there were some machines—Pepys writes of *Hamlet* with scenes and of the wind music that was played when the Angel comes down in *The Virgin Martyr.* The scenes served as a pictorial background for action; they were not necessarily changed with every shift of the locus of action; and notations such as *"Tavern," "Court," "Wood," "Palace,"* indicate that producers and audiences soon came to accept stock scenery. Productions of the sort that Davenant had envisioned seem to have been beyond his financial reach, and he died in 1668 without having produced a real extravaganza.

Killigrew's Drury Lane Theatre was not ready until 1663. The auditorium was semicircular, with sloping floor, two galleries, and boxes on each side of the stage. The stage itself consisted of a deep, level-floored apron and a proscenium arch; extending from the arch to the rear wall was an upward-sloping floor, the area of shutters, relieves, and the backcloth. Two proscenium doors on each side opened on the apron, and the boxes over the doors could be used in performance. This building was destroyed by fire in 1672. The second Drury Lane Theatre was not ready until 1674 (see Plate 23). For reasons of economy it was relatively plain. A section of the theater appears to be given in a drawing by Sir Christopher Wren at All Souls College, Oxford. "A slightly raked apron stage extends 17 feet from the proscenium arch, leaving about 15 feet of stage depth behind. In this back portion of the stage provision is made for four side-wings (or flats) and there are three grooves behind for 'shutters.' Over the apron on each side are two boxes, beneath which are two doors. The pit slopes upward" (Allardyce Nicoll, *Development of the Theatre,* 1927, p. 163). The one extant engraving of the interior of this theater, showing the frontispiece to Perrin's *Ariane* (1674), is clearly untrustworthy in details, the apron, for example, being far too shallow. In scenes and machines, this house could never compete with Dorset Garden, built by the Duke's Company and opened in 1671. The front elevation and something of the interior of Dorset Garden are known from the engravings in Settle's *Empress of Morocco* (1673; Q 1674). These show the

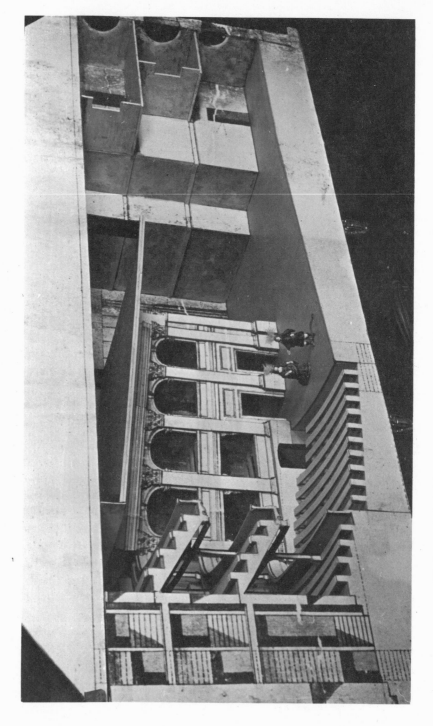

PLATE 23. Playhouse designed by Christopher Wren (*c.* 1674). Model reconstruction by Richard Southern.

ornate fixed frontispiece that constituted the proscenium arch, the music-
room—above the proscenium arch—and a portion of the apron.

The main elements of the Restoration stage were the apron, the proscenium arch, and the area between the proscenium arch and the back
wall of the theater. The apron was customarily called *"the stage,"* and
here most of the action took place. Here actors were most visible and
audible. The proscenium arch was an elaborate structure, with heraldic
or emblematic embellishments. Then came the area that stage directions
and promptbooks refer to as *"the house."* In the early years of the Restoration, this served as a background for performers on *"the stage."* Occasionally actors would enter here and would then come forward and
speak. But within four or five years, playwrights had learned to construct
plays in which action was dramatic because the mechanical and scenic
possibilities of shutters, wings, cut scenes, and relieves were recognized
and utilized. By 1700, the staging of a play or an opera could be a very
complicated business.

Reference has already been made to the proscenium doors and to the
windows or boxes or balconies above them. At Drury Lane and Dorset
Garden there were at least two doors on each side of the stage, and I think
no more than two, for contemporary stage directions name the *"Upper
Door"* and *"Lower Door"* and no others. There are plays in which lad-
ders are set up against the windows or balconies—as for an elopement;
two or more actors are seen in these areas, but they usually descend before
participating in the action.

The stage curtain presents a number of problems, for there were, in
fact, several kinds of curtain, each with one or more uses. The main curtain hung between the proscenium arch and the house. It was customarily
raised or opened after the prologue and closed at the end of the performance. In time, it came to be called *"the great curtain."* Front curtains had
been known in England since at least 1605; sometimes they were decorated, sometimes plain. Some, in one piece, appear to have been raised,
while others were dropped to the floor of the stage. Some, in two pieces,
were hung on rods; and others were drawn up in French valances. The
great curtain was probably in one piece and was raised.

By 1667, plays began to include scenes requiring very elaborate settings,
and frequently a stage direction prescribes that the curtain shall close in
preparation for such a scene and open again when the action is to begin.
For the sake of convenience, many of these scenes occur at the end or the
beginning of an act, and the use here of a curtain led some early com-

mentators to suppose that on occasion the theaters used "act curtains." Now we understand that the interim curtain was employed for the sake of spectacle.

Another kind of curtain was employed almost exclusively in operas. It will be remembered that when the brilliant audience assembled in the Teatro Olimpico in 1585 for the opening performance of *Oedipus,* a curtain was suspended between the audience and the stage, and for a long interval the nobles and their ladies had leisure for mutual admiration. Then the curtain opened, so that the beauty of the stage could be observed. In much the same way, English producers designed and erected ornate frontispieces to stand before the proscenium arch, and in front of this was placed a pair of heavy curtains. The drawing up of these curtains in French valances was the first part of the ritual of operatic performance. The frontispiece and the opening set are described in detail in the Restoration quartos and folios, so that readers, like the audience in the theater, might experience the thrill of the spectacle.

Yet a third kind of curtain was used on the Restoration stage. This was the so-called *"drop curtain,"* that appeared in France as early as 1664. The earliest positive reference to it in England seems to be in *The Prophetess* (Dorset Garden, 1690): *"a Curtain falls representing the entrance into an inner part of a Magnificent Pallace. A noble Arch; behind it two Embroidered Curtains, part of the first ty'd up on either Side, the farthest Curtain hanging down. . . ."* Though the function of the drop curtain was similar to that of the interim curtain, it had two advantages: drop curtains could be placed, it would seem, at any convenient location to cover the mounting of special effects; and they gave a pictorial preparation for the action that was to follow. The idea was as old, at least, as *The Masque of Blackness* (1605), in which a landscape of woods and hunters was *"drawne uppon a doune right cloth, strayned for the scene,"* which opened *"in manner of a curtine."* With the last of the pre-Wars masques, the use of a painted curtain may have been forgotten until the idea was borrowed late in the century from France.

Somewhat akin to the curtains were the gauze transparencies. These were used in Jacobean masques (Jonson's *Hymenaei* had *"tralucent"* elements), and their retention on the Restoration stage is proved by a stage direction in Duffett's burlesque (Lincoln's Inn Fields, 1673) of the operaticized *Macbeth* (Dorset Garden, 1673; Q 1674): *"Thunder and lightning is discover'd, not behind Painted Tiffany to blind and amuse the Senses, but openly, by the most excellent way of Mustardbowl and Salt-*

Peter." Gauzes may well have been used to produce the effect of mist or fog, as in Powell's *Brutus of Alba* (Dorset Garden, 1696; Q 1697): *"Coreb waves his Wand, and a Misty Cloud rises out of the Earth. . . ."* This piece of business probably made use of a part of the machinery introduced in 1692 in *The Fairy-Queen: "The Scene changes to a Garden of Fountaines. A Sonata plays while the Sun rises, it appears red through the mist, as it ascends it dissipates the Vapours, and is seen in its full Lustre; then the Scene is perfectly discover'd. . . ."* Later in this opera, the most famous of all Restoration gauze curtains is introduced: *"a transparent Prospect of a Chinese Garden."*

About the subject of shutters, grooves, wings, and borders, the evidence is at best fragmentary. It has been noted that the second Drury Lane seems to have had three pairs of shutters and four wings. For the production of *Sir Patient Fancy* in 1678, Dorset Garden must have had four sets of two grooves each, with space between the sets for the discovery of people and properties. This is a far cry from the earliest Restoration stages, where action proceeded on the apron against a painted background that lent atmosphere but might remain unchanged as action shifted from the headquarters of one army to the headquarters of its enemy. Plays with unusual or exotic settings might be provided with appropriate scenes, but these, being expensive, were kept for later use in plays where their appropriateness might be questionable. When John Downes records that *Macbeth* was revived in 1673 "in all it's Finery, as new Cloath's, new Scenes . . . ," the entry has importance, for we may infer that many plays lacked the finery of new costumes and new scenes.

It must be assumed that the theaters learned very quickly some of the advantages that might accrue from spacing the grooves for shutters widely enough apart to permit the placing—and discovery—of people and properties between them. As early as 1663, Sir Samuel Tuke plays a mystifying game with audiences and readers alike by making the action of *The Adventures of Five Hours* (Lincoln's Inn Fields) turn repeatedly on the opening and shutting of scenes and on the use of doors other than the four that opened on the apron. Another device was to separate a group, sending one or more actors toward the back of the house and closing them off with shutters so that action might continue *in situ;* this might be varied by bringing one or more characters forward and closing shutters behind them, so that action might proceed in a new area. Thus in Mrs. Trotter's *Agnes de Castro* (Theatre Royal, 1695), in V. i: *"Elvira asleep on a Couch, Bianca weeping by her; Alvaro advances. The King enters to him, and the Scene shuts."* This leaves the King and Alvaro in conversation. Later, after others have come on stage, *"Scene opens, Elvira wakes and starts up."* Note that there is no dropping of the curtain. A part of the enjoyment of a play was watching the shutters open and close.

Until one follows the example of Dr. Richard Southern and reconstructs the production of a Restoration play, as he did of *Sir Patient Fancy*,[4] he will have little appreciation of the skill and speed with which properties can be manipulated, the locus of action shifted, and the whole extent of the stage utilized, from apron to backcloth.

Most of the shutters were probably flat, for there are frequent references to *"A flat Scene of Tents"* or *"the new flat scene"*. But some of them appear to have been built in two planes, for there were "rooms" with practicable chimneys—chimneys, that is, in which a person might hide. Certain stage directions indicate that for a time it was conventional to refer to a pair of shutters as a door, on which one might knock, and which one might open or close. But others show just as clearly that shutters came to be fitted with practicable doors and also windows, with obvious advantages to playwrights and actors.

In contrast to the solid shutters were those that were pierced or cut out. Many of these were landscapes, with the effect of trees, arbors, isolated pieces of shrubbery, and the like, behind which or through which people might walk or hide, observe action downstage, or be observed by those downstage. All this lent fluidity and verisimilitude.

There is good reason to believe that a change of shutters was not necessarily accompanied by a shifting of wings and cloud borders. The best evidence is, perhaps, a stage direction in *Albion and Albanius* (Dorset Garden, 1685; F 1685): *"The Scene is a Poetical Hell. The change is total. The Upper Part of the House as well as the Side Scenes."* On the assumption that anything spelled out in such detail is a departure from custom—something to be called especially to the attention of the audience and the reader—we may infer that audiences were expected to ignore wings and borders most of the time. As on the Continent, wings were apt to be architecture, boscage, or rocks. But not all wings were conventional. In Lee's *Theodosius* (Dorset Garden, 1680; Q 1680), where the backscene represented *"an Altar richly adorn'd; before it Constantine, suppos'd kneels, with Commanders about him," "The side Scenes shew the horrid Tortures, with which the Roman tyrants persecuted the Church."*

---

[4] [*Changeable Scenery: Its Origin and Development in the British Theatre*, London, 1952, pp. 146-53.]

The stage directions for the total change of scene in *Albion and Albanius* contain an element that has not yet been discussed. The change affected *"The Upper Part of the House as well as the Side Scenes."* This means that clouds, cloud borders, and other things above the first level were shifted to harmonize with wings and the normal backcloth. It also means, as other stage directions prove, that there were both lower and upper backcloths, and perhaps also lower and upper shutters. At stage level, there was a prospect of the Royal Exchange. Above, and independent of it, was a pair of flats representing clouds, for these opened to reveal Juno's peacock chariot—as in *L'Educatione d'Achille* (Turin, 1650) or *L'Unione per la Peregrina* (Turin, 1660)—which then moved slowly forward and downward. (It may be remarked that the peacock chariot appeared again in *The Fairy-Queen,* 1692, and *Brutus of Alba,* 1696.) Shutters on two levels are new only in detail: Inigo Jones had such things, and in Davenant's *Salmacida Spolia* of 1640 he employed "upper back shutters which were also hung in grooues and changed as ye others did" (British Museum Lansdowne MS. 1171).

The term *"relieves"* occurs as early as 1606 in Jonson's *Masque of Hymen,* and with varied spellings and some variations in meaning it continues to appear throughout the 17th century; but the nature of the relieve scene and its location on the stage were baffling until Southern's brilliant examination of the evidence in *Changeable Scenery* (pp. 70 ff.). Now it appears that relieves were placed in the space between the shutters and the backcloth. A relieve setting consisted of two or more flat cut-out pieces, set one behind the other, with a ground-row to cover the foot of the foremost piece, and probably side relieves attached to the back of the frame supporting the shutters. The elements of the relieves had flat painted surfaces; they were not bas-reliefs and were not worked in the round. The backcloth of sky and possibly clouds served as background. Relieve scenes were always discovered, never set up or struck in view of the audience. Shutters opened or the curtain rose to discover relieve scenes; music played while spectators considered them; then dialogue began. Later, shutters closed or the curtain fell, and the scene could be struck.

A recurring stage direction calls attention to a scenic effect that was developed during the period. In *The Prophetess* (Dorset Garden, 1690), one setting is described as *"A long Walk in the middle of a great Wood; at the farther end is a Prospect of Dioclesian's Grange in a delightful Valley."* A much earlier play at the same theater, Mrs. Behn's *Sir Patient*

Fancy (1678), has a similar stage direction: *"Scene Changes to the long street. . . ."* Note the definite article: this is a setting that has been used before. Southern (pp. 151-52) makes the plausible suggestion that Dorset Garden had at the back of the house a sort of alcove annexed to the building, "similar to the 'inner stage' of the Elizabethans," an arrangement found in many later English theaters, and that *"the long street"* extended into this alcove. *"The long street"* deserved its name, for from Settle's *The World in the Moon* (1697) we know that *"the Extent of the House"* was fifty feet.

A word must be said about music and lighting. The earliest attempt to bring the orchestra down from the elevated Elizabethan music-room and put it between stage and audience in the continental fashion was in Killigrew's first Drury Lane, 1663. Pepys, a musician, reported that the musicians were so far below the stage as to be only partly audible, and what could be heard was distorted. Soon the music was back in its accustomed position, and there it remained in the public theaters—see the plates in *The Empress of Morocco*—until the opening performance of the operatic *Tempest* in 1674: *"The Front of the Stage is open'd, and the Band of 24 Violins, with the Harpsicals and Theorbo's which accompany the Voices, are plac'd between the Pit and the Stage."* It would be pleasant to think that this became the customary location of the orchestra, but evidence between 1674 and 1700 is lacking.

It has been argued that the new playhouses of the Restoration had footlights similar to those appearing in the 1662 engraving of Kirkman's *The Wits*. The evidence for footlights in the Hall Theater at Whitehall lends some credence to the conjecture. The *Wits* engraving also shows chandeliers similar to those in the theaters of 18th-century London, and it is tempting to think they were to be found in Drury Lane and Dorset Garden. These, with candles installed behind the proscenium arch and the wings, would provide ample illumination for the "house." The apron stage seems to have received adequate illumination from the lighting of the auditorium, for in a scene of supposed darkness Pepys watched an understudy walk through his role reading his lines from the actor's part held in his hand. In the first scene of *The Tempest, "the whole House is darken'd";* later, *"the Lights return."* Perhaps these effects were secured by extinguishing candles whose position was hidden from the audience and lighting them again; or some of the fixtures may have been provided with shields, as described by Sabbattini. But in *Oedipus* (1678) we read that *"the Stage was wholly darkened"* and that with equal suddenness *"the stage [was] made bright"*—this was no casual or gradual process. Is there any reason why chandeliers may not have been hoisted up to the roof and as quickly lowered? In *The Prophetess* (1690), *"a Machine descends, so large it fills all the Space, from the Frontispiece of the Stage to the farther end of the House. . . . In it are Four several Stages, representing the Pallaces of two Gods, and two Goddesses. . . ."* This structure would have interfered with ordinary chandeliers; it must have had its lighting built in, like the structure Inigo Jones designed in 1609 for the House of Fame in Jonson's *Masque of Queens*.

From the references that have been given, it is clear that new effects and unusual machines are most likely to be found first in operatic productions, but there are of course exceptions. One such novelty appears in *The Fairy-Queen* (1692). In Act IV there is a Garden of Fountains. After the sun rises and dissipates the mists, *"the Scene is perfectly discovered, the Fountains inrich'd with gilding and adorn'd with Statues: The view is terminated by a Walk of Cypress Trees which lead to a delightful Bower. Before the Trees stand rows of Marble Columns, which support many Walks which rise by Stairs to the top of the House; the Stairs are adorn'd with Figures on Pedestals, and Rails; and Balasters on each side of 'em. Near the Top, vast Quantities of Water break out of the Hills, and fall in mighty Cascade's to the bottom of the Scene to feed the Fountains which are on each side."* This I take to be the description of an elaborate backscene organically related to the wings. *"In the middle of the Stage,"* continues the stage direction, *"is a very large Fountain, where Water rises about twelve Foot."* This is clearly a practicable fountain. And so must be, in Act V, *"a Fountain, throwing up Water, which falls into a large Basin."* We shall do well to recall that about this time at Bartholomew Fair was a booth whose alternate name was "Sandys's Water-Works" and that, in the reign of Queen Anne, Crawley's Booth at Smithfield was featuring "several Fountains playing water during the time of the Play." Someone, I take it, had devised a new and spectacular variety of hydraulic entertainment, and it had its appeal for both aristocratic and plebeian Londoners.

The general situation is summed up by the anonymous writer of the Preface to *The Fairy-Queen* (1692) which, like that of Dryden's *Albion and Albanius,* gives a succinct history of opera, comparing its position in Italy, France, and England. "That a few private Persons should venture on so expensive a Work as an Opera, when none but Princes, or States exhibit 'em abroad, I hope is no Dishonour to our Nation: And I dare affirm, if we had half the Encouragement in England, that they have in other Countries you might in a short time have as good Dances in England as they have in France, though I despair of ever having as good Voices among us, as they have in Italy. These are the two great things which Travellers say we are most deficient in."

That verdict is not without honor, and this review of staging in England from 1642 to 1700 might conclude on that note, were it not for the fact that history is not always neat. Consider a passage in Settle's *The World in the Moon* (1697):

The Scene a Wood, near Thirty Foot high, the Paintings meeting in Circle; all the Side-Pieces and Back-Scene cut through, to see a farther Prospect of a Wood, continued to the Extent of the House. An Imperial Bed appears on the Stage of Crimson Silk, enrich'd and furl'd with Gold, and other Ornaments; with a Bed and rich Counterpane. Tom lying in it. . . .
[Dialogue].
Two Dancers enter, who are immediately interrupted by Thunder.
           [*The Bed and all the Furniture drops down under the Stage.*]

Then:

Frank Wildblood. Ay, *Joe,* now thou hast entertain'd us—This was a Masterpiece.
Hayns. Nay, as simple as I stand here, this very Machine came over from *France.*
Ned Stanmore. From *France?*
Hayns, [*sic*] *Alamode de Paree.* I can assure ye. For I'll tell you; I the Engineer-Royal of the King's House, and my Brother-Engineers of the Duke's House, went over into *France* together; and this Machine, and a few Clouds of Clouts, was all we brought over for Two Thousand Guineas.
Frank Wildblood. Nay, such an Engineer-General deserves Encouragement. Pray Mr. *Hayns,* let me present you with Five Guineas.

Surely this scene is satiric, for properties had vanished through trap doors for a hundred years; and the allusion to purchase of properties in France must be a hit at Thomas Betterton, who had been sent on such errands. What Settle wishes, I think, is to direct attention to certain novelties first used in this production. In his letter of dedication, Settle had written "That the Model of the Scenes of this Play, are something of an Original: I am sure I have removed a long Heap of Rubbish, and thrown away all our old French Lumber, our Clouds of Clouts, and set Theatrical Paintings at a much fairer Light. . . . For as I dare confidently averr, the Prospect of this Stage will put all the old Rags out of Countenance. . . ."

What are some of the details featured in the stage directions? In an early scene, there was a *"Silver Moon, near Fourteen Foot Diameter";* in Act V, *"Through the Center, and advancing Twenty Four Foot high, is an Ascent of Marble Steps."* In the first stage direction quoted above, the Wood was *"near Thirty Foot high, the Paintings meeting in a Circle."* In II. i, *"During a Symphony of Musick, a Palace of Cynthia, near Twenty Foot high, appears within the Clouds. . . ."* Later, *"The Scene draws, and discovers a magnificent Pallace, consisting of Seven Arches, extending near Thirty Foot high. . . . the Visto continued with a new Order of Dorick Pillars of Egyptian Marble, terminating with a Triumphal Arch."*

The emphasis in each stage direction is upon size. These measurements must have been unusual or they would not have been mentioned, for the stage directions were written to serve as program-notes for readers of the quarto, serving the same purpose as the printed descriptions of the Jacobean masques. But surely size was not all. Settle's first reference is to painting. Did his Silver Moon rotate like the Mikrokosmos in Jonson's *Hymenaei?* Perhaps a clue lies in the stage direction for Cynthia's Bower, the setting of the whole fifth act:

> *Being a Prospect of Terras Walks on Eight several Stages mounted one above another, each Stage contains a Range of Stone-work extending from side to side, decorated with Paintings in Fresco of Heroick History; over each Piece of Painting are carved Rails and Banisters with Pedestals: On Thirty Two Pedestals are carved Sixteen Golden Flower-Pots, and Sixteen Statues of Gods and Goddesses, viz. Jupiter, . . . Psyche. Through the Center, and advancing Twenty Four Foot high, is an Ascent of Marble Steps. This Sett of Scenes is encompass'd round with Arborage-work, circled round with double Festoons of Flowers tyed up in Ribbons of Gold, terminating at Fifty Foot deep, being the Extent of the House, with a Prospect of a Garden above the highest Terras.*
>
> *Above Fifty Figures are seen upon the several Terras's, some of which Descend upon the Stage for the Entertainment.*

Whatever Settle's innovations, it becomes certain that the competition between the London playhouses combined with the outspoken desire to equal or surpass the theatrical achievements of France and Italy to bring sooner or later to the London stage the best in continental theory and practice plus a considerable element that was the product of native ingenuity.

Richard II at Covent Garden

[1964]

ONE of the minor treasures in the Folger Shakespeare Library from the Warwick Castle Collection of Shakespeariana is what at first glance seems to be a theatrical promptbook, bound into which are the two earliest extant sketches of stage settings for one of Shakespeare's plays. The play is *Richard II;* the period is early 18th century; and the transcriber is John Roberts, who also made the sketches. Only one of the drawings has been reproduced,[1] and there has been no discussion of the theatrical problems involved in the production or of the prompt text.

The book consists of leaves of *Richard II* abstracted from a copy of the Second Folio of 1632, with manuscript changes in diction, passages marked for omission, and a number of lines of text supplied in manuscript that are wanting in the print.[2] On a fragment of the original cover the transcriber has written boldly, "K. Rich^d: 2^d. Correct' cum Libr' Theatr'. Jn°. Roberts."

Before identifying Roberts or proceeding further into stage history, it is desirable to describe the book and trace its history. It is a blank book consisting of twenty-seven unnumbered leaves of heavy paper, with the margins ruled in red. There is a flyleaf, front and back, of lighter paper. The leaves are approximately 10″ × 11¾″ in size. The 19th-century bind-

---

[1] In W. M. Merchant's *Shakespeare and the Artist* (Oxford University Press, 1959), p. 41—see also p. 181 for comment; and again in the festival program of the American Shakespeare Festival Theatre and Academy (1962), p. 28.

[2] It will be recalled that the text of the play in F1 was printed from one of the later quartos, with the Abdication Scene supplied from an authentic manuscript. Some revisions were made in the text, and eight passages, totalling fifty lines, were cut. See W. W. Greg, *The Shakespeare First Folio* (Oxford, 1955), pp. 236 ff., for details.

Shakespeare Quarterly, XV, no. 2 (Spring 1964), 161-75.

ing is three-quarter red morocco with a dark brown cloth resembling watered silk. Tipped in on the rectos of twelve leaves are the leaves of the Second Folio bearing the text of *Richard II*. Since these are about 12½″ tall, each one is folded over at the top or the bottom and so are the sketches. Pasted on fol. 3ʳ is a Drury Lane playbill for the performance of *Richard II* on 23 October 1815. On the verso is a colored print of Edmund Kean as Richard II, published on 26 June 1815 by T. Palsor. The next leaf is made up as a title-page: "The Play | Of | Richard yᵉ II. | Original Edition | 1623. | T. Purland." The ornamental capitals *T, P, O, O,* and *E* and the owner's name, printed in several colors, have been cut out and pasted in position, with the other letters supplied in manuscript. There is a fancy border of baroque design printed in red and gold, cut out and pasted down like the initials. In the lower left corner is the memorandum, "Done in a day Sep.: 11: 1847," in Purland's hand. On leaves 7 and 8 respectively are pasted reproductions of the Shakespeare arms and signatures and of scenes in Stratford. On leaf 9, within double rules of red ink, is inlaid part of the original heavy gray paper cover of Roberts's transcript, measuring 7⁵⁄₁₆″ × 4⁷⁄₁₆″. It bears the title supplied by Roberts and quoted above. (On the verso of the fragment, in Purland's hand: "N.B. — by Shakespear. | the 1ˢᵗ Edition — | a prompter's Book —".) Above the inlay are two clippings from newspapers, one dated in manuscript "Aug. 2, 1729" and the other "Sept. 4, 1731." Their contents will be considered later. At the foot of the page Purland has written:

The prompter's book of Drury Lane Theatre 1727. Roberts was Cibbers prompter, and also an Actor and Commentator of Shakspeare: His name appears in Fieldings company at Bartholomew Fair in 1731; and that of his wife in 1729. Their names are frequent in 1730 at Drury Lane, and 1733 at the Hay-Market, and Goodman's-Fields 1734.

The first leaf of text (pp. 23-24 of F2) is tipped along its inner margin to fol. 11. On the verso of fol. 12 is Roberts's sketch of the Combat Scene, titled and marked for insertion facing p. 25 of F2. The leaf bearing pp. 25-26 is on fol. 13. The other leaves of text follow in order until fol. 20, which bears the sketch of the setting for the Parliament Scene, marked for insertion facing p. 38. The last leaf of F2 text, pp. 45-46, is on fol. 24, leaving fols. 25-27 blank.[3]

[3] In F2 the text of *Richard II* ends on p. 45, and *1 Henry IV* begins on p. 46. It may be remarked that the sketch of the Parliament Scene actually faces the blank verso of fol. 19, not p. 38, which is on the recto of fol. 19.

A label of the Warwick Castle Shakespeare Library is pasted inside the front cover. In the upper left corner is a printed slip from a bookseller's catalogue; and on the recto of the flyleaf is an unsigned memorandum by James Orchard Halliwell-Phillipps:

The text of this prompt copy is from the second folio of 1632, not from the first of 1623. It is rendered particularly curious by the insertion of the old rough drawings of the stage dispositions of the Combat Scene & the Parliament Scene, showing exactly how they were placed on the stage in Roberts' time, 1727. These are the earliest relics of the kind I know of.

Theodosius Purland (6 January 1805–16 August 1881), who put the book in its present form, was a London dentist with antiquarian interests, particularly in places of amusement. According to the sale catalogue of Puttick and Simpson for 20 August 1852, "the greater part of [his] Library and Literary curiosities" were to be sold by auction because their owner was "leaving England."[4] Lot 134 in the 1852 sale is Roberts's *Richard II,* sold to "Boone" for 14s. The clipping pasted inside the front cover is from a Puttick and Simpson catalogue. Apparently the book passed from Boone to Halliwell-Phillipps to the Earl of Warwick, and thence to Marsden J. Perry and ultimately to Henry Clay Folger.[5]

Presumably Purland acquired the marked copy of *Richard II* in the process of forming his theatrical library and in 1847 mounted it in a scrapbook, as described above.[6] And for doing this he may be forgiven several

[4] I am greatly indebted to Miss Eleanor Pitcher for examining this and a later catalogue (Puttick and Simpson, 16 March 1882) at the British Museum for me and for hunting out at Hodgson's in Chancery Lane their catalogue of Purland's dramatic and miscellaneous books auctioned on 14-17 March 1882.

[5] The biographical information about Purland has been collected from *N&Q,* 6th ser., V (1882), 168-69, 293, 317; VI (1882), 154-55. An article in *N&Q,* CLXXXVI (1944), 96, describes a neat little engraving of Purland in costume of *c.* 1855, on the back of which are the words, "Theodosius Purland Esq., Member of the B.A.A. [British Archaeological Association]." The initial inquiry of 4 March 1882 by "J. R. D." describes Purland as "Ph.D. M.A. &c." and calls him a friend of William Upcott, J. J. Fillinham, Thomas Wright, Roach Smith, and F. W. Fairholt. Frederick S. Boas replied that Purland practised as a dentist from 1830 to 1881, residing for the last thirty years in Mortimer Street, Cavendish Square. "Calcuttensis" reports that he saw an *os calcis* of Edward IV in Purland's possession, and "A. H." adds that he knew Purland when in Wilson Street, Finsbury, where he distracted young patients with ingenious gadgets moved by clockwork.

[6] The identification of Purland's hand is confirmed by notations in *Alsatian eccentricities, 1700-1782, collected by T. Purland,* "Being a collection of cuttings from newspapers, containing relations of murders and robberies, reports of trials, dying speeches, together with portraits of celebrated criminals, views, *etc.*" (British Museum shelf-list 1243.k, 2 vols., 4°. Apparently the Museum did not purchase Purland's collection of water colors of Vauxhall Gardens or his notes thereon.

inaccuracies. Purland erred, for example, in stating that the printed text Roberts marked was from the First Folio. He erred also in stating that Roberts was prompter at Drury Lane and that the promptbook he transcribed was used at that theater. It is less easy to forgive him for failing to record how *Richard II* came into his possession or the names of previous owners (if he knew them). There is a gap of a century between the making of Roberts's transcript and Theodosius Purland.[7]

Where was *Richard II* actually presented about 1730? How came it to be revived? And who was Roberts? The early stage history of *Richard II* is sketchy. After the performance by the King's Men at the Globe on 12 June 1631, there is no record of the play on the stage until Nahum Tate's alteration was produced about 1680-81.[8] In 1719-20, Lewis Theobald's alteration was presented at Lincoln's Inn Fields seven times, and during the next two seasons was revived for three performances. The production Roberts was concerned with was at Covent Garden in 1738, the first known attempt to perform Shakespeare's unaltered text in over a hundred years. As Professor Emmett L. Avery has related,[9] credit for John Rich's revival of *Richard II* was given at the time to the unknown members of the Shakespeare Ladies Club. In the three preceding seasons, their insistence had increased the number of performances of Shakespeare's plays at Drury Lane, Covent Garden, and the New Haymarket until they comprised 14.0%, 17.0%, and 22.2% of the total. In 1737-38, after the Licensing Act had closed all the playhouses except Drury Lane and Covent Garden,

[7] On the scrap of the original cover is a scrawl that Mrs. Laetitia Yeandle of the Folger Library staff doubtfully reads as "Robt Attkin". Another scrawl, occurring on the back of the sketch of the Combat Scene, suggests "Robt Atkin" or "Atkins". On p. 33 in the white space to the left of the center rule is more scribbling, this time in pencil and in a different hand. The only word may possibly be "Ireland". The writing differs greatly from that of W. H. Ireland, the forger. The same hand has doodled in the bottom margin of the page: "dp", "dp*er*", "d". At the foot of p. 45, the hand has written "d O[?]d" and "d&", and, in the top margin of p. 32, several forms of ampersand. In the left margin of p. 32 are "ds" and more doodling. There was a Mrs. Atkins (sometimes called Widow Atkins) at Covent Garden, the Haymarket, and Lincoln's Inn Fields in various capacities in the 1720's and 1730's; and in the 1750's there was a dancer named Atkins at Drury Lane; but there is no traceable connection between these people and *Richard II*. The scribbles do not look like the work of the kind of person who would pay to have a promptbook transcribed.

[8] See below for comments on its suppression.

[9] "The Shakespeare Ladies Club," *SQ*, VII (1956), 153-58. A. H. Scouten, *The London Stage, Part 3* (Southern Illinois University Press, 1961) I, cxlix-clii, discusses the Shakespearian revivals, names the plays that were revived with the number of performances, and in his calendar gives the casts; see also his "The Increase in Popularity of Shakespeare's Plays in the Eighteenth Century," *SQ*, VII (1956), 189-202.

27.7% of the performances at Covent Garden were Shakespearian. *Richard II* was brought out on 6 February 1738 and repeated nine times in little more than a month; a benefit performance on 2 May was the last in that season. In the following year, there were four revivals. After the next revival, on 23 October 1739, the play vanished from the boards until Macready appeared in a more or less faithful version at Newcastle in 1812-13.[10]

John Roberts deserves a few words. On the testimony of Thomas Davies, it has been customary to identify him as the author of *An Answer to Mr. Pope's Preface to Shakespear . . . By a Stroling Player* (1729).[11] There is no doubt that Davies, who was an actor at the Haymarket in 1736 and was always closely connected with the stage, had opportunity to know Roberts, and there is no reason to question his attribution of the pamphlet.[12]

If Roberts wrote *An Answer,* he must have had good store of audacity, for he begins his attack with a clever misquotation of the *Dunciad Variorum,* I, 5-6, and gives his readers considerable amusement by his mock-modest ridicule of Pope's judgment in the matter under discussion. Roberts's defense of actors reveals that he had used a Shakespeare Folio, a Jonson Folio, Heywood's *Apology for Actors,* Gerard Langbaine, and Sir Richard Baker—to name some of the more important sources of his

[10] See A. H. Scouten, *Part 3,* II, 701-6, for a notice derived from the *London Daily Post* of 6 February, which states that the play had not been acted "these Forty Years" and promises "proper decorations. Likewise a New Prologue address'd to the Ladies." This is probably the prologue printed in the *Daily Post* of 10 February. Scouten gives the original cast: King—Delane; York—Stephens; Gaunt—Johnson; Bolingbroke—Ryan; Norfolk—Walker; Carlisle—Chapman; Aumerle—Hallam; Salisbury—Lyon; Scroop—Aston; Bushy—Rosco; Bagot—Salway; Green—Arthur; Northumberland—Bridgewater; Piercy—Hale; Ross—Ridout; Willoughby—A. Ryan; Surry—Houghton; Fitzwalter—Stevens; Earl Marshall—Mullart; Queen—Mrs. Horton; Dutchess of York—Mrs. Hallam; Dutchess of Gloster—Mrs. James. To these, Thomas Davies adds three other names: Richard Yates as the attendant who fetches a mirror, Michael Stoppelaer as the Abbot of Westminster, and Nathanael Clarke as the Groom (*Dramatic Miscellanies,* I (1784), 175, 180, 192).

[11] Writing of the London theaters during the time when Wilks, Booth, and Cibber were managing Drury Lane, Davies describes the indignation of the public that Wilks should advance his protege, John Mills, at the expense of older and better actors, such as Booth and George Powell, and records that "Roberts the player, author of a letter to Mr. Pope concerning some passages in his preface to Shakspere," told him of a protest that had occurred during a performance of *Macbeth* (*Dramatic Miscellanies,* II, 132).

[12] Some difficulty arises, however, in the acceptance of Roberts as an eyewitness of the event recounted by Davies. Though Mills lived until 1736, Powell's last season was 1714, and it is easier to believe that Roberts (who first appears in theatrical records in 1721) handed on to Davies a story that circulated among theatrical people than that, as a boy, he should have heard the outburst.

information about Tudor and Stuart actors. He was surprisingly well read in 17th-century drama.

In the years between 1721 and 1750, there were several men named Roberts in the London theaters: a box-keeper at Goodman's Fields in 1731; a dancer at Covent Garden in 1736 and a singer there in 1743 and afterwards; and a singer named Ellis Roberts[13] at Drury Lane who is named in the same bill as "Mr. Roberts" for 5 May 1733. Usually it is possible to distinguish between these people and the Mr. J. Roberts who had a benefit at Covent Garden on 17 May 1739 and whom I take to be "Roberts the player" of Davies and the scribe of *Richard II*. He is first named among actors at Drury Lane in 1721-22, but the first named role recorded is that of Roberto in *Love in a Forest* on 9 January 1723 at Drury Lane.[14] He was a minor actor, moving from Drury Lane for a season to Haymarket (before 9 November 1730), then back to Drury Lane in 1731, and after March 1734 to Covent Garden; in 1735-36 he went to the New Haymarket. Here, surprisingly enough, Fielding assigned him comic leads in such plays as *Pasquin*. It is unnecessary to follow his career in detail. There are intervals when his name is not to be found in the casts of any of the theaters, and it has been suggested that he had accidents or misfor-

---

[13] This is perhaps the Roberts who sang at Covent Garden on 26 October 1737, 3 January 1738, *etc.,* but Scouten lists no singer of this name at *Part 3,* II, 680.

[14] Emmett L. Avery, ed., *The London Stage, Part 2* (Southern Illinois University Press, 1960), II, 638, 704 and *passim.* See also Scouten, *Part 3, passim,* and George Winchester Stone, ed., *Part 4* (1962), *passim.* Professor Avery, who has ransacked his notes in my behalf, directs attention to a passage on p. 6 of *The Theatric Squabble; or, the P—ntees* (1733):

> Next *Rob—ts* grave, and slow, moves surly on
> With Arms across, and damns th'ungrateful Town:
> Dull, droning, one long irksome Stile he keeps,
> Drawling he dreams, and the tir'd Audience sleeps;
> Imperfect too, with Spleen and Vapours vext,
> He gravely asks the Prompter—*What is next?*

This is less favorable than the estimate in Thomas Cooke's *Comedian, or Philosophical Enquirer* (October 1732, p. 39), which calls him "a just Speaker; but he seems to want Strength of Voice to go thro a passionate Part." For this reference and several others about Roberts and his wife, I am indebted to Professor Philip Highfill. Aaron Hill entertained enough hope for Roberts to address one of his Original Letters to him on 3 November 1733. This praises his carriage, the harmony, distinctness, and articulation of his speech, and his gravity but suggests that he improve his breathing to avoid a cracking voice, advises him to acquire "the musical variation, which will flow from a change, with the changing passions," and urges "a gayer, shorter, less deliberate, and more lively *tread,* according to the spirited fierceness, or soft amorous vivacity, of the part" he acts in (*Works,* 1753, I, 168-70).

tune or sickness.[15] Perhaps it was during one of his periods of inactivity on the stage that Roberts marked the copy of *Richard II* and copied the two diagrams. Roberts is listed at Covent Garden from 1737 to 1743, but Professor Avery informs me that by 1740 he was being paid only 5*s* each acting day. The last notice of him is his inclusion in a company of London actors performing at Richmond and Twickenham in the summer of 1750.[16]

Roberts's wife was an actress. Her maiden and baptismal names are unknown, and she may have been on the stage earlier than the first performance recorded under her married name. This was at Richmond on 29 June 1724, when she had the very small part of Cherry in *The Beaux' Stratagem*—Roberts was at the same theater in three plays in July. She may also have been a dancer in her early years (see the Drury Lane season for 1730-31). The couple appeared frequently, but not always, at the same theaters. They also played in the booths during Bartholomew Fair and the Southwark Fair.[17] And they were from time to time strolling players.

[15] A benefit performance was given for him at Drury Lane on 28 January 1732, he being then "Confined in the Fleet Prison" (*London Stage, Part 3,* I, 186). See also a letter in *The Daily Advertiser* of 2 May 1737:

> Sir,
>   As at every one of our Theatres this Day, there is a Benefit for Persons under Misfortune, 'tis humbly hop'd that the more humane Pursuers of Pleasure will suspend their Curiosity for Vaux Hall for one Day, (out of a hundred) in Favour of so many Unfortunates, who have but the Chance of one single Night to relieve them from Afflictions which perhaps they have long labour'd under. And, as I have somewhere read,
>
>> So humane Worth to God like Heights they'll raise,
>> For the Preserver shares the Maker's Praise
>
> I believe it is fully known, without troubling you with farther Particulars, that among the Number above mention'd, is included
>
> | | Sir, |
> |----------------|-----------------------------|
> | Hay-Market | Your very humble Servant, |
> | Theatre | John Roberts. |

The New Haymarket bill for 2 May offers *The Fatal Curiosity, etc.,* "For the Entertainment of the Antient and Honourable Society of Non-Common Pleas. For the Benefit of Mr. J. Roberts."

[16] Sybil Rosenfeld, *Strolling Players and Drama in the Provinces 1660-1765* (Cambridge University Press, 1939), p. 296.

[17] One of the clippings pasted into *Richard II* gives notice that Mr. Fielding of Drury Lane plans to present *The Beggar's Wedding* at his booth in the George Inn Yard at Smithfield during Bartholomew Fair and names Mrs. Roberts in the case (cf. *London Stage, Part 2,* II, 1042, for 23 August 1729). The other news clipping announces that Fielding, Hippisley, and Hall's booth at Smithfield will continue performances of *The Emperor of China* "till Tuesday next," with Roberts playing the Emperor (cf. *London*

The Swansea Corporation collected 5s from "Mr. Roberts the player" in 1732-33 for the use of the upstairs room in the Town Hall.[18] In 1733, he was with a mixed company from the London theaters at Canterbury; and in 1740 he appeared there in such roles as Macbeth and Lear. He was with the Duke of Grafton's company at Norwich in 1735, playing Othello and similar roles, and he returned to Norwich in 1743. In one visit to Norwich, Mrs. Roberts played Anne to his Richard III.[19] In London, Roberts never had roles that equaled in importance those assigned to his wife at the height of her career. Between 1737 and 1744, for example, she was appearing at Drury Lane as Belvidera in *Venice Preserv'd,* as Andromache in Ambrose Philips's *The Distrest Mother,* and as the Queen in *Richard III* opposite David Garrick.[20] When a group of players revolted from Drury Lane in 1744, Mrs. Roberts remained loyal and even secured a substantial loan for Fleetwood the manager. When order was restored, Fleetwood attempted to weasel out of paying the debt, refused to allow Mrs. Roberts her articled benefit, denied her payment of a large amount of back salary, and then fired her. For his ingratitude and dishonesty, he was attacked bitterly in two pamphlets of 1744, both of which pay high tribute to Mrs. Roberts's abilities as an actress, and one of which advocates casting her as Lady Macbeth, the Queen in *Hamlet, etc.*[21] During the next season, Mrs. Roberts made a single recorded appearance

---

Stage, Part 3, I, 153, for 8 September 1731). See also Sybil Rosenfeld, *The Theatre of the London Fairs in the 18th Century* (Cambridge University Press, 1960), *passim.* She finds Roberts and his wife at Penkethman's booth at Smithfield in 1724 (p. 28). They disappear from her records after 1734 until Roberts is named to play King Henry in *Fair Rosamond* for Adam Hallam at Bartholomew Fair in 1741 (see Scouten, *Part 3,* II, 920).

[18] Cecil Price, *The English Theatre in Wales* (University of Wales Press, 1948), p. 7.

[19] Rosenfeld, *Strolling Players,* pp. 58, 60, 225, 226, 234, 235. Miss Rosenfeld notes that an actress named Anne Roberts died in Norwich in 1740; her relationship to John Roberts is unknown.

[20] During this flourishing period, Mrs. Roberts had her own house in Duke Street, near Lincoln's Inn Fields, as we learn from the announcements of her benefits on 30 April 1739, 16 March 1742, and 24 March 1743. In the first of these, she was Mary Queen of Scots in *The Albion Queens;* in the second, Berinthia in *The Relapse;* and in the third, Calista to Garrick's Lothario in *The Fair Penitent.* The receipts in 1742 were £130, strong testimony to her popularity. See Scouten, *Part 3,* II, 772, 976, and 1043-44. Professor Avery writes me that Mrs. Roberts was the subject of a poem in *The London Daily Post* of 26 September 1737. But when she appeared as Queen Elizabeth in *Richard III* on 1 October 1737, she was "hiss'd"; Scouten, *Part 3,* II, 684.

[21] *The Disputes between the Directors of D–y, and the Pit Potentates* (1744), pp. 16-19; *An Impartial Examen of the Present Contests between the Town and the Manager of the Theatre* . . . (1744), pp. 16, 18, 19.

with Theophilus Cibber's short-lived company at the Haymarket, "her 1st appearance there for 12 years".[22] She is next heard of among a large group of minor actors in 1748-49;[23] and the last trace I have found of her is in a company brought from London to Maidstone by Wignall in June 1757.[24]

The revival of *Richard II* at Covent Garden in 1738 is generally attributed, as we have seen, to the mysterious Shakespeare Ladies Club. But with all the canon to chose from, why did John Rich select *Richard II,* a play whose history was so tumultuous? He can hardly be supposed to have known that in the time of Queen Elizabeth "this tragedy was played 40^{tie} times in open streets and houses", "the Erle [of Essex] himself being so often present . . . with great applause giving countenance and lyking to the same,"[25] or that on the eve of Essex's attempted rebellion his followers paid a bounty to Shakespeare's company for a performance of the play. There may have been no one to tell Rich that on 14 December 1680, in a time of violent political controversy, a version of *Richard II* by Nahum Tate was forbidden performance by the Lord Chamberlain. Undeterred, Tate changed the locus of action (much as Massinger had done with the play now called *Believe as You List*), and it was given under a new name, *The Sicilian Usurper,* and performed twice (18 and 19 January 1681) before authority penetrated the deception and stopped the production.[26] Tate's introductory letter in the quarto of 1681 disclaims awareness of any parallels between the current political situation and events in the play, but G. C. D. Odell[27] was not the only reader to feel that the author did protest too much. In a later period of political disturbance, Lewis Theobald made an adaptation of *Richard II* that managed to escape governmental censure. It opened on 10 December 1719 at Lincoln's Inn Fields and was acted for the last time in the autumn of 1721 (see above).

During the next twenty or thirty years, England was in political turmoil, and dramatic and journalistic attacks upon the government exceeded in ferocity and brutality—but also in wit—anything published to-

---

[22] John Genest, *Some Account of the English Stage* (Bath, 1832), IV, 169. The date was 20 October 1744.

[23] Stone, *Part 4,* I, 61.

[24] Rosenfeld, *Strolling Players,* p. 254.

[25] E. K. Chambers, *William Shakespeare* (Oxford, 1930), II, 326-27, 323. The Deposition Scene was not included in the three quartos printed in the lifetime of the Queen but appeared in the second issue of Q4 (1608).

[26] William Van Lennep, ed., *The London Stage, Part 1* (Southern Illinois University Press, 1965), under date.

[27] *Shakespeare from Betterton to Irving* (New York, 1921), I, 56-59.

day.[28] Fielding's *Pasquin* (5 March 1736; sixty performances by 26 May) and *The Historical Register* (21 March 1737) burlesqued and satirized the government so pointedly that during one performance Sir Robert Walpole went backstage and "corrected" one of the comedians "with his own Hands very severely."[29]

In the following summer, the 574th number (2 July 1737) of *The Country Journal; or, The Craftsman,* featured a letter by "C. C. P. L." to the pseudonymous editor, Caleb d'Anvers, with a sharp attack on the government in the guise of advice about enforcing the Bill for Licensing the Stage. Ostensibly the author was Colley Cibber, Poet Laureate, but within a short time the writer was identified almost with certainty as Nicholas Amhurst. The course of events may be followed in the pages of *The Gentleman's Magazine.* The number for July 1737 gives the Earl of Chesterfield's speech against the Licensing Bill (pp. 409-11), notices and abstracts in cautious terms the letter of C. C. P. L., and adds that the printer of *The Craftsman* is in custody (p. 430). Before 23 July, the premises of the printer were seized, including his account books, publication of *The Craftsman* was stopped for a week, and several people were imprisoned (*G.M.,* pp. 437-38).

Subjected to vitriolic attack in the columns of *The Daily Gazetteer* and *The Gentleman's Magazine,* the writers in *The Craftsman* protested the innocence of their intentions (*G.M.,* pp. 499-500) and named Sir Roger L'Estrange (1616-1704) as the type of minister who endangers liberty (*G.M.,* pp. 500-1). Then they entered a general defense of liberty of the press (*G.M.,* September, pp. 551-52) and proceeded to a discussion of the abuse by Princes of their authority, with pointed quotations from *Measure for Measure* ("O 'tis excellent To have a giant's strength; but it is tyrannous To use it like a giant"; pp. 557-59). As Haines, printer of *The Craftsman,* Amhurst, the reputed author of the offending letter of 2 July 1737, and John Kelly, supposed author of *Fog's Journal,* waged their battles in the courts, *Old Common Sense* (No. 45, 10 December) reported at length the trial in New York of Peter Zenger and printed the arguments of his attorney, Andrew Hamilton, in defense of freedom of the press (*G.M.,* December 1737, pp. 749-50); and *The Craftsman* devoted its No. 602 (21 January 1738) to Zenger, with a recommendation of the relevant tracts

---

[28] For a summary account of the fermenting theatrical situation, see Scouten, *Part 3,* especially "The Licensing Act," "Repertory," and "The Shakespearian Revival," I, xlviii ff., cxxxviii ff., and cxlix ff.

[29] Scouten, *Part 3,* I, 1.

just published in London (*G.M.,* January 1738, pp. 35-36). Such were the laws of the land that Amhurst, the author, was released after a short imprisonment, but Haines, the printer, was found guilty of printing a libel and sentenced to imprisonment for a year and to a fine of £200, and was required to find security for his good behavior for seven years (*G.M.,* May 1738, p. 274). Amidst the war of the journals, *The Gentleman's Magazine* reported the opinion of *Common Sense* (No. 65) that Haines's attorneys had "not much strengthened" the arguments used by Mr. Hamilton "for Mr Zenger the Printer of New-York; whose Tryal, therefore, no Printer ought to be without. . . ." It continued:

If the Judges make new Laws by an ill Construction, or an ill Execution of old ones, I conclude, that Parliaments will soon be found useless, and the Liberty of the People an inconvenience to the Government. (*G.M.,* April 1738, p. 208)

As You Like It and *King John* were quoted, and even some of the "political aphorisms of my Lord Bacon" were reprinted "to keep awake the Anger of the Gazeteers, so much offended with some quotations from Shakespeare" (*G.M.,* June 1738, pp. 297-98, 308-9).

Just what had the author of the letter of 2 July 1737 written that it started such a controversy, and what was his method of attack? He took the position that once a statute is on the books it should be enforced, and then set out to demonstrate his qualifications to serve as licenser of plays. Old plays and new, he argued, were likely to offend chiefly in the areas of Politics, Divinity, and Bawdry; he chose Politics for his domain and gave a series of passages apt for inclusion in an *Index expurgatorius.* The plays quoted from were Jonson's *Sejanus,* Dryden's *Don Sebastian* and *All for Love,* Lee's *Rival Queens, or Alexander the Great,* George Sewell's *Sir Walter Raleigh,* and three plays by Shakespeare: *King John, 2 Henry IV,* and *Richard II.* Several of these had not been seen on a London stage for many years: *Sejanus, Don Sebastian,* and *Sir Walter Raleigh.* There had been seven performances of *The Rival Queens* in the previous season; six of *All for Love;* nine of *King John;* and one performance of Betterton's (?) adaptation of *2 Henry IV.* All four were performed in the 1737-38 season while the trial of Haines was in progress. As for *Richard II,* the announcement of its revival on 6 February 1738 stated that it had "not [been] acted these forty years." Perhaps, as the management claimed, the cause of the revival was the "Desire of several Ladies of Quality," but I suggest that Rich expected audiences to flock into the theater to see the play that had had a crucial role in the events leading to the prosecution of *The Craftsman* and its printer

Shakespeare's *King John* is the first play to be examined in C. C. P. L.'s letter in *The Craftsman,* possibly on the assumption that Londoners might be expected to remember something of it from the nine performances earlier in the year. The writer continues:

The next Play, that falls under my Consideration, is *the Life and Death of King* Richard *the 2d,* written by the *same Author;* which hath not been acted within my Memory, and I think never ought, without considerable Castrations and Amendments; for it not only represents an *obstinate, misguided Prince* depos'd by his *People,* which is agreeable enough to the Principles of the *Revolution;* but likewise contains several Passages, which the *disaffected* may turn to their Account.—I will mention only two or three.

The *King,* speaking of the Duke of *Hereford,* (his Successor, by the Name of *Henry* the 4*th*) makes the following Reflection upon his *Popularity.*

> —Bagot and Greene
> Observ'd his Courtship to the common People;
> How He did seem to dive into their Hearts,
> With humble and familiar Courtesie;
> What Reverence He did throw away on Slaves,
> Wooing poor Craftsmen with the Craft of Souls,
> And patient under-bearing of his Fortune.

It is to be observed that the *King* had used the *Duke of Hereford* very ill; and though He was neither his *Son,* nor his *lawful Heir,* malicious People may apply it to *Princes,* between whom there is a much nearer Relation. I need say no more; but shall leave it to your Judgment whether this Passage ought not to be expunged, as well as the whole first Scene of the second Act; particularly where *John of Gaunt,* Duke of *Lancaster,* foretels the Fate of the King, his Nephew, just before his Death. As You formerly quoted this prophetical Speech in one of your Papers, I shall, repeat only the Conclusion of it.

> This Land of such dear Souls, this dear-dear Land,
> Dear for her Reputation through the World,
> Is now leas'd out, (I dye pronouncing it)
> Like to a Tenement, or pelting Farm.
> England, bound in with the triumphant Sea,
> Whose rocky Shore beats back the envious Siege
> Of watery Neptune, is bound in with Shame,
> With INKY BLOTS, and ROTTEN PARCHMENT BONDS.
> That England, that was wont to conquer others,
> Hath made a shameful Conquest of itself.

This is such a general Reflection upon my *dear Country*, and the whole Mystery of *Treaty-making*, that I think it ought not to be suffer'd to appear even in *Print*, much less to be pronounced upon the *Stage*.

In another Part of the same Scene, *old Gaunt* addresses the *King*, in this licentious Manner, which will likewise admit of very bad Constructions.

> Thy Death-bed is no lesser than the Land,
> Wherein Thou lyest in Reputation sick,
> And Thou too careless, patient as Thou art,
> Commit'st thy annointed Body to the Cure
> Of those Physicians, that first wounded Thee;
> A thousand Flatterers sit within thy Crown,
> Whose Compass is no bigger than thy Hand,
> And yet incaged in so small a Verge,
> The Waste is no whit lesser than thy Land.

At the latter End of this Scene, the following Dialogue passes between *Northumberland, Willoughby* and *Ross;* which is more intolerable than all the rest.

> *Nor.* The King is not Himself, but basely led
> By Flatterers, and what They will inform
> Meerly in Hate 'gainst any of us all,
> That will the King severely prosecute
> 'Gainst us, our Lives, our Children and our Heirs.
> *Ross.* The Commons hath He pill'd with grievous Taxes,
> And quite lost their Hearts. The Nobles hath he fin'd
> For antient Quarrels, and quite lost their Hearts.
> *Will.* And daily new Exactions are devis'd;
> But what O' God's Name doth become of this?
> *Nor.* Wars have not wasted it; for warr'd He hath not,
> But basely yielded upon Compromise
> That, which his Ancestors atchiev'd with Blows.
> More hath He spent in Peace than They in Wars.

This wants no Comment. . .

All the lines quoted in *The Craftsman* were spoken in the 1738 revival except the first seven (those at I. iv. 23-29).

The absence of contemporary reviews of the production of *Richard II* in the journals is partly compensated by the report of Thomas Davies:

When this play was revived at the theatre in Covent-garden, about forty years since, the ancient ceremony which belonged to the single combat was very accurately observed, with all the decorations and arrangements proper to the appellant and respondent, the spectators and the judges. Amongst the latter, the king was seated in a throne of state. The combatants were dressed in complete armour. Two chairs, finely adorned, were placed on opposite sides of the lists: to these they retired after each of them had stood forth and spoken. Bolingbroke was acted by Ryan. Walker personated Mowbray. His helmet was laced so tightly under his chin, that, when he endeavoured to speak, nobody could understand him; and this obstacle occasioned a laugh from the audience: however, this was soon removed, and the actor was heard with attention. In their persons, dress, and demeanour, they presented something like an image of the old trial of right by duel. . . . (*Dramatic Miscellanies,* I, 124-25)

As soon as Richard, intent upon his Irish expedition, had left the stage, the author introduces a political scene between the earl of Northumberland and the lords Willoughby and Ross, full of severe reflections upon the king's misconduct. The writing is not singularly good, but it was greatly distinguished by the particular behaviour of the audience, on the revival of this play, who applied almost every line that was spoken to the occurrences of the time, and to the measures and character of the ministry. (I, 150-51)

Davies then summarizes conditions in the quarrel with Spain and gives Sir Robert Walpole's fears of an insurrection in Scotland by the Scottish and English Tories and Jacobites, predicting, before his death in 1744, that the King would have to fight for his crown.

The more reluctant Walpole appeared to second the wishes of the merchants in commencing hostilities, the more clamorous the people were for letting loose the vengeance of the nation against the Spaniards. When this tragedy was, after being long forgotten, revived, the cry for war was the highest, and the spectators were ready to apply all that was uttered in the theatre to the transactions of the day and to the ministry. The dialogue of Northumberland and his friends furnished ample materials for political innuendo and application. There was in Bridgewater, who personated Northumberland, a most grave and solemn manner of delivering a sentiment, which dwelt fully upon the attentive hearer. When he pronounced the following words,

> The king is not himself, but basely led
> By flatterers,—

the noise from the clapping of hands and clattering of sticks was loud and boisterous. And when Ross said,

> The earl of Wiltshire hath the state in farm,—

it was immediately applied to Walpole, with the loudest shouts and huzzas I ever heard. Likewise the following observation of Northumberland, that the king's revenue was not diminished by war, was met, by the audience, with re-doubled shouts—

> War hath not wasted it; for warr'd he hath not.
> More hath he spent in peace than they in war.

The two following remarkable lines, spoken by Willoughby and Northumberland, were heard with a dead and respectful silence:—

> WILLOUGHBY. The king's grown bankrupt, like a broken man.
> NORTHUMBERLAND. Reproach, and dissolution, hangeth over him.
>
> (I, 152 ff.)

Davies's description of the audience reaction to the topical hits of the play seem ample confirmation of the hypothesis that the choice of *Richard II* for revival was not an accident. The Covent Garden management were venturing greatly in giving the public opportunity to echo the attacks of *The Craftsman*.[30]

What text was used in the revival of *Richard II* at Covent Garden? The pre-Wars promptbook of the King's Men could hardly have survived, and so the promptbook of 1738 must have been a marked copy or a transcript of one of the editions of the play—a quarto, a folio, Rowe, Pope, or Theobald, or one of the inexpensive reprints of Pope's text issued between 1734 and 1736. A clue is provided at I. iii. 268 in a marginal note by Roberts: *"Desunt 14 lines vide Pope's Edition."*[31] And sure enough, the text used proves to be that of Pope. In general, his emendations are accepted, his wording of the stage directions is adopted, lines that he relegated to footnotes are often marked for omission, and twice (at I. iii. 129 and II. ii. 76) lines that Pope had restored from Qq 1-5 are transcribed in the margin. At I. iii. 267, however, Roberts did not insert the fourteen lines referred to in his marginal note, despite his interlinear memo quoted above, nor did he insert four lines Pope had restored from the early quartos at III. iii. 29. There is no comment at I. iii. 238, where Pope had restored two out of four lines missing from Ff and Q6.

The acting version is considerably shorter than the text of the Folios. Three scenes are omitted entirely: I. iv, in which Richard, Aumerle, Greene, and Bagot jest about Bolingbroke's departure and Richard goes to visit the dying Gaunt with the wish that "we may make hast, and come too late"; II. iv, where a Captain tells Salisbury of the dispersal of the

---

[30] This attack at Covent Garden must have seemed the basest ingratitude to Walpole, for his government's Licensing Act had given the two patent theaters a monopoly.

[31] Actually Qq 1-5 supply 26 lines that are not in Ff or Q6; Pope disregarded 12 of these.

Welsh troops; and V. iv, in which Exton decides to murder Richard. Approximately 285 other lines are marked for omission. Sententious passages, speeches of passion that do not forward the action (*e.g.,* I. ii. 58-74, V. i. 37-50), couplets (especially those concluding a speech or a scene), wordplay (as where Gaunt rings changes on his name at II. i. 73-93), and verses rich in imagery make up the bulk of the deletions. At V. iii. 111, Bolingbroke puts an end to the pleas of the Duchess of York with the words, "Good Aunt, arise, I pardon him" (borrowing from line 131), and continues as in line 137. The omission of the Groom's visit in V. v speeds the play towards its close and also eliminates one speaking part (as Exton is eliminated at V. iv and V. v. 113-18, and a servant-messenger at the end of II. ii). The adaptation was made by a practiced hand for the purpose of pruning whatever might retard the action or sound antiquated to the audience.

Most of the changes in diction are the substitution of *Heaven('s)* for *God('s)*. There are a few modernizations (*unavoydable* for *unavoyded*); where Pope has restored a reading from the early quartos or corrected grammar, the acting text often agrees.

One minor change remains for consideration. An entrance direction at II. iii. 67 names "Barkely", and Northumberland says, "It is my Lord of Barkely, as I ghesse." The newcomer, *"Bark.",* speaks only twice, at II. iii. 69 and 74. In Roberts's transcript, "Surrey" and "Sur." are substituted. Since Barkely appears nowhere else, the change may have been made to eliminate a speaking part, for Surrey has a prominent place in IV. i (where, however, he is linked with Richard's party). If this were the reason, Northumberland's line should have been altered correspondingly. Perhaps Roberts overlooked the changed reading.[32]

It has already been mentioned that the stage directions have generally been altered to agree with Pope. The only innovation is, I think, at II. iii. 80, where York enters *"attended."* This wording occurs in print first in Capell (*Comedies, Histories, and Tragedies,* 1767-68). Readers who are familiar with promptbooks of the 18th century will not be surprised to find a scattering of specific indications for entrances. Thus, after I. i. 19,

[32] It seems unlikely that there were political reasons for the change in 1738, for James, the third earl of Berkeley, had died in 1736 and his son Augustus, the fourth earl, does not appear to have gained prominence until 1745, when he held a command against the rebels. It is true that an uncle of the third earl, George Berkeley, was a member of Parliament for many years; of him, the *DNB* states that "He voted against the measures of Sir Robert Walpole." Could there have been a desire to avoid implicating him? The name "Surrey" was innocuous, the last holder of that title having died in 1554.

But since correction lyeth in those hands
Which made the fault that we cannot correct,
Put we our quarrell to the will of heaven,
Who when they see the houres ripe on earth,
Will raine hot vengeance on offenders heads.

Dut. Findes brotherhood in thee no sharper spurre?
Hath love in thy old blood no living fire?
Edwards seven sonnes (whereof thy selfe art one)
Were as seven vialles of his Sacred blood,
Or seven faire branches springing from one roote:
Some of those seven are dride by natures course,
Some of those branches by the destinies cut:
But *Thomas,* my deere Lord, my life, my Gloster,
(One Viall full of *Edwards* Sacred blood,
One flourishing branch of his most Royall roote)
Is crack'd, and all the precious liquor spilt;
Is hackt downe, and his summer leaves all vaded
By Envies hand, and Murders bloody Axe.
Ah *Gaunt*? His blood was thine that bed, that wombe,
That mettle, that selfe-mould that fashion'd thee,
Made him a man: and though thou liv'st, and breath'st,
Yet art thou slaine in him: thou doest consent
In some large measure to thy Fathers death,
In that thou seest thy wretched brother dye,
Who was the modell of thy Fathers life.
Call it not patience (*Gaunt*) it is despaire,
In suffering thus thy brother to be slaughter'd,
Thou shew'st the naked pathway to thy life,
Teaching sterne murther how to butcher thee:
That which in meane men we intitle patience
Is pale cold cowardise in noble brests:
What shall I say, to safegard thine owne life,
The best way is to venge my Glosters death.

Gaunt. Heavens is the quarrell: for heavens substitute
His Deputy annoynted in his sight,
Hath caus'd his death, the which if wrongfully
Let heaven revenge: for I may never lift
An angry arme against his Minister.

Dut. Where then (alas) may I complaine my selfe?
Gau. To heaven, the widdowes Champion to defence.
Dut. Why then I will: farewell old *Gaunt.*
Thou go'st to Coventry, there to behold
Our Cosine Hereford, and fell Mowbray fight:
O sit my husbands wrongs on Herefords speare,
That it may enter butcher Mowbrayes brest:
Or if misfortune misse the first carreere,
Be Mowbrayes sinnes so heavy in his bosome,
That they may breake his foaming Coursers backe,
And throw the Rider headlong in the Lists,
A Caytiffe recreant to my Cosine Hereford.
Farewell old *Gaunt,* thy sometimes brothers wife
With her companion Greefe, must end her life.

Gau. Sister fare well: I must to Couentrie,
As much good stay with thee, as go with me.

Dut. Yet one word more: Greefe boundeth where it
Not with the emptie hollownesse, but weight: (falls,
I take my leave, before I have begun,
For sorrow ends not when it seemeth done.
Commend me to my brother *Edward Yorke.*
Loe, this is all: nay yet depart not so,
Though this be all, do not so quickly goe,
I shall remember more. Bid him, Oh, what?
With all good speed at Plashie visit me.
Alacke, and what shall good old Yorke there see
But empty lodgings, and unfurnish'd walles,
Vn-peopel'd Offices, untroden stones?

And what heare there for welcome, but my grones?
Therefore commend me, let him not come there,
To seeke out sorrow that dwels every where:
Desolate, desolate will I hence, and dye,
The last leave of thee, takes my weeping eye.   *Exeunt.*

Scæna Tertia.
The Lists at Coventry. ——

Enter Marshall, and Aumerle.

Mar. My L. *Aumerle,* is *Harry Hereford* arm'd?
Aum. Yea, at all poynts, and longs to enter in.
Mar. The Duke of Norfolke, sprightfull and bold,
Stayes but the summons of the Appealants Trumpet.
Au. Why then the Champions, are prepar'd, and stay
For nothing but his Majesties approach.   *Flourish.*

Enter King, Gaunt, Bushy, Bagot, Greene, &
others: Then Mowbray in Ar-
mor, and Heralds.

Rich. Marshall, demand of yonder Champion
The cause of his arrivall heere in Armes,
Aske him his name, and orderly proceed
To sweare him in the justice of his cause.
Mar. In Gods Name, and the Kings, say who thou art,
And why thou com'st, thus knightly clad in Armes?
Against what man thou com'st, and what's thy quarrell,
Speake truely on thy knighthood, and thine oath,
As so defend thee heaven, and thy valour.
Mow. My name is *Tho. Mowbray,* Duke of Norfolke,
Who hither come engaged by my oath
(Which heaven defend a knight should violate)
Both to defend my loyalty and truth,
To God, my King, and his suceeding issue,
Against the Duke of Hereford, that appeales me:
And by the grace of God, and this mine arme,
To prove him (in defending of my selfe)
A Traitor to my God, my King, and me,
And as I truly fight, defend me heaven.

Enter Bullingbrooke in Armour.

Rich. Marshall: Aske yonder Knight in Armes,
Both who hee is, and why he commeth hither,
Thus placed in habiliments of warre:
And formally according to our Law
Depose him in the justice of his cause.
Mar. What is thy name?& wherfore com'st thou hither
Before King *Richard* in his Royall Lists?
Against whom com'st thou? and what's thy quarrell?
Speake like a true Knight, so defend thee heaven.
Bull. Harry of Hereford, Lancaster, and Derbie,
Am I: who ready here do stand in Armes,
To prove by heavens grace, and my bodyes valour,
In Lists, on *Thomas Mowbray* Duke of Norfolke,
That he's a Traitor foule and dangerous,
To God of heaven, King *Richard,* and to me,
And as I truely fight, defend me heaven.
Mar. On paine of death, no person be so bold,
Or daring hardie as to touch the Listes,
Except the Marshall, and such officers
Appointed to direct these faire designes.
Bull. Lord Marshall, let me kisse my Soveraigns hand,
And bow my knee before his Majestie:
For *Mowbray* and my selfe are like two men,
That vow a long and weary pilgrimage,

   c   Then

PLATE 24. A page of text in John Roberts's "transcript" of the Covent Garden Promptbook of *Richard II* (1738). Folger Shakespeare Library.

Roberts has written "M.D.P.S."—Middle Door, Prompt Side (*S* is covered by a blot of ink). After the initial stage direction at II. ii is "P.S."; after line 40, "O.P."—Opposite Prompt; and again after the stage direction at line 71, "O.P." At the opening of II. iii, Bolingbroke and Northumberland enter "O.P."

There are two important changes. The heading of I. iii, *"Scaena Tertia,"* is altered to *"Scaena* The Lists at Coventry" (Plate 24); and the initial scene of Act IV is marked: *"Actus Quartus, Scaena Prima.* Parliament Scene." (The unitalicized words are in manuscript.) To right and left of the added words at IV. i (but not at I. iii) is a circle with dot in the center to indicate a change of scenery.

The sketches by Roberts that face these two pages of text are the earliest of their kind, and they have an authority far greater than the engraved illustrations in Rowe's edition of Shakespeare in 1709 or those in the similarly illustrated editions of other Elizabethan and Jacobean playwrights published about this time.[33] Some of these have been thought to derive from sketches made during rehearsals or performance, and this may well be the case; but all have suffered an inevitable sea change (great or small) at the hands of engravers.[34]

In both sketches of settings at Covent Garden the chair of state is at the center of the back stage (Plates 25-26). Davies spoke with approval of the historical accuracy of the Combat Scene (see pp. 253-54). The arrangement was traditional. The setting of the Parliament Scene has high documentary support. At back stage center is the canopied chair of state, approached by three steps. A Cardinal sits on a stool at each side of the bottom step. Extending downstage is a long table, on which rest the Purse and the Mace, symbols of Majesty, with the Chancellor at the upper end, a Secretary at the lower, and a Judge seated on a cushion on either side. Along a diagonal line from near the foot of the dais to the outer front of the stage are ranged, on one side, the robed figures of Bolingbroke, Northumberland, Percy, and Fitzwater, and then twelve Bishops and twenty-five Civilians. Opposite, in similar formation, are Aumerle, Surrey, Wil-

[33] More authoritative, too, than the engraved frontispieces to the contemporary plays published separately in the first half of the 18th century.

[34] See Merchant, pp. 20-55, for a discussion of theatrical elements in engraved illustrations of English plays before 1740. See also A. C. Sprague, *Shakespeare and the Actors* (Harvard University Press, 1945), especially pp. 162-69, for some of the illustrations in Rowe's Shakespeare. The Henry Peacham drawing of some of the dramatis personae of *Titus Andronicus,* however suggestive of stage costume, cannot be considered to represent any stage setting seen by an Elizabethan audience (see Chambers, I, 312 ff., and Plate XI).

loughby, and Scroop, robed; then Carlisle, the Abbot of Westminster, and Civilians; next to the Civilians are Fryars with crosses, and at lower left are Gentleman Usher and Black Rod. This was such a sight as was familiar to those who had sat in Parliament or had seen the engraving of Queen Elizabeth seated in Parliament that faces p. 126 of Robert Glover's *Nobilitas politica vel civilis* (1608; Plate 27), or the revised plate with James I instead of Elizabeth facing p. 68 of Thomas Milles's *Catalogue of Honor* (1610). The same setting was perhaps more readily accessible in the engraved frontispiece of Sir Simon D'Ewes, *The Journals of All the Parliaments During the Reign of Queen Elizabeth* ... (1682).[35] What the theater provided, and what the audience expected, was a traditional setting. And its focus was the chair of state, the throne. Its position was central and dominating, and placed elsewhere it would, I think, have invited criticism.

Comment on the location of the thrones leads inevitably into a discussion of their use and placing on the English stage, not only at this time but during the Restoration period and, earlier, in the Elizabethan. It is not difficult to establish the fact that during the last decades of the 17th century and afterwards the front curtain was often lowered to cover the setting of the stage for formal scenes. Thrones could in these conditions be brought on and removed at will. There was no need to let them stand on the stage throughout a performance, ignored alike by actors and audience except when in use. The practice may have been different on the earlier platform stages. Jonson's reference to the coming down of a creaking throne has influenced some writers to argue that such chairs of state were always, or customarily, lowered through the trap-door in the heavens to a place at the center of the back stage. Others think that they were placed on stage before a play began, there to remain unnoticed save when required in the business of a scene. Yet others think that thrones were ordinarily placed in the closed inner stage before the opening of a scene and removed after the curtains closed at the scene's ending. It has also been suggested that on occasion they appeared in the upper stage or atop the (perhaps temporary) structure that extended forward from the façade of the tiring house.[36] I

[35] It served also as the frontispiece of his *A Compleat Journal of the Votes, Speeches and Debates, Both of the House of Lords and House of Commons* ... (1693).

[36] See, for example, George F. Reynolds, *The Staging of Elizabethan Plays at the Red Bull Theater 1605-1625* (New York, 1940), and "*Hamlet* at the Globe," *Shakespeare Survey 9* (1956), 49-53; John C. Adams, *The Globe Playhouse* (Harvard University Press, 1942), pp. 192, 335-39; C. Walter Hodges, *The Globe Restored* (London, 1953); Irwin Smith, *Shakespeare's Globe Playhouse* (New York, 1956), p. 111; Bernard Beckerman,

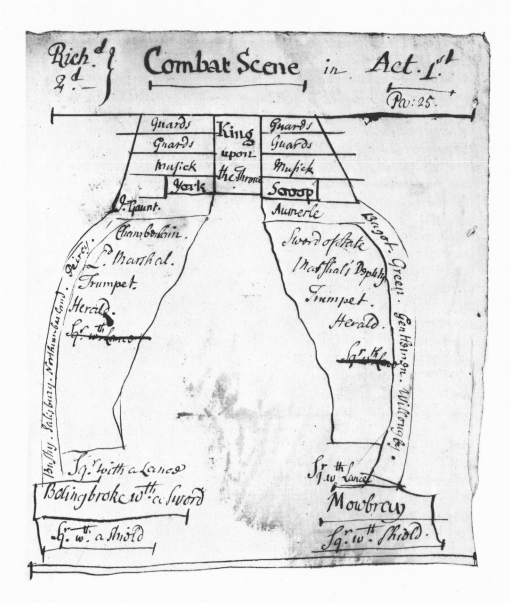

PLATE 25. The Combat Scene in *Richard II* (I. iii) as staged at Covent Garden on 6 February 1738. Folger Shakespeare Library.

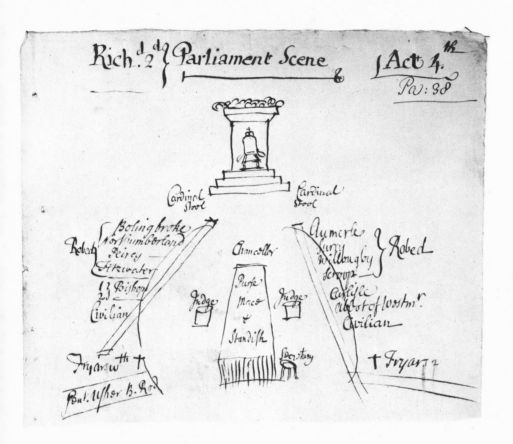

PLATE 26. The Parliament (i.e., Deposition) Scene in *Richard II* (IV. i) as staged at Covent Garden in 1738. Folger Shakespeare Library.

PLATE 27. Queen Elizabeth and Parliament. Engraving in Robert Glover, *Nobilitas politica vel civilis* (1608). Folger Shakespeare Library.

find especially cogent Professor Beckerman's discussion of the staging of group scenes at the Globe:

> It is apparent . . . that in the case of 156 of the 166 group scenes, the organizing principle is ceremony or duty. Movement and arrangement, though not formal, are not artificial. Rather, they reflect circumstances of Elizabethan life. (p. 171)

And so I like to think that the attempt in 1738 to recapture the ceremonial effects of the Combat and Parliament Scenes is a continuation of an age-old stage tradition. In the Elizabethan productions of *Lear* I. i, of *Hamlet* I. ii, II. ii, and V. ii, of *Henry V* I. ii, of *Merchant* IV. i, and elsewhere, the throne, the chair of state, should have been upstage center, flanked by appropriate dignitaries and attendants, as represented in Glover and Milles and D'Ewes—and in the sketches of the Covent Garden stage for *Richard II* in 1738. These are a reflection of some of the circumstances of Elizabethan life, and by their very ceremoniousness they lend an awful dignity: trial by combat, with an appeal to Heavenly Justice; and the impious uncrowning of an anointed king, God's vicegerent in England.

In recollecting the production, Davies emphasizes the use of "complete armour" by the two champions. Whence it was borrowed or whether it was authentic of the late 14th century is not known (Froissart tells that Bolingbroke's armor was made by Milanese smiths and Norfolk's by German craftsmen), but this must be recognized as a conspicuous example of the attempt at historical costume. As such, it lends weight to the arguments of Mr. Hal H. Smith that from Elizabethan times the theaters often used national or historic or emblematic costume to enhance dramatic effects.[37] When the Duke's Company presented the Earl of Orrery's *Henry V* in 1664, "This Play," writes John Downes, "was Splendidly Cloath'd: The King [Harris], in the Duke of York's Coronation Suit: Owen Tudor [Betterton], in King Charle's [*sic*]: Duke of Burgundy, in the Lord of Oxford's, and the rest all New."[38] The verisimilitude was, I fancy, a continuation of Elizabethan stage practice and a striking anticipation of the ceremoniousness in Covent Garden's *Richard II*.

In its several ways, the 1738 revival of *Richard II* was an important event, and we may feel grateful to the unknown lover of the stage that employed John Roberts to prepare a text "Correct cum Libr' Theatr'."

Shakespeare at the Globe (New York, 1962), pp. 165, 171, 209, and Appendix C, ii; and *Merchant*, *op. cit.*, pp. 180-81.

[37] "Some Principles of Elizabethan Costume," *Journal of the Warburg and Courtauld Institutes*, XXV (1963), 240-57.

[38] *Roscius Anglicanus* (1709), pp. 27-28.

Shakespeare in the United States

[1964]

F SHAKESPEARE belonged to the United States by birth instead of by inheritance, the 400th anniversary of his birth could not have been celebrated more widely or enthusiastically. It is not irrelevant to consider what his works have contributed to American culture, and what Americans have contributed to Shakespeare in the library and on the stage. To dispose first of some of the fringe benefits, it may be suggested that much innocent pleasure has accrued from the cultivation of Shakespeare gardens containing all the herbs, flowers, and trees named by the poet. An attempt to naturalize all the birds he mentions has had less happy results, though it must be acknowledged that the starlings imported by Eugene Schieffelin in 1880 have taken literally the injunction to be fruitful and multiply and replenish the earth.

It seems unlikely that Shakespeare would have been known to many of the colonists in the early, perilous years, whether they sought fortunes in Virginia or a religious haven in Plymouth. Nor is it likely that many copies of Shakespeare were to be found among their books. Theology, law, and treatises about agriculture and the crafts were the prime requisites. With increases in population, in prosperity, and in security, came houses with libraries, some leisure for reading, and a small flourishing of literary interests, particularly among those who had been sent back to England for education. Cotton Mather is reputed to have owned a Shakespeare First Folio. A copy of *Macbeth* is named in 1699 among the effects of one Captain Arthur Spicer of Richmond County, Virginia. The earliest literary allusions to the plays (probably attributable to Professor William Dawson of William and Mary College) occur in *Poems on Sev-*

Publications of the Modern Language Association of America, LXXIX (1964), 513-18.

eral Occasions By a Gentleman of Virginia, published in Williamsburg in 1736. William Byrd of Westover had one of the Shakespeare folios in his library at the time of his death in 1744.[1]

Familiarity with Shakespeare was not limited to those who possessed a play or a set of his works. Anthologies printed in England fell into the hands of Seaborn Cotton and Elnathan Chauncey, who copied out lines from Shakespeare about the middle of the 17th century. The almanac makers frequently printed short excerpts from the plays in their pages throughout the 18th century. And cultured readers plundered the works for apt quotations. These turn up in the private correspondence of the Founding Fathers in such forms as to indicate their general currency. Several of the Signers of the Declaration of Independence had editions of Shakespeare in their libraries, and John Adams and Thomas Jefferson were not alone in knowing their Shakespeare intimately. For Jefferson, as for Sir Philip Sidney, literature was to be read for its moral benefits, and he recommended to a friend the study of *Lear* and *Macbeth,* which instilled morality more effectively than could ethics or divinity.

William Scott's famous *Lessons in Elocution,* published in New Haven in 1799, included as illustrative material many of the most famous soliloquies and orations in Shakespeare. This book went through many editions and was widely imitated, for if there was little time to cultivate the reading and writing of literature, there was ample incentive to practice oratory, both legal and political. Boys and young men, especially those on the frontier, had access to few books, and those they had were chewed and digested. Long passages of Shakespeare that Abraham Lincoln memorized out of Scott's *Elocution* stayed with him to his death and were put to practical use throughout his years in the White House. Even people to whom plays and the theater were abhorrent memorized and quoted moral and oratorical speeches from Shakespeare.

The publication of Shakespeare's works began in Boston and New York with the reprints of English editions of single plays: *Hamlet* (1794, 1804—the earlier date is of the Boston edition), *Richard III* (1794, 1804), *Twelfth Night* (1794), *The Merchant of Venice* (1811). There seems to have been an early edition of *The Merry Wives of Windsor* in Boston, and an adaptation of *The Comedy of Errors* called *The Twins* was published in Philadelphia in 1787.

---

[1] [William Parker, of Portsmouth, New Hampshire, had a copy of the First Folio in his possession in 1791. It is now in the Scheide Library, Princeton University (no. CXXXVI in Lee's *Census*).]

Then in 1795 Bioren and Maden began the publication of Shakespeare's *Works* in Philadelphia. A Boston edition appeared in 1802-4. This was published in parts, the first such venture with Shakespeare in America. Subscribers paid 38 cents for each part; others, 50 cents. The edition was reprinted in book form. And thereafter the American market was flooded with reprints of the better—or poorer—English editions. In settled communities a set of Shakespeare volumes on the shelf gave a cultural cachet to the family, and enterprising publishers often made the purchase easy by offering sets by subscription, to be delivered one part at a time in paper covers, as with the Boston edition of 1802-4.

A more genuine testimony to the enjoyment of the plays was their presence in the captain's library aboard American ships that sailed the seven seas and in the ox carts and covered wagons that crossed the plains. Shakespeare and the Bible went everywhere. W. T. Hamilton, a fur trapper, has recorded that in 1842 a trapper from Kentucky gave him a copy of Shakespeare in what is now Wyoming, and the fondness for Shakespeare of Jim Bridger, another Rocky Mountain man, is well authenticated.

After an unsuccessful attempt to establish a theater in Williamsburg in 1715-16, the earliest reference to a performance of Shakespeare in the Colonies is in New York in 1730, when *Romeo and Juliet* appears to have been presented. The theatrical history of Shakespeare really begins in 1750 in New York with *Richard III* (Cibber's adaptation, of course, which held the stage until about 1900). Williamsburg saw the same play in 1751. It was given in Annapolis in 1752 and in Philadelphia in 1753. Charleston had a performance of *Lear* in 1764. Positive evidence exists that fourteen of Shakespeare's plays (including Garrick's *Catharine and Petruchio*) were performed 173 times before 1776. These recorded performances can be but a small fraction of those actually given. Many people in the principal cities could know Shakespeare almost as well from the stage as from the library. George Washington, who had an edition of Shakespeare on his shelves, may typify those who patronized the theater but are not known to have been avid readers of the plays.

The smaller, newer communities were not necessarily neglected. In the wake of the Hallams, who came to Williamsburg in 1752, has come a never-ending succession of actors from the English and Irish theaters. Enlisting local talent, the actors worked their way westward, living off the country by giving plays along the way. Extant playbills show a performance of *Hamlet* in such an unlikely place as Huntsville, Tennessee, in

1826; *Richard III* and *The Merchant of Venice* in Milledgeville, Georgia, in 1834; and *Hamlet* and *Othello* in Montgomery, Alabama, in 1835. Taking boat from Cincinnati (where there was a theater by 1801), the touring actors might go to St. Louis and thence southward to New Orleans.

As the frontier moved westward, the theater followed after. The discovery of gold in California in 1848 brought it leapfrogging into San Francisco and Sacramento. Another gold rush swept it into Colorado. And the trek of the Mormons led to the development of the first church-operated playhouses in Utah as early as 1856.

Virginia and Maryland were the only two original Colonies with no legislation against the stage. In Pennsylvania there had been strong Quaker opposition. And in New England Puritan objections had imposed severe restrictions: *Othello* was presented once in Newport, Rhode Island, as a "moral dialogue" (the same device Sir William Davenant had employed before the opening of the theaters by Charles II), and in Providence in 1762 David Douglass billed plays as moral dialogues in his Historical Academy. The Mormon leaders took the position that music and the drama should be cultivated for their recreational values, and people with talent found themselves assigned to the practice of these arts. Announcements reveal that children were at first encouraged to attend by being admitted for half price. By 1866, however, it was noticed that babies were causing the kind of disturbance that might have been predicted, and a new list of prices was posted: "Infants in arms, $10.00."

In a few cities and states, theatrical records have been collected and published; but most of the early playhouses have vanished, and the records have been lost. We have taken too little care of this, and the neglect should be remedied by a multitude of regional studies and then a comprehensive history of the theater in the United States.

In contrast to the many British actors who have been popular here, few American actors have stormed the English stage. One of the earliest was Ira Aldridge, who at the age of seventeen left his native New York City, never to return. His first London appearance was at the Royal Coburg in 1825. After a short time in London, the African Roscius, as he billed himself, toured in the provinces and in Ireland and Scotland until the middle of the century and then went on to the Continent for spectacular successes in Germany, Russia, and the Balkans. One of the thirty-three memorial seats in the Royal Shakespeare Theatre at Stratford-upon-Avon bears his name. Edwin Forrest went to London in 1834-35 and was acclaimed. Charlotte Cushman played there with success in 1845, and

Anna Cora Mowatt in 1849. Edwin Booth made an excellent impression in 1860. It was Daly's New York production starring John Drew and Ada Rehan that in 1888 restored Shakespeare's version of *The Taming of the Shrew* permanently to the English stage.

Playing chiefly in the principal cities, but also touring indefatigably, Robert Mantell, Richard Mansfield, and Walter Hampden, among others, helped keep Shakespeare's plays before the American public during the opening decades of this century. The names and careers of John and Lionel Barrymore, Jane Cowl, and Katharine Cornell are too well known to require comment.

The passing of the repertory theater in America, after the advent of the motion picture, ushered in generations of audiences for whom the living stage had no meaning and of performers who had no idea of how to read or act Shakespeare. However, in the last twenty years the development of festivals in San Diego, Pasadena, Ashland (Oregon), Antioch College, the University of Colorado, and Stratford (Connecticut)—to mention only the more prominent—has given young actors the opportunity to perform under expert direction on stages that often approximate that of the Globe, and many of them have profited enormously. They have acquired skills not needed on the naturalistic or experimental stage. Some of them are learning to read blank verse beautifully. Their audiences, in turn, have found anew the enjoyment of Shakespeare in the theater. Tens of thousands of school children have discovered for the first time the delights of *Romeo* and *Hamlet* and *Macbeth*. Seen on open stages, the plays are revealing forgotten or unsuspected beauties of construction and other evidences of the craftsmanship of their author, long obscured by the elaborate settings of proscenium-arch stages.

The editions of Shakespeare found in cultivated homes in the young republic were imports from Britain or reprints. Then in 1836 O. W. B. Peabody of Boston published his seven-volume *Dramatic Works,* based on Singer's British edition but with independent reference to the First Folio. Eleven years later, Gulian C. Verplanck brought out another independent edition in New York, *Shakespeare's Plays: With His Life.* The third distinctly American edition, *The Works of William Shakespeare* (1857-66), was that of Richard Grant White, who was prominent in denouncing the forgeries of J. P. Collier. Then in 1871 H. H. Furness published the first volume of his New Variorum Edition of Shakespeare, *Romeo and Juliet,* a landmark in American Shakespeare scholarship. By 1913 he had added sixteen more plays, and Mrs. Furness had compiled a *Concordance to the*

Poems. H. H. Furness, Jr., added two more plays before his death. Then in 1928 the project was entrusted to the Modern Language Association of America, under whose sponsorship six more titles have been published and other volumes are in preparation. No other independent text by an American editor came out until the appearance of *The Complete Works* (1906) edited by W. A. Neilson. Of the editions that have appeared since World War I, each has its weak and strong points. Four tendencies have been manifest. The first is illustrated by the American Arden and the Yale editions, which compete with others for private reading and class use by printing one play to a volume and providing background and explanatory material in introductions and notes; they have independent texts. The second, which may be typified by Hardin Craig's *Complete Works* and G. B. Harrison's *Shakespeare: 23 Plays and the Sonnets,* bring together in one volume a vast amount of commentary and illustration but use a conventional text: these are intended primarily as college texts. The third is the paperbacks, which may be independent texts or reprints of, say, the Globe; a volume will contain one or perhaps two plays, but sometimes more. Some are attractively printed on good paper; others have little typographical appeal. All are inexpensive, and if they do not kill each other off they may help revive the general reading of Shakespeare. The last type to be mentioned consists of the text of one play and a collection of essays or studies, sometimes accompanied by problems and study questions. On a newsstand today it is almost as easy to find a play of Shakespeare as a detective story.

Although courses in English literature were not a part of the curricula of schools and colleges in the period after the American Revolution, there is abundant evidence that Shakespeare was read. The morals of the young, and especially of young ladies, were protected by exposing them to collections of the Beauties of Shakespeare or to the castrated versions of Mr. Bowdler. The *Tales* as written by Mary and Charles Lamb circulated freely, as they still do. Literary people, such as Washington Irving and William Gilmore Sims, were much in Shakespeare's debt, and James Russell Lowell wrote critical essays about him.

Then as now Americans traveling in England made a pilgrimage to Stratford, and some left their signatures in the Visitors' Books of the Birthplace. One pilgrim, Maun-gwu-Daus, of the Chippewa Tribe, paid his tribute in verses that were printed in Stratford-upon-Avon on 5 February 1848:

Indians of North America
Heard the name that shall not decay,
They came and saw where he was born,
How great is the sound of his horn.

They respect and honor his grave
As they do the grave of their brave;
Rest thou great man under these stones,
For there is yet life in thy bones.

Thy Spirit is with Mun-nid-do,
Who gave thee all thou didst do:
When we are at our native home
We shall say, "We have seen his tomb."

Shakespeare was introduced into the schools through selections included in the "readers" that began to appear in the 1820s. Often these selections are to be found, with little or no identification of source, in the chapters dealing with elocution. William H. McGuffey, for example, had a dozen or more famous passages in his Fourth to Sixth Readers issued in the 1840s. During the next decade, the elocutionists worked out elaborate schemes for the proper delivery of King Henry V's speech at Harfleur, with musical notation and indications of appropriate gestures.

Except for the "readers," there was little instruction in Shakespeare in the schools until after the Civil War. An exception is the course in which the plays served as a text in Emma Willard's Troy Female Seminary in the 1830s. Doubtless good teachers in other schools used passages from the plays, either to emphasize a point of morality or to illustrate the depiction of the passions. The Hartford School certainly had readings in the classics as early as 1848. By 1890, such courses were usual throughout the country.

The texts used were probably editions of single plays by W. J. Rolfe, who states in his edition of *The Works* in 1871-96 that the notes had been used twenty years earlier by his own classes (he published a separate *Julius Caesar* in Boston in 1867), or by H. N. Hudson. Hudson's edition of *The Works* came out in Boston in 1851-56, and he was issuing separate editions of *As You Like It* as early as 1870 and of *Julius Caesar* by 1877. It is interesting to note that while Hudson used the text of the Chiswick Shakespeare, Rolfe claimed the First Folio as his basic text. Another small volume may also have been used in the schools: *The Shakespearean Reader* of John W. S. Hows, first published in 1850. The title-pages of

1860 and later state that it is intended for "schools, colleges, and family reading."

The earliest reference to Shakespeare in a college or university catalogue is that of 1855 at the University of Virginia, where McGuffey included aesthetics and rhetoric in his courses in moral philosophy, with Shakespeare among the texts. In 1857, the new School of History and General Literature used Shakespeare for philological study. A little later, the scientific course at Michigan included a semester of Shakespeare, permitting Datus C. Brooks to give attention to aesthetic, philological, oratorical, and historical considerations. Harvard's first genuine offerings in English literature (in 1872-73) included courses by F. J. Child, one in philology based on Chaucer and Shakespeare, and another in composition and literature in which *Hamlet* was one of the set texts. There is no need to follow the history of the increase of courses in English literature (including Shakespeare) in other places of learning. At Yale in 1860, as earlier at Michigan, the Scientific School took the step before the Classical School. Cornell had a Shakespeare course in 1868; Princeton, in 1869; The Johns Hopkins, in 1877; and Columbia, in 1882. Often the approach was severely philological. The study of Shakespeare as dramatic artist came considerably later.

Shakespeare being such a late-comer into the college curriculum, it is not surprising that American library collections of Shakespeare and Shakespeariana were of small importance during most of the nineteenth century. In 1723 Harvard had one of Rowe's editions, and by 1773 it had added Pope's edition of 1728. By 1770 the Library Company of Philadelphia had two critical works, Upton's *Critical Observations* (1748) and Heath's *Revisal of Shakespeare's Text* (1765). The first major collection of Shakespeariana is that purchased in London in 1845 by Charles C. Jewett, the young Librarian of Brown University. This consisted of 196 volumes of commentary and criticism. In 1860 were added 150 volumes that had been purchased at the Burton sale in New York. By way of contrast, it may be noted that in 1835 the Library Company of Philadelphia seems to have had 13 editions of the collected plays and 19 single plays, as well as 29 titles of criticism. At Harvard by 1834 there were 8 collected editions, 1 separate play, and 13 volumes of commentary. Yale in 1845 had in four libraries a total of 17 collected editions of the plays, 1 volume of poems, and 11 books of criticism.

Serious textual studies could not be attempted by Americans until copies of the early editions were at hand. The Boston Public Library took the lead in providing these by acquiring the library of Thomas Pennant Barton in 1873. This contained a set of the four folios, 18 quartos published before 1623, and more than 20 others dated earlier than 1700, all of the important editions from Rowe (1709) to the Variorum of 1821, and 1100 volumes of non-Shakespearian material, including nearly 600 editions of early plays. Before 1880, the James Lenox collection of the four folios and some 40 early quartos was in the New York Public Library. In 1911, the Elizabethan Club at Yale was established by Alexander Cochrane with a nucleus of 27 early Shakespeare quartos from the Huth Library. Scholarly work had been going on in Philadelphia since before 1871 in the Furness household, whose holdings of early editions (a set of the folios and no fewer than 22 quartos ranging from the *Hamlet* of 1611 to that of 1703) and collateral volumes were to be transferred to the Library of the University of Pennsylvania in 1932.

Meanwhile, the opening to the public of the great collections of Henry E. Huntington in 1925 began the transformation of American Shakespearian scholarship—indeed, of English Renaissance scholarship—by making available not only copies of the Shakespeare folios and quartos but an important collection of background material, English and Continental. That transformation was accelerated by the dedication of the Folger Shakespeare Library in 1932, with the incomparable Shakespearian collection of Henry Clay Folger. The Folger collection was soon (1938) to be supplemented by the great collection of early English books from the library of Sir Leicester Harmsworth.

The foresight and generosity of a number of wealthy Americans have enriched immeasurably the cultural resources of this country. Witness the Pierpont Morgan Library in New York (opened to the public in 1924); the John H. Wrenn Library at the University of Texas; the J. K. Lilly Library at Indiana; the Newberry Library in Chicago—and these by no means exhaust the list.

The university libraries have not been idle, whether privately endowed or state supported. Strong collections of Shakespeare and Shakespeariana are to be found at Harvard, Yale, Princeton, Pennsylvania, Illinois, Brown, Michigan, Wisconsin, and elsewhere—in fact, several other university libraries have one or more of the folios and a few quartos. Shakespearians in many areas of the United States can find helpful working collections within reach. Only in the Southeast, the South Central, the Rocky Mountain, and the Northern Pacific regions does one have to travel more than a few hundred miles to reach an important collection.

It must not be supposed that the only American collectors of Shakespeare and Shakespeariana have been those whose libraries are now administered for public use. William E. Burton, the actor, had 1500 such volumes at his sale in 1860. Augustine Daly had a set of the folios and valuable theatrical material at his death in 1899. At the dispersal of the tremendous library of Robert Hoe, III, there were four Shakespeare folios and nine quartos. E. D. Church's fine Shakespeariana went intact to Henry E. Huntington, along with his Americana. Huntington also absorbed the three folios and several quartos of F. R. Halsey. When the great Devonshire collection of early English literature, including the four Shakespeare folios and 57 quartos, went to Huntington, Marsden J. Perry is reported to have said that he would abandon the field, since he could not enjoy primacy. Perry had acquired the remarkable J. O. Halliwell-Phillipps books and manuscripts in 1884; to these he had added the MacGeorge set of folios and many other extremely desirable items. Much of the Halliwell-Phillipps material was bought by Folger in 1907, and the rest of the Shakespeariana was dispersed in 1919. William A. White's Shakespearian holdings were of the finest. Because of his desire that scholars might know what rare books were available in this country, he published a handlist of his Elizabethan library in 1914 and issued a catalogue of the expanded collection in 1926. He was noted for his generosity in giving scholars access to his treasures. In this he rendered a service that was impossible for H. C. Folger. The latter bought as rapidly and as widely as his resources permitted over a period of forty years, but the volume of his purchases was so great that as rapidly as they could be examined and listed they were packed and stored against the day when a library should be built to house them. Since he died before the construction of his library, he never had the pleasure of using his purchases or even seeing them on shelves; thus when he wrote inquirers that the books were inaccessible, he was telling the literal truth. At White's death, 100 people subscribed some $200,000 to buy the Shakespeare quartos and other Elizabethan books for Harvard. These collectors and others whose taste and avidity brought many treasures of the Shakespearian age to America do not enjoy the fame of men like Morgan, Huntington, and Folger, but without their book collecting, our institutional collections could not have become what they are.

[Behind the great collectors were, of course, the often forgotten antiquarian bookdealers. They existed from the early days of the Republic, but the first to achieve international stature and reputation was Henry

Stevens of Vermont. In Colonial America, men of learning and taste like William Byrd, James Logan, and Dr. Benjamin Rush bought through English agents in their areas of special interest. Thomas Jefferson's fine library became the nucleus of the Library of Congress. It would not be wide of the mark, however, to say that these men bought for use. There were a few copies of the First Folio edition of Shakespeare's plays in the United States in the early decades. In addition to the Parker-Baker-Scheide copy mentioned above (note 1), there was a copy in the possession of Francis C. Gray about 1836; Charles Chauncey acquired his copy before 1849; and the actor, W. E. Burton, owned a copy about 1850.[2] It was, I think, the publicity given to the purchase by James Lenox in 1847 of a copy of the Gutenberg Bible that focused attention upon the collection of great books for their own sake. Bibles and Americana had long been the areas of greatest competition among American collectors. After Henry Stevens appeared on the scene, this competition was intensified. At the same time, interest was stimulated in many other kinds of books and manuscripts. The collectors were usually very busy men of affairs, like John Carter Brown, James Lenox, and John Jacob Astor, whose previous reliance had been upon book catalogues from Europe and the few rather elementary bibliographies then available. The energy, intelligence, and swashbuckling tactics of Henry Stevens changed all this and began a new era. By chance it was not he who consummated the purchase of Lenox's Gutenberg Bible (that triumph is credited to Wiley and Putnam), though he had initiated the deal. In that same year, 1847, Lenox rejected Stevens's offer of a set of four Shakespeare Folios because of the condition of one of them; but ten years later he bought a set from Stevens and also twenty-nine Shakespeare play-quartos.[3] The methods developed with such success by Henry Stevens of Vermont were imitated and refined by the great antiquarian bookdealers who followed: men like George D. Smith, Gabriel Wells, and Dr. A. S. W. Rosenbach. By their diligence and expertise these men and their professional rivals hunted out the treasures that graced and made famous the shelves of the great collectors' libraries.]

  [2] [See Sir Sidney Lee's *Census of Extant Copies* . . . (Oxford University Press, 1902). The Parker-Baker-Scheide copy is no. 136; Gray, no. 31; Chauncey, no. 118; Burton, no. 145; and Astor, no. 43.]
  [3] [Stevens records a letter of 16 June 1847 from the London dealer, William Pickering, to the effect that an unnamed American had bought from him a set of Shakespeare Folios "many years since." See *Recollections of James Lenox* . . . , ed. Victor H. Paltsits (New York Public Library, 1951), Note 9, pp. 38-39.]

During the last quarter of the 19th century there was a flourishing exchange of information and ideas between Americans like Grant White, J. Parker Norris, and H. H. Furness and the active Shakespearians in England. Not much Shakespeare criticism was published in this country before the First World War, for the raw materials of research were not to be found on this side of the Atlantic. It is instructive to compare the editions cited in footnotes and bibliographies of even the good books and scholarly articles on Shakespeare published up to 1925 with those listed a few years later, after the opening of the Huntington Library. What American scholarship did get into print received little attention abroad. Even after J. S. P. Tatlock, Felix E. Schelling, W. W. Lawrence, T. M. Parrott, A. H. Thorndike, O. J. Campbell, R. A. Law, H. T. Price, and their compeers had reached the height of their powers, they were read chiefly in their own country. The biographical discoveries of C. W. Wallace and, later, Leslie Hotson could scarcely be ignored. In due course, G. L. Kittredge and E. E. Stoll were invited to address English audiences, but it was nearly 1930 before the important American studies in Shakespeare biography and criticism and the Elizabethan stage were sought out as a matter of course by foreign scholars. It was the brilliant work done on the textual and bibliographical problems of the folios and quartos and bibliographical theory that first commanded international attention. But now the names of the scholars mentioned above, and those of J. Q. Adams, George F. Reynolds, M. P. Tilley, Hyder Rollins, and of the better Shakespearians yet living and producing are well known to all serious students about the world. For there is no phase of Shakespeare studies they have not illuminated.

In this year, when the 400th anniversary of Shakespeare's birth has been celebrated so widely in America, with a National Committee to lead the way and give assistance and encouragement, with elaborate programs at the established festivals and countless special commemorations, it is encouraging to observe that special programs and special exhibits began early in January and are continuing through December; actually, there are still some being scheduled for 1965. More people in this country are now enjoying Shakespeare than ever before. More people are coming to realize that Shakespeare's England was the England of the colonists at Jamestown and Plymouth. Published photographs and television programs are storing our memories with scenes of Shakespeare's England. There are a thousand reminders that Shakespeare is a vital element in our heritage and culture.

It is pleasant to discover that when this country was nearing the final struggles of its Civil War, a citizen brought to the attention of his fellow members of the New England Historic Genealogical Society the fact that the twenty-third of April would be the 300th anniversary of the birth of William Shakespeare. He wrote in part as follows:

It is understood that appropriate notice of this event will be taken in England. But I have yet to learn that any measures have been inaugurated in this country for the celebration of that day. Should it be suffered to pass by without something being done by way of commemoration in this Western World, the neglect cannot fail, in my opinion, to cause us disgrace.

England was, it is true, the birthplace of the greatest writer in our language, but he belongs to us as much as to the land of his nativity. There are probably fifty readers of him in the United States to one reader in England.

After indicating that scientific and literary people—those that might have been expected to take the lead—had remained silent, he proposed that the Society should do something and stated the reasons why such action would be logical.

. . . English history is our history till within less than two hundred and fifty years, it is measurably our history till within less than a century; and even now we have no small sympathy in the public movements of our father-land. . . .

These facts, and others which might be named, seem to render it proper that this Society should celebrate in some way the three hundredth anniversary of his birth. And should it so happen that ours should be the only celebration of this event in America, or even in New England, it will redound much to the credit of this Society, and be a pleasant thing in our annals for posterity to read.

It is a matter of record that the Genealogical Society voted to celebrate.

Excerpta quaedam per A.W. adolescentem

[1967]

I N THE Second Dialogue of *The Humours and Conversations of the Town* (1693), young Madam Townlove and elderly (past thirty!) Madam Thinkwell are discussing the social activities of London.

> TOWNLOVE. I'm glad, my dear, that you approve plays, which you have not in the Country
>
> THINKWELL. 'Tho we have 'em not Acted, we may read them without the temptations of the Pit, which is better; and then we cull 'em, and trouble not our selves with such as are not worth reading. . . . (p. 128)

The opinion of Madam Thinkwell is so entirely consonant with the experience of James Wright (1643-1713), to whom the satire is generally ascribed,[1] as to increase the probability of the attribution to him. Two other of James Wright's publications, *Country Conversations* (1694) and *Historia Histrionica* (1699), have endeared him to historians of the 17th-century English theater.[2] Long ago Thomas Warton remarked of him:

During the fluctuations of government, and afterwards, he was attached to the

---

[1] See Brice Harris's Introduction to the 1961 edition, Scholars' Facsimiles and Reprints.

[2] It is tempting to guess that James Wright was the "ingenious Gentleman of the Middle-Temple" referred to in Bernard Lintott's statement in *The Post-Boy* of 3 March 1710/11 about the sources of the texts for his reprints of Shakespearian poems:

> Some of these Miscellanies were printed from an Old Edition, which Mr: Congreve oblig'd me with; others from an ingenious Gentleman of the Middle-Temple, who is pleas'd to leave his old Copy with me, to shew to any Person that has a mind to gratify this [*sic*] Curiosity therewith.

See Hyder E. Rollins, ed., Variorum Shakespeare, *Poems*, p. 381.

Studies in Honor of DeWitt T. Starnes, ed. T. P. Harrison, Archibald A. Hill, Ernest C. Mossner, and James Sledd (University of Texas Press, 1967), pp. 117-29.

principles of monarchy in their most extensive comprehension; and from this circumstance he might also have derived a predilection for the theatre which he had seen oppressed by the republicans.[3]

Earlier in the same paragraph, Warton had offered a shrewder conjecture:

His early and long residence in London, contributed to furnish him with informations for dramatic history; and his attention to the stage, and knowledge of the older actors and the ancient playhouses might have originated from his father. (p. 602)

This statement can, I think, be shown to come very close to the truth.

About 1655, when James was twelve years old, his father, Abraham Wright (1611-90; see *DNB*), was persuaded to leave his rural retreat in Peckham, County Surrey, and come to London to serve as unofficial minister of St. Olave's in Silver Street, where he remained until 1659. During these years young James may have acquired information about the playhouses and some of the pre-Wars actors, but there is reason to believe that his familiarity with plays and his interest in the theater may have been imparted to him by his father before 1655.

When Abraham Wright was expelled from his fellowship at St. John's College, Oxford, in 1648 because of Royalist convictions, he became tutor to the son of Sir James Grime (or Graham) at Peckham, and it may be presumed that James Wright, who had no formal education at school or university, received from his father all his education prior to his admission to New Inn in 1666. One of the means of instruction used by Abraham Wright seems to have been a commonplace book entitled *Excerpta quaedam per A. W. adolescentem,* which I propose to describe briefly.

The manuscript[4] was purchased for the British Museum as item 120 in the 21 August 1858 sale of books and manuscripts formerly owned by Dr. Philip Bliss; and it is now designated as Add. MS. 22608. Bliss had acquired this and other manuscripts and books originating with Abraham and James Wright from the holdings of William Bromley, Esq., of Baginton, County Warwick, to whom James Wright had bequeathed them, and Bromley's engraved armorial bookplate is in this and several other items in the British Museum. The manuscript consists of some 120 leaves, with contents as follows:

---

[3] *Poems upon Several Occasions . . . by John Milton* (London, 1785), "Corrections and Supplemental Observations," p. 603.

[4] It is a pleasure to record my gratitude to President Mark Curtis of Scripps College for suggesting that the manuscript might be worth examining.

fols.   3-30   "out of ye History of Willi Martyr esquire and recorder of Exeter"

        31-36^v "Out of ye History of ye reagne of King Henry ye seventh. S^r ffrancis Bacon./"

        37-42 "Out of ye Annals of King Henry ye 8th written by ffrancis [Godwin] B^p of Hereford and translated by Morgan Godwin gent:"

        43-68^v "Out of ye History of Queen Elizabeth written by Mr Camden, translated by R: N: Edit. 1630."

    [two blank unnumbered leaves]

    69-101^v [Excerpts from plays]

    101^v-10^v [Partly in cipher: Out of the Holy War by Fuller]

    110^v [Partly in cipher: Out of the epistle]

    111-13^r [Excerpts from plays]

    113^v-16^v [Poems, miscellanea]

    117-19^v "Out of Stafford's Niobe. . . ."

It is the contents of fols. 69-109^v and 111-13 that are of immediate concern.

The earliest reference to the manuscript known to me is in *Historical Papers, Part 1*, edited by Philip Bliss and Bulkeley Badinel for the Roxburghe Club and published by William Nichol in 1846. Items 2 and 3 are "Novissima Straffordii, Some Accounts of the Proceedings against, and Demeanor of, Thomas Wentworth, Earl of Strafford . . . written in Latin, in imitation of the style of Tacitus, by Abraham Wright, Vicar of Okeham in Rutlandshire"; and "The same, translated into English by James Wright, Barrister at Law, the Historian of the County of Rutland." These were printed from the original manuscripts then in the possession of Bliss.[5] In their account of Abraham Wright, the editors record that while he was a scholar of St. John's College, Oxford, he was

Esteemed a good critical and classical scholar, and having a correct ear, and an excellent voice, was selected to address King Charles the First, and his Queen, when they were entertained by Archbishop Laud, in the [new] library of St. John's College, August 30, 1636.

They add that Wright, entering holy orders, preached before the University and, especially, at St. Mary's before Charles I while the King resided in Oxford. After listing some of Wright's books, Bliss and Badinel continue:

Besides the MS. account of Strafford now printed, we have seen a volume of MS. Collections made by Wright in his youth, probably when at college, which

[5] See item 221, *Novissima Straffordii*, in the catalogue of the Bliss sale cited above.

is here mentioned, because it contains some early and original criticisms on Shakespeare. He has transcribed, in addition to large extracts from historical writers, several scenes and passages, that appear to have pleased him, in the plays of Ben Jonson, Beaumont and Fletcher, Shirley, and Shakespeare, appending a short opinion of each play. We give one of these notices, as sufficiently brief and characteristic. (p. vi)

Then follows Wright's opinion of *Othello*.

Students of Shakespeare seem to have ignored the opportunity thus afforded, and all interest in the manuscript was lost for eighty years. Then George Thorn-Drury attempted to follow the trail but found the scent too cold.[6]

Before considering the excerpts from plays and Abraham Wright's opinions of them, three less important matters should be disposed of. The first is a reminder of Wright's dramatic and critical qualifications. He is said to have acted in George Wilde's *Love's Hospital* at St. John's on 29 August 1636, and to have written a comedy entitled *The Reformation*. The latter is supposed to have been lost in the fire in Middle Temple in 1679, when James Wright's books and manuscripts were consumed. Abraham Wright is said to have been an avid collector of play-manuscripts, and it is conjectured that these also perished in the fire. If the twenty-eight plays listed on fol. 111 of *Excerpta quaedam* belonged to him, he had a modest collection of 17th-century printed drama.[7] Next, it should not be forgotten that he had a lively appreciation of style. His *Five Sermons of Five Several Styles or Waies of Preaching* (1656) was published to demonstrate the need of an educated clergy at a time when "inspiration" was generally accepted as the only qualification to preach.[8]

---

[6] In his edition of Abraham Wright's *Parnassus Biceps* (London, 1927, p. vii) he mentions the *Excerpta quaedam* but admits that "no trace of it can now be found." His search may have been prompted by the reprint from *Historical Papers, Part 1* of Wright's criticism of *Othello* that C. M. Ingleby had contributed to *The Shakespeare Allusion Book* (1909), I, 411.

[7] There are two lists on the page. The first, consisting of twenty-five titles, is written consecutively, the authors are named, and each play is classified as comedy, history, *etc.* Below it the titles only are arranged in two columns, and three more plays are named. The second list appears to have been written at some time later than the first; following each title (except *The Contention for Honor and Riches*) is a page-reference to the place in *Excerpta* where quotations are transcribed.

[8] The first sermon, in the style of Bishop Lancelot Andrewes, had been preached before King Charles; the second, in the style of Bishop Joseph Hall, before the University at Wright's ordination; the third, in the style of Jasper Mayne and Christopher Cartwright, before the University; the fourth, Presbyterian in style, at St. Paul's in London; and the fifth, Independent, never preached. The sermons varied in length: Andrewes, 20

The third subsidiary matter is Abraham Wright's use of *Excerpta* for purposes of instruction. At the top of the first page (fol. 69) of dramatic excerpts, and in the margins, Wright, at some period after the original transcription, has written several instructions and introduced a number of markings to guide a young reader:

[*See*] pa. 168 of yr[*or* ye] papers.

Marke Montague Sydnam ... ye voiage to ye Levant. Herberts poems. Maine's and Shirley's play. My pap ⟨ ⟩

ffelthams resolves ...

see pa: 168 of y^r papers.

And for words y^t are newe y^r Inglish dictionary will alone suffice, and make more use of this then you have done, for this is sydnams way and every o ⟨ ⟩

In the right margin, in a different ink:

Marke Sydnam for penning Epistles and imitate him xxx take out of these some sett expressions (as y^t, put them to a gaze, and a sta ⟨ ⟩ . . . and make common vse of them vpon their several occas ⟨ ⟩

And in the left margin:

those places markd ⟨t⟩h⟨us⟩+either   or in my books are not phrases but ex-|⟨p⟩ressions and lines.

It is a temptation to conjecture that these imperatives were written for young James, who was being taught how to write decent English by reading and imitating specified authors and the excerpts from plays as well as the plays themselves. This exercise would have been the foundation of James Wright's love of the drama.[9]

We come at length to the excerpts themselves and, what is much more interesting, the individual criticisms of a man specially qualified to form

---

pages; Hall, 16 pages; Mayne and Cartwright, 25 pages; Presbyterian, 89 pages; and Independent, 64 pages.

[9] The authors referred to appear to be Bishop Richard Montague, Humphrey Sydenham, Sir Henry Blount (*A Relation of the Voiage to the Levant*), George Herbert, Jasper Mayne, James Shirley, and Owen Feltham.

The page is extremely difficult to read, and I have not attempted to record every word. For some reason, Wright sometimes increases the difficulty by substituting letters. For example, *newe* appears as *nffxxff; Epistles* as *Epkstlffs; these* as *thffsff;* and *expressions* as *ffxprffssklns.* In the body of the transcriptions, *per* and *pro* are frequently indicated by the familiar Elizabethan contraction, the letter *p* with a curved line crossing the descender; and initial *com* and *con* are often represented by a sort of reversed *c*.

literary judgments. They were written, it would seem, not earlier than 1639,[10] the year in which Fuller's *Holy War* was published, long excerpts from which precede the quotations from Henry Shirley's *Martyred Soldier* (1638) and James Shirley's *Royal Master* (1638), the last two plays to be quoted from. It is not easy to postulate a date for the pedagogic notations. Humphrey Sydenham's sermons appeared in print between 1626 and 1638; Richard Montague's books, between 1622 and 1640; and Feltham's *Resolves,* between 1623 and 1635; Blount's *Voyage* is dated 1636. Only one of Jasper Mayne's plays was in print as early as 1639, and it was 1648 before a second was published. Poems by Herbert were available as early as 1633, but others are dated in their first editions as late as 1662. If all the instructions were written at one time, a somewhat dubious assumption, the earliest possible date would be 1648. Since James Wright was then only five years old, the instructions about the use of the quotations as a text were probably written at least from seven to ten years later.

It is a safe assumption, I think, that Wright quoted from books on his own shelves.[11] His method of quoting makes difficult the identification of the edition he used, as the examples to be quoted later will make clear, but the page references he supplies indicate that Jonson's *Bartholomew Fair* and *The Staple of News* were in the editions of 1631, and certain quotations show the probable use of the 1637 quarto of *Hamlet* and the certain use of the second quarto of *Othello* (1630).

As might be expected, some plays are given greater space than others. The excerpts from seven of the plays occupy only one page (fractions of a page are ignored): Shirley's *Traitor, Hyde Park,* and *Contention for Honor and Riches,* Beaumont and Fletcher's *Elder Brother* and *King and No King,* Webster's *White Devil,* and Massinger's *New Way to Pay Old Debts.* Two pages are given to *Hamlet,* Beaumont and Fletcher's *Maid's Tragedy,* Davenant's *Platonick Lovers,* and Shirley's *School of Compliment* and *Wedding.* Almost half of the plays are allowed three pages: *Othello,* Jonson's *Staple of News,* Webster's *Devil's Law Case* and

---

[10] In *The Shakespeare Allusion Book, Excerpta quaedam* is dated "about 1637 (or earlier)," the editors having failed to take into account the dates of publication of the plays excerpted by Wright. Their suggestion must have seemed plausible, for in 1637 Wright was twenty-six years old.

[11] A note in the top left margin of fol. 111, next to the first list of plays, suggests that it may have been written after Abraham Wright was residing in London in 1655: "see for Shirleys plaies at y⁰ marigold in y⁰ yard," *i.e.,* in St. Paul's Churchyard. This may indicate that he was still buying plays, or that he was guiding his young son to a shop that stocked them.

Duchess of Malfi, Davenant's *Wits*, Beaumont and Fletcher's *Philaster*, *Faithful Shepherdess*, and *Scornful Lady*, Henry Shirley's *Martyred Soldier*, and James Shirley's *Changes, Bird in a Cage*, and *Young Admiral*. Four pages are given to James Shirley's *Lady of Pleasure;* his *Grateful Servant* occupies five pages; and his *Royal Master* and Jonson's *Bartholomew Fair,* six pages.

Any literate person with a little industry can copy lines out of a play. The results will reveal something of the interests and the taste of the compiler, but may be without general or enduring worth. The value of Abraham Wright's *Excerpta quaedam* lies, in my opinion, in the short critiques appended to the quotations. Of Stafford's *Niobe,* the nondramatic work that makes its appearance in the section devoted to plays, this, in part, is what Wright has to say:

A well pend booke for ye most part in respect of lines ye matter being but common, and ye expressions sometimes are too ranting and play-like for so serious a peece as hee intended it for. . . .

Massinger fares poorly. The verdict on *A New Way to Pay Old Debts* is:

A silly play. ye plot but ordinary . . . for the lines they are very poore, noe expressions but onely plaine downright relating the matter; wthout any new dress either of language or matter.

Davenant's two plays rate higher. Of *The Platonick Lovers:*

An indifferent good play for plot and lines, but most of ye plot lies in ye last act. Theander and Eurithea good Parts for Platonick lovers, such as Randolph's chast M^{rs} is. . . .

Of *The Wits:*

A very good comedie for plot and lines, in either farre exceeding his Platonick lovers.

Wright's observations on three of Webster's plays illustrate his awareness of the different points of view from which a play may be judged: fable, structure, unity, character development, meter and diction, and theatrical effectiveness. *The Duchess of Malfi:*

A good play, especially for ye plot at ye latter end, otherwise plaine. in his language he uses a little too much of scripture, as in ye first act speaking of a captaine full of wounds hee saies hee had like ye children of Israel among [*illegible*]. . . . And wch is against ye lawes of ye scene ye business was 2 yeeres a doing as may bee p*er*ceeud by ye beeginning of ye 3^d act; where Antonio has 3 children by ye Dutchess, when in ye first act hee had but one.

The White Devil:

But an indifferent play to read, but for ye presentments I beeleeue good. ye lines are to much riming. . . . [Wright praises the scene of the murder of the Duke.]

The Young Admiral is "A very good play, both for lines and plot, ye last being excellent in wch hee seems to follow Barclaies Argenis or ye like history. . . ."

We come at length to Wright's criticism of the two plays by Shakespeare. That of *Othello*[12] will occasion no surprise:

Othello by Shakespeare.

A very good play both for lines and plot, but especially ye plot. Iago for a rogue and Othello for a iealous husband 2 parts well pend. Act: 3 ye scene betwixt Iago and Othello, and ye 1 sce: of ye 4 Act between ye same shew admirably ye villanous humour of Iago when hee p[er]suades Othello to his ielousy.

But Wright's estimate of *Hamlet* is sharply at variance with the received opinion that in the 17th century this was the most popular[13] of Shakespeare's plays:

Hamlet. a Tragedie by Shakespeare.

But an indifferent play, ye lines but meane: and in nothing like Othello. Hamlet is an indifferent good part for a madman. and ye scene in ye beginning of ye 5 act beetweene Hamlet and ye grauemaker a good sceane but since betterd in ye ielous lovers.

Before sampling the lines transcribed from *Hamlet* and *Othello,* I think Wright deserves to have it pointed out that he did not simply cull the phrases, sentences, and striking bits of dialogue that appealed to him. Some of the other things he did may be illustrated from *The Staple of News.* The line, "A broken sleeue keepes ye arme backe," is paraphrased,
sleeve
"is ashamed to shew his ~~arme~~ likewise to play a peepe-arme." Opposite·

---

[12] It was printed by Bliss and Badinel in *Historical Papers, Part 1* (1846).

[13] Note, however, that according to Thomas Rymer, "from all the tragedies on our English stage, *Othello* is said to bear the bell away"; see also G. E. Bentley, "Indeed, in the allusions through 1680, *Othello* is Shakespeare's most popular play" (*Shakespeare and Jonson: Their Reputations in the Seventeenth Century Compared,* 1945, I, 113-14).

the line about the "fine Poet" who wrote "Dumb Rethoricke, and silent Eloquence" is the notation, "Daniel," *i.e.,* Samuel Daniel—the identification is confirmed by Jonson's editors. The reference to Silver Street is explained thus: "a vsurer is said to bee bred in silver-street, a good region of money." And towards the end of the play, "a wooden collar" is glossed as a pillory. As the passages to be quoted below will show, Wright sometimes adapts a phrase or inserts words to give a statement a general application. Occasionally he gives the setting of a quoted passage or includes a stage direction. He combines lines, and several times when transcribing dialogue he identifies the speakers as A and B.[14]

The Devil's Law Case:

But an indifferent play, ye plot is intricate enough, but if rightly scanned will bee found faulty, by reason many passages doe either not hang together, or if they doe it is so sillily that no man can p[er]ceive them likely to be ever done....

The Beaumont and Fletcher plays receive mixed praise and censure. *Philaster* is called "A good play ... ye plot is good especially ye discovering of Bellario, and worthy ye imitating. ...." *A King and No King* is "a good play, but especially for ye plot wch is extraordinary, and so strange y^t no man can thīcke what it would come to till ye latter end of ye last act. ...." *The Maid's Tragedy* is "a very good play, and better than ye other 2." Wright praises the scene "betwixt Evadne and Amintor at their going to bed" and the scene of Aspatia's mourning. "All ye 3^d Act very good especially ye scene twixt Amintor and Melantius. ...." *The Scornful Lady* is "a very good play, especially for ye humours. ...." But *The Faithful Shepherdess* is "but an indifferent play. ... ye plot faulty in this y^t Thenot was not brought clearly, and y^t ye honour of Clarin wch hee did more than suspect was not vindicated."

To judge by the number of James Shirley's plays in Wright's list and quoted from, Shirley must have been his favorite playwright. For many of the plays, he had words of praise, but he was not blind to their faults, and some of his observations were acute. Thus of *The Changes:* "But an ordinary play. ye lines nothing neare so good as those in his other plaies: ye plot but plaine, and ye same humour in many parts. ...." *The Grateful Servant* is given higher praise: "A good play, ye plot well *con*trived and smooth: ye lines full of complement, as indeed all his are, and I believe purposely so studied by him for to take ye court. ...."

[14] At the foot of fol. 69, Wright has written: "Note hereafter y^t A: and B: stand for ye speakers."

Out of ye Tragedie of Hamlet Prince of Denmarke
by Will: Shakespeare.

Thinking our state disioint and out of frame. x to p*er*severe in obstinate
condolement, is a course of impious stubbornness, and shewes a will most in-
correct to heauen, an vnderstanding simple and vnschoold

A. staid hee not long. B. While one wth moderate hast might tell an hundred

Ile speake to it though hell it selfe should gape and bid mee hold my peace.

ffor dalliance, hold it a fashion and a toy in blood, a violet in youth, forward
not p[er]manent, sweet not lasting, ye p*er*fume and suppliance of a minute
noe more.

Giue thy thoughts no tongue, nor any vnp*ro*portioned thought his act.
take each mans censure, but reserue thy iudgēent.

ye custom of healths is more honourd in ye breach than ye obseruance xx to
be a drunkard takes from our atchieuments though p*er*formd at hight y^e
pith and marrow of our attribute.

            .   .   .   .

tell me thou dreadful spirit, why thy canonized bones hearsed in death haue
burst their cerements? why ye sepulchre, wherein wee saw thee quietly interred, hath op't his ponderous and marble iawes, to cast thee vp againe,
what makes thee so horridly to shake our disposition wth thoughts beyond y^e
reaches of our soules.

I haue some impartment to you he [*hoc est*] I haue something to tell you

            .   .   .   .

remember thee! I thou poore ghost while memorie holds a seat
in this distracted globe, remember thee,
yea from ye table of my memorie
ile wipe away all triuiall fond records,
all saws of bookes, all formes, all pressures past
y^t youth and obseruation copied there,
and thy *com*mandment all alone shall liue,
wthin ye book and volume of my braine
vnmixt wth baser mettal.

what a peece a worke is man, how noble in reason,
how infinite in faculties, how express and admirable in action, how
like an angel in apprehension,
and yet to mee what is this quintessence of dust. . . .

This wont please ye million, he [*hoc est*] ye vulgar   xx ye vnner'ud
body, he [*hoc est*], ye old.

I am not pigeon liuerd and lacke gall.   xx when you act, in yᵉ very torrent,
and as I may soe say,
Whirlwind of yʳ passion you must acquire and beget a temperance, yᵗ may giue
it smoothness. . . .

. . . .

Too much of water hast thou poore Ophelia, and therefore I forbid my teares
(speaking of one drownd)

How absolute yᵉ knaue is, wee must speake by yᵉ card, or equivocation will
vndoe vs. (speaking by yᵉ card is meant speaking precisely, distinctly.)

Wast Hamlet wrongd Laertes? neuer Hamlet,
if Hamlet from himselfe bee tane away
And when hee's not himselfe does wrong Laertes,
then Hamlet does it not, Hamlet denies it,
who does it then? his madness. Ift be soe,
Hamlet is of yᵉ faction yᵗ is wrongd,
His madness is poore Hamlets enemie.

Out of yᵉ Tragedy of Othello by Shakespeare

Thou yᵗ hast had my purse as if yᵉ stringes were thine.
A fellow all most dambd in a faire wife. xx you that were iust now soe
hasty are now beleed and calmd.

. . . .

Some seruants there are
who traind in formes and visages of duty,
keepe yet their hearts attending on themselues,
throwing out shewes of service on their Lords.

Let not the outward action demonstrate yᵉ native art and figure of yᵉ heart.

A ramme is said to tupp yᵉ ewe. And a horse to cover a mare.

Sʳ you are one of those, yᵗ will not serue god if the deuil bid you.

. . . .

an extravagant and wheeling stranger of here and euery where.

. . . .

A maiden neuer bold: of spirit so still and quiet, yᵗ her motion blusht at her
selfe.

It must needs bee yᵗ wᵗʰ some mixtures powerful o're the blood; or wᵗʰ some
dram coniurd to this effect, hee wrought vpon her.

. . . .

While you liue euer make yʳ foole yʳ purse. xx hee holds mee well, he [*hoc est*], has a good opinion of mee.

.   .   .   .

If it were now to die, twere now to bee most happy, for I feare
my soule hath her *con*tent so absolute
y^t not another comfort like to this
succeeds in unknowne fate.

And this and this ye greatest discord bee, y^t ere o^r hearts shall make. he [*hoc
est*] ye discord of kisses.

.   .   .   .

Looke where hee comes, not poppy, nor mandragora,
nor all ye drowsy sirrops of ye world
shall euer medicine thee to y^t sweet sleepe,
wch thou owed'st yesterday.

.   .   .   .

were they as prime as goates, as hot as munkies,
as salt as wolues in pride.

.   .   .   .

But there where I haue garnerd vp my heart, to bee discarded thence or keepe
it as a cesterne for toades to knot and gender in.

ye bawdy wind y^t kisses all it meets

.   .   .   .

A. would you doe such a thing for all ye world. B. ye world's a huge thing,
it is a great price for a smal vice.

Othello V.ii.1-22, 260-83, and 339-57 are quoted with only three minor
variations from the Q text.

A puny, a Quat, a whipster. all ye same for a feeble weake fellow.

I kissd thee ere I killd thee, noe way but this,
killing my self to die vpon a kiss.

The *Excerpta quaedam* of Abraham Wright introduces a hitherto
unknown 17th-century commentator on English drama. There is, I think,
no comparable body of dramatic criticism of such early date.[15] And no

---

[15] [Professor G. Blakemore Evans has called attention to the comments of an unidentified, well-educated man on five plays of Shakespeare (as well as on twenty-three other
plays and some fifty other English books) in Bodleian MS. Eng. Misc. c. 34. These are
in a commonplace book and can be dated between 18 April 1687 and 4 May 1688. This
commentator quotes a few lines from several plays and passes judgment on such things
as plot, construction, characters, sentiments, wit, and diction. See "A Seventeenth-century
Reader of Shakespeare," *RES*, XXI (1945), 271-79.]

one else before Dryden criticized plays from so many different points of view. It is much to be regretted that Wright did not leave us a considered discourse on Jacobean and Caroline drama—perhaps he did and it was lost in the Middle Temple fire. What has survived deserves to be printed *in extenso*.[16] Wright's opinions, written for his private delectation, give a clearer picture of what educated and cultured gentlemen of the 17th century thought about the popular plays of the time than is to be found elsewhere.

[16] [Wright's critical opinions have now been published by Professor Arthur C. Kirsch, in "A Caroline Commentary on the Drama," *MP*, LXVI (1969), 256-61.]

John Shakespeare's "Spiritual Testament"

[1967]

HE "Spiritual Testament" of John Shakespeare, like the Office Book of Sir Henry Herbert, Master of the Revels, is a lost document. According to report, the six-leaf manuscript was found by Joseph Mosely on 27 April 1757 while working on the roof of the western Shakespeare house in Henley Street. With the knowledge of Shakespeare's collateral descendant, Thomas Hart, who then occupied the building, Mosely gave the document to Mr. Payton of Shottery. In 1784, John Jordan offered a transcript to *The Gentleman's Magazine,* which did not publish it. Then Payton sent the original, minus the first leaf, through James Davenport, the vicar, to Edmond Malone, who made a transcript and printed it in his 1790 edition of Shakespeare (I. 2. 162-66). No one knows what happened to the missing first leaf or to the five leaves sent to Malone.

Before Malone's 1790 edition came from press, he sought additional information about the manuscript from Jordan, who was vague and inconsistent in his replies but did send Malone a transcript of the contents of the missing first leaf from a copy transcribed by Mosely. Malone decided from its diction that the text of this leaf was spurious, but nevertheless he included it among "Emendations and Additions" in the 1790 edition (I. 2. 330-31). By 1796 Malone had concluded that the "Spiritual testament" was not pertinent to the biography of William Shakespeare: "I have since obtained documents that clearly prove it could not have been the composition of any one of our poet's family, as will be fully shown in his Life."[1]

---

[1] *An Inquiry into the Authenticity of Certain Miscellaneous Papers* (London, 1796), p. 195. Repeated substantially in Boswell's Variorum Shakespeare (1821), II, 517

Shakespeare Quarterly, XVIII (1967), 197-205.

Boswell could not find the documentary evidence, however, and assumed that Malone might have had John Shakespeare the shoemaker in mind.[2]

Malone seems to have entertained no doubts about the genuineness of the five leaves sent him, for he and others recognized that it must be a copy of some religious formulary.[3] Confirmation was not supplied until 1923, when Father Herbert Thurston found in the British Museum the unique copy of a tract published in Mexico City in 1661 that agreed closely in text with the five leaves sent Malone.[4] This is entitled, *Testamento o Vltima Voluntad del Alma. Hecho en Salud para Asegurarse el Christiano de las tentaciones del Demonio, en la hora de la muerte. Ordenado por San Carlos Borromeo, Cardenal del Titulo de Santa Praxedis, y Arçobispo de Milan.* Con Licencia, en Mexico. Por la Viuda de Bernardo Calderon, en la calle de San Agustin, Año de 1661. It is a quarto of four unsigned, unpaged leaves, with the press-mark 4404. h. 3. The name of the testator, Philipe Monardes, is written five times in the spaces left blank for that purpose.

Once the identity of the author was known, it was discovered that the British Museum had also a manuscript testament in MS. Egerton 443, fols. 68-72, datable *c.* 1690, and a unique edition in Romansch published in Banaduz in 1741.[5]

---

[2] Variorum Shakespeare, II, 517, n. 2.

[3] This summary account is based on that in E. K. Chambers, *William Shakespeare* (Oxford, 1930), II, 380-81.

[4] "A Controverted Shakespeare Document," *The Dublin Review,* CLXXIII (1923), 165. Thurston made a translation of the Spanish text and also of an Italian version, but the date and location of the Italian edition are not known to me. Useful discussions of the "Spiritual Testament" will be found in John de Groot, *The Shakespeares and "The Old Faith"* (New York, 1946), and Heinrich Mutschmann and Karl Wentersdorf, *Shakespeare and Catholicism* (New York, 1952); this is a translation of their *Shakespeare und Katholizismus,* 1950. See also M. D. H. Parker, *The Slave of Life* (London, 1955), pp. 239-40, 251.

[5] The manuscript text is headed, "Testamento y vltima voluntad del alma hecho en salud, para asegurarse el christiano de las Tentaciones del demonio en la hora de la muerte Ordenado por San Carlos Borromeo, Cardenal del titulo de Sa. Praxedis y Arzobispo de Milan." The name of the testator, Maria Theresa de Cardenas, is written four times in the scribal hand in the appropriate places and signed at the end by the testator. The Romansch edition, with press-mark 885. i. 12, is entitled, *La Suentra Veglia del' Olma en Fuarma de Testament, de Far Enten Vita per Sigirar la Olma dels Tentaments digl Nauscha Spirt, Sin l'Vra della Mort. Fagia de S. Carli Barro Meo Cardinal, & Erzuescho de Miloun.* Con Lubienzia dels Superius. Squicciau â Banaduz, de Matthias Moron gl' Onn. 1741. It is a 12mo, signed) (12. The text of the Testament, which ends on 8ᵛ, is followed by three prayers in Latin and three in Romansch. The prayers have no counterpart in the Spanish or English texts. No name has been written in the blanks.

To these three exemplars, De Groot has added an undated 17th-century edition published in Mexico City by the Widow of Bernardo Calderon and two other Mexican editions dated 1785 and 1797.[6] Three other editions in Spanish may now be added, all published in Mexico City in the first half of the 18th century:[7]

Testamento ó Ultima Voluntad del alma Hecho en salud, para asegurarse el Christiano de las tentaciones de el Demonio en la hora de la muerte. . . . En Mexico, por los Herederos de la Viuda de Francisco Rodriguez Lupercio, en la puente de Palacio. Año de 1708.

Testamento o Vltima Voluntad de el alma, hecho en salud, para asegurarse el Christiano de las tentaciones de el Demonio en la hora de la muerte. . . . En Mexico, por los Herederos de la Viuda de Miguel de Ribera, en la Empedradillo, año de 1715.

Testamento o vltima voluntad del alma. Hecho en salud, para assegurarse el Christiano de los tentaciones del Demonio, en la hora de la Muerte. . . . En Mexico, por Francisco de Rivera Calderon en la Calle de S. Augustin. Año de 1730.

It is interesting that all but one of these early editions originated in Mexico, and significant that the Spanish manuscript of *c.* 1690 referred to above is in a volume of "papers chiefly relating to the Inquisition and to the clergy in the West Indies." The formulary must have been very popular among Spanish Catholics, and doubtless editions published in Spain will eventually come to attention.

It remained for De Groot to link the venerated author of the Testament, Carlo Borromeo (who died in 1585 and was canonized in 1610), directly with English Catholics of the late 16th century. He noted that Fathers Robert Parsons and Edmund Campion were entertained by Borromeo as they passed from Rome through Milan on their way to England in 1580 and connected this event with a letter from Dr. William Allen, rector of the English College in France, to Father Alphonsus Agazzari, rector of the English College in Rome:

Father Robert [Parsons] wants three or four thousand or more of the Testaments, for many persons desire to have them.[8]

[6] P. 230, n. 27, citing Vincente de P. Andrade, *Ensayo Bibliográfico Mexicano del Siglo XVII,* p. 319, item 495.

[7] See Nicolas Leon, *Bibliográfia Mexicana del Siglo XVIII, Part V* (Mexico City, 1908), p. 35, nos. 195, 196; *Part III* (Mexico City, 1906), p. 70, item 35. It will be observed that the editions of 1661 and 1730 came from the same shop.

[8] The date of the letter, 23 June 1581, precludes a reference to the Rheims New Testament, which was not in print until March, 1582 (De Groot, pp. 81, 88). In any

It may be supposed, then, that printed or manuscript copies of Borromeo's Testament were smuggled into England by the Jesuit missionaries and distributed as they had opportunity.

Now, at last, an English printing of this formulary has come to light. It occurs in an unique book of devotions recently acquired by the Folger Shakespeare Library [call number, *STC* 5645.5]:

> *The Contract and Testament of the Soule.*
> [ornament]
> Permissu Superiorum, 1638

This is a 32mo, signed A-D^8, and the words, "Permissu Superiorum," suggest publication on the Continent. This is the earliest surviving text of the Testament, as well as the only authentic English text. For the first time we can know what should have appeared on the missing first leaf of the manuscript sent to Edmond Malone

"The Testament of the Soule. Made by S. Charles Borrom. Card. & Arch. of Millan" begins on C6^v and ends on D8^v (pp. 42-64). Below the head-title just quoted are two numbered paragraphs of general information, entitled, "An Aduertisement to the deuout Reader." Next come two sentences of instruction, followed by the preamble to the Testament. The Testament of fourteen numbered articles follows. Then the testator is instructed to sign a confirmatory declaration, and lastly to say the Pater Noster, Ave Maria, and the Creed.

The missing first leaf of the manuscript sent to Malone should have contained the first and second articles, and part of the third. In the reprint of the 1638 English text that follows, this part of the text, previously unknown, will be printed in italics. The remainder of the text will be in roman. There are very few differences between the printed Articles and those in Malone's version. When Malone's edition of the manuscript differs from the 1638 text, the variant will be printed in italics within square brackets immediately following the reading from which it differs. Variants in spelling and punctuation are ignored.

---

case, it is preposterous to think that Parsons could have hoped to get so many printed books into England without detection.

The Testament of the Soule.

Made by S. Charles Borrom.
Card. & Arch. of Millan.

An Aduertisement to the
deuout Reader.

1. The deuout Person who will make use of this spirituall Writing, for the good of his soule, let him read, or heare it read often, especially when he hopes he is in state of Grace, after Confession & &[9] Cōmunion. And let him keep it in some place of note, & neere vnto him: & when he goeth any iourney, let him carry the same alwayes with him to haue it ready vpon all occasions. And whē he shall fall sicke, after Cōfession let him renew, by reading, or hearing read, this Testamēt, in presence of others, confirming finaly what he hath formerly at other times promised, & bequeathed for the good of his Soule.

2. This Testament may be made by all sorts of Persons, & at al times, writing or causing to be written their Names, at the end of the Protestations following, in manner of subscription, or sealing.[10] And he that cannot write, let him make a Crosse (†) thus or some such marke.

---

*Kneeling, standing, or sitting in deuout manner, before some Altar, or Oratory, say as followeth

In the Name of the Father, & of the Sonne, and of the holy Ghost. Amen.

I N.N. a most miserable Sinner, knowing my selfe to be mortal, & borne to dye, without knowing the houre, where, when, or how; to the end that I be not surprised vpō a sudaine am resolued through the help, and aide of my sweet Sauiour, to make my selfe ready for this vncertaine Houre, seeing he vouchsafeth me now a fit time. Wherfore sincerely from the bottom of my Hart, I giue the world to vnderstād of this my last Wil & testament, in māner following.

I.

First, I heere protest, and declare in the sight, & presence of Almighty God, Father, Sonne, and holy Ghost, three Persons, & one God; and of

---

[9] The repetition occurs as the last word on C5 and the first word on C6ᵛ.
[10] [The letter *l* here failed to print.]

the B.V. Mary, and of all the holy Court of Heauen, that I will liue and dye obedient vnto the Catholike, Romaine, & Apostolicke Church, firmely belieuing all the twelve Articles of the Fayth taught by the holy Apostles, with the interpretation, & declaration made thereon by the same holy church, as taught defined & declared by her. And finally I protest, that I do belieue all that, which a good & faithfull Christian ought to belieue: In which faith I purpose to liue & die. And if at any time (which God forbid) I should chāce by suggestion of the diuell to do, say, or thinke cōtrary to this my beliefe, I do now for that time, in vertue of this present act, reuoke, infring, & annull the same, & will that it be held for neither spokē, or done by me.

II.

Secondly. By this my last Will I protest, that, at my death I will receiue the Sacramēts of Pennance, & Confession; the which if by any accident I should not be able to haue, or make, I do in vertue of this present, resolue from this instant, for that time, to make it frō my hart, accusing my selfe of all my sins cōmitted in Thought, Word, & Worke, as wel against God as against my selfe and my neighbour, whereof I do repent me with infinite sorrow, & desire time of penance, bitterly to bewaile the same, for that I haue offēded my Soueraigne Lord & God, whome I ought to loue and serue aboue all things. The which I now firmely purpose, with his grace, to do as lōg as I shall liue, without euer more offending him.

III.

Item. I do protest, that at the end of my life, I will receiue the most Blessed Sacrament for my Viaticum, or last iourney, that by meanes of so diuine a Pledge, I may perfectly recōcile & vnite my selfe vnto my Lord. The which if throgh any accidēt, I should not then be able to performe, I do now for that time, declare, that I will receiue it, at least spiritually in wil, adoring & most hūbly beseeching my Sauiour, that he will be pleased to assist me in so dāgerous a voyage & [*to*] defend me from the snares, & deceits of my infernal Enemies, & to conduct me to the secure Hauen of his Eternall Blisse.

IV.

Item. I [*I John Shakspear doe*] protest that I wil also passe out of this life, armed with the last Sacrament of Extreme Vnction: the which if through any let, or hinderance, I should not then be able to haue, I do now also for that time demaūd, & craue the same; beseeching his diuine Majesty that he wil be pleased to anoint my Senses both internall and external, with the sacred oile of his infinit Mercy, & to pardō me al my sins committed, by Seeing, Speaking, Tasting [*feeling*], Touching [*smelling*], Smelling [*hearing*], Hearing [*touching*], or [*or by*] any other way whatsoeuer.

V.

Item. I [*I John Shakspear*] do by this present protest, that I will neuer[11] through any temptation whatsoeuer, despaire of the diuine Goodnes, for the multitude and greatnes of my sinnes, for which although I cōfesse, that I haue deserued Hel; yet wil I stedfastly hope in Gods infinit Mercy, knowing that he hath hertofore pardoned many grieuous [*as great*] sinners [*sinners as my self*], whereof I haue good warrant, sealed with his sacred mouth, in holy Writ, wherby he pronounceth, that he is not come to call the iust, but sinners.

VI.

Item. I [*I John Shakspear do*] protest that I do not know, that I haue euer done any good worke meritorious of life euerlasting: & if I haue done any, I [*I do*] acknowledge that I haue done it with a great deale of negligence, & imperfection; neither should I haue bin able to haue done the least, without the assistance of his diuine grace. Wherfore let the diuell remaine confounded, for I do in no wise presume to merit heauen by such good Workes alone: but through the merits, & bloud of my Lord and Sauiour Iesus, shed vpon the Crosse for me most miserable sinner.

VII.

Item. I [*I John Shakspear do*] protest by this present Writing, that I will patiētly endure, & suffer all kind of infirmity, sicknesse, yea & the paine of death it selfe: wherin if it should happē, which God forbid, that through violence of paine & agony, or by subtility of the Diuell, I should fall into any impatience, or tēptation of blasphemy, or murmuration against God or the Catholike Fayth, or giue any signe of bad exāple, I do henceforth, & for that present, repent me, & am most hartily sorry for the same: & I do renounce all the euill whatsoeuer, which I might haue then done, or said,

[11] [The second letter *e* here failed to print.]

beseeching his diuine Clemency, that he will not forsake me in that grieuous & painefull Conflict [*agony*].

VIII.

Item. By vertue of this present Testament, I [*Item, I John Shakspear*] do
pardon all the iniuries and offences that any one hath euer done vnto me,
either in my reputatiō, life, goods or any other way whatsoeuer, beseeching sweet Iesus to pardon thē for the same: & I [*I do*] desire, that they
wil doe the like by me, whome I haue offended, or iniured in any sort
howsoeuer.

IX.

Item. I [*I John Shakspear do*] heere protest, that I do render infinit
thankes to his diuine Maiesty, for all the benefits that I haue receiued, as
wel secret as manifest, & in particular, for the benefit of my Creation, Re-
demption, Sanctification, Conseruation, & Vocation to the holy knowledge of him, and his true Catholike fayth: but aboue all, for his so great
expectation of me to pennance, when he might most iustly haue taken me
out of this life, when I least thought therof [*of it*]: yea euē then, when I
was plūged in the durty puddle of my sins. Blessed be therfore & praysed,
for euer & euer, his infinite Patience and Charity.

X.

Item. I [*I John Shakspear do*] protest, that I am willing, yea I do infinitly
desire, & humbly craue, that of this my last Will & Testament the glorious,
& euer Virgin Mary mother of God, Refuge and Aduocate of sinners
(whome I honour specially aboue all other Saints) may be the chiefe Exe-
cutresse, togeather with these other saints my Patrons, [   ] [*saint
Winefride*] all whom I inuoke, and beseech to be present at the houre of
my death, that she & they may cōfort me with their desired presence, and
craue of sweet Iesus, that he will receiue my soule into peace.

XI.

Item. In vertue of this presēt writing I [*I John Shakspear*] do likewise
most willingly, & with all humility cōstitute, & ordaine my good Angell,
for for[12] Defender & Protectour of my Soule in the dreadfull day of iudg-

---

[12] The repetition occurs only in the printed text, as the last word on D5ᵛ and the
first word on D6ʳ.

ment, when the finall sentence of eternall life or death shalbe discussed, & giuen: beseeching him, that as my soule was by my Creatour cōmitted [*was appointed*] to his custody, & protection when I liued; euen so he wil vouchsafe to defēd the same at that houre, & conduct it to eternall Blisse.

XII.

Item. I [*I John Shakspear*] do in like manner pray, & beseech all my deare friends, Parēts, & kinsfolks, by the bowels of our Sauiour Iesus Christ, that since it is vncertaine what lot will befall me, for feare notwithstanding least by reason of my sinnes, I be to passe, & stay a lōg while in Purgatory, they will vouchsafe to assist and succour me with their holy praiers, & satisfactory workes, especially with the holy Sacrifice of the Masse, as being the most effectuall meanes to deliuer Soules from their tormēts & paines; frō the which, if I shall by Gods gracious goodnes, & by their vertuous works be deliuered, I do promise that I wil not be vngrateful vnto thē, for so great a benefit.

XIII.

Item. [*I John Shakspear doe*] By this my [*my last*] will & Testament, I [*testament*] bequeath my soule assoone as it shall be deliuered, & loosned frō the prison of this my body, to be entōbed in the sweet & amorous Coffin of the Side of Iesus Christ: & that in this life-giuing-Sepulcher it may rest, & liue perpetually inclosed in that eternall habitatiō of Repose, there to blesse for euer and euer, that direfull Iron of the Launce, which like a sharp cutting Rasour [*a charge in a censore*] formed [*formes*] so sweet and pleasant a monument, within the sacred breast of my Lord & Sauiour.

XIV.

Lastly, I [*Item, lastly I John Shakspear*] do protest, that I will willingly accept of death, in what manner soeuer it may, or shall [*it may*] befal me, conforming my wil vnto the will of God; accepting of the same in satisfaction for my sinnes, & giuing thankes vnto his diuine Maiesty for the life he hath bestowed vpon me: & if it please him to prolong, or shorten the same, blessed be he also a thousand thousand times, into whose most most[13] holy hands I cōmend my soule, my [*soul and*] body, my life, & my

---

[13] The repetition occurs only in the printed text, as the last word on D7ᵛ and the first word on D8ʳ.

[*and*] death: and I beseech him aboue all things, that he neuer permit any change to the [*be*] made by me [*me John Shakspear*], of this my foresaid [*aforesaid*] Will, and Testament. Amen.

§. Heere let him, write his Name and Quality, as followeth: [*not in Malone's version*]

I [   ] [*I John Shakspear*] haue made this present Writing of Protestation, Confession and Charter, in presence of the Blessed V. Ma. [*virgin mary*] my Angell guardian, & all the celestiall Court as Witnesses heerunto: the which, my meaning is, that it be of full value, now presently, & for euer, with the force and vertue of Testament, Codicil, & Donation, in case [*cause*] of death; confirming it a new, being in perfect health of soule and body, & signed with mine owne hād, carrying also the same continually [*same*] about me: and for the better declaration hereof, my Will & intention is, that it be finally buried with me, after my death.

Hauing made this protestation, let him say deuoutly, [*not in Malone's version*] Pater, Aue.[14] Creed. FINIS. [*Pater noster, Ave maria, Credo. jesu, son of David, have mercy on me. Amen.*]

The genuine text of Articles I and II and the first part of Article III should be compared with that supplied to Malone and printed by him[15] and also with the conjectural text prepared by Mutschmann and Wentersdorf from Thurston's translations of the Spanish and Italian versions.[16]

This is not the place to study the history or the variations in the text of Borromeo's Testament, but it may be noted that the English edition of 1638 and the Romansch version of 1741 are closer together in organization and content than either is to the Mexican edition of 1661. Paragraph 2 of "An Aduertisement" appears as "Avisament" on the verso of the title-page in Romansch. Then comes "La Fuorna," which is Paragraph 1 of "An Aduertisement." This is followed by "Meditatiuns," an outline of the contents of the Testament; there is no corresponding section in the English version. The numbered Articles that follow are in the same order and have the same general content, but the Romansch version has nothing to correspond to Article XIII of the English text, so that its no. 13

[14] The letter *u* or *v* here failed to print.

[15] See his edition of Shakespeare (1790), I. 2. 330-31.

[16] See *Shakespeare and Catholicism,* pp. 389-91. On pp. 395-97 the spurious text is given in modern spelling. This may also be found unmodernized in De Groot, pp. 66-67.

is the equivalent of English Article XIV. The two Spanish versions, which are practically identical, omit English Article XII but include a prayer for the Pope, "Guarde el Papel en su escritorio".

It is not unreasonable to believe that Borromeo's formulary was sent to England, for the author's reputation was widespread. He is supposed to have written the Testament during a time of plague in Milan (1576-78), and its influence on Catholic devotional books was almost instantaneous. The English translations of Gaspar Loarte's *The Exercise of a Christian* adopt some of Borromeo's paragraphs.[17] Compare with Article I these lines from Loarte's "A Protestation to be made in time of sicknesse . . ." (*STC* 16642, Bb5-5^v):

I protest heere, before Almightie God my Maker and Redeemer, before the blessed Virgine Mary, and all the whole Courte of Heauen: namelie, before my Guardian Angell, and all that are here assistant about me, that by Gods grace, I minde to liue and die in this faith which I haue heere protested, according as the Holy Catholicke and Romane Church doth vnderstand & take it. . . . And if any worde that soundeth contrary hereunto, should by dotage or lacke of iudgement escape out of my mouth, I protest here, that I doe not acknowledge it as mine, but will die and liue in that faith which at this present I haue protested.

There are also borrowings from Borromeo in several editions of the Jesus Psalter. The first sentence of "A protestation verie profitable to be made by the sicke" (*STC* 17273, Douay, 1613, R7-7^v) is not a close rendering of Article VIII, but sentences in "A praier for the sicke person to say after his beleefe" (*STC* 17273, R7^v-8) are surely adapted from Article I:

O almightie & merciful Iesu, I protest before thee, and before al the court of heauen, that I haue a wil and a desire to finish my life in this faith, wherein of necessitie euerie child (obedient to our Mother the holie Church) ought to die.

Further, my sweet Sauiour, I protest to beleeue wholie, and vniuersallie, al which is contained in the Catholike faith, and that which a true and faithful Christian ought to beleeue: that if it happen by assaults of the Deuil, or by violence of sicknesse, I come to thinke, say, or doe anie thing contrarie to this purpose, I doe reuoke it at this present, & protest that I giue no consent to anie such thought, word, or worke.

The prayers appear, with little difference, in *STC* 17265 (? Douay, 1595), *STC* 17266 (Calice, 1599), *STC* 17275.2 (1616), and *STC* 17276.2 (1625).

---

[17] I have used two editions in the Folger Shakespeare Library: *STC* 16641.8, dated 1579, and *STC* 16642, dated 1579 (?). The echoes in Loarte were first noticed by Father Thurston (*The Month*, May 1882).

It is likely that they will be found in *STC* 17263 and 17264 and all the other editions of this book of devotions.[18]

To conclude, the five leaves of the Spiritual Testament sent to Malone must have been genuine, even though the identity of the testator cannot now be established. The disappearance of the document robs us of valuable information. The watermarks in the paper would not only help date the document but would show where the paper had been made. A testament smuggled in for distribution by Parsons and Campion or their successors would probably be written on Italian paper; the paper used in an English transcript would be more likely French or Dutch in origin. An imported testament might be expected to be written in italic, whereas a local transcript would probably be in secretary script. If in the body of the document the name "John Shakspear" was written in the same hand as the text, the testament was certainly a local product; but if it differed, the testator used a prepared form, whether of foreign or English origin. We should like especially to know whether the name in the paragraph following Item XIV was a signature or was in the same hand that wrote it in the body of the document. If it was scribal, did the testator affix his mark, as instructed? And if there was a mark, did it correspond to that used by John Shakespeare, gentleman, in signing documents of the borough of Stratford-upon-Avon? It would be helpful to know whether the testament was a form with John Shakespeare's name written in blanks left for that purpose, for Item XII has the testator beseech his parents, among others, to pray for the delivery of his soul from purgatory. Since the poet's father had no parents living in 1581, the earliest date the testament might have been in distribution in England, it might be expected that "parents" would have been omitted from a local, specially prepared transcript; but if a blank form was filled in, the testator might not have felt free to alter the text. It is a great pity that Malone was not aware of the inferential information to be gleaned from the five leaves and that, failing to insure its preservation, he did not print a minute description of it.

[18] I am indebted to Professor Leo Hughes for examining *STC* 17265 and 17266 at the British Museum and to my former colleague, Mrs. Beverly Shell Kirsch, for checking a number of details for me when I was absent from Washington.

The Year's Contributions to Shakespearian Study: Textual Studies [1948–65]

[1948]

NY year in which three volumes of the New Cambridge Shakespeare are published can be accounted profitable for the students of Shakespeare's text. Perhaps the choice of titles (*1* and *2 Henry IV* and *Henry V*) was fortuitous, but a careful reading of these plays in peculiarly appropriate in these postwar years, and their publication has the same timelessness that John Dover Wilson discovers in Shakespeare's composition of *Henry V*.

In a word [he writes], *Henry V*, so apposite in theme and spirit, as I and many others discovered, to the dispatch of a great expeditionary force in 1914, was actually written for a similar occasion in 1599 [the invasion of Ireland under the Earl of Essex]. Yet it would have been written in any case about this time, and the occasion was for Shakespeare a stroke of luck. . . . For the zenith of the play is not the victory—that is lightly passed over, and (in itself miraculous) is ascribed to God alone—but the King's speeches before the battle is joined, the battle which all but the King think already lost. Every line of what Henry then says breathes the English temper, but one above all—

We few, we happy few, we band of brothers.

If History never repeats itself, the human spirit often does: Henry's words before Agincourt, and Churchill's after the Battle of Britain, come from the same national mint.

The choice of subject by E. M. W. Tillyard for his most recent contribution to the interpretation of Shakespeare may have followed naturally upon his publication of *The Elizabethan World Picture*, but it is as likely to have been dictated by his own unquiet of mind about the place of Brit-

Shakespeare Survey 1 (1948), 127-31.

ain in a chaotic world. In his erudite and provocative book entitled *Shake-speare's History Plays*, Tillyard pleads for the reading of these plays as two tetralogies and argues with particular effectiveness that the later series, *Richard II* to *Henry V*, can only be understood textually and aesthetically if it be granted that *Henry IV*, though in two parts, is one play, and that Shakespeare had *Henry V* in mind when he began writing *Richard II*. In this he and Dover Wilson are in substantial agreement. (Venturing into the field of bibliography, Tillyard guesses (pp. 216-17) that the two parts of *The Troublesome Raigne* (1591) may be bad quartos of an early play by Shakespeare which he later revised as the Folio text of *King John*.)

The New Cambridge volumes should be read in conjunction with Tillyard's volume and with the editor's own *The Fortunes of Falstaff*, which appeared in 1943, and his article, "The Origins and Development of Shakespeare's *Henry IV*."[1] In the latter, Wilson rejects Tillyard's admittedly "hazardous and revolutionary" suggestion that Shakespeare "may well have written early versions of the plays of the second tetralogy, *Richard II, Henry IV*, and *Henry V*, now lost but recast in the plays we have. Further, *The Famous Victories of Henry V* [entered in the Stationers' Register in 1594; earliest surviving quarto dated 1598] may well be an abridgement of Shakespeare's plays on the reigns of Henry IV and Henry V," for the reason that both 1588, when Tarleton was acting in a play about Henry V at the Red Bull, and 1592, when Nashe refers to a play on this subject, are incredibly early dates. He also argues that the Lord Cobham who protested the debasement of Oldcastle's name was William Brooke, who became Lord Chamberlain on 8 August 1596 and died on 6 March 1597. This was suggested by H. N. Paul in Hemingway's Variorum edition (p. 355) and would be easy to accept if Leslie Hotson is correct in his belief[2] that "the two parts of *Henry IV* must be pushed back into the season of 1596-7."

There is general agreement that Shakespeare's foul sheets served as copy for the First Quarto of *1 Henry IV*. This survives in a single sheet, sig. C, which came to light in the binding of a copy of Thomas's *Rules of Italian Grammar* and passed into the hands of Halliwell-Phillipps. His note, dated 25 May 1867, records that it was found "some years ago." Because F reads "President" at II. iv. 32, where Q has "present", Wilson insists that Q6 (1613), which was used in printing F, must have been col-

---

[1] *The Library*, 4th ser., XXVI (1945-46), 2-16.
[2] *2 Henry IV*, Variorum edition, pp. 354-55.

lated with the promptbook; but the emendation is required by the context and is hardly beyond the powers of whoever purged the text of oaths....

In 2 *Henry IV* Wilson has made extensive use of M. A. Shaaber's admirable Variorum edition (1941). Q was set from Shakespeare's foul papers, and F from a literary transcript of the promptbook, possibly in the hand of Ralph Crane. At some time unknown to us, Shakespeare's intention of having two royal processions in V. v was abandoned, as is shown by F's shortened stage direction at line 5, though with no change in the second speech of the First Groom; Wilson follows Q in retaining all of Shakespeare's pageantry. This pious gesture is a dramatic reminder that a Shakespeare drama is not one, but many plays: the ideal play as the author conceived it; the text as written; the tidied-up fair copy, later marked and perhaps abridged for representation; the imperfect rendition on the stage; and the printed text or texts, which may represent one or more of these versions, either "maimed, and deformed" or "perfect in their limbes."

The first textual problem in the play is the presence in many copies of Q of a cancel sheet (not a half-sheet, as stated by Wilson) with the text of a scene (III. i) that had at first been omitted. In an article entitled "The Cancel in the Quarto of 2 *Henry IV*,"[3] the present writer concluded from the evidence of paper, typography, punctuation, and spelling that the cancel was printed by Simmes shortly after Q was first put on sale and suggested that if the publishers did not voluntarily prepare the cancel, Shakespeare or a representative of his company may have procured its insertion. Wilson conjectures with great plausibility that the scene was omitted because the single leaf containing it had been accidentally left behind at the playhouse; thus it was not part of the manuscript licensed for printing, and when the cancel was inserted the content of the scene proved to be so dangerous that Q was not reprinted.

The second textual problem is to account for the omission in Q of about 170 lines of text preserved in F. Since these all relate to the deposing of Richard, modern writers have agreed that the censor or the publishers deleted them to avoid trouble with the authorities. Editors usually reprint Q, restoring the excised passages from F. Hitherto no one has explained satisfactorily how III. i, containing the most explicit references to Richard, escaped the censor's pencil. Wilson's brilliant conjecture that the

---

[3] *Studies in Honor of A. H. R. Fairchild,* ed. C. T. Prouty (University of Missouri Press, 1946), pp. 67-80. [Reprinted in the present volume, pp. 67-80 above.]

leaf with this scene was never seen by the censor is probably the final word on the subject.

In *Henry the Fifth,* his third and latest volume to be considered, Wilson dismisses the "bad" Quarto of 1600 with a brief characterization of it as "a 'reported' version, probably supplied by traitor-actors, of performances —perhaps in a shortened form for provincial audiences—of the play as acted by Shakespeare's company," and refers his readers to detailed discussions by Hereward T. Price, E. K. Chambers, W. W. Greg, and G. I. Duthie. The Folio text is accepted as a reprint of "the manuscript exactly as Shakespeare handed it to his company . . . in 1599," *i.e.,* Shakespeare's foul papers, not the fair copy prepared from them for use as a promptbook.

Starting with the concluding couplet in II. Prologue,

> But till the king come forth, and not till then,
> Unto Southampton do we shift our scene,

Wilson and Duthie, who is associated with him in the preparation and annotation of the text, construct the hypothesis that originally Shakespeare kept his promise to continue the story of Falstaff but that the absence of Will Kemp from 1599 to 1602 left the company without a suitable actor and necessitated the excision of the role of Falstaff and the recasting of portions of the play before it was ever produced. With considerable plausibility they argue that II. i and iii, which are located not in Southampton or France but in London, are interpolations, written to prepare for and recount the death of Falstaff, and that the Jamy-Macmorris episode at III. ii. 63 ff. and Henry's long soliloquy after the departure of Erpingham at IV. i. 34 are additional fillers to replace the lost matter of Falstaff. In some of the episodes, for example that of the leeks, they suppose Pistol was substituted for the Fat Knight, and they cite as proof Pistol's lines, "News have I that my Doll is dead i' th' spital Of malady of France," rejecting the usual emendation of "Doll" to "Nell" on the ground that Shakespeare failed to bring this speech into accord with the revised text.

In an almost exactly contemporaneous study entitled "With Sir John in It,"[4] J. H. Walter advances the same hypothesis, adds the Boy's soliloquy (III. ii. 28-53) to the list of interpolations, and supplies many details overlooked by Wilson and Duthie. He observes that the absence of Kemp did not prevent the Chamberlain's Men from performing "Sir John Old

[4] *MLR,* XLI (1946), 237-46.

Castell," *i.e.*, Part 1 or 2 of *Henry IV,* on 6 March 1600 and could hardly have kept Shakespeare from introducing Falstaff in *Henry V.* Instead, Walter supposes that the Master of the Revels deleted the Falstaff scenes out of deference to Lord Cobham and that Shakespeare was enforced to alter his play accordingly.

The survival of irregularly distributed "Shakespearian" spellings, as in II. iii, the textual disorder of such passages as II. i. 27-31 and 105-6 and III. i. 22-25, and the difficulties in nearly all the scenes in which Pistol and Fluellen appear suggest to Walter that there has been extensive revision and that, though the copy for F was in general in a scribal hand, the passages cited, and others, were printed from Shakespeare's manuscript.

If it was Cobham's protest, instead of the temporary defection of Kemp that necessitated the excision of Falstaff, it is possible that Shakespeare took the unlicensed fair copy and interpolated his revisions in the margins or on loose leaves of paper. In that case, this manuscript, a fair copy of which was afterwards licensed for acting and marked for prompt use, and not Shakespeare's original foul sheets, served as copy for F. It was not a consistently revised text, as Walter points out: Pistol's recommendation to Nym to marry Doll Tearsheet (II.i. 74-79) ignores Falstaff's claim to her; and his reference to Doll and his advancing years (V. i. 79 ff.) would be more appropriate to Falstaff than to Pistol; again, one of the speeches assigned to Pistol, "Master Fer! I'll fer him, and firk him, and ferret him" (IV. iv. 29-30), has a definitely Falstaffian ring. Walter suggests plausibly that the reversed order of IV. iv and v in Q is correct and that F errs because of the confused state of the copy. Doubtless some of the inconsistencies and defects were eliminated in the preparation of the promptbook.

The volume of *Studies in Honor of A. H. R. Fairchild,* referred to above, contains two other studies of direct interest to Shakespearians. The first (pp. 9-35) is an admirable exposition by Giles E. Dawson of the nature of Elizabethan copyright and a summary of the sometimes tempestuous history of "The Copyright of Shakespeare's Dramatic Works" to the death of perpetual copyright in 1774. He shows that there never was a copyright of the collected Works and that each successive publisher of the Works, whether an individual or a syndicate, owned no more than a majority of the separate plays.

The second essay (pp. 119-32) is an acute and closely reasoned study by Harry R. Hoppe, *"John of Bordeaux:* A Bad Quarto that never Reached Print," based on Renwick's edition of the manuscript for the Malone Society. Hoppe is clearly right in his insistence that the text results from the combined efforts of reporter-dictators and a scribe, rather than of a reader-dictator and a scribe, as Renwick suggested. Other "bad" texts are available only in printed versions; Hoppe's observations and conclusions are important because the play under examination is a manuscript, in which the mental and physical processes of the compilers frequently reveal themselves. . . .

The survival of proof-sheets in early editions of Shakespeare has generally been attributed to accident. A new and more plausible explanation is offered by Francis R. Johnson in "Printers' 'Copy Books' and the Black Market in the Elizabethan Book Trade,"[5] namely that the sheets are found in "copy" books, one or more of which were allowed to workmen in Elizabethan printing-shops. Starting with the litigation that followed the printing of Dowland's *Second Book of Songs or Ayres* in 1600, Johnson traces the recorded history of the "ancient custom" of allowing "copy" books and produces a short but valuable chapter on a neglected phase of early printing, illustrated by references to the proof-sheets in the First Folio and other dramatic texts and to the remarkable Folger Library fragment of the first edition of *The Passionate Pilgrim*.

[1949]

The New Cambridge Shakespeare moves one volume nearer completion with the publication of *Macbeth,* a play that challenges and receives John Dover Wilson's best efforts. Textually the edition has the same virtues— and faults—that W. M. T. Dodds describes so acutely in the first four pages of a memorable review[1] of two earlier plays in the series, pages that should be read by every Shakespeare specialist, particularly those who contemplate editing one of the plays. Miss Dodds points out what has long been realized, that the fourfold aims and methods of the edition are mutually incompatible. These are, in Miss Dodds's words:

(1) To advance textual study.
(2) To advance the literary appreciation of the general reader.

[5] *The Library,* 5th ser., I (1946-47), 97-105.
[1] *"King Henry IV: Parts I and II,"* MLR, XLII (1947), 371-82.

Shakespeare Survey 2 (1949), 145-48, 150, 152-53.

(3) To present to the general reader a text embodying the results of specialist methods at present beyond that reader's ken.

(4) To give due weight to literary considerations, as well as to strict textual analysis, in arriving at an established text.

The matter of prime importance [Dodds continues] is the incompatibility of the first and third aims when handled in the way here chosen. A little reflection on the immediately practicable as distinct from the ultimately desirable makes plain their incompatibility within one and the same edition, were both to be *consistently* pursued: one cannot simultaneously advance an unfinished study and present its final or even its agreed results to a public to whom textual study must be rather mediated than laid out for scrutiny. . . . As long as critical method kept within the comprehension of the general reader, and editors were in fact required to be no more than especially gifted general readers, they could in one and the same edition appeal to scholar and general reader alike. But the new critical methods of the scholar are beyond the ken of the ordinary reader; therefore, what must be offered him is decision. One cannot at the same time offer the scholar what he needs: the material for decision (the presentation of alternatives, specialized debate, the tentative solution submitted for consideration).

But to assert that a New Cambridge text "is highly controversial and carries no guarantee by textual scholars" (Dodds, p. 373) is not to deny the brilliance of many of the editor's observations and conjectures or the eloquence of his aesthetic appreciation. The New Cambridge continues to be the most stimulating as well as the most controversial of editions.

Wilson conjectures boldly that *Macbeth* was first written next after *Hamlet,* about 1601 or 1602, and performed in Edinburgh, where he supposes Shakespeare to have taken refuge after the Essex revolt. In the second detail he was admittedly anticipated by Fleay; in the first, though the fact is not mentioned, by J. M. Robertson in *Literary Detection* (1931), who employed, among other proofs, the evidence adduced by J. M. Nosworthy and accepted by Wilson.

The full-length text, Wilson believes, was abbreviated by Shakespeare himself for use in a performance in 1606 before James I and King Christian of Denmark; later (about 1610 or 1611) it was altered by Thomas Middleton, two of whose songs are partly quoted in III. v and IV. i. . . .

The editor of *Macbeth* cannot evade three questions: (1) what, if any, scenes have been lost; (2) to what extent did Middleton contribute to the text; and (3) is Simon Forman's account a forgery? Wilson's answers to the first were in many instances anticipated in the edition of J. Q.

Adams (Houghton Mifflin, 1931), which "did not come into [his] hands until November 1946, when [his] edition was already in the press." And if, as both editors believe, Shakespeare altered a full-length play for a court performance, these two scholars are doubtless right in their conjectures about omitted and truncated scenes. J. M. Nosworthy points out, however,[2] that in his use of sources Shakespeare "has woven all the tractable material into his main plot, and left it at that" (p. 108); "if the cumulative evidence can point to any conclusion it is that *Macbeth* was never anything but a short play" (p. 115). This thesis becomes the more acceptable when we recall that Shakespeare constantly imposes upon his audience a belief in the actuality of his dramatis personae by having them allude to incidents that are not represented on the stage. Thus, after we have heard Lady Macbeth unsex herself in preparation for Duncan's murder (I. v. 39-54) and promise her husband that if he will "only look up clear" he may "leave all the rest to [her]" (I. v. 71, 73), we really do not need to *see* her go armed to the King's chamber to accord her full belief when (II. i. 12-13) she mutters, "Had he not resembled My father as he slept, I had done it."

Middleton's part in *Macbeth,* which is limited by Sir Edmund Chambers to three passages, II. v, IV. i. 39-43, and IV. i. 125-32, is scarcely augmented by Wilson (cf. p. xxiv). On this subject, too, Nosworthy, who at all points is conservative, has several interesting observations.[3] It is his opinion that the Hecate speeches were introduced only to smooth the insertion of Middleton's two songs, and, poor as the links are, he would not deny them to Shakespeare. His suggestion that "possibly [Hecate] had encroached gradually on the territory of the Weird Sisters for years," involves him in all sorts of difficulties. It implies that theatrical manuscripts of *Macbeth* bearing successive alterations were in existence in or about 1663 or 1664, when Davenant staged his adaptation, a supposition for which there is only one shred of evidence: the inclusion of the full texts of Middleton's songs in the first printing of this version.[4]

[2] "*Macbeth* at the Globe," *The Library,* 5th ser., II (1947), 108-18.

[3] "The Hecate Scenes in *Macbeth,*" *RES,* XXIV (1948), 138-39. See also his "Shakespeare and the Siwards," *ibid.,* pp. 139-41.

[4] Only the initial phrases of the songs are printed in the Folio (III. v. 33 s.d. and IV. i. 43 s.d.), yet when the operatic *Macbeth* was presented in 1673, their complete texts were somehow available. The success of the revival prompted William Cademan to issue a quarto with the Folio text, which he seems to have attempted to pass off as the operatic version by inserting one of Middleton's songs and as much of Davenant's lyrical interpolations as could be pirated. In 1674 Philip Chetwind, publisher of the Third

The genuineness of Simon Forman's *Bocke of Plaies* was called in question many years ago, but despite A. K. McIlwraith's emphatic rejection of S. A. Tannenbaum's contention that J. P. Collier forged it, it was eminently worth while for Dover Wilson and R. W. Hunt to search out the history of the manuscript and state at length the reasons for accepting it as genuine.[5] At the request of Wilson, I examined the *Bocke* in the summer of 1947 with the proofs of his and Hunt's notes before me, and I think it would be sheer perversity to question the document further....

In discussions of Shakespeare's text it is customary to speak of the reading of the First Folio, but in reality the text of this literary monument has never been established; nor can it be, until every extant copy, however fragmentary, has been minutely collated. This would be a prodigious labor, even if all the copies were housed together, as they are not. In 1941 Charlton Hinman began collating the text of *Othello* in the Folger Library collection of First Folios and, coming upon a page that bears the original proof-reader's marks, was enabled to explain a crux that had previously baffled editors.[6] Convinced by this experience that his text could not be sound if he relied upon the collation of a limited number of Folios, and well aware of the time and labor required to collate the some 230 extant copies, Hinman set about devising a machine that would throw upon a screen alternate images of the same page in two copies of a Folio in such a way as to disclose the slightest variation in the settings of type. A preliminary account of this device was read at the Modern Language Association meeting in 1946.[7] The working model, which uses microfilm copies, speeds up collation fifty times. A variant of the device now under construction will permit the direct comparison of pages of a book without recourse to photography. With these two machines a scholar may with some confidence undertake the collation of all the surviving copies of the

---

Folio, printed the Davenant alteration in full. Yet the only manuscript of Middleton's *Witch,* from which the two songs were extracted, is nontheatrical—it is a transcript in the hand of Ralph Crane which the author presented to his friend, Thomas Holmes, and which, presumably, always remained in private hands. How did Davenant recover the two Middleton songs? [John P. Cutts, in "The Original Music to Middleton's *The Witch,*" *SQ,* VII (1956), 203-9, suggests that the manuscript copies of the music used in the theater were found in the possession of the King's Musicians.]

[5] See *RES,* XXIII (1947), 193-200.

[6] See *The Library,* 4th ser., XXIII (1942-43), 101-7.

[7] See "Mechanized Collation: A Preliminary Report," *PBSA,* XLI (1947), 1-8. See also his "Why 79 First Folios?" a paper read before the Bibliographical Society of the University of Virginia on 6 June 1947 and later distributed by the Society in mimeographed form.

Folio. Not until Hinman's bibliographical work shall have been completed will it be legitimate to speak of *the* reading of the First Folio. . . .

The literary scholar whom Helge Kökeritz would require to master
Elizabethan phonology before he ventures to edit Shakespeare must also
become a specialist in "The New Bibliography," as F. P. Wilson called it
in *Studies in Retrospect*.[8] Two of the principal contributions to the bibliographical study of Shakespeare in the past year stem from Greg's monumental study, *The Variants in the First Quarto of King Lear* (1940). In
"An Examination of the Method of Proof Correction in *Lear*,"[9] Fredson
Bowers takes issue with some of Greg's conclusions about the precise
method employed by Nicholas Okes in printing and proof-reading *Lear*,
and in a long-needed companion study, "Elizabethan Proofing,"[10] he attempts a generalized description of how Elizabethan printers proofed
their books. Bowers applies to *Lear* the method applied in its elemental
form to a simple textual problem in Middleton and Dekker's *Roaring
Girle*,[11] in which by identifying the various settings of the running-titles
and tracing their reappearance in the Quarto he is able to bring to light
hitherto unnoted details about the sequence of formes in the press. Since
both Greg and Bowers are "dealing only with probabilities and trying to
demonstrate that one set of assumptions is more normal and thus more in
accordance with the evidence than another," their expositions require the
reader's closest attention. And if in the light of newly discovered facts
Bowers has been able to modify certain of Greg's conclusions, it is likely,
I think, that further study may lead to modification of several proposals
by Bowers, who tends, for example, to assume that when Okes was printing *Lear* all the employees and facilities of the shop were continuously
available for this one book, whereas in all likelihood the printing of a
small play-quarto was only one of a number of jobs in progress.

After a careful examination of the bibliographical peculiarities of the
Second Quarto of *Othello* (1630), Charlton Hinman disposes finally of
its pretensions to textual authority.[12] He demonstrates that the compositor

---

[8] Oxford University Press, for the Bibliographical Society, 1945, pp. 76-135. [The
allusion is to Professor Kökeritz's "Five Shakespeare Notes," *RES*, XXIII (1947), 310-20.]

[9] *The Library*, 5th ser., II (1947-48), 20-44.

[10] In *Joseph Quincy Adams Memorial Studies*, ed. James G. McManaway, Giles E. Dawson, and E. E. Willoughby (Washington, 1948), pp. 571-86.

[11] See my "Thomas Dekker: Further Textual Notes," *The Library*, 4th ser., XIX
(1938-39), 176-79. [Reprinted in the present volume, pp. 31-33 above.]

[12] "The 'Copy' for the Second Quarto of *Othello*," in *Joseph Quincy Adams Memorial
Studies*, ed. McManaway, Dawson, and Willoughby (Washington, 1948), pp. 373-89.

of Q2 worked from a copy of Q1 containing the inner forme of sheet I in the uncorrected state into which had been written numerous corrections and short additions derived from F or from a conflation of Q1 and F. And interleaved in the copy were slips of paper on which were transcribed the longer insertions from F. Incidentally, the copy of F used by the editor of Q2 contained one uncorrected forme. The independent readings in Q2 may in future be treated as variations introduced by the compositor or as the emendations of a not-too-careful Caroline editor.

[1950]

A survey of recent textual work on Shakespeare may begin appropriately with companion essays by colleagues at the University of Pennsylvania, one the editor of the Variorum 2 *Henry IV* and the other the prospective editor of the Variorum *Richard II*. Rarely does one find the problems of an editor more delightfully explained. M. A. Shaaber[1] notes the deficiencies of current editions of Shakespeare and describes the potential benefits of several types of edition not now in existence. "It is a strange anomaly," he points out, "that, while the standard editions of most Elizabethan authors print the spelling of the contemporary books and manuscripts from which it is derived, there has never been a complete edition of Shakespeare in the old spelling. . . . Indeed I think there is room for an edition which would reproduce the most authoritative text of each play with no editing at all except to correct undoubted mistakes and make good undoubted omissions. This would serve chiefly as a convenient substitute for facsimiles. Just so it would be welcome, since there is no complete set of reliable facsimiles of the Quartos and all facsimiles are expensive." Shaaber is confident that "in the future we can make better texts of Shakespeare than we have today," and he illustrates the possibility by showing how little attention has been paid to the editorial policies and practices of the First Folio by the citation of passage after passage in the Fifth Quarto text of *1 Henry IV* that has been altered in the Folio. Pollard's judgment about the absence of "editorial meddling" in the latter has been reversed by Greg, who is of the opinion that the plays "under-

---

[1] "Problems in the Editing of Shakespeare: Text," *English Institute Essays 1947* (Columbia University Press, 1948), pp. 97-116.

Shakespeare Survey 3 (1950), 143-44, 147-50, 152.

went a good deal of modernization, and general tidying up in spelling, punctuation, grammar, meter, and so on." "But what has never been done," concludes Shaaber, "is to go beyond general statements or illustrations drawn from a single play and to define the editorial work done on the Folio on a broad scale."

Matthew W. Black[2] concerns himself with *explication du texte*. "The interpreters of Shakespeare . . . have as a body been myriad-minded in the worst sense of the word: they have never, as a body, agreed on which meaning they should seek; and I think it could be demonstrated that not one of those who have been large-minded enough to set up a principle has succeeded in adhering to it in every instance. . . . Yet ever and anon the best of them, at their best, have struck out a comment or a paraphrase so manifestly, convincingly right that we say instinctively, 'That is what Shakespeare meant.' " How difficult it may be to discover Shakespeare's intention, Black's charming essay illustrates in a penetrating discussion of the images, rhetoric, and the operation of Shakespeare's memory and mind in certain passages of *Richard II*.

The preoccupation of Hereward T. Price with his forthcoming Variorum edition of *Titus Andronicus* and the publication of J. Dover Wilson's volume of the play in the New Cambridge edition[3] have combined to focus attention as never before upon this early play, which some admirers of Shakespeare would gladly exclude from the canon. The positions of the two editors are antipodal. Price, who has as yet published only fragmentary reports of his studies, accepts *Titus Andronicus* as the exclusive work of Shakespeare, but gives no hint of his regard for it as poetry or play. Distaste is clearly manifested in Wilson's introduction, the first purpose of which is to deny to Shakespeare more than a reviser's share, as other commentators have done ever since Ravenscroft in 1687 called the play a "heap of Rubbish" to which Shakespeare had given "only . . . some master touches to one or two of the principal parts or characters"; the second purpose of the introduction being to assert, with Symons, Robertson, and Mark Van Doren, that many of the Shakespearian passages, filled with "tawdry rant" or "bleating pathos," are "burlesque and melodramatic travesty."

The external evidence is all in favor of those who hold with Price, for Meres ascribed the play to Shakespeare in 1598 and Heminges and Condell included it in the First Folio and, moreover, inserted an admittedly

[2] "Problems in the Editing of Shakespeare: Interpretation," *ibid.,* pp. 117-36.
[3] Cambridge University Press, 1948.

Shakespearian scene (III. i) which was available only in manuscript. In support of his case, Price[4] argues that throughout the text of the First Quarto (1594) are to be found the same spellings, and particularly the elided and clipped forms, which Shakespeare habitually used to guide the pronunciation of the actors in the reading of his lines. Using the two narrative poems, *Venus and Adonis* and *Lucrece,* which must have been printed from holograph copy, and also the "good" quarto texts of seven early plays for purposes of comparison, he examines metrical spellings, as "grac'd," "facde," "sentst" (but "beleevest"), "tirde," "thou'st"; and phonetic spellings, as "batchiler," "semitars," "cote" (quote), "Iubiter"; and his tentative conclusion is that "we find the same general pattern [in the poems] as in *Titus* and the Quartos. No text is altogether consistent with itself nor does any text resemble the general pattern in every detail. But there is enough general likeness to support the theory that these Quartos all belong to one family. The ground for their resemblance to one another which makes them a family is that they are printed from the same kind of copy, which was a manuscript written by Shakespeare himself. To this family of texts we have every right to add *Titus Andronicus."*

For the sake of argument it might be granted that the First Quarto of *Titus* was printed from a manuscript in Shakespeare's hand without admitting more than that in the process of revising or enlarging the play Shakespeare had done more than recopy it from beginning to end with the insertion of a few passages. The spellings might be his, but only portions of the verse. On the other hand, one may inquire whether Price has analyzed the spelling in each of his chosen texts and made due allowance for the fact that a given quarto may be the work of two or more compositors, each of whom may be expected to have modified the copy-spellings according to his own preferences and habits—or the need to justify a line. Can one be sure that each compositor whose work is preserved in the texts under discussion followed his copy with equal fidelity? To what extent does the age or the dialect of the compositor alter the copy-spelling? Were there no changes in orthographical styles in the decade after 1594? How many of the spelling-habits now attributed to Shakespeare are shared equally by other writers of the time? Price is aware of some of these difficulties, but I am doubtful that he has taken them sufficiently into account. (The misspelling *Epeon* for *Hyperion* at V. ii. 56 which suggests to Price that the manuscript was hard to read and

---

[4] "The First Quarto of *Titus Andronicus," English Institute Essays 1947* (Columbia University Press, 1948), pp. 137-68.

the compositor ignorant of classical words probably appeared in the manuscript in the phonetic form *Epion* = Ep*er*ion.) . . .

We pass directly from Shakespeare's least admired and poorest tragedy to his grandest, *King Lear,* edited by G. I. Duthie.[5] The play survives in two substantive texts, the version in the "Pied Bull" quarto of 1608 and that of the First Folio. It is Duthie's purpose, after establishing the genetic relationship between the two, to produce a text that will be the closest possible approximation to what Shakespeare wrote—hence his title, *Shakespeare's King Lear*—and in the compilation and presentation of the evidence he makes strenuous demands, both on himself and on his readers.

Though entered normally in the Stationers' Register, the "Pied Bull" quarto provides a text that is obviously inferior to that of such "good" quartos as *Much Ado* and *Merchant* but is definitely superior to that of such "bad" quartos as the first editions of *Romeo* and *Hamlet*. It is intermediate, like that of *Richard III,* with which Duthie finds it has much in common.

He agrees with Alexander Schmidt and W. W. Greg that the First Quarto of *Lear* is a reported text, but he rejects shorthand as the means by which the text was reported. There being no role or combination of roles which is consistently better than the rest, Duthie concludes, as did David Patrick in the case of *Richard III* (1936), that no one actor or small group of actors produced the text but that the whole company joined in a communal effort, dictating their lines as accurately as might be, while a scribe recorded them, probably in the form of prose, with a minimum of punctuation. "The actors thus virtually gave a performance of the play, and upon this 'performance' the Q text entirely depends. The actors made such mistakes as they doubtless habitually made in performances in the theater—anticipation and recollection, inversion, the introduction of gratuitous exclamations, vocatives, connectives, *etc.,* synonym-substitution, vulgarization, metrical breakdown, omission, patching." The scribe's report would have been unsuited for regulating a performance, and so it is necessary for Duthie to suppose that a transcript was prepared for use as a promptbook; cursorily edited, however, and placed in the hands of a compositor, the first draft could readily become the sort of text we find in the "Pied Bull" quarto. All this is conjectured to have taken place while the King's Men were on tour, probably in 1605-6. The

---

[5] *Shakespeare's King Lear: A Critical Edition* (Oxford, 1949).

patience and skill with which Duthie presents his evidence are calculated to win assent.

Curiously enough, however, the editor has nothing to say about how the scribe's first draft was released to the publisher, or by whom; and there is little speculation about why this rough manuscript (the equivalent of an author's foul papers) was sold, rather than the prompt-copy conjectured to have been derived from it. Nathaniel Butter's entry of his copy in the Stationers' Register suggests that there was nothing surreptitious in his acquisition of his copy, yet an experienced printer should have recognized the difference between such a manuscript as has been described and a normal book of the play or even a set of author's foul sheets. It remains to be discovered who was the agent that sold the manuscript of *Lear* to its publisher.

The origin of the Folio text has long been known—a copy of the First Quarto in which one or more sheets were in the uncorrected state (see Greg's monograph, *The Variants in the First Quarto of King Lear,* 1940) and which was corrected by reference to a playhouse manuscript that had suffered certain deletions. Duthie works relentlessly through the two substantive texts in order to record all differences between the texts, accepting Greg's paradox that the authenticity of the text is least assured when the two agree.

The resultant text is avowedly eclectic. The Folio is accepted as copy-text, but the Quarto always lies open upon the table. Responsibility for every departure from the Folio is accepted by the editor, and he would be the first to recognize that not every student of *Lear* will concur in all of his decisions. Insofar as the variants in the Quarto are concerned, and in particular the variants that result from stop-press corrections, there is not likely to be much or violent disagreement. Greg's analysis of the variants in the twelve extant copies of the First Quarto is used to good advantage (Duthie does not concern himself with the strictly bibliographical problems as elucidated by Greg in his monograph or more recently by Fredson Bowers), though Duthie and he do not always agree on the authoritative reading.

The weakness in Duthie's attempt to produce a definitive text of *Lear* with the Folio version used as copy-text is in his neglect of the Folio itself. Nowhere does he name the particular copy of the Folio (or the facsimile, as the case may be) which he made his copy-text. He does not take into account the fact that, if in the twelve surviving copies of the first Quarto eight out of the twenty formes present textual variants, variants resulting from proof-reading and press-correction may surely be expected in the seventeen formes of the Folio text as preserved in more than 200 extant copies. I happen to know that a minute collation of the text of another play in more than fifty copies of the first Folio has led to the discovery of variants in half of the formes, and when the nature of the printer's copy for the Folio text of *Lear* is recalled, it becomes incredible that proof-reading should not have resulted in the introduction of variants quite as noteworthy as those in the First Quarto which have been so meticulously evaluated. Not that Duthie may reasonably be expected to collate 200 odd copies of the Folio before making his text. The task is at present physically and financially impossible. But it should be recognized once and for all that until all the Folios have been collated, it is not possible to speak or write of *the* Folio reading. Let one example suffice. At V. iii. 170 the first Quarto reads:

> My name is *Edgar,* and thy fathers sonne,

Duthie reads, without comment;

> My name is Edgar and thy Fathers Sonne,

Now this last is the reading in certain copies of the Folio and also in the Methuen Facsimile; in other copies, however, and in the Lee Facsimile, there is a comma after *Edgar,* as in the first Quarto. The difference is not, as might be supposed, a case of press-correction but simply a matter of inking. In certain copies, the comma was too lightly inked to print.[6] This variant is inconsequential,[7] but collation of as few as a dozen copies might bring to light substantive variants in the Folio of the sort which were introduced by Duthie's "Scribe E" when he corrected a copy of the Quarto for the printer—in a word, such collation may be expected to recapture authentic Shakespearian readings now unknown.

In a detailed study[8] Harry R. Hoppe solves many of the puzzles in the First Quarto of *Romeo and Juliet.* The records of John Danter's brief and troubled career as a printer and publisher supply details that Hoppe

---

[6] I am indebted to Charlton Hinman for calling this variant to my attention.

[7] Omission of the comma in all copies of the Folio might have been the result of the choice of the compositor or of deliberate alteration by Duthie's "Scribe E." Its presence in some copies and absence in others as a result of press-correction would have to be explained as a deliberate insertion or removal of type, depending on the direction of the change.

[8] *The Bad Quarto of Romeo and Juliet: A Bibliographical and Textual Study* (Cornell University Press, 1948).

integrates with the facts known about Lord Hunsdon's Men and enable him to date the publication of this text, for which there is no entry in the Stationers' Register, within narrow limits. Danter appears to have begun work between 9 February and 17 March 1597 but to have been compelled by the seizure of his types and presses after only sheets A to D had been completed to turn the job over to another man, possibly Edward Allde, who printed sheets E to K in a different measure with types of a smaller size. Hoppe's account of the bibliographical peculiarities of the Quarto supersedes previous studies.

The stigmata of memorial reconstruction are so manifest and numerous that Hoppe disposes readily of earlier hypotheses that the First Quarto represents a preliminary draft or that it is the result of shorthand reporting. Instead, he believes that this Quarto is a reported text that derives ultimately from performances of a version like that preserved in the Second Quarto. His analyses of the evidence are enriched by a clear statement of the difficulties an Elizabethan actor had in becoming letter-perfect in a role (he never did) and by voluminous parallels from other "bad" quartos.

The widely variant versions of II. vi and part of V. iii in the two Quartos are accounted for by the supposition that the actors who reconstituted the text had recently participated in the performance of an abbreviated text from which these lines had been largely or entirely omitted and that they were compelled to reconstruct the passages in question from their vague recollections of earlier performances of the complete text.

The First Quarto seems to Hoppe to require only about twelve actors and no musicians, as against the twenty players required for a performance of the Second, which introduces instrumental music, and he cites numerous textual modifications to meet the needs of the smaller troupe. He notes, however, as did Greg before him, the presence of echoes of passages in the uncut version. At least one of the reporters could produce tolerable blank verse at a need, and this he did with greatest success when he was least trammeled by remembered phrases of the authentic text. The paucity of unmistakable mishearings suggests that oral dictation, in which one person acts as scribe while others dictate their parts, did not play an important part in the transmission of the text; rather, the scribe was one of the actor-reporters, whose familiarity with the play and whose poetic skill enabled him to correct obvious errors.

The actors whose lines are most accurately reproduced played Romeo and Paris, one or the other being present in all but seven scenes. Of these seven, six are badly reported; the exception is I. iii, which, with portions of

I. ii, is partly set in the Second Quarto from the corresponding pages of the First Quarto. The average of good lines in the episodes in which Romeo or Paris appears is generally 50 per cent or higher; in other episodes it seldom rises above 35 per cent. This is important, for it clears the book-keeper of the guilt that has sometimes been imputed to him in the theft of texts from Shakespeare's company.

Hoppe suggests diffidently that Gabriel Spencer and William Bird, who early in 1597 transferred from some London company (possibly the Chamberlain's) to the newly reorganized Pembroke's, may well have been the actor-reporters. The Chamberlain's Men, who were in a shaky position following the death of the first Lord Hunsdon in July 1596, may, he thinks, have dropped some of their hired men before going on tour, including Spencer and Bird. (It may be objected, however, that *Romeo* is most likely to have been given in abbreviated form only while the company was in the provinces and that this touring version is probably the one chiefly represented in the First Quarto—if so, the defecting actors must have accompanied the traveling company on at least part of its journey before being dropped.) Chettle is named as a third potential reporter of the First Quarto.

If all of Hoppe's points have not been proved with equal finality, for the necessary data are sometimes wanting, he is always careful to point out the difficulties. He seems not quite decided whether the copy for the First Quarto was prepared originally for use as a promptbook or for sale to a publisher, or for both purposes, and there are typographical links between the two Quartos that are not yet adequately discussed. But the book is a valuable contribution to Shakespeare scholarship....

The initial volume of *The Papers of the Bibliographical Society of the University of Virginia* contains two articles of direct Shakespearian interest. Philip Williams adds one more bit of information about the "Pied Bull" quarto of *Lear* in a neat demonstration[9] that the text was set by one compositor. And Giles E. Dawson continues his investigation[10] of 18th-century editions of Shakespeare's plays and of the printinghouse practices that frequently appear to have been followed on the shady side of the law. As Shakespeare was the most pirated playwright in his own day, so he seems to have continued to be in the 18th century. It is a thing to be wondered at that the works of a century-dead playwright should have been the

---

[9] "The Compositor of the 'Pied Bull' *Lear*," *Papers of the Bibliographical Society of the University of Virginia* [*Studies in Bibliography*], 1 (1948-49), 59-68.

[10] "Three Shakespeare Piracies in the Eighteenth Century," *ibid.*, pp. 47-58.

focal point in the battle which upset the old concepts of copyright and helped establish new ones.

In another paper[11] Dawson relates some of the practices of the 17th-century publishers and states his belief that the system "worked fairly well. . . . A copyright could change hands quite smoothly and quite securely without any entry being made in the Register. . . . And the members of the Stationers' Company were undoubtedly well satisfied with a system of copyright which relied to a large degree upon common gossip, verbal agreements not recorded, and informal notes not preserved."

[1951]

Unless a work of art is to be studied in absolute terms as a timeless contribution to human culture, there can be no thorough understanding and appreciation of it until it has been fitted into a chronological pattern that will relate it to the other works in its canon and throw light on the development of the mind of the artist. Nor can a writer be studied intelligently without reference to the age in which he lived, the other writers of the time, and the events and movements which molded, or were molded by, them. It is the neglect or ignorance of this fundamental truth which leads to the framing of the questions one frequently hears: "What does it matter who wrote 'Shakespeare'? We have the plays, haven't we?" No rational account of the development of Elizabethan literature can be written unless we recognize that the author of "Shakespeare" was a man who flourished at precisely the time of William Shakespeare of Stratford—neither earlier nor later—and accept the overwhelming evidence that William Shakespeare of Stratford is the author of the works then and now attributed to him. But the biographical records of playwrights of that age being scanty, there are gaps in the history and puzzles in the chronology of all the writers which continue to challenge our best efforts.

In particular, there is the blank in William Shakespeare's history which represents the years between the birth of Hamnet and Judith in 1585 and the penning of Greene's *Groatsworth of Wit* in 1592. Somehow during that interval, Shakespeare became an actor and acquired what

---

[11] "Copyright of Plays in the Early Seventeenth Century," *English Institute Essays 1947* (Columbia University Press, 1948), pp. 169-92.

Shakespeare Survey 4 (1951), 153-56, 160, 162-63.

Greene considered a dangerous proficiency in writing plays. Now comes Leslie Hotson[1] with the proposition that in that interval Shakespeare flowered as a lyrical poet and wrote over a hundred of his sonnets. For his assumption that we fail to understand the topical allusions of the Sonnets only because we do not know the detailed history—and I should add the intimate gossip—of the times, he finds support in the prefatory remarks of John Benson, publisher of the *Poems* in 1640:

> In your perusall you shall finde them Seren, cleere and eligantly plaine, such gentle straines as shall recreate and not perplexe your braine, no intricate or cloudy stuffe to puzzell intellect, but perfect eloquence. . . .

Benson, presumably, lived close enough to Shakespeare's time for the allusions to be recognized, and so for him, as for other cultured readers, the Sonnets and their story are supposed to have been pellucid. If this be true, editors should accord a more profound respect than is usual to the order in which Benson reprinted the Sonnets, since it varies radically from that in the Quarto of 1609.

But how credible is Benson's statement? Doubt has been expressed by Hallett Smith,[2] who shows that the quoted words were adapted by John Benson from a commendatory poem addressed by Thomas May to Joseph Rutter in praise of his pastoral tragicomedy, *The Shepheards Holy-Day,* a book published by Benson in 1635. It is conceivable that when Benson read the Sonnets in the course of reprinting them he was struck by the remarkable applicability of Thomas May's phrases; but it seems much more likely, as Smith says, that while writing a publisher's blurb for his book Benson came upon or remembered the passage and, finding it good, adapted it with no thought that three hundred years later his plagiarism would win him esteem as a serious critic of literature.

The contemporary events to which Hotson finds specific references in Sonnets 107, 123, and 124 occurred during the years 1586-89; for the allusions to be most effective, the Sonnets in question should, he thinks, have been written almost at once; and he argues that if these three Sonnets can be dated before 1590, the hundred odd which precede them in Thorpe's edition must have antedated them in composition. Let us ex-

---

[1] *Shakespeare's Sonnets Dated and Other Essays* (London, 1949).

[2] " 'No Cloudy Stuffe to Puzzell Intellect': A Testimonial Misapplied to Shakespeare," *SQ,* I (1950), 18-21. [But see Josephine Waters Bennett, "Benson's Alleged Piracy of *Shakespeare's Sonnets* and Some of Ben Jonson's Works," *Studies in Bibliography,* XXI (1968), 235-48.]

amine the Sonnets in turn. In Number 107, the crucial lines are in the second quatrain:

> The mortall Moone hath her eclipse indur'de,
> And the sad Augurs mock their owne presage,
> Incertenties now crowne them-selves assur'de,
> And peace proclaimes Olives of endlesse age.

Rejecting the identification of the "mortall Moone" as Queen Elizabeth, Hotson revives the unexplained suggestion of Samuel Butler that the reference is to the Armada, and by quoting from English and continental books published from 1588 to 1642 in which the line of battle of the Armada is likened to a crescent moon, he attempts to show that Sonnet 107 celebrates the great naval victory of '88.

It is not always possible to pin down an Elizabethan poet when he plays at topical allusions. In the first place, it is unsafe to assume that he would employ the allusion only in the months following the event; and in the second place, he may have two or more events in mind. The conduct of Edmund Spenser may be cited, who in the political allegory of Book V of *The Faerie Queene* lets his hero Artegall represent now Lord Grey of Wilton and now Sir John Norris; and an interval of some twenty years separated the events which Spenser works into his narrative. Perhaps Shakespeare did have in mind the crescent-shaped alignment of the Armada, but his patriotic emotion at its mortal eclipse may easily have been recollected in the tranquillity of a later decade. He may just as readily have been thinking of his queen, for as the Countess de Chambrun reminds us,[3] Mrs. Stopes long ago discovered that courtiers could and did speak of the waning and even the eclipse of Elizabeth, within her lifetime, as in the letter of 9 July 1595 from Sir Thomas Cecil to Sir Robert Cecil, his brother (Historical Manuscripts Commission Reports, *Hatfield Manuscripts,* V, 273):

I left the moon in the wane at my last being at the Court; I hear now it is a half moon again, yet I think it will never be at the full, though I hope it will never be eclipsed, you know whom I mean. . . .

This was written when Elizabeth was approaching the dangerous period of her grand climacteric. The Virgin Queen would have blazed with anger against the author, if the letter had ever come before her eyes; but it passed between brothers, and the writer risked no more in using the phrase

[3] *TLS,* 31 March 1950, p. 201.

than Shakespeare did in the Mortal Moon Sonnet, which circulated only among his private friends until six years after it was beyond the power of the Queen to do him injury.

It is the belief of the Countess, furthermore, that Hotson has mistaken the theme of the Sonnet, which is, as J. R. asserted as long ago as 1848, the deliverance of the Earl of Southampton from the Tower by James as soon as he learned of Elizabeth's death. This and other interpretations of the supposed allusions are given at length by Hyder E. Rollins in his Variorum edition of the *Sonnets* (1944). . . .

Hotson's proposed dating is momentous, because it confronts us with the proposition that Shakespeare's lyric genius matured as early as 1589. We need go no further than Chatterton and Tennyson for proof of the early flowering of the lyric poet. The dramatist, in contrast, matures slowly, gaining skill in his craft only after repeated trials, and producing great drama only with the slow acquisition of insight into the hidden motives of mankind and an almost godlike comprehension as well of Cressid's frailty as of Lear's purgation. An early date for the Sonnets would clear away the rivalry between advocates of Pembroke and of Southampton as the Fair Youth, for in 1586 each was too young; and if Hotson can produce a convincing candidate for this honor, he will go far towards establishing his dates.

Some problems yet remain, however. *Venus and Adonis* and *Lucrece* bear every sign of having been published as soon as written. And few will be inclined to agree, as Hotson urges, that their poetic immaturity, as compared with the Sonnets, is the result of Shakespeare's having "written down" to the level of appreciation of the youthful Earl of Southampton, to whom they are dedicated. It is difficult to believe that the man who possessed the metrical skill and emotional power to write Sonnets 71, 73, and 87, for example, could have done no better four years later than the "unpolisht lines" of *Venus and Adonis*.

If Shakespeare wrote his sonnets by 1589, he was indeed, as Hotson says, not following the vogue of sonnet-writing but rather was the leader of the fashion. A revolutionary thesis, this: but can it be sustained by a close comparison of the early sonnet cycles? Could Shakespeare's sonnets have circulated before 1590 among his private friends without leaving recognizable traces of their influence on the other sonnet writers? Sidney is indebted to Watson, and after the publication of *Astrophel and Stella* in 1591 there is a sudden outpouring of sonnets, each poet learning from his predecessors. Shakespeare, too, seems to learn, and some of his sonnets, as 130, are an expression of his reaction against conventions that have become stereotyped. But this sonnet, too, along with the others to the Dark Lady, must apparently be put back "in the poet's youth" (p. 35). I am reluctant to believe that Shakespeare could at the same time set the fashion in sonneteering and ridicule its conventions. Until grounds more relevant can be established, I shall adhere to a more conservative dating. . . .

Ever since A. W. Pollard divided Shakespeare quartos into two categories, called "good" and "bad," scholars have grappled with the problems of the bad quartos. The relations of *The First Part of the Contention* (1594) to the Folio text of 2 *Henry VI* have been studied by Peter Alexander (1929), Madeleine Doran (1929), and others with results that are valuable for their own sake and are also helpful in their exemplification of some of the newly developed textual and bibliographical techniques. A significant contribution has been made by John E. Jordan,[4] whose methods of procedure are likely to be adapted to the study of other bad quartos. The acute reasoning which leads to his rejection of Alexander's suggestion that the actors who played Warwick and Suffolk-Clifford compiled the reported text, and of Chambers's hypothesis that the bookkeeper was the culprit, is worthy of commendation. Figures are adduced to prove that the actor who "doubled" the roles of Armorer, Spirit, Lord Scales, Mayor, and Vaux is the most likely reporter of the text of *The First Part of the Contention*. This bit player was a man trusted with several parts who doubtless had the opportunity to examine the prompt-copy (p. 1112). "He would have been able to see much of the stage business and know the action fairly well, but he would not be expected to know it so thoroughly as the prompter. He would have heard many of the lines and would probably remember ones that struck him, but only the general purport of many. . . . He would reasonably confuse prose and verse, as well as misplace lines and misascribe speeches . . ." (p. 1108).

On one minor point I disagree with Jordan and his predecessors. In the Folio, the Queen says to Eleanor: "Give me my Fanne"; the Quarto version is: "Give me my glove." "Since there appears to be no reason for making the change in business," writes Jordan, "the difference is probably a mistake, and certainly the stage manager would have known exactly what he had to have ready to be dropped, although someone else may have remembered only that something was dropped." I propose a very different explanation. A London producer would impress his sophis-

---

[4] "The Reporter of *Henry VI*, Part 2," *PMLA*, LXIV (1949), 1089-1113.

ticated audience by supplying a fan suitable to be carried by a Queen; a touring company could hardly be expected to have such a property; and I fancy that the text and the business were changed accordingly. . . .

The First Quarto of *Troilus and Cressida* exists in two issues, in the second of which a half-sheet, signed ¶, containing title-page and an address to the reader, replaces the original title-page, A1. Since the text of the play begins on A2, it may be assumed that A was the first sheet to be printed off, yet at least part of the type remained undistributed long enough for the last seven lines of the title-page to be used in printing the cancel title. Now Philip Williams seeks[5] to discover when and how the cancel half-sheet was printed. Examination of the running-titles on the three pages of text in the final half-sheet M2 and of the watermarks in M2 and ¶2 satisfies him that half-sheet imposition was not used, but that George Eld printed the cancel on the unused half-sheet of M. Absolute proof of this is, I think, impossible, but Williams establishes its probability. He might have strengthened his case, in my opinion, by insisting that the decision to insert the cancel was made almost as soon as printing began, for otherwise the type of the original title-page would almost certainly have been distributed as soon as sheet A had been perfected. . . .

Except to the specialist, the discovery of and application to textual problems of new techniques of bibliographical study are apt to seem vermiculate scholarship. Yet each new bit of information about the printing and publication of books is potentially as valuable to the literary critic as the products of pure scientific research may be to the physician. There are random allusions to the supposition that in the early days of printing each compositor was expected to possess a set of wooden composing-sticks of varying measures. It is known that by the time of Moxon's *Mechanick Exercises* (1683) every compositor had one of the new adjustable metal composing-sticks. In his bibliographical examination of Restoration plays, Fredson Bowers has utilized this knowledge to good advantage. In a report[6] he calls attention to several books in which marked differences in the length of line may be a clue to the proper allocation of the type-setting to two or more compositors. The advantages are obvious, particularly in determining how and when cancels and anomalous leaves or gatherings were printed. It is also a little easier now to study the spelling and punctuation habits of compositors and to estimate their relation to apparent cor-

[5] "The 'Second Issue' of Shakespeare's *Troilus and Cressida,* 1609," *Studies in Bibliography,* II (1949-50), 25-33.
[6] "Bibliographical Evidence from the Printer's Measure," *ibid.,* pp. 153-67.

ruptions in the text. . . . It is to be hoped that quartos printed while wooden composing-sticks were still in use will also be studied systematically, for speech-tags, marginal stage directions, and mixed passages of prose and verse in them present difficulties that have no close counterpart in most of the later play-quartos.

[1952]

Though it is customary to speak of Nicholas Rowe as the first editor of Shakespeare, the editing began at least as early as the First Folio. Evidence is not wanting that those responsible for this volume were at some pains to publish better texts than had been available previously. A case in point is *King Lear,* a play printed in the Folio from a copy of the "Pied Bull" Quarto that had been elaborately corrected by reference to the playhouse manuscript. Somewhat the same thing was done with *Troilus and Cressida,* a play of which the slightly longer Folio text differs repeatedly from that of the Quarto. Final proof of this fact is presented by Philip Williams,[1] who is thus able to dismiss once and for all the rival hypothesis that the printer of the First Folio used an independent manuscript. In the 1609 Quarto of *Troilus,* the printer followed certain conventions in the use of roman and italic types; so did the printer of the Folio, though the conventions were not necessarily the same. The Quarto was set by two compositors with easily recognizable habits of spelling and treatment of speech-headings; so was the Folio text of *Troilus,* as E. E. Willoughby demonstrated twenty years ago. Now Williams reports the discovery of so many cases in which the Folio agrees—abnormally—with the Quarto in the use of italic and roman types, in the abbreviation of speech-headings, and in idiosyncratic spellings, that one, and only one, explanation will suffice: a marked copy of the Quarto served as printer's copy for the Folio.

Unaware of Williams's paper, which had not yet come from press, Miss Alice Walker published a study[2] of a different aspect of the textual problem of *Troilus.* It has long been known that Jaggard encountered some obstacle to the printing of *Troilus,* which was intended to follow *Romeo*

[1] "Shakespeare's *Troilus and Cressida*: The Relationship of Quarto and Folio," *Studies in Bibliography,* III (1950-51), 131-43.
[2] "The Textual Problem of *Troilus and Cressida,*" MLR, XLV (1950), 459-64.

Shakespeare Survey 5 (1952), 144-47, 151-52.

and Juliet in the Folio. After three pages of text had been put in type (pages gg3ᵛ-4ᵛ), the play was laid aside. The last page of *Romeo,* which had occupied gg3ʳ, was reset on the first recto of a new quire, Gg, with *Timon of Athens* following on the verso. When it was possible to resume printing *Troilus,* the economical Jaggard salvaged leaf gg4, containing the second and third pages of *Troilus,* but he had to cancel leaf gg3. A hitherto unprinted Prologue to *Troilus* was used to fill the recto formerly occupied by the concluding lines of *Romeo,* and on the verso of the cancel Jaggard put a resetting of the first page of *Troilus.* The canceled leaf (gg3) survives in five copies of the Folio. A few unimportant variants have been found by Miss Walker between the first and the second settings of the first three pages of *Troilus* in the Folio; between the Quarto text and the first setting in the Folio the variants are likewise few and unimportant. But beginning with the fourth page of the Folio text she finds a great many substantive differences between Quarto and Folio. She concludes that in the interval while Jaggard was working out a solution of the difficulty which had interrupted work on *Troilus* he had been supplied (presumably by John Heminges and Henry Condell) with a copy of the Quarto into which someone had copied the superior readings, the corrected speech-headings, the more adequate stage directions, and the new passages of text which differentiate the Folio from the Quarto. But for the delay, she guesses, the Folio would have preserved merely an uncorrected reprint of the Quarto text. Another possibility, which she does not suggest, is that Heminges and Condell interrupted Jaggard's work on *Troilus* so that they might have time to collate the Quarto with a manuscript and thus provide a superior text.[3]

Not all the variants introduced into the Folio text are superior; so Miss Walker offers the hazardous conjecture that a different hand had supplied these in the marked copy Jaggard used, beginning with the fourth page of the Folio. This may be correct, but it complicates the problem by introducing an otherwise unknown agent, and it is hardly susceptible of proof. Perhaps Williams, or someone else, will be able to account for the inferior variants as the work of a copyist or of the Folio compositors.

Sir Walter Greg's latest contribution to editorial theory will prove of the utmost value to future editors, as it will dismay most of those who have hitherto done editorial work in this period. In a closely reasoned and amply illustrated essay[4] read at the English Institute in New York in

[3] [But see below, pp. 340-41.]
[4] "The Rationale of Copy-Text," *Studies in Bibliography,* III (1950-51), 19-36.

1949, he gives a new definition to the term *copy-text* and prescribes new methods of procedure for editors. The heart of the essay is contained in the following passage:

It is therefore the modern editorial practice [in dealing with English Renaissance printed texts] to choose whatever extant text may be supposed to represent most nearly what the author wrote and to follow it with the least possible alteration. But here we need to draw a distinction between the significant, or as I shall call them "substantive," readings of the text, those namely that affect the author's meaning or the essence of his expression, and others, such in general as spelling, punctuation, word-division, and the like, affecting mainly its formal presentation, which may be regarded as the accidents, or as I shall call them "accidentals," of the text.

This distinction, as he points out, is not arbitrary or theoretical, for scribes and compositors of the period tended to react differently to the two categories: they attempted to reproduce the "substantives," but the "accidentals" were regarded as within their own power. This is sound but revolutionary doctrine. It means, for example, that the editors of the Variorum *Faerie Queene* erred in selecting the 1596 edition of *The First Three Books,* even though Spenser altered single words, supplied missing phrases and lines, and wrote new stanzas to alter the concluding incident of Book III. It can be demonstrated that Spenser did not supply Richard Field with a new manuscript of the poem for the 1596 edition; instead he revised a copy of John Wolfe's edition of 1590, introducing such new readings as he desired but ignoring many of the typographical and other errors in 1590, including those in the errata list. Since the authoritative text is that which most nearly reproduces the manuscript of the author, the quarto of 1590 should have been used as the copy-text. Spenser's substantive changes in 1596 should have been inserted. In this, as in all other reprinted texts, there are many doubtful readings, possibly introduced by the printer, which require the exercise of editorial intelligence and taste, for as Greg warns, the editing of a text cannot be reduced to a foolproof mechanical procedure: "No juggling with a copy-text will relieve the editor of the duty and necessity of exercising his own judgment." This pithy essay should be read by everyone seriously concerned about the purity of Shakespeare's text.

In a manner as gay as it is earnest, Peter Alexander discusses the punctuation of Shakespeare's text.[5] Editors are frequently called upon, as

[5] "Shakespeare's Punctuation" (Annual Shakespeare Lecture), *Proceedings of the British Academy 1945,* XXXVI (1950), 61-84.

in the case of *Hamlet,* to decide between the punctuation of a good quarto and that of the Folio. Which should be accepted? Or does the punctuation lie within the power of the editor? After a swift review of editorial attitudes towards Shakespeare's text, and particularly its punctuation, Alexander advances the proposition that the editors of the First Folio tried, at least in some plays, to impose upon the copy-text a punctuation that would make the plays easy reading. In the plays that were printed from Shakespeare's own manuscripts, however, such as the good Second Quarto of *Romeo* and of *Hamlet* and the Folio text of *Coriolanus,* there is observable a different style of punctuation, lighter, more fluent perhaps, but, if its principles might be discovered, no less adequate than the other and perhaps more authoritative. Some of the principles governing this other style (Shakespeare's own, Alexander suggests) were discovered inductively by Alfred E. Thiselton, but generally the subject has been neglected, despite Percy Simpson's investigation in 1911 and desultory studies by others of more recent date. It is not easy to formulate Shakespeare's habits of punctuation, because printing-houses were even then attempting to secure a measure of uniformity in punctuation as in spelling. Alexander's challenge is one that should no longer be declined. . . .

One of the imponderables in editing Shakespearian texts is the proof-reading of the original editions. It may be assumed, I think, that Shakespeare read the proofs of *Venus and Adonis* and *Lucrece,* but the conditions of dramatic composition and publication were such that it is improbable he had the opportunity to read the proofs of any of his plays published in quarto before 1616. Naturally he did not see proofs of the First Folio; but did anyone else read its proofs? And, if so, how carefully were they read? The only two pages of Folio proof known until recently have been described by E. E. Willoughby[6] and Charlton Hinman;[7] now Hinman has discovered a third page of Folio proof, this time in the course of collating the text of *Lear* in the Folger Library First Folios with the mechanical device of his own invention. In the account[8] of his discovery, Hinman points out that again only one page in the forme, p. 292 in *King Lear,* bears the proof-reader's marks; that in the three pages of proof only one error marked for correction would require the reader to

[6] [*The Printing of the First Folio of Shakespeare* (Oxford University Press, for the Bibliographical Society, 1932). *Antony and Cleopatra,* sig. xx6ᵛ.]

[7] ["A Proof-Sheet in the First Folio of Shakespeare," *The Library,* 4th ser., XXIII (1942-43), 101-7. *Othello,* sig. vv3ʳ.]

[8] "Mark III: New Light on the Proof-Reading for the First Folio of Shakespeare," *Studies in Bibliography,* III (1950-51), 145-53. [*King Lear,* sig. qq6ᵛ.]

consult the copy from which the text had been set; and that the corrector of the press seems to have been concerned, in all three pages, with the niceties of typography and elimination of obvious typographical errors rather than with the intention of the author. Hinman's account should be read at length, but two other points may be mentioned here. One is that in the conjugate page, 281, which bears no corrector's marks, one press-correction was, nevertheless, made: two types that were riding high and taking too much ink were adjusted at the same time that the five corrections were made on page 282 pursuant to the marked instructions of the proof-reader. The second is that the uncorrected states of the two pages of which Hinman has discovered marked proof are found in Folger Folios nos. 15, 31, 47, 48, and 69 and in the Chatsworth copy, used by Sir Sidney Lee for his facsimile, but in no others. This fact suggests that Jaggard's shop had a method of segregating corrected from uncorrected states of the formes of the First Folio, a thing hitherto unsuspected. Much remains to be learned of Renaissance methods of proofing. . . .

Incidental to the preparation of his critical edition of *King Lear,* G. I. Duthie made an exhaustive study of the systems of shorthand used in England before 1607, when the First Quarto of that play was published. His findings are given in a book[9] whose importance is out of all proportion to its size. Timothy Bright's *Characterie* and Peter Bales's *Brachygraphie* are shown to be too crude and cumbersome for use by a pirate of a play. John Willis's *Stenographie* was a better system, but not even its inventor claimed more for it than that with it a man "well practized in this Art, may write *Verbatim,* as fast as a man can treateably [*i.e.,* deliberately, distinctly, intelligibly] speake." Whereas,

if the speaker from whose mouth we note, be very swift of deliverie, so that he transporteth our imagination beyonde the indevour of our handes; it shall not be amisse to write only the Verbes & Substantives, and other Words essential to the speech delivered, reserving a space for the rest which are of lighter circumstance, to be supplyed with Penne immediately after the speech is ended.

The difficulties of a stenographic reporter in the playhouse can be readily imagined: swift speech, rapid action, entrances and exits, and much that is calculated to transport the imagination beyond the endeavor of the hands. In a word, there was no adequate method of reporting plays by shorthand in Shakespeare's day—certainly the text of the First Quarto of *Lear* was not so reported. . . .

[9] *Elizabethan Shorthand and the First Quarto of King Lear* (Oxford, 1949).

The great figures in Shakespearian scholarship are often too remote geographically or academically to be more than names to their contemporaries. The opportunity to know two of these men better, one dead, the other living, is afforded by J. Dover Wilson's revelation of the private character as well as the intellectual stature of the late Alfred W. Pollard,[10] and the lively and entertaining introduction by an unnamed admirer to the more-than-octogenarian Percy Simpson.[11] Both sketches should be read, as much for their literary quality as for the portraits they paint.

[1953]

Textual and bibliographical studies of Shakespeare were more numerous and more important than usual in 1951-52. The major publication of the year is surely the second volume of *A Bibliography of English Printed Drama to the Restoration*[1] by Sir Walter Greg. This is one of the works for which must be reserved the adjective "monumental." Of direct interest to Shakespearians are the entries relating to *Othello*, first printed in 1622, and the plays which were published for the first time in 1623 in the First Folio. But the *Bibliography* is too well known and too widely used to need praise. It is not inappropriate at this point to return thanks for the reissuing of Greg's *The Editorial Problem in Shakespeare*,[2] which has long been out of print. The second edition contains a few corrections in the text and nine pages of prefatory matter in which the author takes account of a decade of textual studies. . . .

Another kind of editorial activity . . . is illustrated in "An Approach to the Problem of *Pericles*"[3] by Philip Edwards. In reading it, one senses the excitement which drives bibliographers and textual critics to "live laborious days," for despite the modest wording of his title and the tentativeness with which he states his conclusions, Edwards has

[10] In *Proceedings of the British Academy 1945*, XXXVI (1950), 257-306. In this same volume are tributes to J. W. Mackail (pp. 245-55) and Oliver Elton (pp. 317-44).

[11] *A List of the Published Writings of Percy Simpson* (Oxford, 1950).

[1] Oxford University Press, for the Bibliographical Society, 1951.

[2] Oxford, 1951.

[3] *Shakespeare Survey 5* (1952), 25-49.

come very near to the solution of the chief problems of *Pericles,* if indeed he has not found it. *Pericles* was printed three times in quarto format in Shakespeare's lifetime and thrice more by 1635, yet it was not included in the First or Second Folios. It is a moving play, as all who have witnessed a performance can testify. Its kinship with the Romances in theme and situation is very close, and many of its lines, particularly in Acts III-V, are right Shakespeare. The problem is further complicated by the existence of a prose history of Pericles, published in 1609, which claims to give the story as it had been acted by Shakespeare's company. It has been generally assumed that Shakespeare had a collaborator or that he revised, at least in part, another man's play. In the absence of objective evidence and another text with which to compare the First Quarto of *Pericles* (1609), for it alone has any authority, scholars have been guided by taste and their subjective impressions.

Using several of the techniques of modern analytical bibliography, Edwards finds that three different compositors were engaged in setting the type, notes their habits of spelling and punctuation, and ascertains their varying abilities to set prose and blank verse, and, especially, to deal with the lineation of hypermetrical verse. Next he tabulates the pages set by each compositor, checking his results against the evidence of the running-titles. After this, he is ready to discuss the nature of the copy used in printing the Quarto. This, he believes, was a memorial reconstruction of a play written wholly by Shakespeare. Taking the capacities of the three compositors into account, he is then able to suggest boldly that the qualitative differences between Acts I and II on the one hand and Acts III-V on the other are traceable to the two agents who reconstructed the text. As to Wilkins's novel, it too is a report of a performance of Shakespeare's play, eked out with passages borrowed from Twine's earlier prose history. So on occasion a modern editor can confidently lift a short passage from Wilkins to fill a gap in the reported texts of agents A and B. We are left to infer that difficulty about the copyright made it impossible to include *Pericles* in the First Folio.

On the evidence in hand, Edwards has been brilliantly successful. It is to be regretted that he had not the space to publish all his detailed evidence. In my opinion he is wrong in suggesting that the type was set in two different shops, even though one compositor used one sort of type and put 37 lines on a page while the other two set

35 lines in a different sort. The distribution of work among the three men is such that they must all have worked in the same shop.[4]

The most valuable contribution of modern scholarship to the study of Shakespeare is the painstaking effort to discover exactly what kind of manuscript or printed copy lies behind the early quartos and folios, so as to determine the precise authority of each line and eventually to produce a perfect text. Not, alas, the text that Shakespeare intended in his fair copy or even the text, cut and adapted, that one might have heard in a letter-perfect performance at the Globe or Blackfriars. But something far less precious, and yet a text that would be preferred above anything now in print, namely, one in which proper allowance has been made for the idiosyncrasies of scribes, compositors, and proof-readers, and for the contamination of superior copy by inferior. Edwards's paper is a good example of this kind of scholarship. In a series of articles aimed in the same direction, some of which will win fuller acceptance than others, Alice Walker has compared the quarto and folio texts of a number of plays, with startling results. She reasons[5] by analogy from *Richard III*, the Folio text of which was printed, except for two passages, from a copy of Q6 corrected by reference to a theatrical manuscript. The text of the two exceptions was set directly from leaves abstracted from a copy of Q3 that bore prompt-notes and had at some time been inserted in the promptbook to supply a deficiency. Apparently Jaggard strongly preferred to have his men supplied with printed copy rather than manuscript, if we may judge by what was done with this play and with *Lear*. Did the same thing happen, Miss Walker inquires, to 2 *Henry IV*, *Othello*, and *Hamlet?*

In the case of 2 *Henry IV*, the Quarto gives every indication of having been printed from Shakespeare's foul papers, in which certain cuts had been marked. The text of the Folio supplies the omissions and differs in other respects so much that M. A. Shaaber, the Variorum editor, argues for the use of a manuscript based on the promptbook. It is Miss Walker's opinion that the Folio's errors in speech-tags could not have originated in the promptbook or a transcript of it. Though differing somewhat from those in the Quarto, they bear to them a pe-culiarly close relationship. And so it is with certain unusual spellings. Her conclusion is that the Quarto was printed from foul papers and the

---

[4] [Since this was written, John Crow has convinced me that Edwards was correct in supposing that the type was set in two different shops.]

[5] "Quarto 'Copy' and the 1623 Folio of 2 *Henry IV*," *RES*, II (1951), 217-25.

Folio from a copy of this text which had been collated with a fair copy of the foul papers. The suggestion that this fair copy was made by a person unknown, in which some passages were tidied up, and which served as the basis for the promptbook and the players' parts, I find difficult to accept. The process is too complicated. The copy for the Quarto was legitimately obtained, and when a scene was inadvertently omitted by the printer someone was scrupulous enough to have an expensive cancel inserted to supply the deficiency. If the foul papers were in such shape that an intermediary transcript had to be made (see p. 223) before it was safe to proceed with the original promptbook, why were these later sent to the printer of the Quarto instead of this hypothetical transcript? And how did the printer manage to produce so good a text as we find in Q? Granting that the Folio contains erroneous speech-tags and duplicates some unusual readings in the Quarto, may it not be well to assume that a copy of the Quarto, whose text was known to have been curtailed, was amplified by reference to the promptbook itself, with insufficient attention to the correction of minor errors, inconsistencies, and irregularities?

Continuing her attack upon received opinions about the group of plays for which there seem to be two substantive texts, Miss Walker turns next to *Othello*.[6] Collation has driven her to the conclusion that the "well-recognized inferiority of the Quarto text was due not to scribal errors but to memorial contamination" (p. 16), which is not to be charged against the actors but was rather "the work of a bookkeeper who relied on his knowledge of the play as acted and on his invention where memory failed" (p. 24). She is persuaded by the frequency of common errors, the orthographical evidence, and variant readings that a copy of the Quarto was corrected by reference to a manuscript which she refrains from identifying. Admitting that there is no positive bibliographical proof that the Folio was set, at least in part, from the Quarto, she yet urges that in no other way can we account for the preservation of "so many common accidental features." Some of the instances she cites are difficult to explain otherwise. While, however, her challenge cannot be ignored, her explanation will not be widely accepted unless a more detailed study reveals bibliographical dependence of the one text upon the other.

The third play for which Miss Walker attempts to discover new textual

[6] "The 1622 Quarto and the First Folio Texts of *Othello*," *Shakespeare Survey* 5 (1952), 16-24.

relationships is *Hamlet*.[7] Here again she starts with the assumption that printed copy for the Folio was supplied by Jaggard whenever possible. But before attacking the supposedly independent authority of the Second Quarto and Folio texts, her ultimate objective, she reminds us of certain typographical resemblances between the first two Quartos and insists that the latter was set from a corrected copy of the former to the end of the First Act, and thereafter from manuscript. This is decidedly iconoclastic. Turning finally to the Folio, Miss Walker questions its independent authority because in a score of words there is almost complete identity between the Second Quarto and Folio readings, not to mention frequent agreement in pointing. It seems incredible to her that a compositor working from Shakespeare's foul papers in typesetting the Quarto text should so frequently preserve the same accidentals (to use Greg's term) as have likewise survived the process of copying the foul papers and (1) preparing the promptbook, (2) transcribing this for the Folio, and (3) setting it in type. How much simpler if a copy of the Second Quarto was corrected from the promptbook and used in printing the Folio text! The simplicity Miss Walker attains is to be distrusted. As an example of the new difficulties resulting from acceptance of her thesis, consider her explanation of the inferior readings found in the Folio. These have hitherto been attributed to the debasement that is unavoidable when a text is transcribed or printed; Miss Walker would place the chief responsibility on Jaggard's compositors but assigns part of it to a bookkeeper who, in "renewing" a promptbook that must surely have been worn out between 1602 and 1622, "admitted into the new promptbook what was customarily spoken on the stage instead of what was originally set down in the 'parts' " (p. 336). Before agreeing, we must remind ourselves that there is no historical evidence whatever that the *Hamlet* promptbook needed replacement; then we must decide whether to allow three staggering assumptions: (1) that if the old promptbook were replaced by a new one the scribe would go to the trouble of assembling and copying out the players' parts instead of transcribing the tattered original; (2) that these players' parts had been modified (by the actors?) so as to include gags and other debasements; and (3) that the bookkeeper would prefer and write down his own recollections of what had been spoken on the stage rather than follow

---

[7] "The Textual Problem of *Hamlet*: A Reconstruction," *RES*, II (1951), 328-38.

his copy, thus introducing "the anticipations, recollections, and inter-polations which require explanation in the F text" (p. 336).

To do justice, it must be added that Miss Walker admits not having examined later quartos to see whether one of these might have been used in printing the Folio, but she maintains this does not weaken her case that the Folio was printed from a corrected Quarto. Obviously, all the evidence must be examined again, for Miss Walker would persuade us that instead of being blessed with three substantive texts, one "bad" and two "good," we are plagued by the sudden realization that we hold a much less secure textual position.

The newly chosen editor of the Oxford or "McKerrow" Shakespeare, G. I. Duthie, continues his study of good and bad quartos in an important article[8] about *Romeo and Juliet,* which he is editing for the New Cambridge Shakespeare. His initial assumptions are that the First Quarto is a reported text, that back of the Second Quarto is a Shakespearian manuscript, and that a few passages in Q2 were printed directly from Q1. These assumptions are shared by most Shakespearians. Duthie's contributions are threefold. First, he argues that not Shakespeare's foul papers but a transcript of them served as the basic copy for the Second Quarto. This not very fully substantiated opinion is buttressed by Duthie's second proposition, which is that the scribe kept his eye constantly on the First Quarto and, finding the text faithfully reported on leaves B3 and B4, simply tore them out and inserted them in the proper place in his transcript, taking care to cancel everything except the lines from I. ii. 57 to I. iii. 36. At several other places, and this is the third innovation, he noticed that the text of the First Quarto could be altered to agree with Shakespeare's manuscript by interlineation or marginal correction and again he removed leaves (the Prologue, D1, E1, and G3) from his copy of the Quarto, edited them, and inserted them in his transcript. Elsewhere this scribe relied exclusively on Shakespeare's foul papers, and the Second Quarto, printed from his transcript, is the only authoritative text. In the main, Duthie's hypotheses provide the best explanation of the bibliographical and textual relationships between the two texts, but some may remain unconvinced that the copy for the Second Quarto did not consist of leaves from the First Quarto and Shakespeare's foul papers. His account of the use of italics in printing the Nurse's lines is less lucid than, for example,

[8] "The Text of Shakespeare's *Romeo and Juliet," Studies in Bibliography,* IV (1951-52), 3-29. The article is adapted from a paper read at the English Institute in September 1950.

Sir Walter Greg's in *The Editorial Problem in Shakespeare* (1942), a book to which he does not refer.

Of equal interest is Duthie's discussion of how an editor should prepare the text of this play. A thoughtful consideration of it should be compulsory for everyone engaged in editorial work in this period and will be enlightening to everyone who wants to read Shakespeare in the best possible text. . . .

The false dating of several Shakespeare quartos by Thomas Pavier and William Jaggard was proved in 1908 and 1910, but the controversialists of those years would have welcomed the discovery recently made by Allan H. Stevenson.[9] At the Huntington Library he has found a leaf in the Church copy of *Henry V* (dated "1608") with a watermark dated 1617 or 1619, and in the Church copy of *Sir John Oldcastle* (dated "1600") a leaf dated 1608. The value of the discovery at this late date is, as Stevenson says good-humoredly, largely sentimental; but it enables him to make several acute observations about intrusive watermarks. For a revolutionary discovery, one should read Stevenson's other article in the same volume (pp. 57-91), "Watermarks Are Twins." The fact that watermarks were, and are, made in pairs is a commonplace among papermakers and historians of papermaking, but English and American bibliographers have been unaware of it, though, as Stevenson demonstrates, it may be used to advantage.

One of the more recalcitrant plays in the canon is *Troilus and Cressida*. In recent years we have learned the truth about the canceled leaves in the First Folio, the relationship of the Quarto and Folio texts, and the nature of the change in quality of the Folio text that begins with the fourth page and continues to the end of the play. But how was Jaggard able to resume the printing of the play after once having had to abandon it? Sir Walter Greg supplies the answer[10] and prints in tabular form the variants that occur in the first three pages in the Folio and also those that are found in the later pages. When Henry Walley, who had entered *Troilus* in the Stationers' Register in 1609 in defiance of the grand possessors, refused to come to terms with Jaggard, the latter discontinued printing the play and substituted *Timon*. Walley's continued stubbornness drove Jaggard to the discovery that he already had a sort of claim to ownership of the copy by virtue of being the

---

[9] "Shakespearian Dated Watermarks," *Studies in Bibliography*, IV (1951-52), 159-64.
[10] "The Printing of Shakespeare's *Troilus and Cressida* in the First Folio," *PBSA*, XLV (1951), 273-82.

successor to the late James Roberts, who had registered *Troilus* conditionally in 1603. Furthermore, Jaggard had the good fortune to come into possession of (or gain access to) a manuscript of the play that differed markedly from the Quarto and had a hitherto unprinted prologue. His legal position thus fortified, Jaggard resumed printing, inserted the prologue, altered the Quarto text to conform to his manuscript, and included some forty or fifty lines missing from Walley's quarto. . . .

The Shakespeare Association (London) continues its series of collotype facsimiles of Shakespeare Quartos with the publication of *Hamlet* (1603)[11] from the British Museum copy. Now for the first time scholars can collate the two extant copies of this First Quarto, for the Huntington Library copy is already available in facsimile. Sir Walter Greg's Introductory Note gives the history of the two copies and notes the variant readings in the two states of both formes of sheet B. It is interesting that an 18th-century hand has twice corrected "weasel(l)" to "Owsle (Owstle)" on G1, lines 25 and 26 (III. ii. 396-97), for the same emendation occurs in both of the promptbooks of John Ward, grandfather to Mrs. Siddons, and in a Folger Library copy of *Hamlet* (1703) partly marked for prompt use.

[1954]

This has been a notable year in textual studies; perhaps later generations will call it revolutionary. When has scholarly tradition been called so sharply in question as in F. P. Wilson's lecture, "Marlowe and Shakespeare"?[1] "Was it Shakespeare and Marlowe," he inquires, "who first gave dignity and coherence to the historical play and raised it above the level of a chronicle? So we have always been taught to believe; but when we look for these early chronicle plays written before the Armada, where are they? . . . Many play-titles have survived [from the 1580s], and a few plays, and if we go by these we are forced into this surprising conclusion: that there is no certain evidence that any popular dramatist before Shakespeare wrote a play based on English

---

[11] *Hamlet, First Quarto, 1603* (Shakespeare Quarto Facsimiles No. 7, London, 1951).
[1] *Marlowe and the Early Shakespeare* (Oxford University Press, 1953), pp. 105, 106, 108.

history." And after dismissing the pretensions of *The Famous Victories of Henry the Fifth* and several of its ilk, he continues: "My conclusion is, though I am frightened at my own temerity in saying so, that for all we know there were no popular plays on English history before the Armada and that Shakespeare may have been the first to write one." This is heady wine of a new orthodoxy with which to fortify oneself before venturing into the mazes of collaboration and revision that are detailed in the plays recently edited by John Dover Wilson. . . .

In three closely reasoned articles Fredson Bowers addresses himself to several matters of more than casual interest. The importance of facsimile editions is undisputed, but what kind of facsimile should an editor produce?[2] Except for the use of the general reader, it is no longer sufficient to reproduce the pages of one exemplar, unless it be unique, for every copy of an early book consists of an indiscriminate collection of uncorrected and corrected sheets. The ordinary conditions of proof-reading were such, however, that the so-called corrected formes give a text that in the essentials may be less faithful to the author's intention than the compositor's first setting of type. In most cases, then, if it cannot be proved that the author is responsible for alterations in the type or that the press-corrector consulted the manuscript copy, an editor can, paradoxically, give the best facsimile text by reproducing the uncorrected states of the formes. Shakespeare folios and quartos not being generally accessible, most detailed study has to be based upon facsimiles. It is urgent, therefore, as I pointed out fourteen years ago, that publishers of facsimiles should modernize their policies in order to meet the needs of modern scholarship.

In the second paper[3] Bowers states concisely the editorial position in each of the plays of Shakespeare and then demonstrates with ease that not a single play now exists in print with as sound a text as it is possible to establish. If this proposition astounds the lay reader, it should not dismay the scholar. In twoscore years, so much has been learned about the nature of dramatic manuscripts and printinghouse methods that editorial practice has lagged. This is particularly true of the last ten years, when so many new discoveries have been made about the spelling habits of compositors, the methods of proof-reading, the nature

---

[2] "The Problem of the Variant Forme in a Facsimile Edition," *The Library,* 5th ser., VII (1952), 262-72.

[3] "A Definitive Text of Shakespeare: Problems and Methods," in *Studies in Shakespeare,* ed. Arthur D. Matthews and Clark M. Emery (University of Miami Press, 1953), pp. 11-29.

of printer's copy, and the choice of the most authoritative text. This paper should be read by everyone who has a serious interest in Shakespeare and especially by every college and university teacher and every prospective editor.

The third paper[4] is an apologia, intended to dispel the anxieties of those who suspect that the current elaboration in bibliographical description "may so widen the division between the bibliographer and the student of literature that it will be impossible even for the textual critic to use without difficulty some of the technical devices now employed in the analysis of the physical makeup of a book," or of those others who fear the establishment of "a conception of pure bibliography, written by bibliographers for bibliographers."

Bowers defines (1) enumerative or compilative bibliography, (2) historical bibliography, (3) analytical bibliography, (4) descriptive bibliography, and (5) critical or textual bibliography; affirms the right and duty of the bibliographer to discover and record everything that can be ascertained about the production of a book, whether or not it has immediate utility; and asserts the interdependence of bibliographical and textual investigation and the necessity to employ both in literary study. . . .

Studies of the habits of Jaggard's compositors A and B may seem to fall into the category of vermiculate scholarship, but not as they are pursued by Alice Walker. In the seventh and latest volume in the series of "Shakespeare Problems,"[5] she continues to examine the minutiae of six plays which survive in two or more relatively independent texts and further develops her theory that Jaggard had a marked preference for printed over manuscript copy, especially after the long interruption from 1621 to 1623 in printing the First Folio. The little book is packed with so much matter—one is tempted to say dynamite—that it is necessary to select only a few illustrative details and leave the rest for thoughtful reading. The 1622 Quarto of *Othello,* she believes, "was a memorially-contaminated text, printed from a manuscript for which a bookkeeper was possibly responsible and based on the play as acted"; a copy of it was collated with a more authoritative manuscript for use in printing the Folio. Through Act I, the good Second Quarto of *Hamlet* (1604/5) was printed from a corrected copy of the bad First Quarto (1603); then

    [4] "Bibliography, Pure Bibliography, and Literary Studies," *PBSA*, XLVI (1952), 186-208.
    [5] *Textual Problems of the First Folio: Richard III, King Lear, Troilus and Cressida, 2 Henry IV, Hamlet, Othello* (Cambridge University Press, 1953).

the printer turned directly to Shakespeare's foul papers. Before the Folio was begun, the original promptbook had been replaced by a transcript, which, being at one further remove from the foul papers deviated yet more from Shakespeare. A copy of the Second Quarto, already contaminated by the First Quarto readings, was collated with this second promptbook for Jaggard's use in the Folio, but it was not given the same responsible, scrupulous treatment that *Lear* received, for the reason that the King's Men had at this date no manuscript comparable in authority or accuracy to Roberts's quarto of 1604/5. In the case of *Lear,* Miss Walker joins Leo Kirschbaum in rejecting G. I. Duthie's notion that the text of the "Pied Bull" Quarto was the product of a communal act of memory by Shakespeare's company and proposes an entirely new theory: that most of the Quarto represents a transcript of Shakespeare's foul papers, dictated by one minor actor to another (the boys who played Goneril and Regan are prime suspects) and recorded in a horribly illegible hand. In I. i, II. iv, and V. iii, where these actors appear prominently, the text is not only debased as described above but contaminated by reliance of the culprits upon very fallible memories. Later a copy of the Quarto was collated with the promptbook for use in printing the Folio. If all this be true, the "Pied Bull" Quarto has much greater potential authority than now accorded it and editors must rid themselves of their timorous distrust and more boldly conflate the two texts to recapture Shakespeare's lines.

The treatment of *Richard III* is extensive and startling. Miss Walker agrees with Patrick, Greg, and McKerrow that the Quarto was printed from a manuscript based on a memorial reconstruction by the King's Men. There is intimation that the promptbook was lost prior to 1602. In 1621 a Shakespearian autograph of the play was found defective and pieced out with segments of the Third Quarto; but when Jaggard resumed printing the Folio in 1623 it was decided to supply him with printed copy, the Sixth Quarto as it happened, collated with the author's manuscript and patched with the same fragments of the Third Quarto mentioned above. Along with these theories about the transmission of the text is a detailed study of the kind of errors habitually made by compositors A and B and a calculation of the corrupt readings in the Second to the Sixth Quartos which the collator failed to alter by reference to his manuscript. The number is shocking—approximately 140. By contrast, modern editors emend only about 10 readings. It is instructive to see how these figures are arrived at. It is more important to understand their implications and the general trend of Miss Walker's arguments. Their moral is that in future editors must be ever more bold. Editorial work must henceforth be characterized by a new kind of liberty of emendation. This will differ from the eclecticism indulged in by the great editors of the 18th century and their less robust imitators. Supported by modern bibliographical and textual criticism, it will demand of editors the exercise of the finest critical discrimination, especially in those areas where substantive texts are suspect.

[1955]

Charlton Hinman, who has already published descriptions of two pages of First Folio proof discovered in the course of collating with his machine the copies of F in the Folger Shakespeare Library, announces the discovery of yet another page.[1] It is possible that others may come to light before he finishes collating the entire collection of Folger copies a year or two hence. Meanwhile, on the basis of the collation of a third of the plays in F in some twenty copies, he publishes some statistics that are startling in their implications and points to certain inferences that may be drawn from them and an examination of the four known examples of Jaggard's proofs.

First of all, there is the possibility that more than one man marked proof-corrections; this should be neither unexpected nor surprising in the case of so large a volume. Second, proportionately more pages of *Romeo* contain stop-press corrections than do pages of nearby plays— already twelve of the twenty-five pages have been found in two states. Third, the corrections on each page of *Romeo* are relatively few in number and trifling in quality, with the result that the text is lamentably inferior. Fourth, when formes are known in two or more states, the proof-reading was tardy and the percentage of uncorrected copies is high. Hinman is led to conjecture that "to some extent the typesetting, but above all the proof-reading that went into the Folio text of *Romeo*

---

[1] "The Proof-Reading of the First Folio Text of *Romeo and Juliet*," *Studies in Bibliography*, VI (1954), 61-70. [*Romeo and Juliet*, sig. ff6ᵛ. See p. 332 above.]

Shakespeare Survey 8 (1955), 153-54.

and Juliet, is of a special order, clearly differentiating this play from most of the plays nearby. A particular *attitude* towards the *Romeo* text would seem to have prevailed in the printing-house . . . , as if the compositor and the proof-reader alike . . . were but too well aware that they were here perpetuating only the reprint of a reprint of the play." This brings us to a fifth observation, that collation to date of the Folio texts adjacent to *Romeo* has produced "not a single variant [page] in *Coriolanus,* only four variant pages in *Titus,* no variants whatever in *Timon,* four variant pages in *Julius Caesar,* and one variant page in *Macbeth:* a total of nine variant pages in these five whole plays as compared with twelve in *Romeo and Juliet* alone." Of these five adjacent plays, only *Titus* appeared in an earlier edition. Do Hinman's statistics mean that special attention was given to the typesetting and proof-reading of plays set from manuscript and then being printed for the first time? And is it permissible to think that such plays as *Julius Caesar,* of which F is the only text, have been printed with a high degree of accuracy?

Two things have combined to usher in a new age of textual criticism in Shakespeare. The earlier in point of time was recognition of the fact, dimly and only reluctantly apprehended even yet, that copies of the First Folio differ among themselves in hundreds, probably thousands, of readings. The later, and even more important, is that two or more compositors set the type used in printing the First Folio; that they had different ideas about the typographical appearance of a page, as determined by the spacing of stage directions and the handling of lines of verse too long for the narrow columns of F; that each tended to impose his own preferential spelling and punctuation on the text he was setting; and that in consequence it is possible to identify the pages, columns, and with good fortune some shorter passages of text set by each compositor. Better yet, using the methods of Willoughby, Hinman, and Philip Williams (to name only three), it begins to be possible to discover the work habits of Jaggard's compositors and, in particular, to ascertain how accurately each man reproduced his copy in type. The First Folio is no longer a unit. It consists, as we are beginning to find out, of pages printed from type that may be marked off with some confidence into units of work done by men with certain known characteristics and habits of workmanship.

[1956]

In a time like this of feverish activity in the study of Shakespearian texts, it is well to pause for an evaluation of the present state of scholarship and a coordination and consolidation of recent discoveries. This is the more necessary because many of the most rewarding investigations have been of a highly technical nature, requiring the discovery and application of new and ever more rigorous bibliographical techniques and an appalling amount of sheer drudgery. The published results of these researches are likely to be caviar to the general. Indeed, the serious scholar who has not had the time to read all the literature of the subject may find the going heavy. He would not, however, be justified in wondering whether the investigators were indulging in intellectual gymnastics for their own pleasure. Should he be tempted to entertain such a frivolous thought, he would be well advised to read Sir Walter Greg's monumental book about the First Folio.[1]

From the first chapter, entitled "Planning the Collection," to the last, dealing with "The Printing," the author asks all the questions that can be imagined, presents and weighs the evidence, and pronounces judgment with the utmost modesty and admirable detachment. It need hardly be said that no one else has the author's intimate knowledge of English Renaissance drama, whether in manuscript or print; but it should be gratefully recorded that Greg has a lively, pungent style, and is completely at ease in the exposition of the most complicated problems. Thus in Chapter IV, "Editorial Problems 2," he writes:

The question whether a particular Folio text was set up from a manuscript or from an earlier print is one which sufficiently patient and minute examination should be able to answer definitely, although in a few cases critics are not yet agreed. But when we probe beyond this comparatively superficial problem, and ask what sort of manuscript was handed to the Folio printer or lay behind the printed edition supplied, or in some cases what sort of manuscript it was by comparison with which that edition was corrected before being used as copy for the Folio, we enter an altogether different field of criticism, a misty mid region of Weir, a land of shadowy shapes and melting outlines, where not even the most patient inquiry and the most penetrating analysis can hope to arrive at any but tentative and proximate conclusions. But if what song the Sirens sang is

[1] *The Shakespeare First Folio: Its Bibliographical and Textual History* (Oxford, 1955).

Shakespeare Survey 9 (1956), pp. 148-51, 153-55.

a question not beyond all conjecture, we may at least hope to form an idea of the manuscripts behind the transmitted texts of Shakespeare's plays that can claim to be reasonable and to possess a measure of plausibility. We shall be wise to pitch our expectation no higher. (pp. 105-6)

The Shakespeare First Folio epitomizes the scholarship of half a century and blocks out the problems that must be solved in the years ahead.

How those problems are to be solved is the chief concern of Fredson Bowers in his Rosenbach Lectures in Bibliography.[2] It must be largely in terms of the nature and authority of the manuscripts from which the plays were printed and of the processes of the printing shops and the characteristics of the printers who converted copy to type and read the proofs. Bowers is not content simply to describe and illustrate the known methods of bibliographical-textual research; he seeks, as always, to penetrate the textual mysteries that yet baffle us. And in so doing, he does not hesitate to challenge received opinion. The characteristics of certain texts have hitherto been most satisfactorily explained as originating in the use of Shakespeare's foul sheets as copy. Bowers demands proof that an Elizabethan playwright ever turned his foul papers over to a company of actors that bought his play.[3] Instead, he argues that the author delivered a fair copy, of which a transcript was then made that served as promptbook, and that it was this author's fair copy that was on occasion turned over to the printer. The suggestion has its attractions, one of which is that such a fair copy might receive partial editorial annotations before the promptbook was prepared. But no such fair copy is known, and Bowers is on unsure ground when he cites the publication by Heywood, Marston, and others of some of their own plays. The fact is that we do not know how these playwrights arranged to put their plays in print and are unlikely at this date to find any new evidence on the question.

It is not clear to me that Bowers takes sufficiently into account the need to have play-manuscripts licensed by the Master of the Revels. With so many plays in repertory, is it likely that players' parts would be copied out and the cast required to memorize them before the prompt-

---

[2] *On Editing Shakespeare and the Elizabethan Dramatists* (University of Pennsylvania Press, 1955).

[3] May it not be pertinent that a portion of text missing from *Bonduca* (British Museum Add. MS. 36758) was by Edward Knight, bookkeeper of the King's Men, "transcrib'd from the foule papers of the Authors wch were found"?

book was ready and *licensed?* It is dangerous to argue from one case, as Bowers does from Daborne's notes to Henslowe.

The book is full of illustrations, many of them drawn from work in progress of which there are otherwise no published accounts. One of these relates to the printing of the "good" Quarto of *Hamlet*. Bowers is confident that compositor X set sheets B-D (Act I) while Y started on sheet E. Thereafter X set F I N O and Y set G H K L M. This leads him to the inference that while X used the "bad" Quarto in conjunction with manuscript copy, Y worked exclusively with manuscript, so that there are no bad-Quarto corruptions whatever in sheets E G H K L M. This may be true, but it seems incapable of proof; we cannot know all the circumstances of printing. On any given day, X may have been ill and Y may have looked at the copy of the bad Quarto X had used in B-D—and probably kept at hand—or Y may at any time have walked across the room and checked or confirmed a reading. It is hazardous to speak in absolute terms.

Two years ago, J. Dover Wilson began a series of essays in response to a plea for a "Textual Introduction to Shakespeare without Tears." The first,[4] as a brief account of how textual study is practiced today, is comparatively easy reading. In the second[5] the needs and limitations of the general reader are subordinated to the desire to state at length the textual hypothesis upon which the author and his collaborating editor G. I. Duthie have made their text of *Romeo and Juliet*[6] in the latest volume of the New Cambridge Shakespeare.

Before commenting on these essays, it will be profitable to glance at a lecture delivered by Wilson at Stratford-upon-Avon under the auspices of the Governors of the Memorial Theatre.[7] A few details need correction or qualification, but otherwise the lecture is for many readers a better statement than the two essays of the series in *Shakespeare Survey*.

These it will be advantageous to consider together, along with the New Cambridge *Romeo* and the edition of this play by Richard Hosley.[8] It is now the belief of J. Dover Wilson and G. I. Duthie that the good Quarto 2 was printed directly from a copy of the bad Quarto 1 in

[4] "The New Way with Shakespeare's Texts: An Introduction for Lay Readers. I. The Foundation," *Shakespeare Survey* 7 (1954), 48-56.

[5] "II. Recent Work on the Text of *Romeo and Juliet*," *ibid., 8* (1955), 81-99.

[6] Cambridge University Press, 1955.

[7] "On Editing Shakespeare, with Special Reference to the Problems of *Richard III*," in *Talking of Shakespeare,* ed. John Garrett (London, 1954).

[8] New Yale Shakespeare, Yale University Press, 1954.

which interlineations, marginal additions, and loose slips of paper had been inserted bearing corrections of the text secured from collation with Shakespeare's foul sheets. They were driven to this desperate position by their decision that direct bibliographical links are to be found between Q2 and every one of the ten sheets of Q1. It is likely, I think, that minute examination of the evidence will incline readers to favor Hosley's acceptance of the more conservative opinion that, except for certain specific passages demonstrably printed from Q1, the copy for Q2 was basically Shakespeare's foul sheets. Certain minor bibliographical links noted by Wilson and Duthie suggest, however, that the compositor(s) of Q2 did refer sporadically to Q1 to verify or clarify a difficult manuscript reading. This is an unhappy situation, but there seems no help for it. It is regrettable that neither edition is able to contribute new information about the agency that reported the Q1 text or the purpose for which the text was prepared. . . .

In his edition of *King John*,[9] E. A. J. Honigmann keeps the promise implied in his discussion of Shakespeare's early plays[10] and, boldly dating his play 1590-91, asserts that it precedes and is the source of *The Troublesome Raigne* (Q 1591). The supporting argument is too long and complicated to be rehearsed in detail, and it might carry conviction were it not for the evident maturity of much of the verse in *John* and, what is of greater moment, the effect on the accepted chronology of the plays up to *Henry IV*. If it could be granted that by the spring of 1591 Shakespeare had already produced at least one version not only of *Richard III, Titus Andronicus,* the Ur-*Hamlet,* and the plays about *Henry VI,* and would in the next year or two add *Richard II, Love's Labour's Lost, Romeo,* and *A Midsummer Night's Dream,* what would be the effect on our ideas of Shakespeare's development as a poet and playwright? Shakespeare's middle years, as we have understood the term, when he should have been actively creative, are made to seem to have been devoted largely to the rewriting of youthful exercises. Honigmann is a redoubtable champion of his cause, and he has found new and amusing evidence to support it; the odds will remain against him, however, until each play in question can be assigned its chronological place in the canon. His treatment of the text of *John* is independent and deserves respectful consideration, as in his reassignment of lines at II. i. 149-51, his new act-division at III. i. 75, and his restoration of

[9] New Arden Shakespeare, London, 1954.
[10] "Shakespeare's 'Lost Source-Plays,' " *MLR,* XLIX (1954), 293-307.

Folio readings that earlier editors have emended. The comments on punctuation, certain "old" spellings, and the retention of "–ed" and "–d" are dubious. . . .

An example of the practical study of text by bibliographical methods is Fredson Bowers's "The Printing of *Hamlet* Q2."[11] This traces the introduction and reappearance of the units of running-titles through the Quarto and confirms, and is confirmed by, the pattern described by John Russell Brown[12] in another "practical" study of the work of Roberts's compositors X and Y in setting *Hamlet* Q2 and *The Merchant of Venice*. These may seem to be no more than intellectual exercises in determining what happened to particular books in a particular shop, but as Brown points out his researches enable us to discard the notion that *Hamlet* was set by a bungling, inexperienced compositor and to differentiate between the stints of two men whose characteristics can be tabulated and whose relative skill can be determined. This is of enormous value, for it helps the eclectic editor to isolate and evaluate doubtful readings. Bowers illustrates the potential value of specific information about compositors and presswork by his suggestion elsewhere that compositor X, who used the bad Quarto in his first stint on Quarto 2 in setting sheets B-D, probably retained the book, so that none of the sheets (after the conclusion of Act I in sheet E) set by Y were subject to contamination.[13] Thus the theoretical studies have practical utility, and the practical studies contribute to the formulation of theory. . . .

Considerable attention has been given to Miss Alice Walker's attempts to prove that the Folio texts of several plays, *Hamlet* and *2 Henry IV* among them, were set from corrected copies of Good Quartos, and that, in consequence, the F texts have much less authority than has been accorded them. Her conclusions have not gone unchallenged. Two painstaking studies, independently pursued but written upon the same basic assumptions and employing essentially the same methods, reassess Miss Walker's evidence for *2 Henry IV* and *Hamlet* and arrive at conclusions diametrically opposed to hers.[14] M. A. Shaaber[15] grants the existence of certain identities in spelling and punctuation between Folio and Quarto texts but is more impressed by the differences. "I think,"

---

[11] *Studies in Bibliography*, VII (1955), 41-50.
[12] "The Compositors of *Hamlet* Q2 and *The Merchant of Venice*," *ibid.*, pp. 17-40.
[13] But see above, p. 349.
[14] See also the dissenting reviews of her book by M. A. Shaaber, *MLN*, LXIX (1954), 436-38, and G. Blakemore Evans, *JEGP*, LIII (1954), 473-76.
[15] "The Folio Text of *2 Henry IV*," *SQ*, VI (1955), 134-44.

he writes, "there is reason to expect a certain amount of agreement, perhaps a good deal, in two texts derived by different lines of transmission from the same original." He is unwilling to concede that Q was referred to by the scribe who, he thinks, made a transcript of the playhouse manuscript for use by the printer (and I judge he would object equally to the suggestion that the compositors of F consulted Q, as has been suggested for Qq 2 and 1 of *Romeo*). Harold Jenkins[16] goes further. Admitting that a number of identical readings listed by Miss Walker are proof that Q2 of *Hamlet* is occasionally the source of F's text, he produces weighty evidence that the F text is wrong in a greater number of readings because Q2 was not followed consistently, and he concludes that a corrected copy of Q2 could not have been used as printer's copy for F. He believes that Heminges and Condell were not satisfied with the Q2 text and accordingly supplied Jaggard with a transcript of the playhouse manuscript and, further, that the scribe consulted a copy of Q2 sporadically. This, with the very important substitution of scribe for compositor, is the same position as for *Romeo*, which Jenkins describes in a gem of understatement as "very inconvenient." "If neither the nature nor the extent of the consultation can be defined," he continues, "it leaves the position of the modern editor hazy and insecure."

[1957]

Working full time, Dr. Horace Howard Furness, the founder of the New Variorum Shakespeare, could at the top of his powers edit a play in three years. His current successors must not only fit their editorial labors into full-time professional schedules but must grapple with a much more formidable volume of commentary and with textual problems of a complexity undreamed of in the leisurely days of Furness. In consequence, they live for many years with their plays and, as in the case of Matthew W. Black with *Richard II*,[1] achieve an admirable mastery of material and ripeness of scholarship. These qualities are the more de-

---

[16] "The Relation between the Second Quarto and the Folio Text of *Hamlet*," *Studies in Bibliography*, VII (1955), 69-83.

[1] *The Life and Death of King Richard the Second* (New Variorum Shakespeare, Philadelphia, 1955).

Shakespeare Survey 10 (1957), pp. 151, 153-58.

sirable because of the editorial necessity to exclude all that is doubtful and to present the rest with severe compression. The only serious loss in the present volume is the skimping of textual and bibliographical material.

As Miss Alice Walker points out in her review,[2] it would have been wiser to base the text (except for the Deposition Scene) on Q1 than on F, and it was a mistake to omit the formal tabulation of variants in Q1 and the discussion of these readings. Black is to be commended for his zeal in collating multiple copies of the quartos of *Richard II* and in particular for securing photostats of the Petworth copy of Q1, that had not previously been examined by scholars. As the editor notes, the Petworth copy is unique, for example, in having forme D (i) in the uncorrected state, with four readings that are corrected in the other three extant copies. Two of these readings (II. i. 194-96, ii. 35-36) are omissions of more than a line, the insertion of which by stop-press correction implies strongly that at least some of the proofs were read with reference to copy. Unfortunately, the editor overlooked four other variants in Petworth D (i). Its "At nothing" (II. ii. 14) is corrected to "With nothing"; "Shews" (II. ii. 21), to "Shew"; "in the" (II. ii. 82), to "on the"; and "his owne" (II. i. 176), to "my owne". This last alteration is a patent error:

Petworth (uncorrected):   About his mariadge, nor his owne disgrace,
Devonshire, Capell (corrected):   About his mariadge, nor my owne disgrace,
First Folio: About his marriage, nor my own disgrace

Failing to note it deprived the editor of restoring the true reading in a passage that has baffled all commentators.[3] . . .

In commenting upon the text of *Julius Caesar*, T. S. Dorsch (New Arden edition, 1955, p. xxv) noted the inaccuracy of speaking of *the* Folio text of a play before the completion of Charlton Hinman's project of collating all the Folger Shakespeare Library copies. This work goes on apace, but in terms of the number of plays completed the progress may seem to the uninitiated to be like that of Hamlet's crab. Hinman's latest interim report[4] discloses that the finding of hitherto unnoticed typographical evidence has necessitated reexamination of many plays previously collated. This has not been a mere duplication of labor. Its

[2] *SQ*, VII (1956), 243-46.
[3] The four variants overlooked by Black in the Petworth copy were first noted by John Crow, who pointed them out to me.
[4] "Cast-off Copy for the First Folio of Shakespeare," *SQ*, VI (1955), 259-73.

first result—and others will be reported later—is the revolutionary discovery that the compositors of the First Folio did not begin at p. 1 and proceed to p. 2 and so on through the twelve pages of the six-leaf quires.

The fact is that no play in the First Folio was set in this way. Independently of both the number of compositors and the number of skeletons employed, the First Folio was set throughout, not by successive pages, but *by formes*. When the compositor had set what was to be page 1 of a given quire, that is, he then set page 12; then page 2 and page 11, then 3 and 10, and so on. Or, and in fact far more often, he first set what were to become pages 6 and 7, then set 5 and 8, then 4 and 9, and so on until he had done 1 and 12—and then proceeded to pages 6 and 7 of the following quire. Or, if two compositors were working, A set page 6 while B set page 7, then A set 5 while B set 8, and so on until A had set page 1 and B page 12, at which point B set page 6 of the next quire while A set page 7—and so on again, but with B now setting the pages, in reverse of their "normal" order, of the first half of the quire, ending with page 1, while A set the others, ending with page 12. The sequence of formes that was followed from quire to quire was not always the same; nor, in quires set by two compositors, did each invariably set exactly the same number of pages as the other. On the contrary, there were many departures from what may be regarded as the usual—or perhaps we should say the ideal—method of working. But setting was nevertheless always by formes rather than by successive pages of text. (p. 261)

This means that before the compositors began work on a play, someone had to cast off the copy, marking the exact word which would appear first on each page of each quire. The casting-off might be relatively easy if the copy were an unmarked quarto or a clean manuscript; it would be less easy if, as in the case of *Lear*, a quarto had been collated with a theatrical manuscript and were filled with interlineations and marginal corrections. It might be equally difficult if the copy were the author's foul sheets. But, easy or difficult, someone did count off the copy, as the photographic illustrations of Hinman's lucid article prove conclusively. Sometimes there were miscalculations, which the compositors learned to deal with by spacing out or compressing their text. Such mechanical adjustments were not necessarily momentous. The changes, however, were not always innocent—see for example the passage from *Antony* about which Hinman is certain "that the copy is not accurately reproduced in this speech" (p. 268).

Whether compositors, when much pressed for space, often solved their problems by tampering with the text in these or other "more drastic" ways I do not know. But there is abundant evidence that the amount of text that could be got comfortably into a page was frequently misjudged; and it would hardly be surprising if, in an already crowded page, something not considered essential were left out. Is this, rather than either imperfect copy or mere careless error on the part of the compositor, the real reason why Folio *Othello* lacks after its fifteenth line (ss3^v a 37, page 310), to the prejudice of both sense and grammar, the part-line "And in conclusion" that appears in Q1? And can it be that some of the verse that is printed as prose in the Folio also represents, not difficult marginal scribblings in the copy, but only another way of dealing with a space problem—of "justifying," as it were, a page rather than a line? And were there still more serious tamperings with the text of the copy—some of them, perhaps, undertaken during the casting-off process itself and so also by other persons than compositors? (pp. 268-69)

The crowding and spacing-out of text constitute what Hinman calls presumptive evidence that copy was cast-off. His absolute proof rests upon the identification of some hundreds of individual types that appear throughout the Folio. The patterns in which these appear and reappear are consistent only with setting by formes. A sample of this evidence is also given in photographic reproduction.

The goal towards which Hinman is pushing is an exact account of how each page (each column of each page, perhaps) of each play in the First Folio was put in type, the identity of the compositor, and the order of the printing. The immediate results of the investigations thus far are, first, to prove triumphantly the validity and utility of this kind of study; second, to focus attention on the collating machine, without which such research is impossible;[5] third, to demonstrate, once and for all it may be hoped, the wisdom and uncanny foresight of Henry Clay Folger in assembling so many copies of the First Folio in one place; fourth, to stimulate a quantity of studies of printing methods in Shakespeare's day, especially of compositorial habits; and fifth, to force a reappraisal of the now shaky editorial position about the nature of the copy used in printing each play in the First Folio.

[5] With machines now in the British Museum, the Bodleian, the Houghton Library, the University of Virginia, and the University of Minnesota, it may be hoped that cognate studies of the First Folio and other books will be undertaken. [There are now (1968) collating machines also at the Newberry Library, the University of Kansas, the University of Texas, Edinburgh University, Wilhelms University at Münster, and elsewhere. So far more than twenty-five machines have been built.]

Not long before his untimely death, Philip Williams read at the English Institute a survey[6] of current work on Shakespeare's text that is notable for its flashes of insight and for the questions it asks. What does it mean, for instance, that the compositors of the First Folio perpetuated the seemingly indiscriminate variations between the *oh* and *o* spellings of the Quarto of *Troilus* but agreed to *o* in *Julius Caesar* and *oh* in *The Comedy of Errors?* Is it permissible to draw inferences about composite authorship of *1 Henry VI* from the fact that in Acts I and II Compositor A, who is conservative in treatment of his copy, spells *Burgundy* but in Act III (coinciding with the introduction of scene-division) always sets *Burgonie?* Or is it dangerous to go further than the supposition that the copy was (for whatever reason) in two or more hands? As for *Henry VIII,* which is often parceled out between Shakespeare and Fletcher on the basis of *'em* and *them* spellings, how heavily must the statistics be discounted because compositor B appears to have felt no compunction about normalizing the spellings of the pronoun in the seven pages he set? Williams gives several other examples to drive home his point about the indispensability of compositor analysis in textual studies.

Another kind of bibliographical evidence that Williams alludes to is a remarkable anticipation of Hinman's discovery about the counting-off of copy in the printing of the First Folio (p. 13). What a pity he did not live to follow up some of the clues so lavishly sprinkled throughout the essay! ...

Several studies of *Hamlet* are now in progress. In the first of two installments,[7] Fredson Bowers essays to discover the precise relation between the "bad" and "good" Quartos. Building upon his earlier work on the printing of *Hamlet* Q2, Bowers attempts to prove that bibliographical links between the two quartos are so close and continuous in sheets B, C, and D of Q2 as to require belief that Q1 was consulted constantly or that an annotated copy may actually have been used as printer's copy. This section of the text, constituting Act I, was put into type by compositor X, many of whose characteristics are now a matter of record. Bowers observes that a number of words that are spelled in Q1 in a form characteristic of X appear in Q2 with different spelling, and he attributes the change to the influence of

---

[6] "New Approaches to Textual Problems in Shakespeare," *Studies in Bibliography,* VIII (1956), 3-14.

[7] "The Textual Relation of Q2 to Q1 *Hamlet* (1)," *ibid.,* pp. 39-66.

manuscript copy. Even stronger proof of manuscript influence is supplied by such a passage as I. v. 55-57. Q2 reads:

> So but though to a radiant Angle linckt,
> Will sort it selfe in a celestiall bed
> And pray on garbage.

Angle linckt (for *Angel linked*) shows that Q1 was presumably consulted:

> So Lust, though to a radiant angle linckt,
> Would fate it selfe from a celestiall bedde,
> And prey on garbage:

The Folio supports *Lust* and *sate* (misprinted *fate* in Q1) and corrects *from* to *in*. Here it is almost impossible to believe that the compositor was using other than manuscript copy. The conclusion of Bowers's case will be awaited eagerly.[8]

Encouraged, perhaps, by Miss Walker's advocacy of annotated quartos as copy for the First Folio, Andrew S. Cairncross examines the printing of *Henry V*.[9] He argues "that the First Folio text of *Henry V* was set up, so far as that was found feasible, from one or more corrected exemplars of the bad quarto." Actually, he believes that a heavily annotated copy of Q3 served as copy but that in emergencies leaves were abstracted from a copy of Q2 to facilitate typesetting. He cites bibliographical links (p. 71) and particularly the spelling of speech-prefixes (p. 72) to show that the introduction of passages from the playhouse manuscript is accompanied by changes in the spelling that persist only until quarto copy is resumed. The facsimiles that Cairncross reproduces to show how annotation might have been effected and how it may explain certain redundancies in the text and other anomalies are impressive. Upon one thing he is insistent: that the quartos were annotated by Jaggard in the printing-house. If this be true, what manuscript supplied the new passages of text? Not the promptbook, surely; on occasion the promptbook was taken to Stationers' Hall to permit entry of a play for publication, but there is no evidence that the King's Men permitted any of their promptbooks to go to a printer. If it was a transcript that Jaggard used to annotate the quartos, why did his compositors not use it as copy?

---

[8] Elsewhere ("Hamlet's 'Sallied' or 'Solid' Flesh: A Bibliographical Case-History," *Shakespeare Survey* 9 (1956), 44-48), Bowers establishes that the correct reading at *Hamlet* I. ii. 129 is "sallied", a rare variant of "sullied".

[9] "Quarto Copy for Folio *Henry V*," *Studies in Bibliography*, VIII (1956), 67-93.

Miss Walker has suggested that Jaggard's shop had a strong pre-ference for printed copy, and Cairncross agrees. He has gone through several of the bad quartos in search of their possible influence on the First Folio. He is confident that earlier theories, such as those about the use of marked quartos as promptbooks, the replacement of lost or worn leaves of a promptbook or other theatrical manuscript with marked pages abstracted from a quarto, and the annotation of quartos by Heminges and Condell (or their agents) for Jaggard's use, are based on misreading of the evidence. The substitution of quartos for manuscript copy was the act of Jaggard. The implication is that Heminges and Condell provided manuscript copy and were unaware of Jaggard's substitution. But in some cases, *Richard III* and *Lear* for example, one copy of a quarto seems not to have sufficed. Cairncross attacks the idea of the use of *one* physical copy of a quarto. In the case of *Lear*,[10] P. A. Daniel erred in thinking that Q1 was the only printed text used in setting Folio *Lear,* as Madeleine Doran pointed out several years ago; the agreements of F with Q1 and Q2 "run in sequences, which are mutually exclusive, and coincide, as we should expect, with the pages of one quarto or the other." The use of more than one copy of a quarto of *Lear* would have been extremely difficult to prove, had not chance provided (we may suppose) a copy each of Q1 and Q2 instead of two copies of either quarto. We still need to discover what manuscript was collated with the quartos and exactly where the scribal work took place (whether in the playhouse or at the printer's). It seems not unlikely that printed copy may have been preferred above manuscript, not only because composition would be swifter, but also because casting-off copy would be easier.[11]

Ever since Heminges and Condell warned purchasers of the First Folio against "stolne, and surreptitious copies" of some of the quartos, there has been controversy about their precise meaning. Most people now agree that some of the pre-Folio quartos are "bad," and there is general agreement about the source and nature of the badness. But many points are still in dispute; so Leo Kirschbaum's treatise,[12] the result of his first-hand examination of the records of the Sta-

[10] "The Quartos and the Folio Text of *King Lear,*" *RES*, VI (1955), 252-58.

[11] Cairncross assumes that compositor B worked alone on *Lear,* but it has been suggested that another man also had a hand. Proof of F's dependence on both Q1 and Q2 predisposes me to think there were two compositors, and I should like to know whether the compositorial pattern matches the Qq pattern.

[12] *Shakespeare and the Stationers* (Ohio State University Press, 1955).

tioners' Company, is a welcome addition to the literature of the subject. He is certainly right that there is no necessary connection between the goodness or badness of a play-text and the validity of the publisher's copyright—the Stationers had little if any concern for the quality of a text that was to be entered for publication. There is grave doubt, on the other hand, about Kirschbaum's belief that publication, and only publication, established copyright. The book must be read for the wealth of detail it contains about the publication of Shakespeare's plays and of all the other plays of the King's Men that got into print. Some of the details are subject to different interpretations than those given by Kirschbaum, but he makes provocative suggestions about the plays that cannot be ignored.

[1958]

During the year, the Shakespeare Association of America has begun an experiment the outcome of which will be watched with interest. Mindful of the fact that neither individuals nor libraries can hope to keep fully abreast of Shakespeare scholarship, and that even the ample volumes of the New Variorum Shakespeare (begun in 1871 by Horace Howard Furness, continued by his son and namesake, and since 1936 issued under the auspices of the Modern Language Association of America) become outdated within a short time of publication, the Shakespeare Association commissioned the compilation of a Supplement to the New Variorum *1 Henry IV* and published it as the summer number of *Shakespeare Quarterly,* with extra copies in cloth covers similar to volumes of the New Variorum.[1] G. Blakemore Evans, the editor of this Supplement, has brought together in variorum form "with some degree of completeness all (mere nonsense aside) that has been written relating to the play from 1935 to July 1955." John Crow's review of the book concludes in part as follows:

It's all notes and no text—the pedant's dream. . . . The book is what it sets out to be; it is intended not to divert, nor even to persuade, but to chronicle. . . . If we wish to know—and teachers of Shakespeare simply have to know—what all the boys have been saying in the last twenty years, this book tells us and tells us admirably. . . . I read it through and was enthralled with it and I shall regard it

[1] *Supplement to Henry IV, Part 1. A New Variorum Edition of Shakespeare* (Shakespeare Association of America, New York, 1956).

Shakespeare Survey 11 (1958), pp. 152-55.

as a necessary part of my library. It led me to much that I had missed; it reminded me of much that had begun to grow hazy in my memory. . . .[2]

If this volume proves sufficiently useful and popular, the Shakespeare
Association of America may be encouraged to bring out Supplements
to 2 *Henry IV* and other of the New Variorum volumes. . . .

The records of the Company of Stationers of London have been
consulted sporadically for a long time in the study of the history of
English literature. Since the publication of Arber's *Transcripts of the
Stationers' Register,* they have been used systematically, especially by
students of English drama. A new body of material was made available
in Greg and Boswell's *Records of the Court of the Stationers' Company
1576-1602* (1930), and W. A. Jackson's edition of Court-Book C (now
in preparation) will add still more to our knowledge. Meanwhile, there
are many things unknown or imperfectly understood. Some of the more
important of these are disclosed and explained in Sir Walter Greg's
James P. Lyell Lectures in Bibliography of 1954-55.[3] These treat of
Decrees and Ordinances, the Stationers' Records, Licensing for the Press,
Entrance and Copyright, Imprints and Patents, the Hand of the
Master of the Revels, and Blocking Entries. Some of these matters
have been in dispute ever since the "blocking entries" of James Roberts
first came to notice. This is a book that must be read by anyone who
wants to know why "good" quartos of *Merry Wives* and *Henry V*
were not published to displace the "bad" ones, as happened in the case
of *Hamlet,* for example; or how Bonian and Walley managed to bring
out an edition of *Troilus;* or whether Edward Blount, as a sort of
successor to Roberts, presented the promptbooks of *Pericles* and *Antony*
at Stationers' Hall; or whether Walkley's *Othello* really had the sanction
of the King's Men (Greg now has some doubts).

An essay of primary importance[4] introduces Compositor E of the
First Folio, whose hitherto shadowy existence was hinted at by E. E.
Willoughby in 1932 and by Philip Williams in 1956. His was a prentice
hand, Charlton Hinman tells us, and most of the pages he set exist in
both an uncorrected and a corrected state: proof of the fact that Jaggard
was aware of E's limitations and tried to catch his worst mistakes. He

---

[2] *SQ,* VIII (1957), 91-94.

[3] *Some Aspects and Problems of London Publishing between 1550 and 1650* (Oxford, 1956).

[4] "The Prentice Hand in the Tragedies of the Shakespeare First Folio: Compositor E,"
Studies in Bibliography, IX (1957), 3-20.

is known only in his work ("The evil that men do lives after them"):
a page of *Titus,* the second setting of the last half-page of *Romeo,* part
of *Troilus,* Act I of *Othello,* ten pages of *Lear,* and one and one half
pages of *Hamlet.* Of this, only *Titus* III. ii was set from manuscript copy;
all the rest was from printed copy, though the ten selected pages of *Lear*
and presumably the page-and-a-half of *Hamlet* were marked copies of
quartos and thus somewhat more difficult. This is the man. The final
identification of Compositor E, who in that title achieves more lasting
fame than if his name and birthplace were known, is not simply a brilliant piece of bibliographical research that could hardly have been ac-
complished without the use of Hinman's collating machine and his vast
accumulation of data about the printing of the First Folio. It gives meaning for the first time to the otherwise fantastically erratic sequence of
formes through Jaggard's press as the Folio moved to tardy completion.

In a poorly lithographed book that deserves formal print and clean
reproductions, John Shroeder makes a valuable contribution to the study
of the First Folio.[5] The book suffers from trying to combine instruction
for the general reader with the solution of highly technical problems,
but this should not detract from the praise of the author's perception
that, by plotting through a thousand pages the course of the box rules
that enclose the two columns of text in the First Folio, it might be
possible to determine the order in which the formes were printed. It is
Shroeder's misfortune that he excluded the center rules from consideration and that he had not a collating machine to single out details that
escape the unaided eye. In consequence of these things and of the fact
that the story told by the rules must be supplemented by the evidence
of broken types and the explanation of the part played by Compositor E
(whose existence was then unproved), Shroeder falls occasionally into
error and has to concede that certain irregularities defy explanation. In
his long review of the book,[6] Charlton Hinman points out the limitations of Shroeder's methods and corrects some of his mistakes but
adds that "Mr. Shroeder has demonstrated conclusively that *Julius Caesar*
was printed before *Romeo and Juliet;* that part of *Richard III* and
the whole of *Henry VIII* were printed only long after the other
Histories and when all of *Macbeth* and part of *Hamlet* had completed
their runs at the press; . . . that, indeed, irregularity was the rule

[5] *The Great Folio of 1623: Shakespeare's Plays in the Printing-House* (Hamden, Conn., 1956).
[6] *SQ,* VIII (1957), 219-22.

rather than the exception throughout the printing of a large part of the great folio of 1623. This is important information, and its discoverer deserves high praise. . . ."

There has been general agreement that Q2 of *Romeo and Juliet* was printed in large part from a manuscript in Shakespeare's hand but that in one long passage, roughly from I. ii. 52 to I. iii. 35, the copy was a corresponding passage in the bad Quarto 1. The terminal points of this passage are controversial, as is the extent to which Q1 may have contaminated Q2 elsewhere. A few hard facts about the printing of Q2 have been quarried by Paul L. Cantrell and George Walton Williams.[7] They give bibliographical evidence that all of Q2 except six pages was set by a compositor called A; the rest, by Compositor B. Then by analysis of the spellings of speech tags in Q1 and Q2 they indicate the very strong probability that specified pages of Q2 were set from manuscript and are presumably free from Q1 contamination (barring, of course, casual consultation of Q1 by A or B). The results of this part of the investigation would be more usable if they had been presented in tabular form. Apart from the value of the study in the examination of the text, it is important as illustrating a new method of attacking a vexing problem. In a companion study[8] Richard Hosley restates convincingly the reasons for rejecting the proposition that Q2 of *Romeo* was set from an annotated copy of Q1 and for believing that Shakespeare's foul sheets served as copy except for the passage, I. ii. 52 to I. iii. 35, which was printed directly from Q1 without annotation. Previous commentators had suggested I. ii. 46, 54, or 58 as the starting point. He gives several good examples of sporadic consultation of Q1 and coins and defines a useful term, *manuscript link* (pp. 133-34).

[1959]

The place of honor in the field of bibliographical and textual studies must be given to the third volume of Sir Walter Greg's *Bibliography*,[1] which exceeds all expectations. Devoted primarily to the collections of

[7] "The Printing of the Second Quarto of *Romeo and Juliet* (1599)," *Studies in Bibliography*, IX (1957), 107-28.

[8] "Quarto Copy for Q2 *Romeo and Juliet*," *ibid.*, pp. 129-41.

[1] *A Bibliography of the English Printed Drama to the Restoration*, vol. III (Oxford University Press, for the Bibliographical Society, 1957.)

plays, it gives a formal description of the Pavier-Jaggard nonce collection of 1619 and the four Shakespeare Folios (pp. 1107-21; see also pp. 1249-58), with a succinct account of significant irregularities and of variant issues and reprints. The Appendix reprints wholly or in part booksellers' lists, early play-catalogues (indexed), and prefaces to plays; it also describes early private collections and gives publication-lists, actor-lists, and author-lists (the last three indexed). Then in eighteen sections there is a wealth of information about such subjects as authors, dedications and commendations, prologues and epilogues (first lines), adaptations and drolls, court performances, people connected with the theaters such as producers, musicians, and choreographers, title-page mottoes, "Quorum fit mentio," and "Notabilia." This is treasure trove indeed, and there are, besides, more than a score of reproductions of engraved portraits of the playwrights. . . .

After Charlton Hinman's demonstration[2] that Jaggard cast off copy and then printed the First Folio of Shakespeare by formes, rather than seriatim, as had hitherto been tacitly assumed, it was natural that investigations would begin in order to discover whether this method was followed in printing books in other formats. One such study by George Walton Williams[3] deals with certain quartos set by a particular compositor in the shop of Thomas Creede between the years 1593 and 1599. Its importance lies in the fact that certain textual and bibliographical problems—as spelling, lineation, and the like—can be attacked with greater confidence if the method of composition can be determined. Williams observes that frequently, but not always, it is possible to prove that composition was by formes by means of "(1) the count of type-pieces of a character as they appear in a sheet or a forme, and (2) the presence of substitutions for the character which indicate that the supply of the character has been exhausted in the course of the work.". . .

The boundaries of the Shakespeare canon are vigilantly guarded, and properly so, but it may be suspected that the popular reluctance to admit that Shakespeare ever had a collaborator is the chief obstacle to the inclusion of *The Two Noble Kinsmen,* despite its acceptance by Coleridge, Bradley, Chambers, and Greg, to name only a few. Employing the method of Edward A. Armstrong,[4] Kenneth Muir[5] finds in the

[2] "Cast-off Copy for the First Folio of Shakespeare," *SQ*, VI (1955), 259-73.

[3] "Setting by Formes in Quarto Printing," *Studies in Bibliography,* XI (1958), 39-53.

[4] In *Shakespeare's Imagination* (London, 1946).

[5] "Shakespeare's Hand in *The Two Noble Kinsmen,*" *Shakespeare Survey 11* (1958), 50-59.

scenes usually attributed to Shakespeare two of the image-clusters (*kite* and *hum*) isolated by Armstrong, and two or three others. One of the more interesting of these involves a reference to the osprey (I. i) in a context of *war, cards, knives, lords, Kings, beds* (= graves), *graves, shadows,* and *actions,* that is to be compared to a similar reference in *Coriolanus* (IV. vii), in a context of *war, breaking the neck, sword, lord,* and *sovereignty,* with *tomb, darkened,* and *action* in nearby lines. This strong confirmation of the attribution of the play to Shakespeare and Fletcher on the title-page of the Quarto (1634) is given further support by the metrical evidence Muir presents. . . .

There have been two welcome additions to the Shakespeare Quarto Facsimiles: *Henry V* (1600) and *Love's Labour's Lost* (1598).[6] Sir Walter Greg's prefatory remarks are, as usual, succinct and authoritative. There has been a change for the worse in the paper in these volumes, with the result that the facsimiles are less legible than those issued earlier. In view of the fact that there is no other series of photographic facsimiles of the Shakespeare Quartos, nor likely to be one, I still wish, as I did in reviewing Facsimile No. 1 many years ago,[7] that snippets of the pages of other copies showing press-variants might be included at the back of each volume to facilitate bibliographical and textual studies.

[1960]

Numbers 11 and 12 of the Shakespeare Quarto Facsimiles[1] are valuable additions to the reference shelves. In No. 11 Sir Walter Greg reproduces in excellent facsimile (the best since No. 7) the unique Bodleian copy of *The True Tragedy of Richard Duke of York* (1595). His marginal references to the Folio text of *3 Henry VI* make easier and more profitable the study of this reported text. No. 12, the first Quarto of *Richard the Third* (1597), reproduced from the Huth copy in the British Museum, is photographically inferior to its predecessor. Greg's collation of the four extant copies and one fragment of the Quarto produces only one true variant (the Folger and Yale copies read cor-

---

[6] Nos. 9 and 10 (Oxford, 1957).

[7] [*MLN*, LV (1940), 634.]

[1] *The True Tragedy of Richard Duke of York 1595* (Oxford, 1958); *Richard the Third 1597* (1959).

Shakespeare Survey 13 (1960), pp. 164-68.

rectly "to" instead of "from" at II. i. 5).[2] The inclusion of a reproduction of sig. A3 of Q2 was well advised, for the two lines (I. i. 101-2) of the received text that appear first in Q2 may well have been printed as a press-correction in some copy of Q1 no longer extant. Early quartos of Shakespeare being so rare and inaccessible, it is strange that more individuals have not collected these fine quarto facsimiles. They bring the reader as close to the original as it is possible to come and afford a variety of unexpected delights. . . .

Following the lead of Philip Williams, who first drew attention to the importance of Jaggard's 1619 Shakespeare Quartos in the study of the First Folio compositors and ultimately of their printer's copies,[3] D. F. McKenzie has made a close study of some 3,200 variants between Q1 of *The Merchant of Venice* and Q2, which was put in type by Folio Compositor B.[4] It was Williams's impression that in *Lear* (1619) B gives "little evidence of the carelessness of which he has been accused, and the few errors that he did make are not those which have been attributed to him in the F text." The results of McKenzie's detailed tabulation and analysis of the variants in *Merchant* (1619) are to the contrary. Excluding substantial changes in stage directions and speech-prefix forms, which "appear to have all the characteristics of planned rather than impromptu editing," and a few readings that may represent press-corrections of Q1 that do not appear in the sixteen or more surviving exemplars, McKenzie finds that B's attitude towards his copy and his habits of work in 1619 ("misdirected ingenuity, deliberate tampering, and plain carelessness") were little different from those in 1621-23. These characteristics, though tedious to enumerate, deserve attention and suggest that the other 1619 Quartos must be scrutinized with equal care. For, as John Russell Brown wrote in his Introduction to the New Arden edition of *The Merchant* (1955), all of the 1619 Shakespeare texts appear to have received the same kind of unauthoritative editing that he observed in that play.[5] The extent of B's mischief

---

[2] Bad inking and loose type caused most of the apparent variations in text (see Greg, p. vi). It would have been more accurate to record the Folger copy as reading "merc" at I. i. 151.

[3] "Two Problems in the Folio Text of *King Lear*," *SQ*, IV (1953), 451-60.

[4] "Compositor B's Role in *The Merchant of Venice* Q2 (1619)," *Studies in Bibliography*, XII (1959), 75-90.

[5] Brown lists (p. xix, n. 1) thirteen of Q2's changes that he had accepted on the assumption that Jaggard had attempted to edit the text. At least eight of these are, however, required by the context, and another, at IV. i. 394, may represent a press-correction in Q1 that existed in a no-longer-extant copy.

in F cannot be safely estimated until all the available evidence has been compiled about his work in other books.

[1961]

There has never been a time, even during the "war" against Walker by Tonson and the rest of the Proprietors, when Shakespeare was so frequently published or widely read. There would seem to be an edition to suit every purse and every taste. Yet never have editors been so self-critical. A sort of revolution began in 1921, with the statement of principles by the editors of the first volume of the New Cambridge Shakespeare. Sixteen years later, the first of the Penguin paperbacks came from press, with an easy text and minimal apparatus. Upon the completion of the last Penguin, the editor[1] still bristles at the mention of "scientific bibliography," which he seems to equate with the paleographical attack upon textual problems. Meanwhile, many school texts continued to reprint the Globe text, with or without modification, and scholars began to debate the theory of editing. McKerrow's *Prolegomena* (1939) led to Greg's *Editorial Problem* (1942), which was followed by essays and monographs on special problems. Peter Alexander's independent text (1951) was followed by C. J. Sisson's (1954), and that in turn by John Munro's (1958). The New Arden volumes (from 1951), in which special editors are given wide leeway, have raised again the question of modernized punctuation and spelling and—by contrast with the new severely scholarly edition of Dekker (from 1953)—have confronted publishers and reviewers with the problem of what to give the serious reader. It is not without significance that in the land where variorum editions are supposed to be anathema, the New Arden retains many variorum features.

There can be no question of the need for more kinds of text than one. Some of the criteria of a critical old-spelling text were stated by Fredson Bowers in his lecture before the Bibliographical Society in 1958.[2] He gives special attention to the methods of the editor and to the

[1] See G. B. Harrison's "An Epilogue," at the end of the concluding volume, *The Narrative Poems* (Harmondsworth, 1959).

[2] "Principles and Practice in the Editing of Early Dramatic Texts," in *Textual and Literary Criticism* (Cambridge University Press, 1960), pp. 117-50, 171-86.

Shakespeare Survey 14 (1961), pp. 157-62, 164-65.

typographical disposition of the apparatus. The general controversy becomes direct and pointed in contiguous essays by John Russell Brown[3] and Arthur Brown,[4] which describe the relative merits of photographic facsimiles, type-facsimiles, diplomatic reprints, old-spelling critical editions, and partly or wholly modernized texts, and also their shortcomings. How will editions of plays in manuscript differ from those of printed texts? What shall an editor do about obsolete spellings that lend flavor or occur in rhyme words or, worse yet, convey a double meaning that is partly lost in any modern form? What is wanted or needed in respect of the retention of original punctuation, capitals, type-variations, and layout? Are the answers of fifty years ago (such as, for example, were embodied in the Rules for Editors of the Malone Society) valid today? Have new techniques of printing or copying changed the picture or given promise of a helpful change? There are no easy answers. Few of the editions of the Elizabethans now in progress or preparation are soundly planned or consistently executed. With every passing year it becomes more imperative that these problems be solved, even at the cost of a break with tradition, so that the different segments of the reading public can find the kinds of edition they need. . . .

The Bibliographical Way[5] is an eloquent apologia for critical bibliography by Fredson Bowers, who quite naturally draws many of his illustrations from the texts of Dekker's plays. Keeping up with Shakespeare is now so strenuous an undertaking that there is danger of neglecting what may be learned from the critical editions of his contemporaries. Bowers has found and solved a number of bibliographical problems in Dekker that have no known counterparts in Shakespeare, but it is foolhardy not to become familiar with the methods by which the problems were solved. In describing that hazardous segment of the bibliographical way where certainty is impossible, so that a choice has to be made between a plausible bibliographical explanation and an equally plausible literary or historical explanation, Bowers has selected the famous "clock" passage in *Richard III,* IV. ii as an illustration. Some eighteen or twenty lines present in the Quartos are absent from the more authoritative Folio text. Editors have conjectured that they were omitted

[3] "The Rationale of Old-Spelling Editions of the Plays of Shakespeare and his Contemporaries," *Studies in Bibliography,* XIII (1960), 49-67.

[4] "The Rationale of Old-Spelling Editions of the Plays of Shakespeare and his Contemporaries: A Rejoinder," *ibid.,* pp. 69-76.

[5] University of Kansas Libraries, 1959.

out of respect to James I or fear of Buckingham. Bowers believes that
Compositor A failed to include them because a miscalculation had
occurred in casting off the copy. In Q3 and Q6, which were used as
printer's copy for F, the passage occurs at the foot of one page and
the head of the next. It could not have been overlooked by eye-skip
or because of mutilation. In F, it should come near the foot of the
second column of page s3^v. This page was set by Compositor A, the
following page, s4, by Compositor B. Bowers assumes that A and B
worked simultaneously on these two pages of the inner forme of the
inside sheet of quire s. He argues that as A neared the end of the
second column of s3^v he discovered he had more text than could be
put on the page. His last line had to be "The most arch deed of pittious
massacre" (IV. iii. 2), because B had begun the following page with
the next line, "That euer yet this land was guilty of." A's only course
was to omit a block of text, the "clock" passage. This seems a plausible
explanation, but is it necessarily the correct one? Reference to the
Folio shows that there are at least a dozen white lines on the page that
might have been used, and at least two places where a line might
have been saved by combining short speeches. Setting three long lines with
turnovers would have saved yet more space. There are other pages in
F where rules are omitted from a scene-heading and long lines printed
with turnovers.[6] Is it likely that A would have left out a long passage
of text rather than remove a few leads and close up the lines of type
so that the passage might be included?[7] He might even have asked
B, whose type was still on the composing table, to remove a few leads
from his columns and fit in an equal number of lines of text. Such
minor adjustments should have been easy for two men working together
on so large a book as F. The bibliographical probability in this case
is no more impressive than the literary or historical.

A more extended and detailed apologia for biblio-textual study of
Shakespeare is found in Bowers's *Textual and Literary Criticism*.[8] The

---

[6] Cf. *Tempest*, p. 1, column a; *Merry Wives*, p. 49, column b.

[7] It may be argued that A did indeed compress the lines of type so that he might
squeeze in as much text as possible, for there are no rules above and below the stage direction *"Enter Tyrrel"* that begins Scene iii in modern texts. But there was never any
intention of marking a new scene at this point in F. *"Scena Tertia"* begins column b of
p. 54, which—to use Bowers's own time scheme—was set by Compositor B long before
A reached the bottom of his second column.

[8] Cambridge University Press, 1959. This consists of the Sandars Lectures in Bibliography for 1957-58 at Cambridge University and a paper read before the Bibliographical

first lecture states and illustrates the fact that editors, publishers, and critics have been shockingly indifferent to the purity of text of the poetry and fiction of the last 250 years. Not even the foremost authors of the present decade can be trusted to recognize their own revisions in works that have gone through several editions (cf. the anecdote about T. S. Eliot, pp. 32-33).

The second lecture, an apparent digression from Elizabethan studies into American literature, demonstrates that the minute study of the physical characteristics of a group of manuscripts can give new information about the date of composition of certain poems in *Leaves of Grass* (1860) and at the same time enable critics to think Whitman's thoughts after him as his ideas ripened and his plans for the volume matured. It becomes possible to form a new estimate of the poet's method of composition and revision. The humble means to this great end consists in part of fitting together in their original patterns the slips of paper of various colors and textures that in their present form, as assembled by Whitman in the course of revision, are interspersed with scraps of galley-proof and lines of manuscript—a glorified literary jig-saw puzzle. There is no such wealth of material for the direct study of the composition of *Hamlet* or the contemplation of how Shakespeare's mind worked. Instead, it is necessary to adopt Polonius's method of indirection and examine compositorial spellings and such vermiculate data.

The significance of the apparent digression is that the labors of the biblio-textual scholar are not to be treated with lofty disdain, as is the fashion in some circles. Chance, patience, perspicacity may at any time yield surprising results. The continuous effort to establish the text of Shakespeare and make it readily available for every reader is of prime importance, if only for the reason that scholars should not view with indifference or complacence even a slight taint of illegitimacy in the poet's brain children.

In Chapter III, Bowers enumerates the groups of variants that require scrutiny and, after naming and appraising the principal editions of Shakespeare now in circulation, illustrates how a modern editor attempts to discover the manner in which his text was transmitted and then to recover the author's words. Studies of this sort take time, for what

---

Society in 1958. See especially the Preface and Chapters I, III, and IV. Chapter II treats of the textual problems of Whitman's *Leaves of Grass* (1860).

seems valid for Shakespeare must be tested by similar studies of other playwrights. Of one thing we may be sure: the definitive text of Shakespeare will not be produced this year or next.

The advocates of textual-bibliographical studies are not without their critics. In reviewing Bowers's *Textual and Literary Criticism,* D. F. McKenzie comments at length[9] on "the author's general assumptions" in the lecture on textual criticism of Shakespeare. The "present achievement [of 'the newer bibliography'] is slight and painfully gained compared with its mooted possibilities." Furthermore, "its very bases appear to many, if not actually suspect, at least a little uncertain, at least in the present state of our knowledge." "It cannot," he continues, "be too frequently stressed how difficult the task of isolating a compositor's work may be. . . . Determination tests, moreover, have too often had indeterminate results: if Folio compositor A is now partly C, and Folio compositor B is like a twin brother to E, may the general reader not view with suspicion any compositor-determination study based on evidence less exhaustive than Dr. Hinman's?" McKenzie's caution is not unprecedented. When Greg and Neidig discovered the truth about the falsely dated Shakespeare quartos of 1619, they were not given universal assent. And when McKerrow modestly offered his *Introduction to Bibliography* (1927) there were literary students who dismissed it lightly. Some of the initial hypotheses of Pollard and Greg have had to be abandoned, and even McKerrow has proved to be occasionally wrong. But what a new world of textual and literary studies there is today because of Pollard and Greg and McKerrow! Bibliographical studies are advancing today as the science of chemistry once did. The spadework may be dull and painful—it is. For one success, there may be many partial and some total failures; for one Hinman, there may be a dozen journeyman bibliographers. But the movement is irresistible. "Prate not of most or least, / Painful or easy!" Not every bombarded atom yields the expected isotope.

If the spelling of an edition of Shakespeare is controversial, how much more so may be the punctuation. From an early date, compositors have exercised considerable independence in the pointing of texts. Commentators write of dramatic punctuation as opposed to other systems, but, for the very good reason that no dramatic manuscript before 1700 that served as printer's copy is in existence, we do not actually know what Shakespeare's habits of punctuation were or what changes com-

[9] *The Library,* 5th ser., XIV (1959), 208-13.

positors introduced. Using the indirect, Polonian approach, D. F. McKenzie examines the work of Jaggard's Compositor B, who in 1619 set *The Merchant of Venice* from the First Quarto of 1600.[10] He tabulates and classifies the 3,200-odd changes in punctuation made by B and finds it possible to generalize cautiously.[11] B's "general tendency was clearly to punctuate heavily," for the most part by the insertion of commas, particularly at the ends of lines. The modern editor must take this fact into account. He will not be able to work confidently, however, until similar studies have been made of other books from Jaggard's shop and especially those set by B. Nor may it be safely assumed that B's habits were unchanging. Philip Williams observed several years ago that when B set Q2 *Lear* from Q1 he exhibited traits that are markedly different from those to be found in his work on *Lear* in the First Folio.

As if the textual problems of *Hamlet* were not sufficiently baffling, Harold Jenkins now attacks the verbal accuracy of F, one of the substantive texts, charging it with theatrical contamination.[12] Sixty-five times when Q2 and F differ in verbal detail, he is confident that the later text has been corrupted by the insertion of non-Shakespearian words. Most of these are repetitions that originated with the actors, though a few such as "*Ham. within.* Mother, mother, mother" in the Closet Scene clarify the obvious. Others are as banal as F's "O, o, o, o," tacked on to Hamlet's dying words, "The rest is silence." These corruptions are charged to the actors, actors whose memories were faulty or who were willing to delay some necessary business of the play while they reenacted an effective piece of stage business. Jenkins is sure that the corruption is not limited to the sixty-five readings he lists and discusses. Nor, indeed, is it found only in *Hamlet*. He cites examples in *Othello* and *Richard II,* as others have done; and the variants of Q1 *Richard III* lend weight to his arguments. There can be no doubt that actors seldom read their lines with perfect accuracy. Doubters should read the text while playing Shakespeare recordings of a performance. There are the same repetitions, insertions of interjections, and paraphrases that Jenkins writes about. Even the best editors retain far too many of these objectionable words, though they are known to be corruptions. They are more apt to purify the text in passages of blank verse than in

[10] "Shakespearian Punctuation—A New Beginning," *RES,* X (1959), 361-70.

[11] Obviously McKenzie knows at first hand the drudgery of some kinds of bibliographical and textual study.

[12] "Playhouse Interpolations in the Folio Text of *Hamlet,*" *Studies in Bibliography,* XIII (1960), 31-47.

speeches written in prose, possibly because meter renders the excrescences
more conspicuous. Sometimes editors justify a suspected reading with
halfhearted apologies; sometimes they retain one because of the power
of tradition. Audiences accustomed to F's hypermetrical

> For *Hecuba?*
> What's *Hecuba* to him, or he to *Hecuba,* . . .

would be as much put out by Q2's

> For *Hecuba.*
> What's *Hecuba* to him, or he to her, . . .

as they—and editors—are reluctant to accept Juliet's "A rose by any other
word would smell as sweete" (Q2; Q1 reads *name*).

What Jenkins is asserting is that the F text of *Hamlet,* and of other
plays too, is not as Shakespeare wrote it. Somehow, in the preparation
of the promptbook, or in the transcription (at some time for some
reason or other) of the promptbook, many locutions invented by the
actors have got into the text. He is well aware of the seriousness
of his charge. As yet, he declines the opportunity to explain how or
when the debasement occurred. . . .

"The careful analyst will occasionally wish to identify the first formes
in a book under investigation; often, perhaps, to check someone else's
assumption that the inner forme was regularly printed first, or to verify
a plausible interpretation of skeletons or press-figures." So begins a
modest note by Kenneth Povey.[13] If one or more unpressed copies be
available, it is possible to examine the pages under the illumination of
a beam of light directed parallel to the surface of the paper and discern
on the first formes small hillocks of ink produced by the indentation
of perfecting types of the second formes. When the condition of a book
permits, one may thus determine priority of formes, distinguish between
concurrent and consecutive perfecting, and discover whether a printer
used common imposition in half-sheets or worked two half-sheets together.[14]

[13] "The Optical Identification of First Formes," *ibid.,* pp. 189-90.
[14] Information is given for the construction of a homemade lamp, and an editorial
note mentions the prospect of a commercial product.

[1962]

During the last fifteen years, there has been curiosity about the minutely detailed study of the Shakespeare First Folio by Charlton Hinman and the machine he invented to facilitate his work. From time to time he has published announcements of the discovery of pages bearing the marks of Jaggard's proof-reader; evidence that the Folio was set by formes and not seriatim, page by page; and the characteristics of an apprentice workman who, unfortunately for scholarship, had a large hand in the setting of the tragedies. These fragmentary interim reports have but whetted interest in the *opus magnum* which was in prospect. Now that this is in process of publication, Hinman has decided to give a hint of some of his conclusions.[1] The first reading of the printed version of his lecture—slightly abridged but not altered substantially—may dismay a little those who do not grasp the significance of some of Hinman's comments or who have not heard in private conversation of some of the discoveries that are not even glanced at in this latest report.[2]

What are some of Hinman's conclusions after collating thirty-six plays in fifty of the Folger Shakespeare Library's copies of the First Folio? (How fortunate that they are in one place for collation!) And what of the capacity and effectiveness of the collating machine? Of the machine it may be said that optical lenses, unlike human eyes, never tire, and that experienced scholars can multiply their output of collation by ten. The machine can scan pages and spot variants in less time than is needed to record them. And scholars may work with the assurance that the machine has not failed to report a variant.

But what of the weightier matters? One result of Hinman's years of study is the discovery that there is no warrant for the confidence, inspired by the discussion of a single page of proof of *Antony and Cleopatra,* that all of the First Folio benefited by careful proof-reading and press-correction. So far as this minute collation has proceeded, he is satisfied that "only 134 of these nearly 900 pages of the Folio which contain Shakespearian text were proof-corrected; and the average

[1] *Six Variant Readings in the First Folio of Shakespeare* (University of Kansas Libraries, 1961).

[2] The description of how the collating machine works will make textual editors eager to use one of the dozen or more examples that have been installed in research libraries in the United States and in England.

Shakespeare Survey 15 (1962), pp. 175-76.

number of changes made even in these 134 was less than four per page. Approximately 750 Folio pages appear not to have been proofed at all" (p. 9). In the comedies, Hinman has recorded about seventy variants that reflect proof-reading; in the histories, about seventy more. The tragedies received more careful attention, but almost half of the some 370 variants in this section "are confined to a mere 70 pages—the pages which prove to have been set by an apprentice compositor" (p. 9).

When we learn that the proof-reader was more interested in typographical niceties (turned types, space-types that took ink, *etc.*) than in errors affecting the sense of the text, and, what is much more serious, that in dealing with substantive errors he relied on native wit instead of consulting his copy,[3] it is tempting to ask, "Is this the promised end?" And if it be, has Hinman spent his years in much ado about nothing?

The discussion of the six variant readings that Hinman has singled out for comment has less significance than some of the things merely alluded to or assumed silently. How is it possible to prove that the Folio was set by formes, and what are the implications of the discovery, as it may affect lineation, omission of words or lines, verbal substitutions? What kind of evidence enables a man to parcel out the typesetting among five compositors, and ascertain their reliability in transmitting text accurately? With what validity can an editor state that a given play—or even a specified portion of a play—was more than usually difficult for the compositor? The answers to these questions, with supporting evidence, will presumably be found in the eagerly awaited book, with who knows what besides.

Meanwhile, a comment on one small point. Hinman makes the observation (p. 5) that uncorrected impressions of formes of the First Folio eventually found their way into different copies of the finished book. "Not, however, into any particular copies. . . . The uncorrected states of the various formes that make up the whole book did not go regularly into the same few copies." In consequence, no particular copy should be expected to contain an unusually high percentage of uncorrected formes. But there is a play-quarto in the Garrick collection in the British Museum so made up, and such a copy of Spenser's *Faerie Queene* in the Tudor and Stuart Club Library at The Johns Hopkins University. Some of the sheets of the latter are of very thick paper. Probably both of these copies were made up as printers' "copy books," partly from sheets

---

[3] Hinman has found only two indubitable cases of consultation of copy by the proof-reader.

that would otherwise have been discarded, partly from sheets of paper of different weight and texture surreptitiously slipped into the press in order to increase the number of "copy books."[4] Remembering these two books, I am perverse enough to hope that some day a copy of the First Folio will be found in which there is just such an extraordinary percentage of uncorrected formes and imperfect sheets.

[1963]

With *1 Henry VI*[1] the New Arden plunges more deeply than before into the treacherous waters of composite authorship. The editor, Andrew S. Cairncross, aligns himself with Peter Alexander in attributing the play wholly to Shakespeare and in dating it earlier than Parts 2 and 3 of *Henry VI*. Because of the very scanty external evidence, an intricate knot of problems, and a vast literature, the subject cannot be discussed here at the length it deserves. Comments on several of the chief points at issue may, however, be helpful.

From the wording of the title-page of the "bad" octavo of *3 Henry VI*, it may be inferred that 2 and *3 Henry VI* belonged to Pembroke's Men; and since the unauthorized texts of *The Contention* (1594) and *The True Tragedy* (1595) contain echoes of *1 Henry VI* (argued first by Alexander, who is joined by Cairncross—see his Appendix III), it may be assumed that this play, too, belonged to Pembroke's, who acted it often enough to mingle phrases of it in the reported texts of *The Contention* and *The True Tragedy*. Now the playhouses were closed by the plague in June 1592, and it seems probable that all three parts of *Henry VI* must have been written a considerable time before that date. Thus far Cairncross, who sets an earlier limit with his citation of borrowings from *The Faerie Queene* (Q 1590). He might have narrowed the limiting dates of composition by using evi-

---

[4] Cf. Francis R. Johnson, "Printers' 'Copy Books' and the Black Market in the Elizabethan Book Trade," *The Library*, 5th ser., I (1946-47), 97-105. [See p. 310 above.] Johnson should have included in his discussion the surviving copies of books that have sheets printed on one side only and others in which there are sheets that show the inked impression of one forme superimposed on the blind (uninked) impression of a different forme.

[1] London, 1962.

Shakespeare Survey 16 (1963), pp. 173-75, 180-81.

dence provided by Alexander and supplemented by G. Blakemore Evans[2] that *The Troublesome Raigne of King John* (Q 1591) contains reminiscences of *1 Henry VI* (and also of *2, 3 Henry VI* and *Richard III*). Then it seems (unlike Hamlet, the investigator of these plays rarely knows greater certainty than *seems*) that Strange's could hardly have bought their *Harey the vj,* performed as "ne" for Henslowe between 1 March and 19 June 1592, from Pembroke's, even though the latter company broke utterly on their provincial tour in 1593. *Harey the vj* must have been a rival to Shakespeare's play. And Nashe's allusion of August 1592 to the popularity of "brave Talbot" may refer to either play or to both.

There is little agreement about the nature of the copy used by Jaggard in printing F. To J. Dover Wilson (1951), it appeared to consist of the manuscripts handed over by the authors (Greene, Nashe, and Peele) to the first company that owned the play, to which their prompter had added occasional stage directions and notations for sound-effects before a fair copy was made to be used as promptbook (*i.e., 1 Henry VI* is to be identified with Henslowe's *Harey the vj*). This manuscript, Wilson thinks, was divided throughout (or at least those parts of it attributed to Greene, the chief plotter) into acts and scenes. When Shakespeare was called upon to revise the play, he rejected certain scenes—the original V. i, for example—and displaced or rewrote others, producing a text in which only Act III has all the scenes numbered. This was transcribed in the preparation of a new promptbook and survived to be used in printing F. Cairncross rejects all this. He postulates a Shakespearian rough draft containing inconsistencies[3] and even self-contradictions (*e.g.,* Exeter's surprise at seeing Winchester in Cardinal's robes at V. i. 28, when he had certainly worn them in Exeter's presence in I. iii, III. iv, and IV. i). To this manuscript the bookkeeper is supposed to have added some stage directions and sound-effects, not always at the right points. At the same time, he indicated certain adaptations to be made in the cast—indicated them but did not actually mark all the changes (*e.g.,* the 2 *Messenger–Lucie* confusion in Act IV). Then the rough manuscript was copied by a scribe who took liberties with the text, transposing words and phrases,

---

[2] In his review of J. Dover Wilson's New Cambridge edition of *1, 2, 3 Henry VI, SQ,* IV (1953), 84-92.

[3] In speech-prefixes primarily, but also in proper names (*Burgonie* as well as *Burgundie*), which Cairncross thinks may have been taken over from the various printed sources.

"improving" the diction, omitting many small words and inserting others, to the detriment of the meter. From this transcript a promptbook was prepared, and many years later it was used as printer's copy for F. The evidence is displayed persuasively, but doubts remain. Is there any other play in which Shakespeare carried over from his sources such contradictory details? Is the supposititious scribe an adequate agent to account for the ametrical lines and the many other indications of heterogeneous copy? Did Shakespeare ever write blank verse as listless as some of that in *1 Henry VI?*

Cairncross relies heavily on Hereward T. Price's brilliant discussion[4] of the structure of *1 Henry VI* and his insistence that no other playwright than Shakespeare had such architectural skill. But granting all this, must one suppose that Shakespeare could not have salvaged scenes written by other poets and fitted them with others of his own composition in conformity to a plan of his own devising?

Acting upon his theory about the authorship of the play and the nature of the manuscript from which it was printed, Cairncross has felt unusually free to amend the text. Some of the changes are justifiable; others appear to go too far in smoothing the meter and improving the language. At III. i. 71, "years" is unaccountably changed to "tears".

Conservative scholarship has resisted efforts to identify passages in Shakespeare's plays as insertions or revisions made by the author after the play took final form and was regularized for production. Now, reversing his earlier position, Brents Stirling adduces bibliographical, textual, and aesthetic evidence that Shakespeare telescoped incidents in Act II of *Julius Caesar* in order to speed the action and increase the dramatic tension.[5] Revision also took place in IV. iii, containing the duplicate accounts of Portia's death. The starting-point of the discovery is the presence in a play with uniform speech-headings of certain passages in which the speech-headings are spelled differently. It has been claimed that in *Caesar* Shakespeare first learned how to write tragedy; by following Stirling step-by-step through his exposition, it is possible to see Shakespeare in the process of improving his art. . . .

The Taming of the Shrew lends itself to a variety of interpretations. It may be played as a boisterous farce in praise of the use of force to assert masculine superiority or it may be acted as almost a high romantic comedy in which the principals, genuinely in love at first sight, must

[4] *Construction in Shakespeare* (University of Michigan Press, 1951).
[5] "*Julius Caesar* in Revision," *SQ*, XIII (1962), 187-205.

wage the eternal battle of the sexes before arriving at a joyous marital equilibrium. It is well known that Shakespeare's play, as preserved in the Folio, dispenses with Christopher Sly, the drunken tinker, *in medias res*, letting the play end with Katherine's assertion of wifely submission. Modern producers, particularly those who may feel twinges of guilt about Petruchio's crudity, avert unfavorable reactions by the audience by borrowing from *A Shrew* the dramatic epilogue in which the awakened drunkard, in his own guise, goes home to put in practice the lesson he has learned in a rare dream. *Dramatic epilogue* is the term coined by Richard Hosley[6] to describe "a short dramatic action following the play proper, normally performed by two or more actors, employing the same fictional situation as that of the induction, and concluding the dramatic action begun in the induction" (pp. 22-23). That is, to describe the kind of scene wanting at the end of *The Shrew* but present in *A Shrew*. Hosley names the 45 Elizabethan plays beginning with an induction, grouping together the 19 that end with a dramatic epilogue and the 26 that lack one. He observes that dramatic epilogues appear to have been out-of-fashion after about 1600. As to whether Shakespeare omitted the dramatic epilogue deliberately or whether it was left out of the Folio by accident, Hosley argues that Shakespeare did not write one. In the concluding scene, 13 (or 12) actors are on stage, not counting servants. Now Hosley assumes that some of these men doubled as Lord or Sly or Lady, and he points out that there was no time for the necessary change of costumes that would have been needed to bring Sly back on stage. It is his belief, furthermore, that Shakespeare would not have wished to blunt the edge of Petruchio's victory by bringing on Sly to point the moral. . . .

It is generally agreed that the modern approach to the study of Shakespeare's text began with Pollard, Greg, and McKerrow about 1909, and that the starting-point was the recognition of the differences between working with classical manuscripts and with printed books. Simultaneous studies by Alice Walker and Sailendra Kumar Sen now remind us that Edward Capell had apprehended a great part of the truth about first editions and reprints as early as 1760, when he chose an authoritative copy-text for each poem in his *Prolusions; or, select Pieces of ancient Poetry*, and that by 1768 (his introduction to *Mr. William Shakespeare his Comedies, Histories, and Tragedies*) his experience with quartos and

[6] "Was There a 'Dramatic Epilogue' to *The Taming of the Shrew*?" *SEL*, I (1961), 17-34.

folios had led him to a position that anticipates that of Pollard, Greg, and McKerrow. Sen[7] points out that on the evidence of duplicated passages of text, erroneous assignment of speeches, the naming of mute dramatis personae, Capell set aside the First Quartos of *Hamlet, Henry V, Merry Wives, etc.* as lacking in authority and accepted the other First Quartos on to that of *Othello* as the equivalent of the author's manuscripts.[8] This was the distinction Pollard made between "good" and "bad" quartos, and for many of the same reasons. Capell even suggested that some of the quartos had been printed from Shakespeare's manuscripts. He denied authority to the later quartos and to folios later than the First, except in particular cases where for undiscoverable reasons a reading might represent the author's intention. Malone (1790), too, recognized the "badness" of the First Quartos of *Romeo, Henry V, Merry Wives,* and *Richard III,* and the "goodness" of the First Folio for the plays first printed therein. The methods of Capell and Malone were, therefore, not eclectic in the older sense, and had their principles been accepted by later editors the modern study of Shakespeare might have begun more than a century before Pollard's *Shakespeare's Folios and Quartos* (1909).

Miss Walker gives a brief account of Capell's life and a lively description of his personality, and leads thence into an examination of his editorial theory and practice. Malone owed much to him, including the idea of aproaching the study of Shakespeare as a literary artist by discovering the order in which his works had been written and thus tracing his development.[9] . . .

An interesting theatrical manuscript, never previously described, directs attention once more to the Witches' Songs in *Macbeth.* It is a

[7] *Capell and Malone, and Modern Critical Bibliography* (Calcutta, 1960).

[8] Miss Walker, "Edward Capell and his Edition of Shakespeare," *Proceedings of the British Academy,* XLVI (1962), 131-45, notes that Capell was aware of the possibility that erroneous readings would be found even in first editions because of the intervention of scribes and printers—that first editions have not the high authority of a holograph manuscript.

[9] In addition to the set of transcripts given by Capell to Trinity College, Cambridge, "the only transcript that survives" (p. 137), there is a uniformly bound set of six volumes of Capell's holograph notes for the edition in the Folger Shakespeare Library (MS. S. a. 17-22). There is also his holograph transcript of *Edward III,* dated 3 October 1753 and 6 November 1753. At the end of the volume is an English epitaph for himself in his own hand, with date of death supplied later. Below this epitaph is written another, in Latin: "Qui literas amas & excolis, tibi qui pro virili consuluit vivens huic consule et tu." [This may be translated as follows: And you there who love and cultivate letters, remember him who, when living, was mindful of you to the best of his ability.]

Restoration transcript of Davenant's adaptation of the play,[10] made, according to Christopher Spencer, the editor, from Davenant's foul papers, independently of the transcript that was supplied to the printer of the First Quarto (1674) of the Davenant version. Reproductions of the title-page, the list of dramatis personae, and three pages of text give an excellent idea of how the manuscript was prepared. The main scribe, A, left blanks for words he could not read; Hands B, C, and D supplied missing words, made a number of interlineations and corrections, and wrote longer passages of revision on nine slips of paper attached by wax to the margins—five of these survive, and stains show where others were once attached.[11] Spencer is probably correct in thinking that the manuscript was intended for use in making the promptbook. His attempts to show that Davenant had a pre-Wars manuscript of *Macbeth,* independent of F1 (1623), and that a song near the beginning of II. v was written by Shakespeare rather than by Davenant are unconvincing.

> The worst of creatures fastest propogate
> Many more murders must this one ensue
> As if in Death were propogation too...

reads to me like purest Davenant.

[1965]

The primary intention of forty years of a bibliophile's life and the bibliographical persistence and acumen of a scholar have come to rich fruition in *The Printing and Proof-Reading of the First Folio of Shakespeare,*[1] which Charlton Hinman tells us could never have been written unless Henry Clay Folger had hunted out and brought together an unprecedented number of copies for scholarly use. Nor could it have been written unless Hinman had invented his now famous collating ma-

---

[10] *Davenant's Macbeth from the Yale Manuscript: An Edition, with a Discussion of the Relation of Davenant's Text to Shakespeare's* (Yale University Press, 1961).

[11] Spencer suggests that B made the earliest additions and that C and D, whose hands appear only on the tipped-in slips, followed in that order. Each of them, in his opinion, referred to an independent text of Shakespeare in making his corrections. Hand B may have written the label on the cover, naming Mr. Holden.

[1] 2 vols., Oxford, 1963.

Shakespeare Survey 18 (1965), pp. 186-87, 189-91. Volume 17 (1964), a special quatercentenary number, omitted the customary review of the past year's scholarship.

chine and devoted nearly two decades to the study. Announcing his most important discoveries as they were validated, Hinman removed the element of surprise from his book while simultaneously making the new methods of research available to other scholars. Now we know that the First Folio was not put into type seriatim but by formes; we have a printing schedule that is unlikely to be greatly modified; we know where interruptions occurred in composition and presswork, that five men were engaged, and what pages, columns, and parts of columns they set. Further refinements are needed, as Hinman points out, particularly in recognizing and tabulating the spelling preferences and other characteristics of Compositors C and D. Although the collation of more than fifty copies of the Folio has produced few substantive variants, it has indicated which compositors need to be checked most carefully and has given editors a true understanding of many short or otherwise abnormal lines and greater leeway in rectifying them.

[Professor Hinman has now (1968) rounded out his study of the First Folio by planning and supervising the publication of the Norton Facsimile of *The First Folio of Shakespeare*.[2] In this handsome volume each page is reproduced photographically in the final state of press-correction and is "conjugate" (so to speak) with its forme-mate page reproduced in the same state of correction. Reproduction is of the highest quality. The facsimiles are full-size and without sophistication of any kind. Casual stains are left untouched, but great care was exercised to select pages for photographing that are relatively even in the inking and that are least affected by show-through. They were chosen from no fewer than twenty-nine of the eighty copies of the First Folio in the Folger Shakespeare Library. Hinman's introductory essay states the importance and authority of the text of the First Folio and describes Jaggard's methods of printing and proofreading it. An appendix reproduces typical examples of uncorrected and corrected pages (including two that bear the marks of Jaggard's proof-reader), and another identifies which of the twenty-nine copies of the Folio was the source of each of the 908 pages reproduced. A noteworthy feature of the Norton Facsimile is its use for the first time of Through Line Numbering (TLN for short). This gives each line of the text an absolutely standard number by counting the lines of type of the Folio text of each play from beginning to end. For additional convenience of reference, act-, scene-, and line-numbers of the first

[2] [New York: W. W. Norton, 1968.]

edition (1864) of the Globe Shakespeare are noted at the foot of each page.] . . .

Pending his completion of the edition of the Sonnets, the final volume of the New Shakespeare, J. Dover Wilson[3] has paid quatercentenary tribute to his author by publishing the Introduction, an urbane book whose relative informality permits a charming directness of statement. Marshaling expertly the evidence accumulated from Tyler, Beeching, Dowden, Wyndham, and others, Wilson makes a strong case for William Herbert, Earl of Pembroke, as the Fair Youth and for a late dating of the Sonnets, 1597-1606. Wilson's belief that some at least of the Sonnets were secured in manuscript by Thorpe from the Dark Lady, after she realized the Poet had made a final break with her, introduces a new factor into the calculation of how the Sonnets came to be printed. And his inclusion of the descriptions of Pembroke by Clarendon and Aubrey helps to an understanding of how the young earl might win and command the abnegating love of a great poet, though I find it difficult to reconcile the character described by Clarendon with that depicted in Sonnets 87 ("Farewell! thou art too dear for my possessing") and 94 ("They that have power to hurt and will do none"). . . .

One of the very welcome quatercentenary volumes is the attractive facsimile edition of the Poems published by the Elizabethan Club at Yale.[4] It consists of the unique Bodleian copy of *Venus and Adonis,* the Elizabethan Club's own *Lucrece* and *Sonnets,* the Huntington Library's *Passionate Pilgrim* (second edition), and the Folger Shakespeare Library copies of *Passionate Pilgrim* (first edition, fragment) and *Phoenix and Turtle.* The facsimiles are clear, but it was an error in judgment to reprint only portions of the unique fragment of the first printing of *The Passionate Pilgrim.* The editors give a precise account of the first editions of the poems and provide a selected bibliography. "Familiarity breeds consent," the editors say. "The effect of moving easily into the presence of the poem [in a modernized text] is in part an illusion: what we read is not quite the poem, but something that includes spellings, punctuation marks, and even emendations that may keep us at some distance from the original poem" (p. xi). They are aware of the

[3] *An Introduction to The Sonnets of Shakespeare for the Use of Historians and Others* (Cambridge University Press, 1964).

[4] *Shakespeare's Poems: Venus and Adonis, Lucrece, The Passionate Pilgrim, The Phoenix and Turtle, The Sonnets, A Lover's Complaint: A Facsimile of the Earliest Editions,* ed. James M. Osborn, Louis L. Martz, and Eugene M. Waith (Yale University Press, for the Elizabethan Club, 1964).

obstacles interposed by early scribes and compositors and by erratic spelling and inconsistent punctuation, and ask, if *i–j*, *u–v*, and long *s* are modernized, whether it is "mere sentimentality to urge the retention of spellings that offer no service to pronunciation, rhythm, and meaning." Then they illustrate the way in which modern punctuation can spoil the flow of lines and break the natural unity of a quatrain and point to further advantages provided by the original capitalization and spelling. The modern spelling and pointing give an "illusion of familiarity" that may be narcotic. Sometimes the old spellings give just sufficient pause to suggest multiple meanings, and the old pointing may permit the association of phrases with either what precedes or follows, or with both, where modern punctuation closes the door on fluency and interpenetration. . . .

Since bibliographers began to analyze the spelling of Elizabethan texts and construct tables of preferential spellings of the compositors who set them, there has been spectacular progress. This was one of the most heavily used tools, for example, in Hinman's study of the printing of the First Folio. Much more could be done if more manuscripts had survived that served as printer's copy, but there are few survivors like the fragment of Sir John Harington's translation of *Orlando Furioso*.[5] Much more will be done when there has been time to study, not just a few Shakespeare quartos and the First Folio, but the output over a period of years of the shops that printed them, and when works of many other authors have been examined similarly. This time-consuming research is particularly liable to error originating in human frailty, and it may be hoped that techniques will be perfected for the use of electronic computers, which are speedy and tireless. T. H. Hill's attempt[6] to formulate a rationale of the study of Elizabethan spelling proposes some useful technical terms (*spelling-habit, spelling-pattern*) and warns against facile assumptions. One may question whether the average Elizabethan printer's shop had as clear a concept of a "rule of the house" as Hill seems to take for granted. Until the major output of many shops has been studied in depth, will it be possible to characterize a change in spelling by the corrector of the press as an application of the "rule of the house"?

[5] [See W. W. Greg, "An Elizabethan Printer and his Copy," *The Library*, 4th ser., IV (1923-24), 102-18.]

[6] "Spelling and the Bibliographer," *ibid.*, 5th ser., XVIII (1963), 1-28.

A List of the Published Writings of
James G. McManaway

A List of the Published Writings of
James G. McManaway

1931

"The Copy for *The Careless Lovers*," *MLN*, XLVI, 406-9.

1932

The Works of Edmund Spenser (Variorum Edition), vol. I, ed. Frederick Morgan Padelford, Edwin Greenlaw, Ray Heffner, Ernest A. Strathmann, and James G. McManaway, Baltimore, The Johns Hopkins Press.

1933

The Works of Edmund Spenser (Variorum Edition), vol. II, ed. Edwin Greenlaw, Ray Heffner, James G. McManaway, and Ernest A. Strathmann, Baltimore, The Johns Hopkins Press.

1934

" 'Occasion,' *Faerie Quenne* II. iv. 4-5," *MLN*, XLIX, 391-93.
* "Philip Massinger and the Restoration Drama," *ELH*, I, 276-304.
The Works of Edmund Spenser (Variorum Edition), vol. III, ed. Frederick Morgan Padelford, Ray Heffner, and James G. McManaway, Baltimore, The Johns Hopkins Press.

This list runs through 1968. Publications reprinted or in part reprinted in the present volume are starred.

Review: Robert S. Telfer, ed., Massinger's *The Unnatural Combat* (1932), *MLN*, XLIX, 553-54.

Review: Ursula Todd-Naylor, ed., Wycherley's *The Country Wife* (1931), *MLN*, XLIX, 120.

Review: Benjamin T. Spencer, ed., Massinger's *The Bondman* (1932), *MLN*, XLIX, 118-20.

Review: Johanne Stochholm, ed., Massinger's *The Great Duke of Florence* (1933), *MLN*, XLIX, 553-54.

1935

"*Richard III* on the Stage," *TLS*, 27 June, p. 416.

The Works of Edmund Spenser (Variorum Edition), vol. IV, ed. Ray Heffner, Frederick Morgan Padelford, James G. McManaway, and Lewis F. Ball, Baltimore, The Johns Hopkins Press.

Review: Rudolf Kirk, ed., Massinger's *The City Madam* (1934), *MLN*, L, 208.

Review: Robert Withington, ed., *Essays and Characters: Montaigne to Goldsmith* (1933) and *Essays and Characters: Lamb to Thompson* (1933), *MLN*, L, 68.

1936

"MS. of Davenport's 'Policy without Piety'; John Withorn: Sir John Kay," *N&Q*, CLXX, 295.

The Works of Edmund Spenser (Variorum Edition), vol. V, ed. Ray Heffner, Frederick Morgan Padelford, James G. McManaway, and Lewis F. Ball, Baltimore, The Johns Hopkins Press.

1937

"Women and Ships," *TLS*, 20 February, p. 131.

"Words Divided at End of Line," *N&Q*, CLXXII, 157-58.

Review: Edward M. Hinton, *Ireland Through Tudor Eyes* (1935), *MLN*, LII, 467.

1938

"A Chaucerian Fisherman (?)," *MLN*, LIII, 422-23.

"Fortune's Wheel," *TLS*, 16 April, p. 264.

"Survey of the Harmsworth Collection," *Amherst Graduates' Quarterly*, XXVII, 329-36.

* "Thomas Dekker: Further Textual Notes," *The Library*, 4th ser., XIX, 176-79.

The Works of Edmund Spenser (Variorum Edition), vol. VI, ed. the General Editors, James G. McManaway, Dorothy E. Mason, and Brents Stirling, Baltimore, The Johns Hopkins Press.

1939

"Additions to the Harmsworth Collection," *Amherst Graduates' Quarterly*, XXVIII, 102-5.

"A *Hamlet* Emendation," *MLR*, XXXIV, 68-70. (With William B. Van Lennep.)

"Little Crown Street, Westminster," *N&Q*, CLXXVII, 478.

"A Notable Collection of MSS., 1833," *N&Q*, CLXXVI, 63.

Review: Arthur H. Nethercot, *Sir William D'Avenant* (1938), *The Library Quarterly*, IX, 242-44.

1940

"The Folger Library," *South Atlantic Bulletin*, VI, 1-4.

* "The 'Lost' Canto of *Gondibert*," *MLQ*, I, 63-78.

Review: W. W. Greg, ed., *King Lear, 1608; The Merchant of Venice, 1600; The Merry Wives of Windsor, 1602* (Shakespeare Quarto Facsimiles, Nos. 1, 2, 3, 1939), *MLN*, LV, 632-34.

Review: Hazelton Spencer, *The Art and Life of William Shakespeare* (1940), *The Johns Hopkins Alumni Magazine*, XXVIII, 99-100.

1941

"Early Engravings of North American Indians," *American Notes and Queries*, I, 13-14.

"Nerissa's Ring," *American Notes and Queries*, I, 69.

"Newfoundland in Poems and Novels," *N&Q*, CLXXXI, 251.

Review: R. R. Cawley, *Unpathed Waters: Studies in the Influence of the Voyagers on Elizabethan Literature* (1940), *The American Neptune*, I, 321-22.

Review: Cyrus L. Day and Eleanore B. Murrie, *English Song-Books, 1651-1702: A Bibliography* (1940), *MLN*, LVI, 630-31.

Review: Alfred Harbage, *Annals of English Drama, 975-1700* (1940), *MLQ*, II, 141-43.

Review: Baldwin Maxwell, *Studies in Beaumont, Fletcher, and Massinger* (1939), *MLN*, LVI, 144-46.

1942

"The License for Shakespeare's Marriage," *MLN*, LVII, 450-51, 688-89.

Review: W. W. Greg, *The Variants in the First Quarto of King Lear* (1940), *MLR*, XXXVII, 86-88.

1943

"Notes on 'A Key . . . to . . . *Absalom and Achitophel*,'" *N&Q*, CLXXXIV, 365-66.

Review: G. E. Bentley, *The Jacobean and Caroline Stage: Dramatic Companies and Players* (1941), *MLQ*, IV, 245-47.

Review: William A. Neilson and Charles J. Hill, eds., *The Complete Plays and Poems of William Shakespeare* (1942), *MLN*, LVIII, 483-85.

1944

"Nerissa's Ring (3:88 *et al.*)," *American Notes and Queries*, III, 173.

Review: Gladys I. Wade, *Thomas Traherne* (1944), *Thought*, XIX, 729-31.

1945

A Check-List of English Plays, 1641-1700, compiled by Gertrude L. Woodward and James G. McManaway, Chicago, The Newberry Library.

* "Latin Title-Page Mottoes as a Clue to Dramatic Authorship," *The Library*, 4th ser., XXVI, 28-36.

1946

* "The Cancel in the Quarto of 2 *Henry IV*," in *Studies in Honor of A. H. R. Fairchild*, ed. C. T. Prouty, University of Missouri Press, pp. 69-80.

"Shakespeare and the Heretics," in *To Doctor R. Essays Here Collected and Published in Honor of the Seventieth Birthday of Dr. A. S. W. Rosenbach*, ed. Percy E. Lawler, John Fleming, and Edwin Wolf, Philadelphia, pp. 136-53.

1948

* "*The First Five Bookes of Ovids Metamorphosis*, 1621, Englished by Master George Ṣandys," *Papers of the Bibliographical Society of the University of Virginia [Studies in Bibliography]*, I (1948-49), 69-82.

"The Folger Shakespeare Library," *Shakespeare Survey 1*, 57-58 and Plates 15-17, 24.

Joseph Quincy Adams Memorial Studies, ed. James G. McManaway, Giles E. Dawson, and Edwin E. Willoughby, Washington, The Folger Shakespeare Library.

* "The Year's Contributions to Shakespearian Study: Textual Studies," *Shakespeare Survey 1*, 127-31.

1949

"Early English Literature, 1475-1700," in Curt F. Bühler, James G. McManaway, and Lawrence C. Wroth, *Standards of Bibliographical Description*, University of Pennsylvania Press, pp. 63-89.

"The Laurence Olivier *Hamlet*," *SAB*, XXIV, 3-11.

* "The Two Earliest Prompt Books of *Hamlet*," *PBSA*, XLIII, 288-320.

* "The Year's Contributions to Shakespearian Study: Textual Studies," *Shakespeare Survey 2*, 145-53.

Review: John Carter, *Taste and Technique in Book-Collecting* (1948), *MLR*, XLIV, 555.

1950

"Additional Prompt-Books of Shakespeare from the Smock Alley Theatre," *MLR*, XLV, 64-65.

"The Flesh and Blood Shakespeare as an Actor," The Washington *Post*, 23 April.

" 'O Death, Rock Me Asleep,' " *N&Q*, CXCV, 98.

"Recent Studies in Shakespeare's Chronology," *Shakespeare Survey 3*, 22-33.

"Where Are Shakespeare's Manuscripts?" *New Colophon*, II, 357-69.

* "The Year's Contributions to Shakespearian Study: Textual Studies," *Shakespeare Survey 3*, 143-52.

Review: Fredson Bowers, ed., *Studies in Bibliography*, vol. II (1949-50), *PBSA*, XLIV, 75-79.

Review: John W. Draper, *The Twelfth Night of Shakespeare's Audience* (1950), *U. S. Quarterly Book Review*, VI, 151.

Review: Willard Farnham, *Shakespeare's Tragic Frontier* (1950), *U. S. Quarterly Book Review*, VI, 151-52.

Review: E. P. Goldschmidt, *The Printed Book of the Renaissance* (1950), *RN*, III, 21-24; IV (1951), 12-14.

Review: Leonard Unger, *Donne's Poetry and Modern Criticism* (1950), *U. S. Quarterly Book Review*, VI, 415.

Review: W. B. C. Watkins, *Shakespeare and Spenser* (1950), *U. S. Quarterly Book Review*, VI, 416.

1951

* "King James Takes a Collection," in *Essays Honoring Lawrence C. Wroth*, ed. Frederick R. Goff, Portland, Maine, pp. 223-33.

"A New Shakespeare Document," *SQ*, II, 119-22.

"Some Bibliographical Notes on Samuel Daniel's *Civil Wars*," *Studies in Bibliography*, IV (1951-52), 31-39.

"An Uncollected Poem of John Skelton (?)," *N&Q*, CXCVI, 134-35.

* "The Year's Contributions to Shakespearian Study: Textual Studies," *Shakespeare Survey 4*, 153-63.

Review: Lawrence Babb, *The Elizabethan Malady* (1951), *U. S. Quarterly Book Review*, VII, 349.

Review: G. I. Duthie, *Elizabethan Shorthand and the First Quarto of King Lear* (1950), *SQ*, II, 85-86.

Review: Allan Holaday, ed., Heywood's *The Rape of Lucrece* (1950), *JEGP*, L, 267-68.

Review: M. P. Tilley, comp., *A Dictionary of the Proverbs in England in the Sixteenth and Seventeenth Centuries* (1951), *U. S. Quarterly Book Review*, VII, 214-15.

Review: Helen Constance White, *The Tudor Books of Private Devotion* (1951), *U. S. Quarterly Book Review*, VII, 363-64.

1952

"Additional Notes on 'The Great Danseker,'" *MLR*, XLVII, 202-3.

"In Praise of Books," in program of the Exhibition of Rare Books, Monterey, California.

* "The Year's Contributions to Shakespearian Study: Textual Studies," *Shakespeare Survey 5*, 144-52.

Review: J. V. Cunningham, *Woe or Wonder: The Emotional Effect of Shakespearean Tragedy* (1951), *U. S. Quarterly Book Review*, VIII, 23.

Review: Alfred Harbage, *Shakespeare and the Rival Traditions* (1952): "The Two Audiences and Master Will," *N. Y. Times Book Review*, 16 November, p. 6.

Review: G. B. Harrison, *Shakespeare's Tragedies* (1952): "The Deep and Tragic," *N. Y. Times Book Review*, 13 July, p. 12.

Review: Leslie Hotson, *Shakespeare's Motley* (1952), *U. S. Quarterly Book Review*, VIII, 366-67.

Review: Edward Hubler, *The Sense of Shakespeare's Sonnets* (1952): "Speaking of Books," *N. Y. Times Book Review*, 18 May, p. 2.

Review: Harry Levin, *The Overreacher: A Study of Christopher Marlowe* (1952): "A Man of Violence and Genius," *N. Y. Times Book Review*, 26 October, p. 10.

Review: Dorothy and Charlton Ogburn, *This Star of England* (1952): "'Once More Unto the Breach,' The Bard is Under Fire," The Washington *Star*, 7 December.

1953

"Duff 362," *TLS*, 15 May, p. 317.

* "*Songs and Masques in The Tempest*," *Theatre Miscellany*, Luttrell Society Reprints, No. 14 (Oxford), 69-96.

"An Unrecorded English Coranto," *The Library*, 5th ser., VIII, 125-26.

*"The Year's Contributions to Shakespearian Study: Textual Studies," *Shakespeare Survey 6*, 163-72.

Review: Allardyce Nicoll, *A History of English Drama, 1660-1900*, vols. I-III (1952), *MLR*, XLVIII, 461.

Review: Robert G. Noyes, *The Thespian Mirror: Shakespeare in the 18th-Century Novel* (1953), *U. S. Quarterly Book Review*, IX, 293.

Review: A. C. Sprague, *Shakespearian Players and Performances* (1953), *U. S. Quarterly Book Review*, IX, 294.

1954

*"The Colophon of the Second Folio of Shakespeare," *The Library*, 5th ser., IX, 199-200.

*"A Miscalculation in the Printing of the Third Folio," *The Library*, 5th ser., IX, 129-33.

"William Shakespeare," in *The New Century Cyclopedia of Names*, ed. Clarence L. Barnhart, New York, Appleton-Century-Crofts, III, 3571-72.

*"The Year's Contributions to Shakespearian Study: Textual Studies," *Shakespeare Survey 7*, 147-53.

Review: Herbert Farjeon, ed., *The Complete Works of William Shakespeare* (New Nonesuch Edition, 1953), *SQ*, V, 92-93.

Review: Leslie Hotson, *The First Night of Twelfth Night* (1954): "A Comedy for a Queen," *N. Y. Times Book Review*, 12 December, p. 4.

Review: Alice Walker, *Textual Problems of the First Folio* (1953), *PBSA*, XLVIII, 105-7.

1955

"Bibliography," in *Literature and Science*, Proceedings of the Sixth Triennial Congress (1954) of the International Federation for Modern Languages and Literatures. Oxford, Basil Blackwell, pp. 27-35.

Dick of Devonshire, ed. James G. McManaway and Mary Ruthven McManaway, Oxford, The Malone Society.

"Supplements to the New Variorum Shakespeare," *SQ*, VI, 247.

*"The Year's Contributions to Shakespearian Study: Textual Studies," *Shakespeare Survey 8*, 153-59.

1956

Introduction to Irwin Smith, *Shakespeare's Globe Playhouse*, New York, Scribner's, pp. vii-ix.

"A Probable Source of *Romeo and Juliet* III.i.100-1," *N&Q*, CCI, 57.

*"The Year's Contributions to Shakespearian Study: Textual Studies," *Shakespeare Survey 9*, 148-56.

Review: Paul Murray Kendall, *Richard the Third* (1956): "In Defense of a King," *N. Y. Times Book Review*, 26 August, p. 3.

Review: Helge Kökeritz, ed., *Mr. William Shakespeares Comedies, Histories, & Tragedies: A Facsimile Edition* (1954), *MLR*, LI, 588-90.

Review: Allardyce Nicoll, *A History of English Drama, 1660-1900*, vol. IV (1955), *MLR*, LI, 458-59.

1957

"A Casual Recollection of Holinshed?" *N&Q*, CCII, 371.

"Shakespearian Productions in America in 1955-56," *SJ*, XCIII, 145-53.

"The Theatrical Collectanea of Daniel Lysons," *PBSA*, LI, 333-34.

*"The Year's Contributions to Shakespearian Study: Textual Studies," *Shakespeare Survey 10*, 151-58.

Review: J. C. Maxwell, ed., *Pericles* (New Cambridge Shakespeare, 1956), *MLR*, LII, 583-84.

Review: George Speaight, *The History of the English Puppet Theatre* (1956), *SQ*, VIII, 243-44.

1958

"*The Contention* and *2 Henry VI*," in *Studies in English Language and Literature Presented to Karl Brunner on the Occasion of his Seventieth Birthday*, ed. Siegfried Korninger, *Wiener Beiträge zur englischen Philologie*, LXV, 143-54.

"Introduction," in *English Books (Literature, History, Religion, Science) Printed before 1640*, New York, John F. Fleming, pp. 1-2.

Preface to Peter Alexander, ed., *Shakespeare: The Histories* (Heritage Shakespeare), New York, Heritage Press, pp. vii-xviii.

"Writing in Sand in *Titus Andronicus* IV. i," *RES*, new ser., IX, 172–73.

*"The Year's Contributions to Shakespearian Study: Textual Studies," *Shakespeare Survey 11*, 149-55.

Review: Clara Longworth de Chambrun, *Shakespeare: A Portrait Restored* (1958): "The Bard's Good Friends," *N. Y. Times Book Review*, 12 January, p. 33.

Review: William A. Jackson, ed., *Records of the Court of the Stationers' Company, 1602 to 1640* (1957), *PBSA*, LII, 65-67.

1959

*"Elizabeth, Essex, and James," in *Elizabethan and Jacobean Studies Presented to Frank Percy Wilson in Honour of his Seventieth Birthday*, ed. Herbert Davis and Helen Gardner, Oxford, The Clarendon Press, pp. 219-30.

"Marsden Jasiel Perry," in *Grolier 75: A Biographical Retrospective to Celebrate the Seventy-fifth Anniversary of the Grolier Club in New York*, New York, The Grolier Club.

"Queen Elizabeth Crowned with Stars," *N&Q*, CCIV, 35-36.

*"The Year's Contributions to Shakespearian Study: Textual Studies," *Shakespeare Survey 12*, 146-52.

Review: R. C. Churchill, *Shakespeare and His Betters* (1959): "Who Did It If Not Will?" *N. Y. Times Book Review*, 15 March, p. 4.

Review: Sarah A. Dickson, comp., *A Catalogue of the Books, MSS., and Engravings Acquired Since 1942 in the Arents Tobacco Collection at the N. Y. Public Library*, Part I, 1507-1571 (1958), *PBSA*, LIII, 207-9.

1960

*"The Year's Contributions to Shakespearian Study: Textual Studies," *Shakespeare Survey 13*, 162-69.

Review: T. W. Baldwin, *Shakspere's Love's Labor's Won: New Evidence from the Account Books of an Elizabethan Bookseller* (1957), *SQ*, XI, 369-70.

Review: Frank O'Connor, *Shakespeare's Progress* (1960): "With No Applause for Master Will," *N. Y. Times Book Review*, 20 November, p. 62.

1961

"Entertainment for the Grand Duke of Tuscany," *TN*, XVI (1961-62), 20-21.

"The First American Engraving of Shakespeare," *SQ*, XII, 157-58.

"A *Hamlet* Reminiscence in 1660," *N&Q*, CCVI, 388.

*"The Year's Contributions to Shakespearian Study: Textual Studies," *Shakespeare Survey 14*, 157-66.

Review: Levi Fox, *Shakespeare's Town and Country* (1959), *SQ*, XII, 70.

Review: James M. Osborn, ed., *The Autobiography of Thomas Whythorne* (1961), *SQ*, XII, 339.

Review: James M. Osborn, ed., *The Queenes Maiesties Passage Through the Citie of London to Westminster the day before her Coronacion* (1960), *SQ*, XII, 146-47.

1962

* *The Authorship of Shakespeare*, Washington, The Folger Shakespeare Library. Reprinted in *Life and Letters in Tudor and Stuart England* (First Folger Series), ed. Louis B. Wright and Virginia A. LaMar, Ithaca, New York, Cornell University Press for the Folger Shakespeare Library, 1962.

* "Notes on Act V of *Antony and Cleopatra*," *Shakespeare Studies* (Tokyo), I, 1-5.

* "Notes on Two Pre-Restoration Stage Curtains," in *Studies in English Drama Presented to Baldwin Maxwell* [*PQ*, XLI, no. 1], ed. Charles B. Woods and Curt A. Zimansky, Iowa City, State University of Iowa, pp. 270-74.

"Portraits of Shakespeare," in program of the American Shakespeare Festival Theatre and Academy, Stratford, Connecticut, 1962 Repertory Season.

*"The Year's Contributions to Shakespearian Study: Textual Studies," *Shakespeare Survey 15*, 175-82.

Review: Emmett L. Avery, ed., *The London Stage, 1660-1800*, Part 2: 1700-1729 (1960), *SQ*, XIII, 241-43.

Review: Mark Eccles, *Shakespeare in Warwickshire* (1961), *JEGP*, LXI, 635-36.

Review: R. A. Foakes and R. T. Rickert, eds., *Henslowe's Diary* (1961), *University of Toronto Quarterly*, XXXI, 392-93.

Review: George Rylands, director, London Records (recordings of thirteen Shakespeare plays and the Sonnets), *SQ*, XIII, 245-46.

Review: "Paperbacks in Review: The Bard" (miscellaneous paperback editions of books on Shakespeare), *N. Y. Times Book Review*, 27 May, p. 36.

1963

"In Praise of Books," The Ontario-Upland (California) *Daily Report*, 12 August.

"Privilege to Print," *Studies in Bibliography*, XVI, 201-3.

" 'Smoth Tongued Shakespeare,' 1650," *SQ*, XIV, 92.

* "The Year's Contributions to Shakespearian Study: Textual Studies," *Shakespeare Survey 16*, 172-81.

Review: Elemér Hankiss and Elisabeth Berczelli, comps., *Bibliographie der in Ungarn erschienen Theaterkalender XVII-XIX Jahrhundert* (1961), *SQ*, XIV, 85.

Review: Peter Quennell, *Shakespeare: A Biography* (1963): "What Manner of Man was Will?" *N. Y. Times Book Review*, 24 November, p. 1.

Review: W. H. D. Rouse, ed., *Shakespeare's Ovid: Being Arthur Golding's Translation of the Metamorphoses* (1962), *SQ*, XIV, 86.

Review: Arthur H. Scouten, ed., *The London Stage, 1660-1800*, Part 3: 1729-1747 (1961), *SQ*, XIV, 475.

Review: George Winchester Stone, ed., *The London Stage, 1660-1800*, Part 4: 1747-1776 (1962), *SQ*, XIV, 475.

1964

"The Folger Shakespeare Library," *The Library Chronicle*, XXX, 72-76.

Foreword to Irwin Smith, *Shakespeare's Blackfriars Playhouse*, New York University Press, pp. xiii-xiv.

* "L'Héritage de la Renaissance dans la mise en scène en Angleterre (1642-1700)" ["The Renaissance Heritage of English Staging (1642-1700)"], in *Le Lieu théâtral à la Renaissance*, ed. Jean Jacquot, Paris, Éditions du Centre National de la Recherche Scientifique, pp. 459-72.

* "*Richard II* at Covent Garden," in *Shakespeare 400* [*SQ*, XV, No. 2], ed. James G. McManaway, New York, Holt, Rinehart, and Winston, pp. 161-75.

Shakespeare 400 [*SQ*, XV, No. 2], ed. James G. McManaway, New York, Holt, Rinehart, and Winston.

* "Shakespeare in the United States," *PMLA*, LXXIX, 513-18.

"Unrecorded Performances in London about 1700," *TN*, XIX (1964-65), 68-70.

Review: G. Blakemore Evans, ed., *Shakespearean Prompt-Books of the Seventeenth Century*, vol. I (1960), vol. II (1963), vol. III (1964), *SQ*, XV, 434-35.

Review: "Everybody's Shakespeare" (miscellaneous books on Shakespeare), *N. Y. Times Book Review* (pt. 2), 5 January, p. 6.

Review: "A Shelf of Shakespeare for the Layman" (miscellaneous books on Shakespeare), *N. Y. Times Book Review*, 19 April, p. 42.

Review: John Wain, *The Living World of Shakespeare* (1964): "In Celebration of the Nature of Man," *N. Y. Times Book Review*, 1 November, p. 5.

1965

"Introduction," in *In the Beginning Was the Word: Opening an Exhibition of Written and Printed Biblical and Liturgical Texts from the Eighth Century to the Present,* Washington, The Cathedral Rare Book Library, p. 19.

"The Folger Shakespeare Library—Additional Links with Philadelphia," *The Library Chronicle,* XXXI, 23-24.

* "The Year's Contributions to Shakespearian Study: Textual Studies," *Shakespeare Survey 18,* 186-92.

1966

"The Folger Shakespeare Library," in *The Reader's Encyclopedia of Shakespeare,* ed. Oscar James Campbell and Edward G. Quinn, New York, T. Y. Crowell, pp. 235-37.

"Parish Registers of St. Giles Without Cripplegate," *N&Q,* CCXI, 14-15.

1967

* *"Excerpta quaedam per A. W. adolescentem,"* in *Studies in Honor of DeWitt T. Starnes,* ed. Thomas P. Harrison, Archibald A. Hill, Ernest C. Mossner, and James Sledd, Austin, The University of Texas, pp. 117-29.

* "John Shakespeare's 'Spiritual Testament,'" *SQ,* XVIII, 197-205.

Pericles Prince of Tyre (Pelican Shakespeare), ed. James G. McManaway, Baltimore, Penguin Books. Revised edition in *William Shakespeare: The Complete Works* (Pelican Shakespeare), gen. ed. Alfred Harbage, Baltimore, Penguin Books, 1969.

"A Reading in *King Lear,*" *N&Q,* CCXII, 139.

Review: E. A. J. Honigmann, *The Stability of Shakespeare's Text* (1965), *The Library,* 5th ser., XXII, 161-63.

1968

Review: W. W. Greg, *Collected Papers,* ed. J. C. Maxwell (1966), *The Library,* 5th ser., XXIII, 148-49.

Review: Charlton Hinman, ed., *The First Folio of Shakespeare: The Norton Facsimile* (1968): " 'Offer'd to your view cur'd and perfect of their limbes,' " *N. Y. Times Book Review,* 8 December, pp. 4-5.

Review: Rudolf Hirsch, *Printing, Selling, and Reading, 1450-1550* (1967), *RQ,* XXI, 318-19.

Review: Marvin Spevack, comp., *A Complete and Systematic Concordance to the Works of Shakespeare,* vol. I: Drama and Character Concordances to the Folio Comedies (1968), *SQ,* XIX (1968), 393-95.

Index

Index

Abbot, George, 126

Abuses, The (Anon.), 62

Adagia (Erasmus), 186

Adams, John, 266

Adams, Joseph Q., 37 n. 6, 73 n. 14, 75 and n. 21, 276, 311-12

Addison, Joseph, 184

Adelphi (Terence), 6

Adventures of Five Hours, The (Tuke), 233

Æsop, 186, 215-16, 218 (Plates 17-19)

African Roscius, the (Ira Aldridge), 268

Agazzari, Alphonsus, 295-96

Agnes de Castro (Trotter), 233-34

Albion and Albanius (Dryden), 234-35, 237-38

Aldridge, Ira, 268

Alexander, Peter, 327, 331-32, 366, 375-76

Allde, Edward, 62, 321

Allen, William, 295

Alleyn, Edward, 176-77

All for Love (Dryden), 251

Altamira, 18 n. 31

Amhurst, Nicholas, 250-51

Amorous War, The (Mayne), 65

Andrewes, Lancelot, 126

Andria (Terence; tr. Kyffin), 63-64

Anne of Swansea, 97-98, 106

Anne, Queen (James I), 217, 223

Anouilh, Jean, 211-13

Answer to Mr. Pope's Preface to Shakespeare, An (? Roberts), 245

Antony and Cleopatra (Shakespeare), 211, 213-14, 354, 360, 373

Apology for Actors, An (Heywood), 64, 245

Apophthegmata (Erasmus), 186

This is an index of persons and primary sources. Since each class of entry is exclusive of the other, an author should be searched under appropriate title-entries as well as under the author-entry. The list of J. G. McManaway's publications (pp. 385-400) has not been indexed.

Arcadia (Sidney), 178

Arden, Mary, 175

Argalus and Parthenia (Glapthorne), 11

Ariane (Perrin), 229

Ariels Songs in the Play call'd the Tempest, 131, 135, 137-39, 142-43

Armstrong, Edward A., 363-64

Ars sensualium pictus (Komenski), 221

Arthur (actor), 245 n. 10

Ashton, Abdie, 165, 167, 170

Aspley, William, 67 n. 1, 70 n. 11, 71, 73-75

Aston (actor), 245 n. 10

Astor, John Jacob, 275

Astrophel and Stella (Sidney), 178, 326

As You Like It (Shakespeare), 251, 271

Atkins (dancer), 244 n. 7

Atkins, Mrs. (actress), 244 n. 7

Atkins (or Attkin), Rob[t] (name written in John Roberts's *Richard II*), 244 n. 7

Aubrey, John, 181, 186, 382

Avery, Emmett L., 244, 246 n. 14, 247

Bacon, Sir Francis, 198, 201, 206, 251

Badinel, Bulkeley, 281

Baker, David Erskine, 23, 25

Baker, Herschel, 97 n. 5, 106

Baker, Sir Richard, 245

Bald, R. C., 95 n. 2, 109 n. 32

Baldwin, T. W., x

Banister, John, 138, 141

Banquet of Jests, A (Anon.), 194-96

Barker, Russell H., 84 n. 10

Barret, Alice, 19

Barrett, Mistress (relict of William Barrett), 86, 88, 123

Barrett, William, 81, 84, 86-88, 123

Barrymore, John, 269

Barrymore, Lionel, 269

Barry, Mrs. Elizabeth, 197

Bartholomew Fair (Jonson), 285

Barton, Thomas Pennant, 273

Bashful Lover, The (Massinger), 8, 12, 17, 24-25

STUDIES IN
Shakespeare, Bibliography,
and Theater

was composed and printed by
The William Byrd Press, Inc., Richmond, Virginia
and bound by
Russell-Rutter Company, Inc., New York City

The types are Granjon and Cloister Old Style,
the paper is Curtis Rag Text, the cloth Holliston Roxite

Design by Willis Shell